Pro .NET Performance

Sasha Goldshtein
Dima Zurbalev
Ido Flatow

Apress

Pro .NET Performance

Copyright © 2012 by Sasha Goldshtein, Dima Zurbalev, and Ido Flatow

ISBN-13 (pbk): 978-1-4302-4458-5

ISBN-13 (electronic): 978-1-4302-4459-2

President and Publisher: Paul Manning
Lead Editor: Gwenan Spearing
Developmental Editor: Gwenan Spearing
Technical Reviewers: Todd Meister and Fabio Claudio Ferracchiati
Editorial Board: Steve Anglin, Ewan Buckingham, Gary Cornell, Louise Corrigan, Morgan Ertel, Jonathan Gennick, Jonathan Hassell, Robert Hutchinson, Michelle Lowman, James Markham, Matthew Moodie, Jeff Olson, Jeffrey Pepper, Douglas Pundick, Ben Renow-Clarke, Dominic Shakeshaft, Gwenan Spearing, Matt Wade, Tom Welsh
Coordinating Editors: Corbin Collins and Kevin Shea
Copy Editor: Lori Cavanaugh
Compositor: SPi Global
Indexer: SPi Global
Artist: SPi Global
Cover Designer: Anna Ishchenko

Distributed to the book trade worldwide by Springer Science+Business Media New York, 233 Spring Street, 6th Floor, New York, NY 10013. Phone 1-800-SPRINGER, fax (201) 348-4505, e-mail orders-ny@springer-sbm.com, or visit www.springeronline.com.

For information on translations, please e-mail rights@apress.com, or visit www.apress.com.

Apress and friends of ED books may be purchased in bulk for academic, corporate, or promotional use. eBook versions and licenses are also available for most titles. For more information, reference our Special Bulk Sales–eBook Licensing web page at www.apress.com/bulk-sales.

Any source code or other supplementary materials referenced by the author in this text is available to readers at www.apress.com/9781430244585. For more information about how to locate your book's source code, go to www.apress.com/source-code.

To my loving wife Dina, who is the sunshine of my life.
To my parents Boris and Marina, for making all the sacrifices so I don't have to.
—Sasha

To my lovely wife Efrat, for reminding me that a muse is not gone, it is just playing hide and seek.
—Ido

Contents at a Glance

Contents

Foreword

The original Desktop .NET Framework turned 10 years old recently (Feb 2012). I have been on the team since its very inception, and for over half that time I have acted as its performance architect, so that 10th birthday got me thinking about where .NET has been, where it is going, and what's the 'right' way to think about .NET performance. The chance to write a foreword on a book dedicated to .NET performance gave me the opportunity to write these thoughts down.

Programmer productivity has always been and will always be the fundamental value of the .NET framework. Garbage collection (GC) is the single most important feature that boosts productivity, not only because it avoids a broad class of nasty bugs (memory corruption), but also because it allows class libraries to be written without being "cluttered" with error-prone resource allocation conventions (no more passing buffers, or subtle rules about who is responsible for deleting memory). Strong type safety (which now includes Generics) is another important pillar because it captures a broad class of programmer intent (e.g., this list is homogeneous) and allows tools to find many bugs well before the program is ever run. It also enforces strong contracts between software components, which is very important for class libraries and large projects. The lack of strong typing in languages like JavaScript will always place them at a disadvantage as software scales. On top of these two pillars we added a class library that was designed for ease of use (very uniform, simple interfaces, consistent naming conventions, etc.). I am very proud of the result; we have built a system for building code whose productivity is second to none.

Programmer productivity alone is not enough, however, especially for a mature piece of software like the .NET runtime. We want high performance as well, and this is where this book comes into play.

The bad news is that in the same way that you can't expect your program to run correctly the very first time you run it, you can't expect high performance to "just happen" the very first time your program runs correctly. In the same way that there are tools (GC and type safety) and techniques (asserts, interface contracts) that reduce the occurrence of software bugs, there are tools (various profilers) and techniques (perf planning, hot path protyping, lazy initialization) that reduce the likelihood of performance issues.

The good news is that performance follows the 90%-10% rule. Typically well over 90% of your application is *not* performance critical and can be written to maximum programmer productivity (the fewest, simplest, easiest lines of code possible). The other 10%, however, needs careful attention. It needs a plan, and it needs it *before* the code is written. This is what Chapter 1 is all about. To do that planning you need data (how fast are various operations, library calls, etc.), and for that you need measuring tools (profilers), which is what Chapter 2 is all about. These are the cornerstones of any high-performance software project. Heed these chapters well. If you take them to heart, you *will* write high-performance software.

The rest of the book is about the details you need to "know your options" when you are building your performance plan. There is no substitute for a basic understanding of the performance characteristics of the platform you are using, and that is what Chapter 3 (types), Chapter 4 (GC), and Chapter 5 (fundamental libraries) are about. If your prototyping shows that a simple, straightforward .NET implementation does not get you the performance you need, you should first investigate algorithm improvement (Chapter 9) or concurrency (Chapter 6) because these are likely to have the biggest effect. If you still need perf, some .NET specific tricks (Chapter 10) may help. If all else fails, you can sacrifice the programmer productivity for a small fraction of your code and write the most critical pieces in unsafe or unmanaged code (Chapter 8).

The key point I want to stress, however is having a plan (Chapter 1), because that is where it all starts. In this plan you will identify your high volume or performance critical paths and you will spend extra development time to carefully measure, and prototype solutions for these important paths. Next, armed with the measurements from the prototyping and the information in this book, it is typically a very straightforward exercise to get the performance you need. It might be as simple as avoiding common performance pitfalls, or maybe doing simple optimizations. It might be parallelizing your hot path, or maybe you have to write some unsafe code or unmanaged code. Whatever it is, the result is a design that achieves your performance objectives (by doing extra work on 10% of your code) while simultaneously reaping the productivity benefits of .NET on the remaining 90%. This is the goal of the .NET framework: high productivity *and* high performance. You *can* have it all.

So there you have it. The bad news is that performance is not free; you have to *plan* for it. The good news is that it is not that hard, and that by reading this book you have taken the most important step in writing your *high-performance* .NET application.

Good luck and enjoy the book. Sasha, Dima, and Ido did a great job on it.

Vance Morrison
Performance Architect, .NET Runtime

About the Authors

Sasha Goldshtein is a Microsoft Visual C# MVP, and the CTO of SELA Group. Sasha leads the Performance and Debugging team in the SELA Technology Center, and consults on various topics including production debugging, application performance troubleshooting, and distributed architecture. Most of Sasha's experience is in C# and C++ application development, as well as high-scalability and high-performance system architecture. He is a frequent speaker at Microsoft conferences, and the author of multiple training courses: ".NET Performance", ".NET Debugging", "Windows Internals", and many others.
Blog: http://blog.sashag.net Twitter: @goldshtn

Dima Zurbalev is a Senior Consultant at SELA Group's Performance and Debugging emergency response team. Dima's performance optimization and debugging skills enable him to solve seemingly impossible problems for customers, bringing to the table deep understanding of CLR and Windows internals. Most of his development experience revolves around .NET and C++ infrastructure projects, and he has contributed to several open source projects on CodePlex.
Blog: http://blogs.microsoft.co.il/blogs/dimaz

Ido Flatow is a Microsoft Connected Systems MVP, and a Senior Architect at SELA Group. With over 15 years of experience, Ido is one of SELA's Windows Azure and Web experts, specializing in technologies such as WCF, ASP.NET, Silverlight, and IIS. He is a Microsoft certified trainer (MCT), the co-author of Microsoft's Official WCF 4.0 course (10263A), and a frequent speaker at conferences worldwide.
Blog: http://blogs.microsoft.co.il/blogs/idof
Twitter: @IdoFlatow

About the Technical Reviewers

Todd Meister has been working in the IT industry for over fifteen years. He's been a Technical Editor on over 75 titles ranging from SQL Server to the .NET Framework. Besides technical editing titles he is the Senior IT Architect at Ball State University in Muncie, Indiana. He lives in central Indiana with his wife, Kimberly, and their five incisive children.

Fabio Claudio Ferracchiati is a prolific writer and technical reviewer on cutting-edge technologies. He has contributed to many books on .NET, C#, Visual Basic, SQL Server, Silverlight, and ASP.NET. He is a .NET Microsoft Certified Solution Developer (MCSD) and lives in Rome, Italy. He is employed by Brain Force.

Acknowledgments

Writing a book is such a huge undertaking that it would have taken us another year to publish it if not for the unconditional support of our families, friends, and colleagues.

Our manager at SELA Group, David Bassa, has given us all possible help to see this book to completion, and was very understanding when other projects slipped through the tracks when the book's deadlines loomed.

The editorial team at Apress made this project enjoyable and tolerated our second-language English to shape the book as you see it today. Gwenan, Kevin, and Corbin: thank you for your professionalism and patience.

Last but not least, a great many thanks to our families, who have sacrificed countless hours on this book's altar. Without your support, this book would never be published.

Introduction

This book has come to be because we felt there was no authoritative text that covered all three areas relevant to .NET application performance:

- Identifying performance metrics and then measuring application performance to verify whether it meets or exceeds these metrics.

- Improving application performance in terms of memory management, networking, I/O, concurrency, and other areas.

- Understanding CLR and .NET internals in sufficient detail to design high-performance applications and fix performance issues as they arise.

We believe that .NET developers cannot achieve systematically high-performance software solutions without thoroughly understanding all three areas. For example, .NET memory management (facilitated by the CLR garbage collector) is an extremely complex field and the cause of significant performance problems, including memory leaks and long GC pause times. Without understanding how the CLR garbage collector operates, high-performance memory management in .NET is left to nothing but chance. Similarly, choosing the proper collection class from what the .NET Framework has to offer, or deciding to implement your own, requires comprehensive familiarity with CPU caches, runtime complexity, and synchronization issues.

This book's 11 chapters are designed to be read in succession, but you can jump back and forth between topics and fill in the blanks when necessary. The chapters are organized into the following logical parts:

- Chapter 1 and Chapter 2 deal with performance metrics and performance measurement. They introduce the tools available to you to measure application performance.

- Chapter 3 and Chapter 4 dive deep into CLR internals. They focus on type internals and the implementation of CLR garbage collection—two crucial topics for improving application performance where memory management is concerned.

- Chapter 5, Chapter 6, Chapter 7, Chapter 8, and Chapter 11 discuss specific areas of the .NET Framework and the CLR that offer performance optimization opportunities—using collections correctly, parallelizing sequential code, optimizing I/O and networking operations, using interoperability solutions efficiently, and improving the performance of Web applications.

- Chapter 9 is a brief foray into complexity theory and algorithms. It was written to give you a taste of what algorithm optimization is about.

- Chapter 10 is the dumping ground for miscellaneous topics that didn't fit elsewhere in the book, including startup time optimization, exceptions, and .NET Reflection.

Some of these topics have prerequisites that will help you understand them better. Throughout the course of the book we assume substantial experience with the C# programming language and the .NET Framework, as well as familiarity with fundamental concepts, including:

- Windows: threads, synchronization, virtual memory

- Common Language Runtime (CLR): Just-In-Time (JIT) compiler, Microsoft Intermediate Language (MSIL), garbage collector

- Computer organization: main memory, cache, disk, graphics card, network interface

There are quite a few sample programs, excerpts, and benchmarks throughout the book. In the interest of not making this book any longer, we often included only a brief part—but you can find the whole program in the companion source code on the book's website.

In some chapters we use code in x86 assembly language to illustrate how CLR mechanisms operate or to explain more thoroughly a specific performance optimization. Although these parts are not crucial to the book's takeaways, we recommend dedicated readers to invest some time in learning the fundamentals of x86 assembly language. Randall Hyde's freely available book "The Art of Assembly Language Programming" (http://www.artofasm.com/Windows/index.html) is an excellent resource.

In conclusion, this book is full of performance measurement tools, small tips and tricks for improving minor areas of application performance, theoretical foundations for many CLR mechanisms, practical code examples, and several case studies from the authors' experience. For almost ten years we have been optimizing applications for our clients and designing high-performance systems from scratch. During these years we trained hundreds of developers to think about performance at every stage of the software development lifecycle and to actively seek opportunities for improving application performance. After reading this book, you will join the ranks of high-performance .NET application developers and performance investigators optimizing existing applications.

Sasha Goldshtein
Dima Zurbalev
Ido Flatow

CHAPTER 1

■ ■ ■

Performance Metrics

Before we begin our journey into the world of .NET performance, we must understand the metrics and goals involved in performance testing and optimization. In Chapter 2, we explore more than a dozen profilers and monitoring tools; however, to use these tools, you need to know which performance metrics you are interested in.

Different types of applications have a multitude of varying performance goals, driven by business and operational needs. At times, the application's architecture dictates the important performance metrics: for example, knowing that your Web server has to serve millions of concurrent users dictates a multi-server distributed system with caching and load balancing. At other times, performance measurement results may warrant changes in the application's architecture: we have seen countless systems redesigned from the ground up after stress tests were run—or worse, the system failed in the production environment.

In our experience, knowing the system's performance goals and the limits of its environment often guides you more than halfway through the process of improving its performance. Here are some examples we have been able to diagnose and fix over the last few years:

- We discovered a serious performance problem with a powerful Web server in a hosted data center caused by a shared low-latency 4Mbps link used by the test engineers. Not understanding the critical performance metric, the engineers wasted dozens of days tweaking the performance of the Web server, which was actually functioning perfectly.

- We were able to improve scrolling performance in a rich UI application by tuning the behavior of the CLR garbage collector—an apparently unrelated component. Precisely timing allocations and tweaking the GC flavor removed noticeable UI lags that annoyed users.

- We were able to improve compilation times ten-fold by moving hard disks to SATA ports to work around a bug in the Microsoft SCSI disk driver.

- We reduced the size of messages exchanged by a WCF service by 90 %, considerably improving its scalability and CPU utilization, by tuning WCF's serialization mechanism.

- We reduced startup times from 35 seconds to 12 seconds for a large application with 300 assemblies on outdated hardware by compressing the application's code and carefully disentangling some of its dependencies so that they were not required at load time.

These examples serve to illustrate that every kind of system, from low-power touch devices, high-end consumer workstations with powerful graphics, all the way through multi-server data centers, exhibits unique performance characteristics as countless subtle factors interact. In this chapter, we briefly explore the variety of performance metrics and goals in typical modern software. In the next chapter, we illustrate how these metrics can be measured accurately; the remainder of the book shows how they can be improved systematically.

1

Performance Goals

Performance goals depend on your application's realm and architecture more than anything else. When you have finished gathering requirements, you should determine general performance goals. Depending on your software development process, you might need to adjust these goals as requirements change and new business and operation needs arise. We review some examples of performance goals and guidelines for several archetypal applications, but, as with anything performance-related, these guidelines need to be adapted to your software's domain.

First, here are some examples of statements that *are not* good performance goals:

- The application will remain responsive when many users access the Shopping Cart screen simultaneously.

- The application will not use an unreasonable amount of memory as long as the number of users is reasonable.

- A single database server will serve queries quickly even when there are multiple, fully-loaded application servers.

The main problem with these statements is that they are overly general and subjective. If these are your performance goals, then you are bound to discover they are subject to interpretation and disagreements on their frame-of-reference. A business analyst may consider 100,000 concurrent users a "reasonable" number, whereas a technical team member may know the available hardware cannot support this number of users on a single machine. Conversely, a developer might consider 500 ms response times "responsive," but a user interface expert may consider it laggy and unpolished.

A performance goal, then, is expressed in terms of *quantifiable performance metrics* that can be *measured* by some means of performance testing. The performance goal should also contain some information about its *environment*—general or specific to that performance goal. Some examples of well-specified performance goals include:

- The application will serve every page in the "Important" category within less than 300 ms (not including network roundtrip time), as long as not more than 5,000 users access the Shopping Cart screen concurrently.

- The application will use not more than 4 KB of memory for each idle user session.

- The database server's CPU and disk utilization should not exceed 70%, and it should return responses to queries in the "Common" category within less than 75ms, as long as there are no more than 10 application servers accessing it.

▓ **Note**   These examples assume that the "Important" page category and "Common" query category are well-known terms defined by business analysts or application architects. Guaranteeing performance goals for every nook and cranny in the application is often unreasonable and is not worth the investment in development, hardware, and operational costs.

We now consider some examples of performance goals for typical applications (see Table 1-1). This list is by no means exhaustive and is not intended to be used as a checklist or template for your own performance goals—it is a general frame that establishes differences in performance goals when diverse application types are concerned.

Table 1-1. *Examples of Performance Goals for Typical Applications*

System Type	Performance Goal	Environment Constraints
External Web Server	Time from request start to full response generated should not exceed 300ms	Not more than 300 concurrently active requests
External Web Server	Virtual memory usage (including cache) should not exceed 1.3GB	Not more than 300 concurrently active requests; not more than 5,000 connected user sessions
Application Server	CPU utilization should not exceed 75%	Not more than 1,000 concurrently active API requests
Application Server	Hard page fault rate should not exceed 2 hard page faults per second	Not more than 1,000 concurrently active API requests
Smart Client Application	Time from double-click on desktop shortcut to main screen showing list of employees should not exceed 1,500ms	--
Smart Client Application	CPU utilization when the application is idle should not exceed 1%	--
Web Page	Time for filtering and sorting the grid of incoming emails should not exceed 750ms, including shuffling animation	Not more than 200 incoming emails displayed on a single screen
Web Page	Memory utilization of cached JavaScript objects for the "chat with representative" windows should not exceed 2.5MB	--
Monitoring Service	Time from failure event to alert generated and dispatched should not exceed 25ms	--
Monitoring Service	Disk I/O operation rate when alerts are not actively generated should be 0	--

▓ **Note**   Characteristics of the hardware on which the application runs are a crucial part of environment constraints. For example, the startup time constraint placed on the smart client application in Table 1-1 may require a solid-state hard drive or a rotating hard drive speed of at least 7200RPM, at least 2GB of system memory, and a 1.2GHz or faster processor with SSE3 instruction support. These environment constraints are not worth repeating for every performance goal, but they are worth remembering during performance testing.

When performance goals are well-defined, the performance testing, load testing, and subsequent optimization process is laid out trivially. Verifying conjectures, such as "with 1,000 concurrently executing API requests there are less than 2 hard page faults per second on the application server," may often require access to load testing tools and a suitable hardware environment. The next chapter discusses measuring the application to determine whether it meets or exceeds its performance goals once such an environment is established.

Composing well-defined performance goals often requires prior familiarity with performance metrics, which we discuss next.

Performance Metrics

Unlike performance goals, performance metrics are not connected to a specific scenario or environment. A performance metric is a measurable numeric quantity that reflects the application's behavior. You can measure a performance metric on any hardware and in any environment, regardless of the number of active users, requests, or sessions. During the development lifecycle, you choose the metrics to measure and derive from them specific performance goals.

Some applications have performance metrics specific to their domain. We do not attempt to identify these metrics here. Instead, we list, in Table 1-2, performance metrics often important to many applications, as well as the chapter in which optimization of these metrics is discussed. (The CPU utilization and execution time metrics are so important that they are discussed in *every* chapter of this book.)

Table 1-2. *List of Performance Metrics (Partial)*

Performance Metric	Units of Measurement	Specific Chapter(s) in This Book
CPU Utilization	Percent	All Chapters
Physical/Virtual Memory Usage	Bytes, kilobytes, megabytes, gigabytes	Chapter 4 – Garbage Collection Chapter 5 – Collections and Generics
Cache Misses	Count, rate/second	Chapter 5 – Collections and Generics Chapter 6 – Concurrency and Parallelism
Page Faults	Count, rate/second	--
Database Access Counts/Timing	Count, rate/second, milliseconds	--
Allocations	Number of bytes, number of objects, rate/second	Chapter 3 – Type Internals Chapter 4 – Garbage Collection
Execution Time	Milliseconds	All Chapters
Network Operations	Count, rate/second	Chapter 7 – Networking, I/O, and Serialization Chapter 11 – Web Applications
Disk Operations	Count, rate/second	Chapter 7 – Networking, I/O, and Serialization
Response Time	Milliseconds	Chapter 11 – Web Applications
Garbage Collections	Count, rate/second, duration (milliseconds), % of total time	Chapter 4 – Garbage Collection
Exceptions Thrown	Count, rate/second	Chapter 10 – Performance Patterns
Startup Time	Milliseconds	Chapter 10 – Performance Patterns
Contentions	Count, rate/second	Chapter 6 – Concurrency and Parallelism

Some metrics are more relevant to certain application types than others. For example, database access times are not a metric you can measure on a client system. Some common combinations of performance metrics and application types include:

- For client applications, you might focus on startup time, memory usage, and CPU utilization.

- For server applications hosting the system's algorithms, you usually focus on CPU utilization, cache misses, contentions, allocations, and garbage collections.

- For Web applications, you typically measure memory usage, database access, network and disk operations, and response time.

A final observation about performance metrics is that the level at which they are measured can often be changed without significantly changing the metric's meaning. For example, allocations and execution time can be measured at the system level, at the single process level, or even for individual methods and lines. Execution time within a specific method can be a more actionable performance metric than overall CPU utilization or execution time at the process level. Unfortunately, increasing the granularity of measurements often incurs a performance overhead, as we illustrate in the next chapter by discussing various profiling tools.

PERFORMANCE IN THE SOFTWARE DEVELOPMENT LIFECYCLE

Where do you fit performance in the software development lifecycle? This innocent question carries the baggage of having to *retrofit* performance into an existing process. Although it is possible, a healthier approach is to consider every step of the development lifecycle an opportunity to understand the application's performance better: first, the performance goals and important metrics; next, whether the application meets or exceeds its goals; and finally, whether maintenance, user loads, and requirement changes introduce any regressions.

1. During the requirements gathering phase, start thinking about the performance goals you would like to set.

2. During the architecture phase, refine the performance metrics important for your application and define concrete performance goals.

3. During the development phase, frequently perform exploratory performance testing on prototype code or partially complete features to verify you are well within the system's performance goals.

4. During the testing phase, perform significant load testing and performance testing to validate completely your system's performance goals.

5. During subsequent development and maintenance, perform additional load testing and performance testing with every release (preferably on a daily or weekly basis) to quickly identify any performance regressions introduced into the system.

Taking the time to develop a suite of automatic load tests and performance tests, set up an isolated lab environment in which to run them, and analyze their results carefully to make sure no regressions are introduced is very time-consuming. Nevertheless, the performance benefits gained from systematically measuring and improving performance and making sure regressions do not creep slowly into the system is worth the initial investment in having a robust performance development process.

Summary

This chapter served as an introduction to the world of performance metrics and goals. Making sure you know *what* to measure and what performance criteria are important to you can be even more important than actually *measuring* performance, which is the subject of the next chapter. Throughout the remainder of the book, we measure performance using a variety of tools and provide guidelines on how to improve and optimize applications.

■ ■ ■

CHAPTER 2

Performance Measurement

This book is about improving the performance of .NET applications. You can't improve something that you can't measure first, which is why our first substantial chapter deals with performance measurement tools and techniques. Guessing where the application's bottlenecks are and jumping to premature conclusions on what to optimize is the worst thing a performance-conscious developer can do and often ends perilously. As we have seen in Chapter 1, there are many interesting performance metrics that can be the central factor to your application's perceived performance; in this chapter we shall see how to obtain them.

Approaches to Performance Measurement

There is more than one right way to measure application performance, and much depends on the context, the application's complexity, the type of information required, and the accuracy of the obtained results.

One approach for testing small programs or library methods is *white-box testing*: inspecting source code, analyzing its complexity on the whiteboard, modifying the program's source, and inserting measurement code in it. We will discuss this approach, often called *microbenchmarking*, towards the end of this chapter; it can be very valuable—and often irreplaceable—where precise results and absolute understanding of every CPU instruction is required, but rather time-consuming and inflexible where large applications are concerned. Additionally, if you don't know in advance which small part of the program to measure and reason about, isolating the bottleneck can be extremely difficult without resorting to automatic tools.

For larger programs, the more common approach is *black-box testing*, where a performance metric is identified by a human and then measured automatically by a tool. When using this approach, the developer doesn't have to identify the performance bottleneck in advance, or assume that the culprit is in a certain (and small) part of the program. Throughout this chapter we will consider numerous tools that analyze the application's performance automatically and present quantitative results in an easily digestible form. Among these tools are *performance counters*, Event Tracing for Windows (*ETW*), and commercial *profilers*.

As you read this chapter, bear in mind that performance measurement tools can adversely affect application performance. Few tools can provide accurate information and at the same time present no overhead when the application is executing. As we move from one tool to the next, always remember that the accuracy of the tools is often at conflict with the overhead they inflict upon your application.

Built-in Windows Tools

Before we turn to commercial tools that tend to require installation and intrusively measure your application's performance, it's paramount to make sure everything Windows has to offer out-of-the-box has been used to its fullest extent. Performance counters have been a part of Windows for nearly two decades, whereas Event Tracing for Windows is slightly newer and has become truly useful around the Windows Vista time frame (2006). Both are free, present on every edition of Windows, and can be used for performance investigations with minimal overhead.

Performance Counters

Windows performance counters are a built-in Windows mechanism for performance and health investigation. Various components, including the Windows kernel, drivers, databases, and the CLR provide performance counters that users and administrators can consume and understand how well the system is functioning. As an added bonus, performance counters for the vast majority of system components are turned on by default, so you will not be introducing any additional overhead by collecting this information.

Reading performance counter information from a local or remote system is extremely easy. The built-in *Performance Monitor* tool (perfmon.exe) can display every performance counter available on the system, as well as log performance counter data to a file for subsequent investigation and provide automatic alerts when performance counter readings breach a defined threshold. Performance Monitor can monitor remote systems as well, if you have administrator permissions and can connect to them through a local network.

Performance information is organized in the following hierarchy:

- *Performance counter categories* (or *performance objects*) represent a set of individual counters related to a certain system component. Some examples of categories include .NET CLR Memory, Processor Information, TCPv4, and PhysicalDisk.

- *Performance counters* are individual numeric data properties in a performance counter category. It is common to specify the performance counter category and performance counter name separated by a slash, e.g., Process\Private Bytes. Performance counters have several supported types, including raw numeric information (Process\Thread Count), rate of events (Print Queue\Bytes Printed/sec), percentages (PhysicalDisk\% Idle Time), and averages (ServiceModelOperation 3.0.0.0\Calls Duration).

- *Performance counter category instances* are used to distinguish several sets of counters from a specific component of which there are several instances. For example, because there may be multiple processors on a system, there is an instance of the Processor Information category for each processor (as well as an aggregated _Total instance). Performance counter categories can be multi-instance—and many are—or single-instance (such as the Memory category).

If you examine the full list of performance counters provided by a typical Windows system that runs .NET applications, you'll see that many performance problems can be identified without resorting to any other tool. At the very least, performance counters can often provide a general idea of which direction to pursue when investigating a performance problem or inspecting data logs from a production system to understand if it's behaving normally.

Below are some scenarios in which a system administrator or performance investigator can obtain a general idea of where the performance culprit lies before using heavier tools:

- If an application exhibits a memory leak, performance counters can be used to determine whether managed or native memory allocations are responsible for it. The Process\ Private Bytes counter can be correlated with the .NET CLR Memory\# Bytes in All Heaps counter. The former accounts for all private memory allocated by the process (including the GC heap) whereas the latter accounts only for managed memory. (See Figure 2-1.)

- If an ASP.NET application starts exhibiting abnormal behavior, the ASP.NET Applications category can provide more insight into what's going on. For example, the Requests/Sec, Requests Timed Out, Request Wait Time, and Requests Executing counters can identify extreme load conditions, the Errors Total/Sec counter can suggest whether the application is facing an unusual number of exceptions, and the various cache- and output cache-related counters can indicate whether caching is being applied effectively.

- If a WCF service that heavily relies on a database and distributed transactions is failing to handle its current load, the ServiceModelService category can pinpoint the problem—the Calls Outstanding, Calls Per Second, and Calls Failed Per Second counters can identify heavy load, the Transactions Flowed Per Second counter reports the number of transactions the service is dealing with, and at the same time SQL Server categories such as MSSQL$INSTANCENAME:Transactions and MSSQL$INSTANCENAME:Locks can point to problems with transactional execution, excessive locking, and even deadlocks.

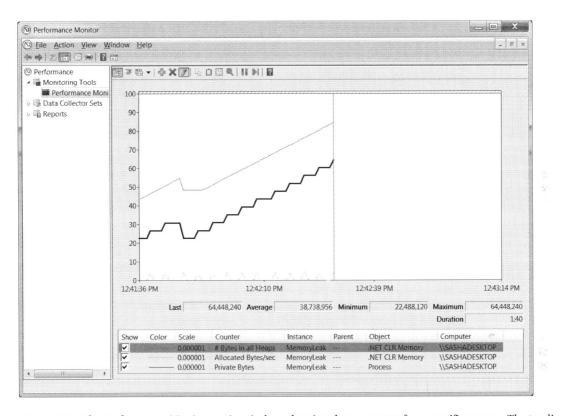

Figure 2-1. *The Performance Monitor main window, showing three counters for a specific process. The top line on the graph is the* Process\Private Bytes *counter, the middle one is* .NET CLR Memory\# Bytes in all Heaps, *and the bottom one is* .NET CLR Memory\Allocated Bytes/sec. *From the graph it is evident that the application exhibits a memory leak in the GC heap*

MONITORING MEMORY USAGE WITH PERFORMANCE COUNTERS

In this short experiment, you will monitor the memory usage of a sample application and determine that it exhibits a memory leak using Performance Monitor and the performance counters discussed above.

1. Open Performance Monitor—you can find it in the Start menu by searching for "Performance Monitor" or run perfmon.exe directly.

2. Run the MemoryLeak.exe application from this chapter's source code folder.

3. Click the "Performance Monitor" node in the tree on the left, and then click the green **+** button.

4. From the .NET CLR Memory category, select the # Bytes in all Heaps and Allocated Bytes/sec performance counters, select the MemoryLeak instance from the instance list, and click the "Add >>" button.

5. From the Process category, select the Private Bytes performance counter, select the MemoryLeak instance from the instance list, and click the "Add >>" button.

6. Click the "OK" button to confirm your choices and view the performance graph.

7. You might need to right click the counters in the bottom part of the screen and select "Scale selected counters" to see actual lines on the graph.

You should now see the lines corresponding to the Private Bytes and # Bytes in all Heaps performance counters climb in unison (somewhat similar to Figure 2-1). This points to a memory leak in the managed heap. We will return to this particular memory leak in Chapter 4 and pinpoint its root cause.

■ **Tip** There are literally thousands of performance counters on a typical Windows system; no performance investigator is expected to remember them all. This is where the small "Show description" checkbox at the bottom of the "Add Counters" dialog comes in handy—it can tell you that System\Processor Queue Length represents the number of ready threads waiting for execution on the system's processors, or that .NET CLR LocksAndThreads\ Contention Rate / sec is the number of times (per second) that threads attempted to acquire a managed lock unsuccessfully and had to wait for it to become available.

Performance Counter Logs and Alerts

Configuring performance counter logs is fairly easy, and you can even provide an XML template to your system administrators to apply performance counter logs automatically without having to specify individual performance counters. You can open the resulting logs on any machine and play them back as if they represent live data. (There are even some built-in counter sets you can use instead of configuring what data to log manually.)

You can also use Performance Monitor to configure a performance counter alert, which will execute a task when a certain threshold is breached. You can use performance counter alerts to create a rudimentary monitoring infrastructure, which can send an email or message to a system administrator when a performance constraint is violated. For example, you could configure a performance counter alert that would automatically restart your process when it reaches a dangerous amount of memory usage, or when the system as a whole runs out of disk space. We strongly recommend that you experiment with Performance Monitor and familiarize yourself with the various options it has to offer.

CONFIGURING PERFORMANCE COUNTER LOGS

To configure performance counter logs, open Performance Monitor and perform the following steps. (We assume that you are using Performance Monitor on Windows 7 or Windows Server 2008 R2; in prior operating system versions, Performance Monitor had a slightly different user interface—if you are using these versions, consult the documentation for detailed instructions.)

1. In the tree on the left, expand the Data Collector Sets node.

2. Right-click the User Defined node and select New ➤ Data Collector Set from the context menu.

3. Name your data collector set, select the "Create manually (Advanced)" radio button, and click Next.

4. Make sure the "Create data logs" radio button is selected, check the "Performance counter" checkbox, and click Next.

5. Use the Add button to add performance counters (the standard Add Counters dialog will open). When you're done, configure a sample interval (the default is to sample the counters every 15 seconds) and click Next.

6. Provide a directory which Performance Monitor will use to store your counter logs and then click Next.

7. Select the "Open properties for this data collector set" radio button and click Finish.

8. Use the various tabs to further configure your data collector set—you can define a schedule for it to run automatically, a stop condition (e.g. after collecting more than a certain amount of data), and a task to run when the data collection stops (e.g. to upload the results to a centralized location). When you're done, click OK.

9. Click the User Defined node, right-click your data collector set in the main pane, and select Start from the context menu.

10. Your counter log is now running and collecting data to the directory you've selected. You can stop the data collector set at any time by right-clicking it and selecting Stop from the context menu.

When you're done collecting the data and want to inspect it using the Performance Monitor, perform the following steps:

11. Select the User Defined node.

12. Right-click your data collector set and select Latest Report from the context menu.

13. In the resulting window, you can add or delete counters from the list of counters in the log, configure a time range and change the data scale by right-clicking the graph and selecting Properties from the context menu.

Finally, to analyze log data on another machine, you should copy the log directory to that machine, open the Performance Monitor node, and click the second toolbar button from the left (or Ctrl + L). In the resulting dialog you can select the "Log files" checkbox and add log files using the Add button.

Custom Performance Counters

Although Performance Monitor is an extremely useful tool, you can read performance counters from any .NET application using the System.Diagnostics.PerformanceCounter class. Even better, you can create your own performance counters and add them to the vast set of data available for performance investigation.

Below are some scenarios in which you should consider exporting performance counter categories:

- You are developing an infrastructure library to be used as part of large systems. Your library can report performance information through performance counters, which is often easier on developers and system administrators than following log files or debugging at the source code level.

- You are developing a server system which accepts custom requests, processes them, and delivers responses (custom Web server, Web service, etc.). You should report performance information for the request processing rate, errors encountered, and similar statistics. (See the ASP.NET performance counter categories for some ideas.)

- You are developing a high-reliability Windows service that runs unattended and communicates with custom hardware. Your service can report the health of the hardware, the rate of your software's interactions with it, and similar statistics.

The following code is all it takes to export a single-instance performance counter category from your application and to update these counters periodically. It assumes that the AttendanceSystem class has information on the number of employees currently signed in, and that you want to expose this information as a performance counter. (You will need the System.Diagnostics namespace to compile this code fragment.)

```
public static void CreateCategory() {
  if (PerformanceCounterCategory.Exists("Attendance")) {
    PerformanceCounterCategory.Delete("Attendance");
  }
  CounterCreationDataCollection counters = new CounterCreationDataCollection();
  CounterCreationData employeesAtWork = new CounterCreationData(
    "# Employees at Work", "The number of employees currently checked in.",
    PerformanceCounterType.NumberOfItems32);
  PerformanceCounterCategory.Create(
    "Attendance", "Attendance information for Litware, Inc.",
    PerformanceCounterCategoryType.SingleInstance, counters);
}
public static void StartUpdatingCounters() {
  PerformanceCounter employeesAtWork = new PerformanceCounter(
    "Attendance", "# Employees at Work", readOnly: false);
  updateTimer = new Timer(_ => {
    employeesAtWork.RawValue = AttendanceSystem.Current.EmployeeCount;
  }, null, TimeSpan.Zero, TimeSpan.FromSeconds(1));
}
```

As we have seen, it takes very little effort to configure custom performance counters, and they can be of utmost importance when carrying out a performance investigation. Correlating system performance counter data with custom performance counters is often all a performance investigator needs to pinpoint the precise cause of a performance or configuration issue.

▨ **Note** Performance Monitor can be used to collect other types of information that have nothing to do with performance counters. You can use it to collect configuration data from a system—the values of registry keys, WMI objects properties, and even interesting disk files. You can also use it to capture data from ETW providers (which we discuss next) for subsequent analysis. By using XML templates, system administrators can quickly apply data collector sets to a system and generate a useful report with very few manual configuration steps.

Although performance counters offer a great amount of interesting performance information, they cannot be used as a high-performance logging and monitoring framework. There are no system components that update performance counters more often than a few times a second, and the Windows Performance Monitor won't read performance counters more often than once a second. If your performance investigation requires following thousands of events per second, performance counters are not a good fit. We now turn our attention to *Event Tracing for Windows* (ETW), which was designed for high-performance data collection and richer data types (not just numbers).

Event Tracing for Windows (ETW)

Event Tracing for Windows (ETW) is a high-performance event logging framework built into Windows. As was the case with performance counters, many system components and application frameworks, including the Windows kernel and the CLR, define *providers*, which report *events*—information on the component's inner workings. Unlike performance counters, that are always on, ETW providers can be turned on and off at runtime so that the performance overhead of transferring and collecting them is incurred only when they're needed for a performance investigation.

One of the richest sources of ETW information is the *kernel provider*, which reports events on process and thread creation, DLL loading, memory allocation, network I/O, and stack trace accounting (also known as *sampling*). Table 2-1 shows some of the useful information reported by the kernel and CLR ETW providers. You can use ETW to investigate overall system behavior, such as what processes are consuming CPU time, to analyze disk I/O and network I/O bottlenecks, to obtain garbage collection statistics and memory usage for managed processes, and many other scenarios discussed later in this section.

ETW events are tagged with a precise time and can contain custom information, as well as an optional stack trace of where they occurred. These stack traces can be used to further identify sources of performance and correctness problems. For example, the CLR provider can report events at the start and end of every garbage collection. Combined with precise call stacks, these events can be used to determine which parts of the program are typically causing garbage collection. (For more information about garbage collection and its triggers, see Chapter 4.)

Table 2-1. *Partial List of ETW Events in Windows and the CLR*

Provider	Flag / Keyword	Description	Events (Partial List)
Kernel	PROC_THREAD	Creation and destruction of processes and threads	--
Kernel	LOADER	Load and unload of images (DLLs, drivers, EXEs)	--
Kernel	SYSCALL	System calls	--
Kernel	DISK_IO	Disk I/O reads and writes (including head location)	--
Kernel	HARD_FAULTS	Page faults that resulted in disk I/O (not satisfied from memory)	--
Kernel	PROFILE	Sampling event—a stack trace of all processors collected every 1ms	--
CLR	GCKeyword	Garbage collection statistics and information	Collection started, collection ended, finalizers run, ~100KB of memory have been allocated
CLR	ContentionKeyword	Threads contend for a managed lock	Contention starts (a thread begins waiting), contention ends
CLR	JITTracingKeyword	Just in time compiler (JIT) information	Method inlining succeeded, method inlining failed
CLR	ExceptionKeyword	Exceptions that are thrown	--

Accessing this highly detailed information requires an ETW collection tool and an application that can read raw ETW events and perform some basic analysis. At the time of writing, there were two tools capable of both tasks: *Windows Performance Toolkit* (WPT, also known as XPerf), which ships with the Windows SDK, and *PerfMonitor* (do not confuse it with Windows Performance Monitor!), which is an open source project by the CLR team at Microsoft.

Windows Performance Toolkit (WPT)

Windows Performance Toolkit (WPT) is a set of utilities for controlling ETW sessions, capturing ETW events into log files, and processing them for later display. It can generate graphs and overlays of ETW events, summary tables including call stack information and aggregation, and CSV files for automated processing. To download WPT, download the Windows SDK Web installer from http://msdn.microsoft.com/en-us/performance/cc752957.aspx and select only Common Utilities ➤ Windows Performance Toolkit from the installation options screen. After the Windows SDK installer completes, navigate to the Redist\Windows Performance Toolkit subdirectory of the SDK installation directory and run the installer file for your system's architecture (Xperf_x86.msi for 32-bit systems, Xperf_x64.msi for 64-bit systems).

▓ **Note** On 64-bit Windows, stack walking requires changing a registry setting that disables paging-out of kernel code pages (for the Windows kernel itself and any drivers). This may increase the system's working set (RAM utilization) by a few megabytes. To change this setting, navigate to the registry key `HKLM\System\CurrentControlSet\Control\Session Manager\Memory Management`, set the `DisablePagingExecutive` value to the DWORD `0x1`, and restart the system.

The tools you'll use for capturing and analyzing ETW traces are XPerf.exe and XPerfView.exe. Both tools require administrative privileges to run. The XPerf.exe tool has several command line options that control which providers are enabled during the trace, the size of the buffers used, the file name to which the events are flushed, and many additional options. The XPerfView.exe tool analyzes and provides a graphical report of what the trace file contains.

All traces can be augmented with call stacks, which often allow precise zooming-in on the performance issues. However, you don't have to capture events from a specific provider to obtain stack traces of what the system is doing; the `SysProfile` kernel flag group enables collection of stack traces from all processors captured at 1ms intervals. This is a rudimentary way of understanding what a busy system is doing at the method level. (We'll return to this mode in more detail when discussing *sampling* profilers later in this chapter.)

CAPTURING AND ANALYZING KERNEL TRACES WITH XPERF

In this section, you'll capture a kernel trace using XPerf.exe and analyze the results in the XPerfView.exe graphical tool. This experiment is designed to be carried out on Windows Vista system or a later version. (It also requires you to set two system environment variables. To do so, right click Computer, click Properties, click "Advanced system settings" and finally click the "Environment Variables" button at the bottom of the dialog.)

1. Set the system environment variable `_NT_SYMBOL_PATH` to point to the Microsoft public symbol server and a local symbol cache, e.g.: `srv*C:\Temp\Symbols*http://msdl.microsoft.com/download/symbols`

2. Set the system environment variable `_NT_SYMCACHE_PATH` to a local directory on your disk—this should be a *different* directory from the local symbols cache in the previous step.

3. Open an administrator Command Prompt window and navigate to the installation directory where you installed WPT (e.g. `C:\Program Files\Windows Kits\8.0\Windows Performance Toolkit`).

4. Begin a trace with the `Base` kernel provider group, which contains the `PROC_THREAD, LOADER, DISK_IO, HARD_FAULTS, PROFILE, MEMINFO`, and `MEMINFO_WS` kernel flags (see Table 2-1). To do this, run the following command: `xperf -on Base`

5. Initiate some system activity: run applications, switch between windows, open files—for at least a few seconds. (These are the events that will enter the trace.)

6. Stop the trace and flush the trace to a log file by running the following command: `xperf -d KernelTrace.etl`

7. Launch the graphical performance analyzer by running the following command:
   `xperfview KernelTrace.etl`

8. The resulting window contains several graphs, one for each ETW keyword that generated events during the trace. You can choose the graphs to display on the left. Typically, the topmost graph displays the processor utilization by processor, and subsequent graphs display the disk I/O operation count, memory usage, and other statistics.

9. Select a section of the processor utilization graph, right click it, and select Load Symbols from the context menu. Right click the selected section again, and select Simple Summary Table. This should open an expandable view in which you can navigate between methods in all processes that had some processor activity during the trace. (Loading the symbols from the Microsoft symbol server for the first time can be time consuming.)

There's much more to WPT than you've seen in this experiment; you should explore other parts of the UI and consider capturing and analyzing trace data from other kernel groups or even your own application's ETW providers. (We'll discuss custom ETW providers later in this chapter.)

There are many useful scenarios in which WPT can provide insight into the system's overall behavior and the performance of individual processes. Below are some screenshots and examples of these scenarios:

- WPT can capture all disk I/O operations on a system and display them on a map of the physical disk. This provides insight into expensive I/O operations, especially where large seeks are involved on rotating hard drives. (See Figure 2-2.)

- WPT can provide call stacks for all processor activity on the system during the trace. It aggregates call stacks at the process, module, and function level, and allows at-a-glance understanding of where the system (or a specific application) is spending CPU time. Note that managed frames are not supported—we'll address this deficiency later with the PerfMonitor tool. (See Figure 2-3.)

- WPT can display overlay graphs of different activity types to provide correlation between I/O operations, memory utilization, processor activity, and other captured metrics. (See Figure 2-4.)

- WPT can display call stack aggregations in a trace (when the trace is initially configured with the `-stackwalk` command line switch)—this provides complete information on call stacks which created certain events. (See Figure 2-5.)

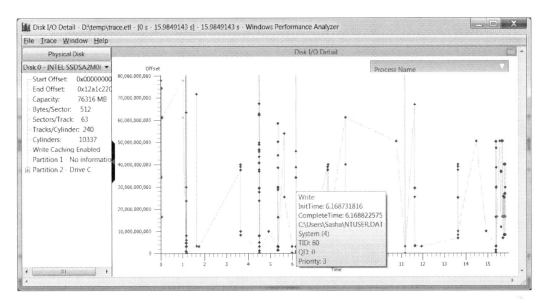

Figure 2-2. *Disk I/O operations laid out on a map of the physical disk. Seeks between I/O operations and individual I/O details are provided through tooltips*

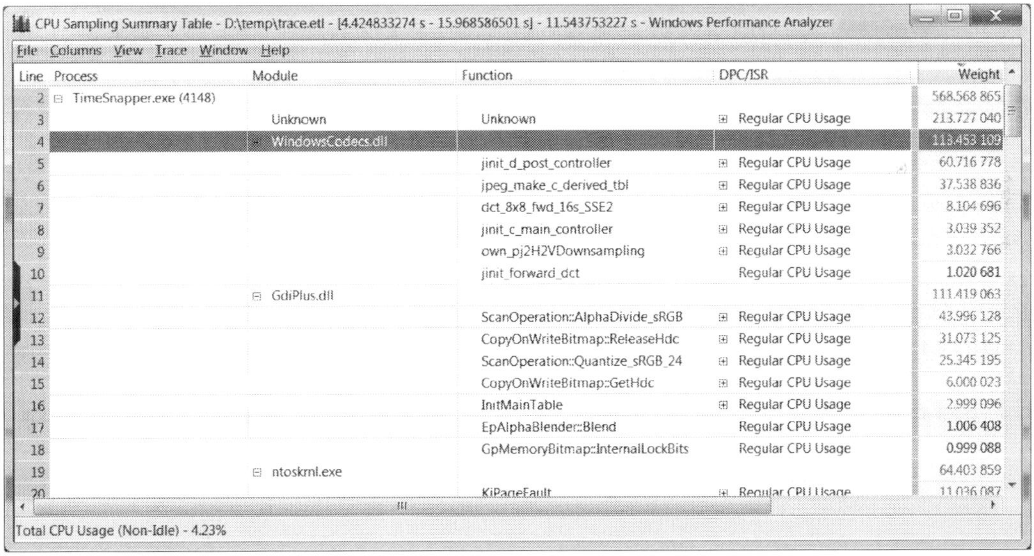

Figure 2-3. *Detailed stack frames for a single process (TimeSnapper.exe). The Weight column indicates (roughly) how much CPU time was spent in that frame*

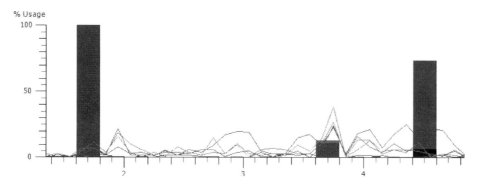

Figure 2-4. *Overlay graph of CPU activity (lines—each line indicates a different processor) and disk I/O operations (columns). No explicit correlation between I/O activity and CPU activity is visible*

Line	Process	Stack	Weight	% Weight	Cou ▲
13		│ │ │ │ │ clr.dll!RunMain	5,013.608 781	10.85	4,9
14		│ │ │ │ │ clr.dll!MethodDescCallSite::CallTargetWorker	5,013.608 781	10.85	4,9
15		│ │ │ │ │ clr.dll!CallDescrWorkerWithHandler	5,013.608 781	10.85	4,9
16		│ │ │ │ │ clr.dll!CallDescrWorkerInternal	5,013.608 781	10.85	4,9
17		⊟ │ │ │ │ │- ?!?	5,012.608 781	10.85	4,9
18		⊟ │ │ │ │ │ │ │- ?!?	5,002.608 960	10.83	4,9
19		⊟ │ │ │ │ │ │ │ │- ?!?	5,000.521 307	10.83	4,9
20		│ │ │ │ │ │ │ │ ?!?	5,000.521 307	10.83	4,9
21		⊟ │ │ │ │ │ │ │ │- ?!?	4,995.442 422	10.81	4,9
22		⊟ │ │ │ │ │ │ │ │ │- ?!?	4,992.411 307	10.81	4,9
23		⊞ │ │ │ │ │ │ │ │ │ │- ?!?	3,989.661 456	8.64	3,9
24		│ │ │ │ │ │ │ │ │ │- mscorlib.dll!System.DateTime.get_Now()	973.931 079	2.11	9
25		⊞ │ │ │ │ │ │ │ │ │ │- ?!? <itself>	19.221 479	0.04	
26		⊞ │ │ │ │ │ │ │ │ │ │- mscorlib.dll!System.DateTime.get_UtcNow()	4.119 320	0.01	
27		⊞ │ │ │ │ │ │ │ │ │ │- clr.dll!ThePreStub	3.041 182	0.01	
28		⊞ │ │ │ │ │ │ │ │ │ │- mscorlib.dll!System.DateTime..ctor(Int64, Syste...	2.024 527	0.00	
29		│ │ │ │ │ │ │ │ │ │- clr.dll!SystemNative::_GetSystemTimeAsFileTime	1.012 264	0.00	
30		⊞ │ │ │ │ │ │ │ │ │- clr.dll!ThePreStub	3.031 115	0.01	
31		⊞ │ │ │ │ │ │ │- clr.dll!ThePreStub	4.045 029	0.01	▼

CPU Sampling Summary Table - d:\temp\trace4.etl - [1.280367413 s - 7.054331998 s] - 5.773964585 s - Windows Performance Analyzer

File Columns View Trace Window Help

Total CPU Usage (Non-Idle) - 12.91%

Figure 2-5. *Call stack aggregation in the report. Note that managed frames are displayed only partially—the ?!? frames could not be resolved. The mscorlib.dll frames (e.g. System.DateTime.get_Now()) were resolved successfully because they are pre-compiled using NGen and not compiled by the JIT compiler at runtime*

■ **Note**   The latest version of the Windows SDK (version 8.0) ships with a pair of new tools, called Windows Performance Recorder (wpr.exe) and Windows Performance Analyzer (wpa.exe), that were designed to gradually replace the XPerf and XPerfView tools we used earlier. For example, wpr -start CPU is roughly equivalent to xperf -on Diag, and wpr -stop reportfile is roughly equivalent to xperf -d reportfile. The WPA analysis UI is slightly different, but provides features similar to XPerfView. For more information on the new tools, consult the MSDN documentation at http://msdn.microsoft.com/en-us/library/hh162962.aspx.

XPerfView is very capable of displaying kernel provider data in attractive graphs and tables, but its support for custom providers is not as powerful. For example, we can capture events from the CLR ETW provider, but XPerfView will not generate pretty graphs for the various events—we'll have to make sense of the raw data in the trace based on the list of keywords and events in the provider's documentation (the full list of the CLR ETW provider's keywords and events is available in the MSDN documentation—`http://msdn.microsoft.com/en-us/library/ff357720.aspx`).

If we run XPerf with the CLR ETW provider (`e13c0d23-ccbc-4e12-931b-d9cc2eee27e4`) the keyword for GC events (`0x00000001`), and the Verbose log level (`0x5`), it will dutifully capture every event the provider generates. By dumping it to a CSV file or opening it with XPerfView we will be able—slowly—to identify GC-related events in our application. Figure 2-6 shows a sample of the resulting XPerfView report—the time elapsed between the `GC /Start` and `GC /Stop` rows is the time it took a single garbage collection to complete in the monitored application.

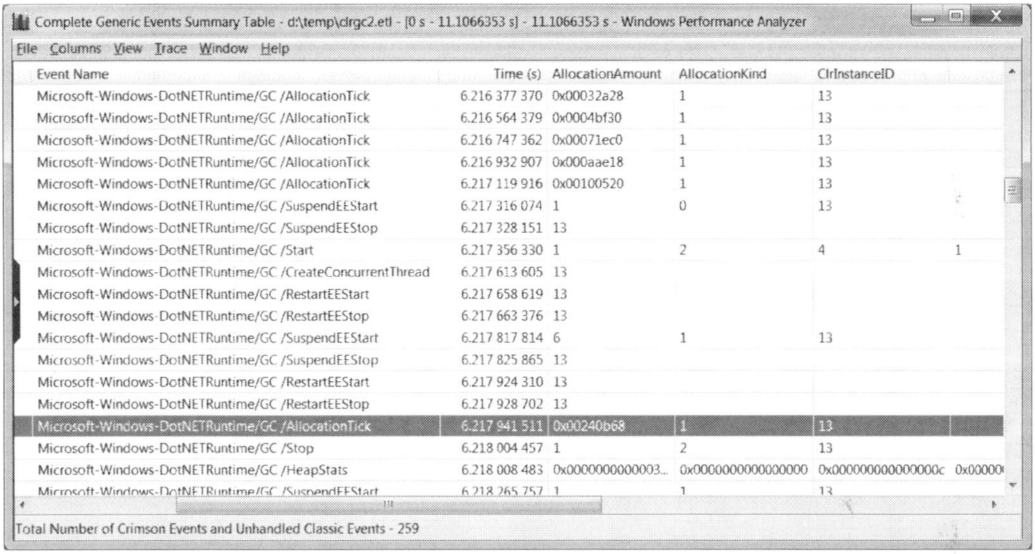

Event Name	Time (s)	AllocationAmount	AllocationKind	ClrInstanceID	
Microsoft-Windows-DotNETRuntime/GC /AllocationTick	6.216 377 370	0x00032a28	1	13	
Microsoft-Windows-DotNETRuntime/GC /AllocationTick	6.216 564 379	0x0004bf30	1	13	
Microsoft-Windows-DotNETRuntime/GC /AllocationTick	6.216 747 362	0x00071ec0	1	13	
Microsoft-Windows-DotNETRuntime/GC /AllocationTick	6.216 932 907	0x000aae18	1	13	
Microsoft-Windows-DotNETRuntime/GC /AllocationTick	6.217 119 916	0x00100520	1	13	
Microsoft-Windows-DotNETRuntime/GC /SuspendEEStart	6.217 316 074	1	0	13	
Microsoft-Windows-DotNETRuntime/GC /SuspendEEStop	6.217 328 151	13			
Microsoft-Windows-DotNETRuntime/GC /Start	6.217 356 330	1	2	4	1
Microsoft-Windows-DotNETRuntime/GC /CreateConcurrentThread	6.217 613 605	13			
Microsoft-Windows-DotNETRuntime/GC /RestartEEStart	6.217 658 619	13			
Microsoft-Windows-DotNETRuntime/GC /RestartEEStop	6.217 663 376	13			
Microsoft-Windows-DotNETRuntime/GC /SuspendEEStart	6.217 817 814	6	1	13	
Microsoft-Windows-DotNETRuntime/GC /SuspendEEStop	6.217 825 865	13			
Microsoft-Windows-DotNETRuntime/GC /RestartEEStart	6.217 924 310	13			
Microsoft-Windows-DotNETRuntime/GC /RestartEEStop	6.217 928 702	13			
Microsoft-Windows-DotNETRuntime/GC /AllocationTick	6.217 941 511	0x00240b68	1	13	
Microsoft-Windows-DotNETRuntime/GC /Stop	6.218 004 457	1	2	13	
Microsoft-Windows-DotNETRuntime/GC /HeapStats	6.218 008 483	0x0000000000003...	0x0000000000000000	0x000000000000000c	0x00000
Microsoft-Windows-DotNETRuntime/GC /SuspendEEStart	6.218 265 757	1	1	13	

Figure 2-6. *Raw report of CLR GC-related events. The selected row displays the* `GCAllocationTick_V1` *event that is raised every time approximately 100KB of memory is allocated*

Fortunately, the Base Class Library (BCL) team at Microsoft has identified this deficiency and provided an open source library and tool for analyzing CLR ETW traces, called PerfMonitor. We discuss this tool next.

PerfMonitor

The PerfMonitor.exe open source command line tool has been released by the BCL team at Microsoft through the CodePlex website. At the time of writing the latest release was PerfMonitor 1.5 that can be downloaded from `http://bcl.codeplex.com/releases/view/49601`. PerfMonitor's primary advantage compared to WPT is that it has intimate knowledge about CLR events and provides more than just raw tabular data. PerfMonitor analyzes GC and JIT activity in the process, and can sample managed stack traces and determine which parts of the application are using CPU time.

For advanced users, PerfMonitor also ships with a library called TraceEvent, which enables programmatic access to CLR ETW traces for automatic inspection. You could use the TraceEvent library in custom system monitoring software to inspect automatically a trace from a production system and decide how to triage it.

Although PerfMonitor can be used to collect kernel events or even events from a custom ETW provider (using the /KernelEvents and /Provider command line switches), it is typically used to analyze the behavior of a managed application using the built-in CLR providers. Its runAnalyze command line option executes an application of your choice, monitors its execution, and upon its termination generates a detailed HTML report and opens it in your default browser. (You should follow the PerfMonitor user guide—at least through the Quick Start section—to generate reports similar to the screenshots in this section. To display the user guide, run PerfMonitor usersguide.)

When PerfMonitor is instructed to run an application and generate a report, it produces the following command line output. You can experiment with the tool yourself as you read this section by running it on the JackCompiler.exe sample application from this chapter's source code folder.

```
C:\PerfMonitor>perfmonitor runAnalyze JackCompiler.exe

Starting kernel tracing.  Output file: PerfMonitorOutput.kernel.etl
Starting user model tracing.  Output file: PerfMonitorOutput.etl
Starting at 4/7/2012 12:33:40 PM
Current Directory C:\PerfMonitor
Executing: JackCompiler.exe {

} Stopping at 4/7/2012 12:33:42 PM=1.724 sec
Stopping tracing for sessions 'NT Kernel Logger' and 'PerfMonitorSession'.
Analyzing data in C:\PerfMonitor\PerfMonitorOutput.etlx
GC Time HTML Report in C:\PerfMonitor\PerfMonitorOutput.GCTime.html
JIT Time HTML Report in C:\PerfMonitor\PerfMonitorOutput.jitTime.html
Filtering to process JackCompiler (1372).  Started at 1372.000 msec.
Filtering to Time region [0.000, 1391.346] msec
CPU Time HTML report in C:\PerfMonitor\PerfMonitorOutput.cpuTime.html
Filtering to process JackCompiler (1372).  Started at 1372.000 msec.
Perf Analysis HTML report in C:\PerfMonitor\PerfMonitorOutput.analyze.html
PerfMonitor processing time: 7.172 secs.
```

The various HTML files generated by PerfMonitor contain the distilled report, but you can always use the raw ETL files with XPerfView or any other tool that can read binary ETW traces. The summary analysis for the example above contains the following information (this might vary, of course, when you run this experiment on your own machine):

- CPU Statistics—CPU time consumed was 917ms and the average CPU utilization was 56.6%. The rest of the time was spent waiting for something.

- GC Statistics—the total GC time was 20ms, the maximum GC heap size was 4.5MB, the maximum allocation rate was 1496.1MB/s, and the average GC pause was 0.1ms.

- JIT Compilation Statistics—159 methods were compiled at runtime by the JIT compiler, for a total of 30493 bytes of machine code.

Drilling down to the CPU, GC, and JIT reports can provide a wealth of useful information. The CPU detailed report provides information on methods that use a large percentage of CPU time (*bottom up analysis*), a call tree of where CPU time is spent (*top down analysis*), and individual caller-callee views for each method in the trace. To prevent the report from growing very large, methods that do not exceed a predefined relevance threshold (1% for the bottom up analysis and 5% for the top down analysis) are excluded. Figure 2-7 is an example of a bottom up report—the three methods with most CPU work were System.String.Concat, JackCompiler. Tokenizer.Advance, and System.Linq.Enumerable.Contains. Figure 2-8 is an example of (part of) a top down report—84.2% of the CPU time is consumed by JackCompiler.Parser.Parse, which calls out to ParseClass, ParseSubDecls, ParseSubDecl, ParseSubBody, and so on.

Name	Exc %	Exc MSec	Inc %	Inc MSec	CPU Utilization	First	Last
mscorlib!System.String.Concat(String,String,String)	15.0	138	15.0	138			
JackCompiler.Compiler!JackCompiler.Tokenizer.Advance()	12.5	115	19.3	177			
System.Core!System.Linq.Enumerable.Contains([Enumerable`1<!!0>,!!0)	8.1	74	8.1	74			
JackCompiler.Compiler!JackCompiler.Parser.ParseTerm()	7.0	64	25.8	237			
JackCompiler.Compiler!JackCompiler.Parser.ParseAddExpression()	4.4	40	36.8	337			
kernel32!?	3.7	34	3.7	34			
mscorlib!System.IO.TextWriter.WriteLine(String,Object)	3.6	33	9.9	91			
JackCompiler.Compiler!JackCompiler.Tokenizer.EatWhile(Predicate`1<wchar>)	2.9	27	3.5	32			
JackCompiler.Compiler!JackCompiler.Parser.ParseMulExpression()	2.5	23	33.5	307	0334334333244330	535.779	1388.363
JackCompiler.Compiler!JackCompiler.Parser.ParseExpression()	2.2	20	43.8	402	0445445444355450	534.779	1388.363
JackCompiler.Compiler!JackCompiler.Parser.IsNextTokenMulOp()	2.2	20	5.3	49	000001000_00_0	582.152	1375.159
JackCompiler.Compiler!JackCompiler.Parser.ParseLetStatement()	2.1	19	39.3	360	0544544434433430	533.779	1388.363
ntdll!?	2.1	19	98.3	901	0211599A9999AA99A991	297.866	1390.272
JackCompiler.Compiler!JackCompiler.Parser.ParseSubCall(Token)	2.1	19	21.6	198	112122222233220	547.779	1389.374
mscorwks!?	2.0	18	2.0	18	001	399.791	519.773
JackCompiler.Compiler!JackCompiler.CCodeGenerator.Assignment(Token,bool)	1.9	17	5.6	51	10000100100000	555.843	1365.522
JackCompiler.Compiler!JackCompiler.Parser.ParseSubBody()	1.9	17	78.5	720	1878798878888881	529.779	1389.374
JackCompiler.Compiler!JackCompiler.Parser.ParseRelationalExpression()	1.9	17	40.9	375	0444445444354440	534.779	1388.363
System.Core!System.Linq.Enumerable.Contains([Enumerable`1<!!0>,!!0)	1.5	14	1.5	14	0 0 0	547.779	1348.705
JackCompiler.Compiler!JackCompiler.Tokenizer.Next()	1.2	11	19.3	177	221121221322110	547.779	1389.374
JackCompiler.Compiler!JackCompiler.Tokenizer.EatWhitespace()	1.2	11	1.7	16	0 0 0 00000	515.773	1382.273

Inset note within CPU Utilization header:

> CPU Utilization over time.
> Total time is broken into 32 buckets and each digit represents its CPU
> _ = no CPU used
> 0 = 0-10% CPU use
> 1 = 10-20% use
> ..
> 9 = 90-100% use
> A = 100-110% use.
> ..
> Z = 340-350% use.
> * = greater than 350% use.

Figure 2-7. *Bottom up report from PerfMonitor. The "Exc %" column is an estimation of the CPU time used by that method alone; the "Inc %" column is an estimation of the CPU time used by that method and all other methods it called (its sub-tree in the call tree)*

Name	Inc %	Inc MSec	Exc %	Exc MSec	CPU Utilization
ROOT	100.0	917	0.0	0	0311599A9999AAA9A991
+Process JackCompiler (1372)	100.0	917	0.0	0	0311599A9999AA9A991
+Thread (4636)	100.0	917	0.2	2	0311599A9999AA9A991
+ntdll!?	98.3	901	2.1	19	0211599A9999AA99A991
|+JackCompiler!JackCompiler.CompilerDriver.Main(String[])	95.3	874	0.2	2	1599A9999AA99A991
||+JackCompiler!JackCompiler.CompilerDriver.DriveCompilerWithCCodeGenerator(String[])	95.1	872	0.5	5	0599A99999A99A991
|| +JackCompiler.Compiler!JackCompiler.Parser.Parse()	84.2	772	0.0	0	2989898988998991
|| |+JackCompiler.Compiler!JackCompiler.Parser.ParseClass()	84.2	772	0.9	8	2989898988998991
|| | +JackCompiler.Compiler!JackCompiler.Parser.ParseSubDecls()	82.0	752	0.1	1	2979898988988881
|| | |+JackCompiler.Compiler!JackCompiler.Parser.ParseSubDecl()	81.9	751	0.5	5	2979898988988881
|| | | +JackCompiler.Compiler!JackCompiler.Parser.ParseSubBody()	78.5	720	1.9	17	1878798878888881
|| | | |+JackCompiler.Compiler!JackCompiler.Parser.ParseStatements()	75.4	691	0.3	3	1878788878888881
|| | | ||+JackCompiler.Compiler!JackCompiler.Parser.ParseStatement()	75.0	688	0.5	5	1877788878888881
|| | | || +JackCompiler.Compiler!JackCompiler.Parser.ParseLetStatement()	30.2	277	1.2	11	0433433323222320
|| | | || |+JackCompiler.Compiler!JackCompiler.Parser.ParseExpression()	20.3	186	0.0	0	0223212222111210
|| | | || | +JackCompiler.Compiler!JackCompiler.Parser.ParseRelationalExpression()	19.5	179	0.3	3	0222212212111210
|| | | || | |+JackCompiler.Compiler!JackCompiler.Parser.ParseAddExpression()	17.7	162	0.1	1	0222221212111110
|| | | || | ||+JackCompiler.Compiler!JackCompiler.Parser.ParseMulExpression()	16.8	154	0.5	5	0222211211111110
|| | | || | |||+JackCompiler.Compiler!JackCompiler.Parser.ParseTerm()	12.9	118	0.8	7	212111111100100
|| | | || +JackCompiler.Compiler!JackCompiler.Parser.ParseDoStatement()	22.0	202	0.1	1	122122222223220
|| | | || |+JackCompiler.Compiler!JackCompiler.Parser.ParseSubCall(Token)	17.3	159	0.1	1	011021112222210
|| | | || | |+JackCompiler.Compiler!JackCompiler.Parser.ParseExpressionList()	8.1	74	0.0	0	01011000011110
|| | | || | ||+JackCompiler.Compiler!JackCompiler.Parser.ParseExpression()	8.1	74	0.3	3	01011000011110

Figure 2-8. *Top down report from PerfMonitor*

The detailed GC analysis report contains a table with garbage collection statistics (counts, times) for each generation, as well as individual GC event information, including pause times, reclaimed memory, and many others. Some of this information will be extremely useful when we discuss the garbage collector's inner workings and performance implications in Chapter 4. Figure 2-9 shows a few rows for the individual GC events.

GC Events by Time													
All times are in msec. Start time is msec from trace start.													
Start Time	GC Num	Gen	Pause	Alloc Rate MB/sec	Alloc MB	MSec GC/ Alloc MB	MSec GC/ Kept MB	Before MB	After MB	Ratio Before/After	Reclaimed	Suspend Time	Type	Reason
551.053	1	0	0.20	7.53	4.15	0.046	2.56	4.15	0.07	55.82	4.07	0.01	NonConcurrentGC	AllocSmall
554.348	2	0	0.09	1341.22	4.15	0.020	0.84	4.23	0.10	42.74	4.13	0.01	NonConcurrentGC	AllocSmall
557.265	3	0	0.08	1465.75	4.15	0.018	0.59	4.25	0.13	33.15	4.12	0.01	NonConcurrentGC	AllocSmall
560.292	4	0	0.08	1405.49	4.15	0.019	0.49	4.27	0.16	27.49	4.12	0.01	NonConcurrentGC	AllocSmall
563.323	5	0	0.09	1406.78	4.15	0.020	0.46	4.31	0.18	23.94	4.13	0.01	NonConcurrentGC	AllocSmall
566.281	6	0	0.08	1449.91	4.16	0.017	0.33	4.34	0.21	20.79	4.14	0.01	NonConcurrentGC	AllocSmall

Figure 2-9. *Individual GC events, including the amount of memory reclaimed, the application pause time, the type of collection incurred, and other details*

Finally, the detailed JIT analysis report shows how much time the JIT compiler required for each of the application's methods as well as the precise time at which they were compiled. This information can be useful to determine whether application startup performance can be improved—if an excessive amount of startup time is spent in the JIT compiler, pre-compiling your application's binaries (using NGen) may be a worthwhile optimization. We will discuss NGEN and other strategies for reducing application startup time in Chapter 10.

▥ **Tip** Collecting information from multiple high-performance ETW providers can generate very large log files. For example, in default collection mode PerfMonitor routinely generates over 5MB of raw data per second. Leaving such a trace on for several days is likely to exhaust disk space even on large hard drives. Fortunately, both XPerf and PerfMonitor support circular logging mode, where only the last *N* megabytes of logs are retained. In PerfMonitor, the /Circular command-line switch takes the maximum log file size (in megabytes) and discards the oldest logs automatically when the threshold is exceeded.

Although PerfMonitor is a very powerful tool, its raw HTML reports and abundance of command-line options make it somewhat difficult to use. The next tool we'll see offers very similar functionality to PerfMonitor and can be used in the same scenarios, but has a much more user-friendly interface to collecting and interpreting ETW information and will make some performance investigations considerably shorter.

The PerfView Tool

PerfView is a free Microsoft tool that unifies ETW collection and analysis capabilities already available in PerfMonitor with heap analysis features that we will discuss later in conjunction with tools such as CLR Profiler and ANTS Memory Profiler. You can download PerfView from the Microsoft download center, at http://www.microsoft.com/download/en/details.aspx?id=28567. Note that you have to run PerfView as an administrator, because it requires access to the ETW infrastructure.

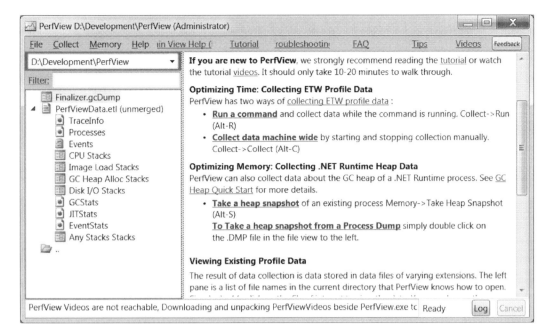

Figure 2-10. *PerfView's main UI. In the file view (on the left) a heap dump and an ETW trace are visible. The links on the main view lead to various commands the tool supports*

To analyze ETW information from a specific process, use the Collect ➤ Run menu item in PerfView (Figure 2-10 shows the main UI). For the purpose of the heap analysis we will perform shortly, you can use PerfView on the MemoryLeak.exe sample application from this chapter's source code folder. It will run the process for you and generate a report with all the information PerfMonitor makes available and more, including:

- Raw list of ETW events collected from various providers (e.g. CLR contention information, native disk I/O, TCP packets, and hard page faults)

- Grouped stack locations where the application's CPU time was spent, including configurable filters and thresholds

- Stack locations for image (assembly) loads, disk I/O operations, and GC allocations (for every ~ 100KB of allocated objects)

- GC statistics and events, including the duration of each garbage collection and the amount of space reclaimed

Additionally, PerfView can be used to capture a heap snapshot from a currently running process or import a heap snapshot from a dump file. After importing, PerfView can be used to look for the types with most memory utilization in the snapshot and identify reference chains that are responsible for keeping these types alive. Figure 2-11 shows the PerfView reference analyzer for the Schedule class, which is responsible (inclusively) for 31MB of the heap snapshot's contents. PerfView successfully identifies the Employee class instances holding references to Schedule objects, while Employee instances are being retained by the f-reachable queue (discussed in Chapter 4).

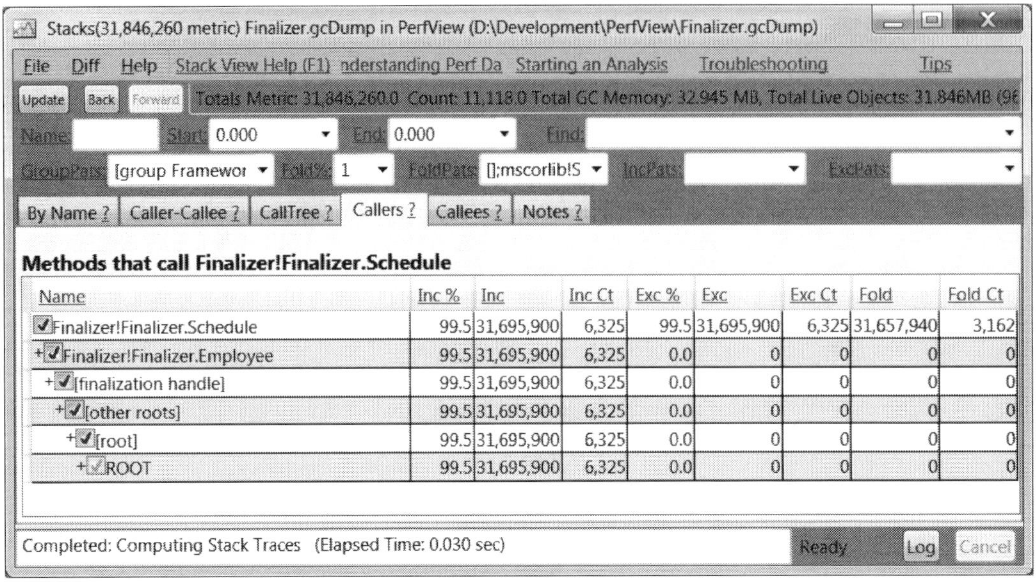

Figure 2-11. *Reference chain for Schedule class instances, responsible for 99.5% of the application's memory usage in the captured heap snapshot*

When we discuss memory profilers later in this chapter, we'll see that PerfView's visualization capabilities are still somewhat lacking compared to the commercial tools. Still, PerfView is a very useful free tool that can make many performance investigations significantly shorter. You can learn more about it using the built-in tutorial linked from its main screen, and there are also videos recorded by the BCL team that exhibit some of the tool's main features.

Custom ETW Providers

Similarly to performance counters, you might want to tap into the powerful instrumentation and information collection framework offered by ETW for your own application's needs. Prior to .NET 4.5, exposing ETW information from a managed application was fairly complex. You had to deal with plenty of details around defining a manifest for your application's ETW provider, instantiating it at runtime, and logging events. As of .NET 4.5, writing a custom ETW provider could hardly be easier. All you need to do is derive from the System.Diagnostics.Tracing.EventSource class and call the WriteEvent base class method to output ETW events. All the details of registering an ETW provider with the system and formatting the event data are handled automatically for you.

The following class is an example of an ETW provider in a managed application (the full program is available in this chapter's source code folder and you can run it with PerfMonitor later):

```
public class CustomEventSource : EventSource {
  public class Keywords {
    public const EventKeywords Loop = (EventKeywords)1;
    public const EventKeywords Method = (EventKeywords)2;
  }

  [Event(1, Level = EventLevel.Verbose, Keywords = Keywords.Loop,
         Message = "Loop {0} iteration {1}")]
  public void LoopIteration(string loopTitle, int iteration) {
```

```csharp
  WriteEvent(1, loopTitle, iteration);
}
[Event(2, Level=EventLevel.Informational, Keywords=Keywords.Loop,
       Message="Loop {0} done")]
public void LoopDone(string loopTitle) {
  WriteEvent(2, loopTitle);
}
[Event(3, Level=EventLevel.Informational, Keywords=Keywords.Method,
       Message="Method {0} done")]
public void MethodDone([CallerMemberName] string methodName=null) {
  WriteEvent(3, methodName);
}
}

class Program {
  static void Main(string[] args) {
    CustomEventSource log=new CustomEventSource();
    for (int i=0; i<10; ++i) {
      Thread.Sleep(50);
      log.LoopIteration("MainLoop", i);
    }
    log.LoopDone("MainLoop");
    Thread.Sleep(100);
    log.MethodDone();
  }
}
```

The PerfMonitor tool can be used to automatically obtain from this application the ETW provider it contains, run the application while monitoring that ETW provider, and generate a report of all ETW events the application submitted. For example:

```
C:\PerfMonitor>perfmonitor monitorDump Ch02.exe

Starting kernel tracing.  Output file: PerfMonitorOutput.kernel.etl
Starting user model tracing.  Output file: PerfMonitorOutput.etl
Found Provider CustomEventSource Guid ff6a40d2-5116-5555-675b-4468e821162e
Enabling provider ff6a40d2-5116-5555-675b-4468e821162e level: Verbose keywords:
0xffffffffffffffff
Starting at 4/7/2012 1:44:00 PM
Current Directory C:\PerfMonitor
Executing: Ch02.exe {

} Stopping at 4/7/2012 1:44:01 PM=0.693 sec
Stopping tracing for sessions 'NT Kernel Logger' and 'PerfMonitorSession'.
Converting C:\PerfMonitor\PerfMonitorOutput.etlx to an XML file.
Output in C:\PerfMonitor\PerfMonitorOutput.dump.xml
PerfMonitor processing time: 1.886 secs.
```

▓ **Note** There is another performance monitoring and system health instrumentation framework we haven't considered: *Windows Management Instrumentation* (WMI). WMI is a command-and-control (C&C) infrastructure integrated in Windows, and is outside the scope of this chapter. It can be used to obtain information about the system's state (such as the installed operating system, BIOS firmware, or free disk space), register for interesting events (such as process creation and termination), and invoke control methods that change the system state (such as create a network share or unload a driver). For more information about WMI, consult the MSDN documentation at http://msdn.microsoft.com/en-us/library/windows/desktop/aa394582.aspx. If you are interested in developing managed WMI providers, Sasha Goldshtein's article "WMI Provider Extensions in .NET 3.5" (http://www.codeproject.com/Articles/25783/WMI-Provider-Extensions-in-NET-3-5, 2008) provides a good start.

Time Profilers

Although performance counters and ETW events offer a great amount of insight into the performance of Windows applications, there's often a lot to be gained from more intrusive tools—profilers—that inspect application execution time at the method and line level (improving upon ETW stack trace collection support). In this section we introduce some commercial tools and see the benefits they bring to the table, bearing in mind that more powerful and accurate tools sustain a bigger measurement overhead.

Throughout our journey into the profiler world we will encounter numerous commercial tools; most of them have several readily available equivalents. We do not endorse any specific tool vendor; the products demonstrated in this chapter are simply the profilers we use most often and keep in our toolbox for performance investigations. As always with software tools, your mileage may vary.

The first profiler we consider is part of Visual Studio, and has been offered by Microsoft since Visual Studio 2005 (Team Suite edition). In this chapter, we'll use the Visual Studio 2012 profiler, which is available in the Premium and Ultimate editions of Visual Studio.

Visual Studio Sampling Profiler

The Visual Studio sampling profiler operates similarly to the PROFILE kernel flag we've seen in the ETW section. It periodically interrupts the application and records the call stack information on every processor where the application's threads are currently running. Unlike the kernel ETW provider, this sampling profiler can interrupt processes based on several criteria, some of which are listed in Table 2-2.

Table 2-2. *Visual Studio Sampling Profiler Events (Partial List)*

Trigger	Meaning	Reasonable Range	Scenario
Clock cycles	The application used a CPU clock cycle	1M—1,000M	Find the methods that are the heaviest users of CPU time (bottlenecks)
Page faults	The application accessed a page of memory that is currently not in RAM and must be fetched from disk (page file)	1—1,000	Find the methods that are causing page faults, i.e. expensive disk I/O instead of accessing memory
System calls	The application used a Win32 API or .NET class that issued a call to an operating system service	1—10,000	Find the methods that are causing user-to-kernel-mode transitions, which are expensive
Last level cache misses	The application accessed a memory location that is not in the CPU cache but could be found in main memory (RAM)	1,000—1M	Find the locations in code that are causing cache misses (see also Chapter 5)
Instructions retired	The application executed a CPU instruction	500K—100M	Similar to clock cycles

Capturing samples using the Visual Studio profiler is quite cheap, and if the sample event interval is wide enough (the default is 10,000,000 clock cycles), the overhead on the application's execution can be less than 5%. Moreover, sampling is very flexible and enables attaching to a running process, collecting sample events for a while, and then disconnecting from the process to analyze the data. Because of these traits, sampling is the recommended approach to begin a performance investigation for CPU bottlenecks—methods that take a significant amount of CPU time.

When a sampling session completes, the profiler makes available summary tables in which each method is associated with two numbers: the number of *exclusive samples*, which are samples taken while the method was currently executing on the CPU, and the number of *inclusive samples*, which are samples taken while the method was currently executing or anywhere else on the call stack. Methods with many exclusive samples are the ones responsible for the application's CPU utilization; methods with many inclusive samples are not directly using the CPU, but call out to other methods that do. (For example, in single-threaded applications it would make sense for the Main method to have 100% of the inclusive samples.)

RUNNING THE SAMPLING PROFILER FROM VISUAL STUDIO

The easiest way to run the sampling profiler is from Visual Studio itself, although (as we will see later) it also supports production profiling from a simplified command line environment. We recommend that you use one of your own applications for this experiment.

1. In Visual Studio, click the Analyze ➤ Launch Performance Wizard menu item.

2. On the first wizard page, make sure the "CPU sampling" radio button is selected and click the Next button. (Later in this chapter we'll discuss the other profiling modes; you can then repeat this experiment.)

3. If the project to profile is loaded in the current solution, click the "One or more available projects" radio button and select the project from the list. Otherwise, click the "An executable (.EXE file)" radio button. Click the Next button.

4. If you selected "An executable (.EXE file)" on the previous screen, direct the profiler to your executable and provide any command line arguments if necessary, then click the Next button. (If you don't have your own application handy, feel free to use the JackCompiler.exe sample application from this chapter's source code folder.)

5. Keep the checkbox "Launch profiling after the wizard finishes" checked and click the Finish button.

6. If you are not running Visual Studio as an administrator, you will be prompted to upgrade the profiler's credentials.

7. When your application finishes executing, a profiling report will open. Use the "Current View" combo box on the top to navigate between the different views, showing the samples collected in your application's code.

For more experimentation, after the profiling session completes make sure to check out the Performance Explorer tool window (Analyze ➤ Windows ➤ Performance Explorer). You can configure sampling parameters (e.g. choosing a different sample event or interval), change the target binary, and compare multiple profiler reports from different runs.

Figure 2-12 shows a summary window of the profiler's results, with the most expensive call path and the functions in which most exclusive samples have been collected. Figure 2-13 shows the detail report, in which there are a few methods responsible for most CPU utilization (have a large number of exclusive samples). Double-clicking a method in the list brings up a detailed window, which shows the application's source color-coded with the lines in which most samples were collected (see Figure 2-14).

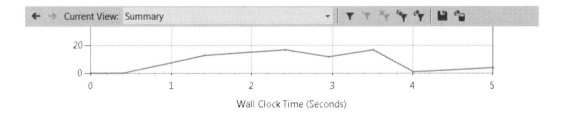

Hot Path

The most expensive call path based on sample counts

Function Name	Inclusive Samples %	Exclusive Samples %
◄▪ JackCompiler.Parser.ParseStatements()	75.95	0.38
◄▪ JackCompiler.Parser.ParseStatement()	75.19	0.00
🔥 **JackCompiler.Parser.ParseDoStatement()**	**27.10**	**0.00**
🔥 **JackCompiler.Parser.ParseLetStatement()**	**25.95**	**0.00**
🔥 **JackCompiler.Parser.ParseIfStatement()**	**13.36**	**0.00**

Related Views: Call Tree Functions

Functions Doing Most Individual Work

Functions with the most exclusive samples taken

Name	Exclusive Samples %
System.String.Concat(string,string,string)	24.81
System.Linq.Enumerable.Contains(class System.Collections.Generic.IEnumerable`1<!!0>,!!...	11.07
System.IO.TextWriter.WriteLine(string,object)	8.02
System.Linq.Enumerable.Contains(class System.Collections.Generic.IEnumerable`1<!!0>,!!...	6.49
_PreStubWorker@4	4.96

Figure 2-12. *Profiler report, Summary view—the call path responsible for most of the samples and the functions with most exclusive samples*

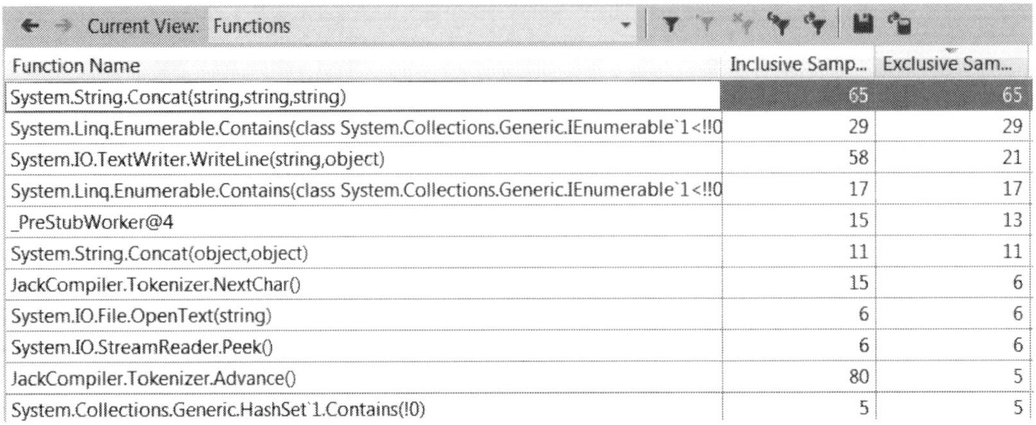

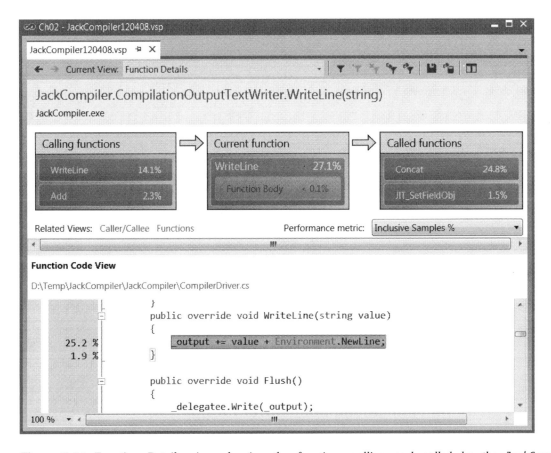

Figure 2-13. *Functions view, showing the functions with the most exclusive samples. The* System.String.Concat *function is responsible for twice as many samples as any other function*

Figure 2-14. *Function Details view, showing the functions calling and called by the* JackCompiler. CompilationOutputTextWriter.WriteLine *function. In the function's code, lines are highlighted according to the percent of inclusive samples they accumulated*

■ **Caution**   It may appear that sampling is an accurate technique for measuring CPU utilization. You might hear claims that go as far as "if this method had 65% of the exclusive samples, then it ran for 65% of the time". Because of the statistical nature of sampling, such reasoning is treacherous and should be avoided in practical use. There are several factors that can contribute to the inaccuracy of sampling results: CPU clock rates can change hundreds of times every second during application execution, such that the correlation between the number of samples and actual CPU time is skewed; a method can be "missed" (underrepresented) if it happens not to be running when many samples were taken; a method can be overrepresented if it happens to be running when many samples were taken but finished quickly every time. To summarize, you should not consider the results of a sampling profiler to be an exact representation of where CPU time was spent, but rather a general outline of the application's main CPU bottlenecks.

The Visual Studio profiler offers more information in addition to the exclusive/inclusive sample tables for every method. We recommend that you explore the profiler's windows yourself—the Call Tree view shows the hierarchy of calls in the application's methods (compare to PerfMonitor's top down analysis, Figure 2-8), the Lines view displays sampling information on the line level, and the Modules view groups methods by assembly, which can lead to quick conclusions about the general direction in which to look for a performance bottleneck.

Because all sampling intervals require the application thread that triggers them to be actively executing on the CPU, there is no way to obtain samples from application threads that are blocked while waiting for I/O or synchronization mechanisms. For CPU-bound applications, sampling is ideal; for I/O-bound applications, we'll have to consider other approaches that rely on more intrusive profiling mechanisms.

Visual Studio Instrumentation Profiler

The Visual Studio profiler offers another mode of operation, called *instrumentation profiling*, which is tailored to measuring overall execution time and not just CPU time. This makes it suitable for profiling I/O-bound applications or applications that engage heavily in synchronization operations. In the instrumentation profiling mode, the profiler modifies the target binary and embeds within it measurement code that reports back to the profiler accurate timing and call count information for every instrumented method.

For example, consider the following method:

```
public static int InstrumentedMethod(int param) {
  List<int> evens=new List<int>();
  for (int i=0; i<param; ++i) {
    if (i % 2 == 0) {
      evens.Add(i);
    }
  }
  return evens.Count;
}
```

During instrumentation, the Visual Studio profiler modifies this method. Remember that instrumentation occurs at the binary level—your source code is *not* modified, but you can always inspect the instrumented binary with an IL disassembler, such as .NET Reflector. (In the interests of brevity, we slightly modified the resulting code to fit.)

```
public static int mmid=(int)
  Microsoft.VisualStudio.Instrumentation.g_fldMMID_2D71B909-C28E-4fd9-A0E7-ED05264B707A;

public static int InstrumentedMethod(int param) {
  _CAP_Enter_Function_Managed(mmid, 0x600000b, 0);
```

```
  _CAP_StartProfiling_Managed(mmid, 0x600000b, 0xa000018);
  _CAP_StopProfiling_Managed(mmid, 0x600000b, 0);
  List <int> evens=new List<int>();
  for (int i=0; i<param; i++) {
    if (i % 2 == 0) {
      _CAP_StartProfiling_Managed(mmid, 0x600000b, 0xa000019);
      evens.Add(i);
      _CAP_StopProfiling_Managed(mmid, 0x600000b, 0);
    }
  }
  _CAP_StartProfiling_Managed(mmid, 0x600000b, 0xa00001a);
  _CAP_StopProfiling_Managed(mmid, 0x600000b, 0);
  int count=evens.Count;
  _CAP_Exit_Function_Managed(mmid, 0x600000b, 0);
  return count;
}
```

The method calls beginning with _CAP are interop calls to the VSPerf110.dll module, which is referenced by the instrumented assembly. They are the ones responsible for measuring time and recording method call counts. Because instrumentation captures every method call made out of the instrumented code and captures method enter and exit locations, the information available at the end of an instrumentation run can be very accurate.

When the same application we've seen in Figures 2-12, 2-13, and 2-14 is run under instrumentation mode (you can follow along—it's the JackCompiler.exe application), the profiler generates a report with a Summary view that contains similar information—the most expensive call path through the application, and the functions with most individual work. However, this time the information is not based on sample counts (which measure only execution on the CPU); it is based on precise timing information recorded by the instrumentation code. Figure 2-15 shows the Functions view, in which inclusive and exclusive times measured in milliseconds are available, along with the number of times the function has been called.

Function Name	Elapsed Inclusi...	Elapsed Exclus...	Number of Calls
JackCompiler.Tokenizer.NextChar()	4,163.71	2,246.36	951,000
JackCompiler.Token..ctor(valuetype JackCompiler.TokenType,string)	2,561.65	1,557.73	463,000
JackCompiler.Tokenizer.Advance()	9,195.09	1,070.54	293,000
JackCompiler.Parser.Match(class JackCompiler.Token)	7,751.63	749.13	171,000
JackCompiler.Tokenizer.EatWhile(class System.Predicate`1<char>)	2,445.82	716.53	144,000
System.Object..ctor()	627.72	627.72	483,000
System.String.op_Equality(string,string)	580.68	580.68	1,161,000
System.String.get_Chars(int32)	481.38	481.38	951,000
JackCompiler.Parser.ParseStatements()	9,734.91	456.07	6,000
System.Predicate`1.Invoke(!0)	501.06	435.24	525,000
JackCompiler.Tokenizer.get_IsAtEnd()	418.59	404.36	293,000
System.Environment.get_NewLine()	391.10	391.10	951,000
System.String.Concat(string,string)	383.15	383.15	1,091,000
System.String..ctor(char[])	342.48	342.48	463,000
JackCompiler.Parser.NextToken()	2,586.89	329.52	121,000

Figure 2-15. The Functions view: System.String.Concat no longer appears to be the performance bottleneck, as our attention shifts to JackCompiler.Tokenizer.NextChar and JackCompiler.Token..ctor. The first method was called almost a million times

■ **Tip** The sample application used to generate Figures 2-12 and 2-15 is not entirely CPU-bound; in fact, most of its time is spent blocking for I/O operations to complete. This explains the difference between sampling results, which point towards `System.String.Concat` as the *CPU* hog, and the instrumentation results, which point towards `JackCompiler.Tokenizer.NextChar` as the *overall* performance bottleneck.

Although instrumentation seems like the more accurate method, in practice you should try to keep to sampling if most of your application's code is CPU-bound. Instrumentation limits flexibility because you must instrument the application's code prior to launching it, and cannot attach the profiler to a process that was already running. Moreover, instrumentation has a non-negligible overhead—it increases code size significantly and places a runtime overhead as probes are collected whenever the program enters or exits a method. (Some instrumentation profilers offer a line-instrumentation mode, where each line is surrounded by instrumentation probes; these are even slower!)

As always, the biggest risk is placing too much trust in the results of an instrumentation profiler. It is reasonable to assume that the number of calls to a particular method does not change because the application is running with instrumentation, but the time information collected may still be significantly skewed because of the profiler's overhead, despite any attempts by the profiler to offset the instrumentation costs from the final results. When used carefully, sampling and instrumentation can offer great insight into where the application is spending time, especially when you compare multiple reports and take note whether your optimizations are yielding fruit.

Advanced Uses of Time Profilers

Time profilers have additional tricks up their sleeves that we haven't examined in the previous sections. This chapter is too short to discuss them in considerable detail, but they are worth pointing out to make sure you don't miss them in the comforts of Visual Studio's wizards.

Sampling Tips

As we saw in the Visual Studio Sampling Profiler section, the sampling profiler can collect samples from several types of events, including cache misses and page faults. In Chapters 5 and 6 we will see several examples of applications that can benefit greatly from improving their memory access characteristics, primarily around minimizing cache misses. The profiler will prove valuable in analyzing the number of cache misses and page faults exhibited by these applications and their precise locations in code. (When using instrumentation profiling, you can still collect CPU counters such as cache misses, instructions retired, and mispredicted branches. To do so, open the performance session properties from the Performance Explorer pane, and navigate to the CPU Counters tab. The collected information will be available as additional columns in the report's Functions view.)

The sampling profiling mode is generally more flexible than instrumentation. For example, you can use the Performance Explorer pane to attach the profiler (in sampling mode) to a process that is already running.

Collecting Additional Data While Profiling

In all profiling modes, you can use the Performance Explorer pane to pause and resume the data collection when the profiler is active, and to generate markers that will be visible in the final profiler report to discern more easily various parts of the application's execution. These markers will be visible in the report's Marks view.

■ **Tip** The Visual Studio profiler even has an API that applications can use to pause and resume profiling from code. This can be used to avoid collecting data from uninteresting parts of the application, and to decrease the size of the profiler's data files. For more information about the profiler APIs, consult the MSDN documentation at `http://msdn.microsoft.com/en-us/library/bb514149(v=vs.110).aspx`.

The profiler can also collect Windows performance counters and ETW events (discussed earlier in this chapter) during a normal profiling run. To enable these, open the performance session properties from Performance Explorer, and navigate to the Windows Events and Windows Counters tabs. ETW trace data can only be viewed from the command line, by using the `VSPerfReport /summary:ETW` command line switch, whereas performance counter data will appear in the report's Marks view in Visual Studio.

Finally, if Visual Studio takes a long time analyzing a report with lots of additional data, you can make sure it was a one-time performance hit: after analysis completes, right-click the report in Performance Explorer and choose "Save Analyzed Report". Serialized report files have the .vsps file extension and open instantaneously in Visual Studio.

Profiler Guidance

When opening a report in Visual Studio, you might notice a section called Profiler Guidance which contains numerous useful tips that detect common performance problems discussed elsewhere in the book, including:

- "Consider using `StringBuilder` for string concatenations"—a useful rule that may help lower the amount of garbage your application creates, thus reducing garbage collection times, discussed in Chapter 4.

- "Many of your objects are being collected in generation 2 garbage collection"—the *mid-life crisis* phenomenon for objects, also discussed in Chapter 4.

- "Override `Equals` and equality operator on value types"—an important optimization for commonly-used value types, discussed in Chapter 3.

- "You may be using Reflection excessively. It is an expensive operation"—discussed in Chapter 10.

Advanced Profiling Customization

Collecting performance information from production environments may prove difficult if you have to install massive tools such as Visual Studio. Fortunately, the Visual Studio profiler can be installed and run in production environments without the entire Visual Studio suite. You can find the profiler setup files on the Visual Studio installation media, in the `Standalone Profiler` directory (there are separate versions for 32- and 64-bit systems). After installing the profiler, follow the instructions at `http://msdn.microsoft.com/en-us/library/ms182401(v=vs.110).aspx` to launch your application under the profiler or attach to an existing process using the VSPerfCmd.exe tool. When done, the profiler will generate a .vsp file that you can open on another machine with Visual Studio, or use the VSPerfReport.exe tool to generate XML or CSV reports that you can review on the production machine without resorting to Visual Studio.

For instrumentation profiling, many customization options are available from the command line, using the VSInstr.exe tool. Specifically, you can use the START, SUSPEND, INCLUDE, and EXCLUDE options to start and suspend profiling in a specific function, and to include/exclude functions from instrumentation based on a pattern in their name. More information about VSInstr.exe is available on the MSDN at `http://msdn.microsoft.com/en-us/library/ms182402.aspx`.

Some time profilers offer a remote profiling mode, which allows the main profiler UI to run on one machine and the profiling session to take place on another machine without copying the performance report manually. For example, the JetBrains dotTrace profiler supports this mode of operation through a small remote agent that runs on the remote machine and communicates with the main profiler UI. This is a good alternative to installing the entire profiler suite on the production machines.

▨ **Note** In Chapter 6 we will leverage the GPU for super-parallel computation, leading to considerable (more than 100×!) speedups. Standard time profilers are useless when the performance problem is in the code that runs on the GPU. There are some tools that can profile and diagnose performance problems in GPU code, including Visual Studio 2012. This subject is outside the scope of this chapter, but if you're using the GPU for graphics or plain computation you should research the tools applicable to your GPU programming framework (such as C++ AMP, CUDA, or OpenCL).

In this section, we have seen in sufficient detail how to analyze the application's execution time (overall or CPU only) with the Visual Studio profiler. Memory management is another important aspect of managed application performance. Through the next two sections, we will discuss allocation profilers and memory profilers, which can pinpoint memory-related performance bottlenecks in your applications.

Allocation Profilers

Allocation profilers detect memory allocations performed by an application and can report which methods allocated most memory, which types were allocated by each method, and similar memory-related statistics. Memory-intensive applications can often spend a significant amount of time in the garbage collector, reclaiming memory that was previously allocated. As we will see in Chapter 4, the CLR makes it very easy and inexpensive to allocate memory, but recovering it can be quite costly. Therefore, a group of small methods that allocate lots of memory may not take a considerable amount of CPU time to run—and will be almost invisible in a time profiler's report—but will cause a slowdown by inflicting garbage collections at nondeterministic points in the application's execution. We have seen production applications that were careless with memory allocations, and were able to improve their performance—sometimes by a factor of 10—by tuning their allocations and memory management.

We'll use two tools for profiling memory allocations—the ubiquitous Visual Studio profiler, which offers an allocation profiling mode, and CLR Profiler, which is a free stand-alone tool. Unfortunately, both tools often introduce a significant performance hit to memory-intensive applications, because every memory allocation must go through the profiler for record-keeping. Nonetheless, the results can be so valuable that even a 100× slowdown is worth the wait.

Visual Studio Allocation Profiler

The Visual Studio profiler can collect allocation information and object lifetime data (which objects were reclaimed by the garbage collector) in the sampling and instrumentation modes. When using this feature with sampling, the profiler collects allocation data from the entire process; with instrumentation, the profiler collects only data from instrumented modules.

You can follow along by running the Visual Studio profiler on the JackCompiler.exe sample application from this chapter's source code folder. Make sure to select ".NET memory allocation" in the Visual Studio Performance Wizard. At the end of the profiling process, the Summary view shows the functions allocating most memory and the types with most memory allocated (see Figure 2-16). The Functions view in the report contains for each method the number of objects and number of bytes that method allocated (inclusive and exclusive metrics are provided, as usual) and the Function Details view can provide caller and callee information, as well as color-highlighted source code with allocation information in the margins (see Figure 2-17). More interesting information is in the Allocation view, which shows which call trees are responsible for allocating specific types (see Figure 2-18).

Functions Allocating Most Memory

Functions with the highest exclusive bytes allocated

Name	Bytes %
System.String.Concat(string,string,string)	89.04
System.String.CtorCharCount(char,int32)	1.66
System.IO.TextWriter.WriteLine(string,object)	1.43
System.String.Concat(object,object)	1.41
JackCompiler.Tokenizer.Advance()	1.03

Types With Most Memory Allocated

Types with the hightest total number of bytes allocated

Name	Bytes %
System.String	95.53
System.Char[]	1.47
JackCompiler.Token	0.65
System.String[]	0.48
System.Byte[]	0.45

Figure 2-16. *Summary view from allocation profiling results*

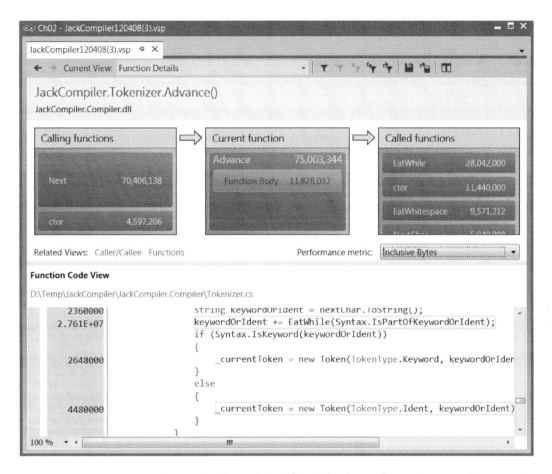

Figure 2-17. *Function Details view for the* `JackCompiler.Tokenizer.Advance` *function, showing callers, callees, and the function's source with allocation counts in the margin*

Name	Inclusive Alloc...	Exclusive Alloc...	Inclusive Bytes	Exclusive Bytes
⊟ System.String	**2,845,239**	**2,845,239**	**1,093,265,124**	**1,093,265,124**
⊟ JackCompiler.CompilerDriver.Main(string[])	2,845,187	1	1,093,263,696	50
⊟ JackCompiler.CompilerDriver.DriveCompilerWithCCodeGenerator(string[])	2,845,186	32	1,093,263,646	2,030
⊟ JackCompiler.Parser.Parse()	2,784,121	3	1,010,376,134	96
⊟ JackCompiler.Parser.ParseClass()	2,784,118	0	1,010,376,038	0
⊟ JackCompiler.Parser.ParseSubDecls()	2,562,113	7	1,003,813,868	392
⊟ JackCompiler.Parser.ParseSubDecl()	2,562,106	5	1,003,813,476	336
⊟ JackCompiler.Parser.ParseSubBody()	2,451,097	4	1,001,493,010	258
⊟ JackCompiler.Parser.ParseStatements()	2,194,061	2	942,643,758	138
⊟ JackCompiler.Parser.ParseStatement()	2,194,059	7	942,643,620	518
⊟ JackCompiler.Parser.ParseDoStatement()	1,181,002	1	348,500,104	38
⊞ JackCompiler.Parser.ParseSubCall(class JackCom	769,001	0	239,248,066	0
⊞ JackCompiler.CCodeGenerator.DiscardReturnVal	12,000	0	100,652,000	0
⊞ JackCompiler.CompilationOutputTextWriter.W	12,000	0	100,652,000	0
⊞ JackCompiler.Parser.ParseLetStatement()	568,042	11	293,084,478	754
⊞ JackCompiler.Parser.ParseIfStatement()	242,001	0	162,622,100	0
⊞ JackCompiler.Parser.ParseWhileStatement()	162,005	3	113,740,320	142

Figure 2-18. *Allocation view, showing the call tree responsible for allocating* `System.String` *objects*

In Chapter 4 we will learn to appreciate the importance of quickly discarding temporary objects, and discuss a critical performance-related phenomenon called *mid-life crisis*, which occurs when temporary objects survive too many garbage collections. To identify this phenomenon in an application, the Object Lifetime view in the profiler's report can indicate in which generation objects are being reclaimed, which helps understand whether they survive too many garbage collections. In Figure 2-19 you can see that all of the strings allocated by the application (more than 1GB of objects!) have been reclaimed in generation 0, which means they didn't survive even a single garbage collection.

Class Name	Instances	Total Bytes All...	Gen 0 Bytes Co...	Gen 1 Bytes Co...	Gen 2 Bytes Co...
System.String	2,845,239	1,093,265,124	1,091,621,562	0	0
System.Char[]	726,008	16,857,070	16,818,660	0	0
JackCompiler.Token	463,000	7,408,000	7,396,640	0	0
System.String[]	189,008	5,484,312	5,486,996	0	0
System.Byte[]	3,005	5,160,090	5,236,770	0	0
System.Char	382,001	4,584,012	4,576,980	0	0
System.Predicate`1	140,001	4,480,032	4,474,080	0	0
System.Object[]	114,006	2,388,732	2,394,728	0	0

Figure 2-19. *The Object Lifetime view helps identify temporary objects that survive many garbage collections. In this view, all objects were reclaimed in generation 0, which is the cheapest kind of garbage collection available. (See Chapter 4 for more details.)*

Although the allocation reports generated by the Visual Studio profiler are quite powerful, they are somewhat lacking in visualization. For example, tracing through allocation call stacks for a specific type is quite time-consuming if it is allocated in many places (as strings and byte arrays always are). CLR Profiler offers several visualization features, which make it a valuable alternative to Visual Studio.

CLR Profiler

CLR Profiler is a stand-alone profiling tool that requires no installation and takes less than 1MB of disk space. You can download it from `http://www.microsoft.com/download/en/details.aspx?id=16273`. As a bonus, it ships with complete sources, making for an interesting read if you're considering developing a custom tool using the CLR Profiling API. It can attach to a running process (as of CLR 4.0) or launch an executable, and record all memory allocations and garbage collection events.

While running CLR Profiler is extremely easy—run the profiler, click Start Application, select your application, and wait for the report to appear—the richness of the report's information can be somewhat overwhelming. We will go over some of the report's views; the complete guide to CLR Profiler is the CLRProfiler. doc document, which is part of the download package. As always, you can follow along by running CLR Profiler on the JackCompiler.exe sample application.

Figure 2-20 shows the main view, generated after the profiled application terminates. It contains basic statistics concerning memory allocations and garbage collections. There are several common directions to take from here. We could focus on investigation memory allocation sources to understand where the application creates most of its objects (this is similar to the Visual Studio profiler's Allocations view). We could focus on the garbage collections to understand which objects are being reclaimed. Finally, we could inspect visually the heap's contents to understand its general structure.

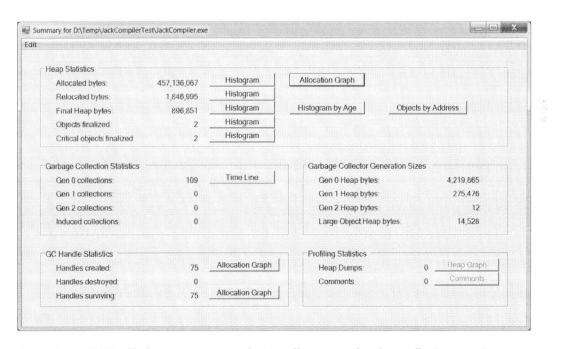

Figure 2-20. *CLR Profiler's main report view, showing allocation and garbage collection statistics*

The **Histogram** buttons next to "Allocated bytes" and "Final heap bytes" in Figure 2-20 lead to a graph of object types grouped into bins according to their size. These histograms can be used to identify large and small objects, as well as the gist of which types the program is allocating most frequently. Figure 2-21 shows the histogram for all the objects allocated by our sample application during its run.

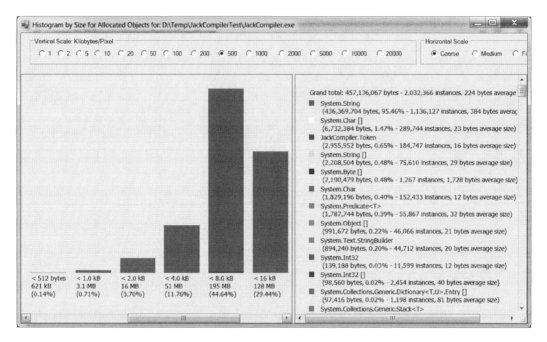

Figure 2-21. *All objects allocated by the profiled application. Each bin represents objects of a particular size. The legend on the left contains the total number of bytes and instances allocated from each type*

The **Allocation Graph** button in Figure 2-20 opens a view that shows the allocating call stacks for all the objects in the application in a grouped graph that makes it easy to navigate from the methods allocating most memory to individual types and see which methods allocated their instances. Figure 2-22 shows a small part of the allocation graph, starting from the Parser.ParseStatement method that allocated (inclusively) 372MB of memory, and showing the various methods it called in turn. (Additionally, the rest of CLR Profiler's views have a "Show who's allocated" context menu item, which opens an allocation graph for a subset of the application's objects.)

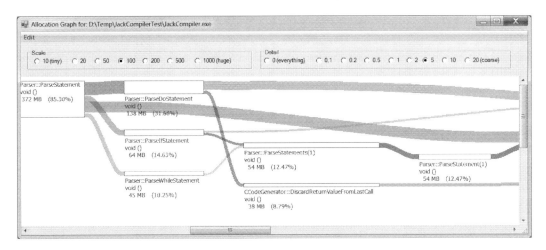

Figure 2-22. *Allocation graph for the profiled applications. Only methods are shown here; the actual types allocated are on the far right of the graph*

The **Histogram by Age** button in Figure 2-20 displays a graph that groups objects from the final heap to bins according to their age. This enables quick identification of long-lived objects and temporaries, which is important for detecting mid-life crisis situations. (We will discuss these in depth in Chapter 4.)

The **Objects by Address** button in Figure 2-20 visualizes the final managed heap memory regions in layers; the lowest layers are the oldest ones (see Figure 2-23). Like an archaeological expedition, you can dig through the layers and see which objects comprise your application's memory. This view is also useful for diagnosing internal fragmentation in the heap (e.g. due to pinning)—we will discuss these in more detail in Chapter 4.

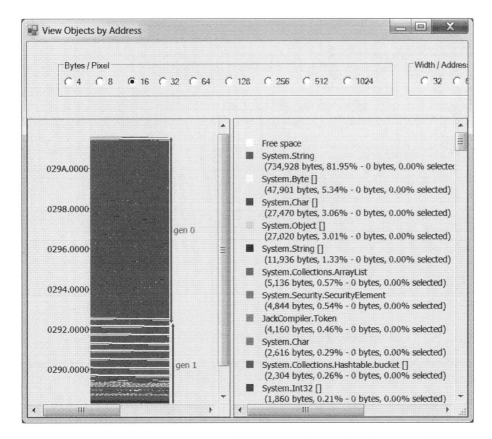

Figure 2-23. *Visual view of the application's heap. The labels on the left axis are addresses; the "gen 0" and "gen 1" markers are subsections of the heap, discussed in Chapter 4*

Finally, the **Time Line** button in the Garbage Collection Statistics section in Figure 2-20 leads to a visualization of individual garbage collections and their effect on the application's heap (see Figure 2-24). This view can be used to identify which types of objects are being reclaimed, and how the heap is changing as garbage collections occur. It can also be instrumental in identifying memory leaks, where garbage collections do not reclaim enough memory because the application holds on to increasing amounts of objects.

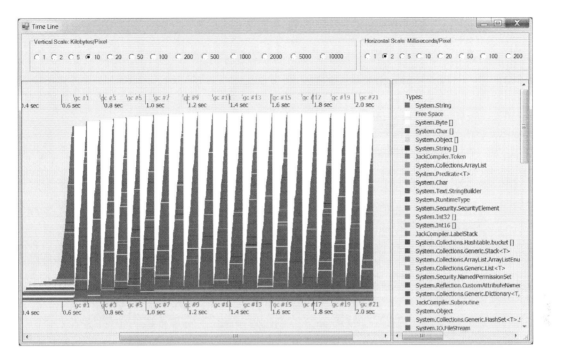

Figure 2-24. *Time line of an application's garbage collections. The ticks on the bottom axis represent individual GC runs, and the area portrayed is the managed heap. As garbage collections occur, memory usage drops significantly and then rises steeply until the next collection occurs. Overall, memory usage (after GC) is constant, so this application is not exhibiting a memory leak*

Allocation graphs and histograms are very useful tools, but sometimes it's equally important to identify references between objects and not call stacks of methods. For example, when an application exhibits a managed memory leak, it can be very useful to crawl its heap, detect the largest object categories, and ascertain the object references that are preventing the GC from collecting these objects. While the profiled application is running, clicking the "Show Heap now" button generates a *heap dump*, which can be inspected later to categorize references between objects.

Figure 2-25 shows how three heap dumps are displayed simultaneously in the profiler's report, showing a an increase in the number of byte[] objects retained by the f-reachable queue (discussed in Chapter 4), through Employee and Schedule object references. Figure 2-26 shows the result of selecting "Show New Objects" from the context menu to see only the objects allocated between the second and third heap dumps.

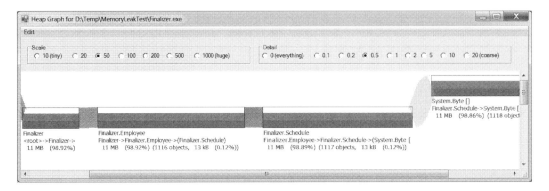

Figure 2-25. *Three heap dumps on top of one another, showing 11MB of byte[ ] instances being retained*

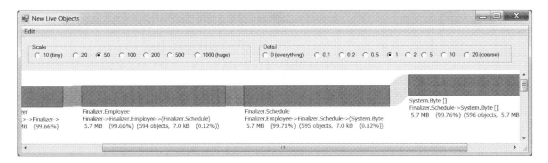

Figure 2-26. *The new objects allocated between the ultimate and penultimate heap dumps, showing that the source of the memory leak is clearly this reference chain from the f-reachable queue*

You can use heap dumps in CLR Profiler to diagnose memory leaks in your applications, but the visualization tools are lacking. The commercial tools we discuss next offer richer capabilities, including automatic detectors for common memory leak sources, smart filters, and more sophisticated grouping. Because most of these tools don't record information for each allocated object and don't capture allocation call stacks, they introduce a lower overhead to the profiled application—a big advantage.

Memory Profilers

In this section we'll discuss two commercial memory profilers that specialize in visualizing managed heaps and detecting memory leak sources. Because these tools are fairly complex, we will examine only a small subset of their features, and leave the rest to the reader to explore in the respective user guides.

ANTS Memory Profiler

RedGate's ANTS Memory Profiler specializes in heap snapshot analysis. Below we detail the process for using ANTS Memory Profiler to diagnose a memory leak. If you would like to follow through with these steps as you read this section, download a free 14-day trial of ANTS Memory Profiler from http://www.red-gate.com/products/dotnet-development/ants-memory-profiler/ and use it to profile your own application. In the directions and screenshots below, we used ANTS Memory Profiler 7.3, which was the latest version available at the time of writing.

You can use the FileExplorer.exe application from this chapter's source code folder to follow this demonstration—to make it leak memory, navigate the directory tree on the left to non-empty directories.

1. Run the application from within the profiler. (Similarly to CLR Profiler, ANTS supports attaching to a running process, starting from CLR 4.0.)

2. Use the Take Memory Snapshot button to capture an initial shapshot after the application has finished initializing. This snapshot is the baseline for subsequent performance investigations.

3. As the memory leak accumulates, take additional heap snapshots.

4. After the application terminates, compare snapshots (the baseline snapshot to the last snapshot, or intermediate snapshots among themselves) to understand which types of objects are growing in memory.

5. Focus on specific types using the Instance Categorizer to understand what kinds of references are retaining objects of the suspected types. (At this phase you are inspecting references between *types*—instances of type *A* referencing instances of type *B* will be grouped by type, as if *A* is referencing *B*.)

6. Explore individual instances of the suspected types using the Instance List. Identify several representative instances and use the Instance Retention Graph to determine why they are retained in memory. (At this phase you are inspecting references between individual *objects*, and can see why specific objects are not reclaimed by the GC.)

7. Return to the application's source code and modify it such that the leaking objects are no longer referenced by the problematic chain.

At the end of the analysis process, you should have a good grasp of why the heaviest objects in your application are not being reclaimed by the GC. There are many causes of memory leaks, and the real art is to quickly discern from the haystack that is a million-object heap the interesting representative objects and types that will lead to the major leak sources.

Figure 2-27 shows the comparison view between two snapshots. The memory leak (in bytes) consists primarily of string objects. Focusing on the string type in the Instance Categorizer (in Figure 2-28) leads to the conclusion that there is an event that retains FileInformation instances in memory, and they in turn hold references to byte[] objects. Drilling down to inspect specific instances using the Instance Retention Graph (see Figure 2-29) points to the FileInformation.FileInformationNeedsRefresh static event as the source of the memory leak.

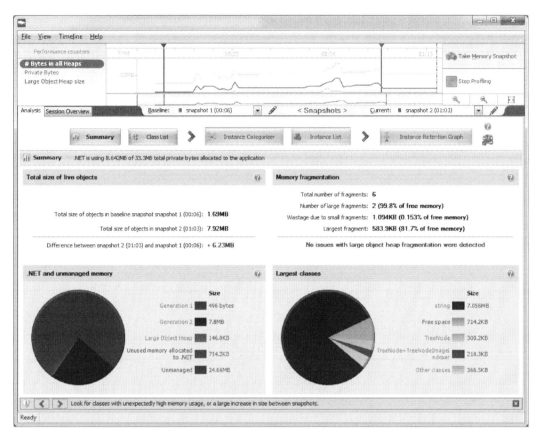

Figure 2-27. *Comparison between two heap snapshots. The total difference between them is +6.23MB, and the largest type currently held in memory is* System.String

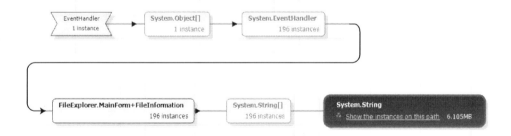

Figure 2-28. *The strings are retained by arrays of strings, which are retained by* FileInformation *instances, which are in turn retained by an event (through* System.EventHandler *delegates)*

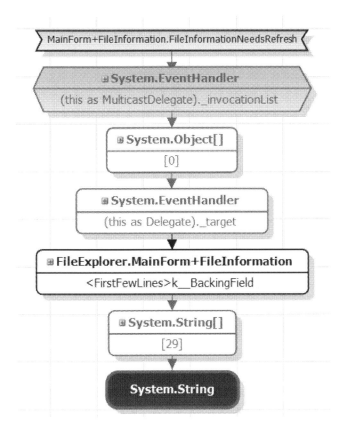

Figure 2-29. The individual string we chose to examine is element 29 in an array of strings, held by the `<FirstFewLines>k__BackingField` field of a `FileInformation` object. Following the references points to the `FileInformation.FileInformationNeedsRefresh` static event

SciTech .NET Memory Profiler

The SciTech .NET Memory Profiler is another commercial tool focused on memory leak diagnostics. Whereas the general analysis flow is quite similar to ANTS Memory Profiler, this profiler can open *dump files*, which means you don't have to run it alongside the application and can use a crash dump generated when the CLR runs out of memory. This can be of paramount importance for diagnosing memory leaks *post mortem*, after the problem has already occurred in the production environment. You can download a 10-day evaluation version from `http://memprofiler.com/download.aspx`. In the directions and screenshots below, we used .NET Memory Profiler 4.0, which was the latest version available at the time of writing.

▓ **Note** CLR Profiler can't open dump files directly, but there is an SOS.DLL command called `!TraverseHeap` that can generate a .log file in CLR Profiler's format. We discuss more examples of SOS.DLL commands in Chapters 3 and 4. In the meantime, Sasha Goldshtein's blog post at `http://blog.sashag.net/archive/2008/04/08/next-generation-production-debugging-demo-2-and-demo-3.aspx` provides an example of how to use SOS.DLL and CLR Profiler together.

To open a memory dump in .NET Memory Profiler, choose the File ➤ Import memory dump menu item and direct the profiler to the dump file. If you have several dump files, you can import them all into the analysis session and compare them as heap snapshots. The import process can be rather lengthy, especially where large heaps are involved; for faster analysis sessions, SciTech offers a separate tool, NmpCore.exe, which can be used to capture a heap session in a production environment instead of relying on a dump file.

Figure 2-30 shows the results of comparing two memory dumps in .NET Memory Profiler. It has immediately discovered suspicious objects held in memory directly by event handlers, and directs the analysis towards the FileInformation objects.

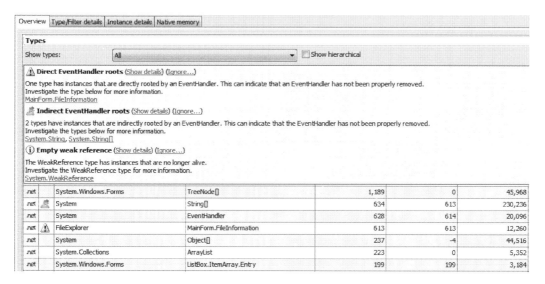

Figure 2-30. *Initial analysis of two memory snapshots. The first column lists the number of live instances, whereas the third columns lists the number of bytes occupied by them. The main memory hog—string objects—are not visible because of the tooltip*

Focusing on the FileInformation objects illustrates that there is a single root path from the FileInformation.FileInformationNeedsRefresh event handler to the selected FileInformation instances (see Figure 2-31) and a visualization of individual instances confirms the same reference chain we have seen previously with ANTS Memory Profiler.

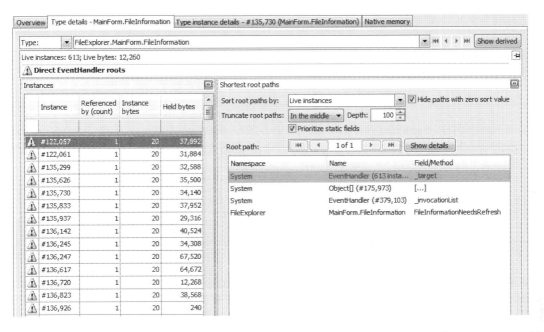

Figure 2-31. *FileInformation instances. The "Held bytes" column lists the amount of memory retained by each instance (its subtree in the object graph). On the right the shortest root path for the instance is shown*

We will not repeat here the instructions for using the rest of .NET Memory Profiler's functionality—you can find excellent tutorials on SciTech's website, `http://memprofiler.com/OnlineDocs/`. This tool concludes our survey of memory leak detection tools and techniques, which begun with CLR Profiler's heap dumps.

Other Profilers

In this chapter, we chose to focus mostly on CPU, time, and memory profilers, because these are the metrics on which most performance investigations focus. There are several other performance metrics that have dedicated measurement tools; in this section we will briefly mention some of them.

Database and Data Access Profilers

Many managed applications are built around a database and spend a significant portion of their time waiting for it to return query results or complete bulk updates. Database access can be profiled at two locations: from the application's side, which is the realm of *data access profilers*, and from the database's side, best left to *database profilers*.

Database profilers often require vendor-specific expertise, and are typically used by database administrators in their performance investigations and routine work. We will not consider database profilers here; you can read more about the SQL Server Profiler, which is a very powerful database profiling tool for Microsoft SQL Server, at `http://msdn.microsoft.com/en-us/library/ms181091.aspx`.

Data access profilers, on the other hand, are well within the domain of application developers. These tools instrument the application's data access layer (DAL) and typically report the following:

- The database queries executed by the application's DAL, and the precise stack trace that initiated each operation.

- The list of application methods that initiated a database operation, and the list of queries that each method has run.

- Alerts for inefficient database accesses, such as performing queries with an unbounded result set, retrieving all table columns while using only some of them, issuing a query with too many joins, or making one query for an entity with *N* associated entities and then another query for each associated entity (also known as the "SELECT N + 1" problem).

There are several commercial tools that can profile application data access patterns. Some of them work only with specific database products (such as Microsoft SQL Server), while others work with only a specific data access framework (such as Entity Framework or NHibernate). Below are a few examples:

- RedGate ANTS Performance Profiler can profile application queries to a Microsoft SQL Server database.

- Visual Studio "Tier Interactions" profiling feature can profile any synchronous data access operation from ADO.NET—unfortunately, it does not report call stacks for database operations.

- The Hibernating Rhinos family of profilers (LINQ to SQL Profiler, Entity Framework Profiler, and NHibernate Profiler) can profile all operations performed by a specific data access framework.

We will not discuss these profilers in more detail here, but if you are concerned about the performance of your data access layer, you should consider running them alongside with a time or memory profiler in your performance investigations.

Concurrency Profilers

The rising popularity of parallel programming warrants specialized profilers for highly concurrent software that uses multiple threads to run on multiple processors. In Chapter 6 we will examine several scenarios in which easily ripe performance gains are available from parallelization—and these performance gains are best realized with an accurate measurement tool.

The Visual Studio profiler in its Concurrency and Concurrency Visualizer modes uses ETW to monitor the performance of concurrent applications and report several useful views that facilitate detecting scalability and performance bottlenecks specific to highly concurrent software. It has two modes of operation demonstrated below.

Concurrency mode (or *resource contention profiling*) detects resources, such as managed locks, on which application threads are waiting. One part of the report focuses on the resources themselves, and the threads that were blocked waiting for them—this helps find and eliminate scalability bottlenecks (see Figure 2-32). Another part of the report displays contention information for a specific thread, i.e. the various synchronization mechanisms for which the thread had to wait—this helps reduce obstacles in a specific thread's execution. To launch the profiler in this mode of operation, use the Performance Explorer pane or Analyze ➤ Launch Performance Wizard menu item and select the Concurrency mode.

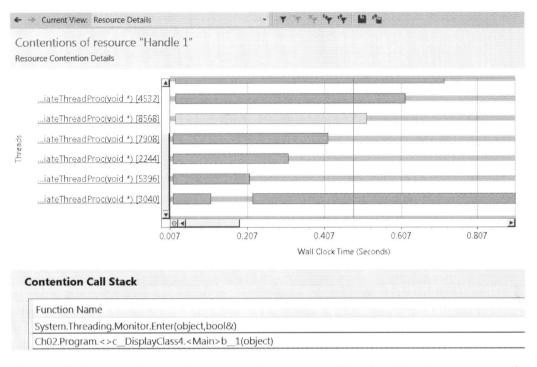

Figure 2-32. *Contention for a specific resource—there are several threads waiting at once to acquire the resource. When a thread is selected, its blocking call stack is listed on the bottom*

Concurrency Visualizer mode (or *multithreaded execution visualization*) displays a graph with the execution details of all application threads, color-coded according to their current state. Every thread state transition—blocking for I/O, waiting for a synchronization mechanism, running—is recorded, along with its call stack and unblocking call stack when applicable (see Figure 2-33). These reports are very helpful for understanding the role of application threads, and detecting poor performance patterns such as oversubscription, undersubscription, starvation, and excessive synchronization. There's also built-in support in the graph for Task Parallel Library mechanisms such as parallel loops, and CLR synchronization mechanisms. To launch the profiler in this mode of operation, use the Analyze ➤ Concurrency Visualizer sub-menu.

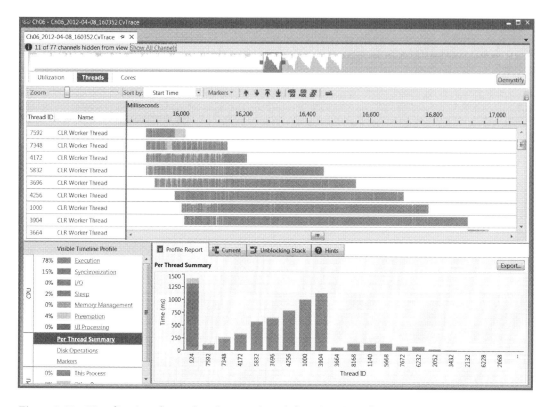

Figure 2-33. *Visualization of several application threads (listed on the left) and their execution. From the visualization and the histogram on the bottom it is evident that work was not distributed evenly between the different threads*

▓ **Note** MSDN features a collection of anti-patterns for multithreaded applications based on Concurrency Visualizer graphs, including lock convoy, uneven workload distribution, oversubscription, and others—you can find these anti-patterns online at `http://msdn.microsoft.com/en-us/library/ee329530(v=vs.110).aspx`. When you run your own measurements, you'll be able to identify similar problems by visually comparing the reports.

Concurrency profiling and visualization are highly useful tools, and we will meet them again in subsequent chapters. They serve as another great evidence of ETW's great influence—this omnipresent high-performance monitoring framework is used across managed and native profiling tools.

I/O Profilers

The last performance metric category we study in this chapter is I/O operations. ETW events can be used to obtain counts and details for physical disk access, page faults, network packets, and other types of I/O, but we haven't seen any specialized treatment for I/O operations.

Sysinternals Process Monitor is a free tool that collects file system, registry, and network activity (see Figure 2-34). You can download the entire suite of Sysinternals tools, or just the latest version of Process Monitor, from the TechNet website at `http://technet.microsoft.com/en-us/sysinternals/bb896645`. By applying its rich filtering capabilities, system administrators and performance investigators use Process Monitor to diagnose I/O-related errors (such as missing files or insufficient permissions) as well as performance problems (such as remote file system accesses or excessive paging).

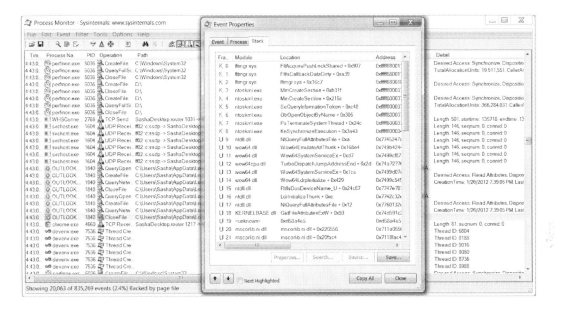

Figure 2-34. *Process Monitor showing several types of events in the main view and the call stack for a specific event in the dialog window. Frames 19 and lower are managed frames*

Process Monitor offers a complete user-mode and kernel-mode stack trace for each event it captures, making it ideal to understand where excessive or erroneous I/O operations are originating in the application's source code. Unfortunately, at the time of writing Process Monitor cannot decode managed call stacks—but it can at least point in the general direction of the application that performed the I/O operation.

Through the course of this chapter we used automatic tools that measure application performance from various aspects—execution time, CPU time, memory allocation, and even I/O operations. The variety of measurement techniques is overwhelming, which is one of the reasons why developers often like to perform manual benchmarks of their application's performance. Before concluding this chapter, we discuss microbenchmarking and some of its potential pitfalls.

Microbenchmarking

Some performance problems and questions can only be resolved by manual measurement. You might be settling a bet about whether it's worthwhile to use a `StringBuilder`, measuring the performance of a third party library, optimizing a delicate algorithm by unrolling inner loops, or helping the JIT place commonly used data into registers by trial and error—and you might not be willing to use a profiler to do the performance measurements for you because the profiler is either too slow, too expensive, or too cumbersome. Though often perilous, microbenchmarking is still very popular. If you do it, we want to make sure that you do it right.

Poor Microbenchmark Example

We start with an example of a poorly designed microbenchmark and improve it until the results it provides are meaningful and correlate well with factual knowledge about the problem domain. The purpose is to determine which is faster—using the is keyword and then casting to the desired type, or using the as keyword and relying on the result.

```
//Test class
class Employee {
  public void Work() {}
}
//Fragment 1 - casting safely and then checking for null
static void Fragment1(object obj) {
  Employee emp = obj as Employee;
  if (emp != null) {
    emp.Work();
  }
}
//Fragment 2 - first checking the type and then casting
static void Fragment2(object obj) {
  if (obj is Employee) {
    Employee emp = obj as Employee;
    emp.Work();
  }
}
```

A rudimentary benchmarking framework might go along the following lines:

```
static void Main() {
  object obj = new Employee();
  Stopwatch sw = Stopwatch.StartNew();
  for (int i = 0; i < 500; i++) {
    Fragment1(obj);
  }
  Console.WriteLine(sw.ElapsedTicks);
  sw = Stopwatch.StartNew();
  for (int i = 0; i < 500; i++) {
    Fragment2(obj);
  }
  Console.WriteLine(sw.ElapsedTicks);
}
```

This is *not* a convincing microbenchmark, although the results are fairly reproducible. More often than not, the output is 4 ticks for the first loop and 200-400 ticks for the second loop. This might lead to the conclusion that the first fragment is 50-100 times faster. However, there are significant errors in this measurement and the conclusion that stems from it:

- The loop runs only once and 500 iterations are not enough to reach any meaningful conclusions—it takes a negligible amount of time to run the whole benchmark, so it can be affected by many environmental factors.

- No effort was made to prevent optimization, so the JIT compiler may have inlined and discarded both measurement loops completely.

- The Fragment1 and Fragment2 methods measure not only the cost of the is and as keywords, but also the cost of a method invocation (to the Fragment*N* method itself!). It may be the cast that invoking the method is significantly more expensive than the rest of the work.

Improving upon these problems, the following microbenchmark more closely depicts the actual costs of both operations:

```
class Employee {
  //Prevent the JIT compiler from inlining this method (optimizing it away)
  [MethodImpl(MethodImplOptions.NoInlining)]
  public void Work() {}
}

static void Measure(object obj) {
  const int OUTER_ITERATIONS = 10;
  const int INNER_ITERATIONS = 100000000;
  //The outer loop is repeated many times to make sure we get reliable results
  for (int i = 0; i < OUTER_ITERATIONS; ++i) {
    Stopwatch sw = Stopwatch.StartNew();
    //The inner measurement loop is repeated many times to make sure we are measuring an
    //operation of significant duration
    for (int j = 0; j < INNER_ITERATIONS; ++j) {
      Employee emp = obj as Employee;
      if (emp != null)
        emp.Work();
    }
    Console.WriteLine("As - {0}ms", sw.ElapsedMilliseconds);
  }
  for (int i = 0; i < OUTER_ITERATIONS; ++i) {
    Stopwatch sw = Stopwatch.StartNew();
    for (int j = 0; j < INNER_ITERATIONS; ++j) {
      if (obj is Employee) {
        Employee emp = obj as Employee;
        emp.Work();
      }
    }
    Console.WriteLine("Is Then As - {0}ms", sw.ElapsedMilliseconds);
  }
}
```

The results on one of the author's test machines (after discarding the first iteration) were around 410ms for the first loop and 440ms for the second loop, a reliable and reproducible performance difference, which might have you convinced that indeed, it's more efficient to use just the as keyword for casts and checks.

However, the riddles aren't over yet. If we add the virtual modifier to the Work method, the performance difference disappears completely, not even if we increase the number of iterations. This cannot be explained by the virtues or maladies of our microbenchmarking framework—it is a result from the problem domain. There is no way to understand this behavior without going to the assembly language level and inspecting the loop generated by the JIT compiler in both cases. First, before the virtual modifier:

```
; Disassembled loop body - the first loop
mov edx,ebx
mov ecx,163780h (MT: Employee)
call clr!JIT_IsInstanceOfClass (705ecfaa)
```

55

```
test eax,eax
je WRONG_TYPE
mov ecx,eax
call dword ptr ds:[163774h] (Employee.Work(), mdToken: 06000001)
WRONG_TYPE:

; Disassembled loop body - the second loop
mov edx,ebx
mov ecx,163780h (MT: Employee)
call clr!JIT_IsInstanceOfClass (705ecfaa)
test eax,eax
je WRONG_TYPE
mov ecx,ebx
cmp dword ptr [ecx],ecx
call dword ptr ds:[163774h] (Employee.Work(), mdToken: 06000001)
WRONG_TYPE:
```

In Chapter 3 we'll discuss in great depth the instruction sequence emitted by the JIT compiler to call a non-virtual method and to call a virtual method. When calling a non-virtual method, the JIT compiler must emit an instruction that makes sure we are not making a method call on a null reference. The CMP instruction in the second loop serves that task. In the first loop, the JIT compiler is smart enough to optimize this check away, because immediately prior to the call, there is a null reference check on the result of the cast (if (emp !=null) ...). In the second loop, the JIT compiler's optimization heuristics are not sufficient to optimize the check away (although it would have been just as safe), and this extra instruction is responsible for the extra 7-8% of performance overhead.

After adding the virtual modifier, however, the JIT compiler generates exactly the same code in both loop bodies:

```
; Disassembled loop body - both cases
mov edx,ebx
mov ecx,1A3794h (MT: Employee)
call clr!JIT_IsInstanceOfClass (6b24cfaa)
test eax,eax
je WRONG_TYPE
mov ecx,eax
mov eax,dword ptr [ecx]
mov eax,dword ptr [eax+28h]
call dword ptr [eax+10h]
WRONG_TYPE:
```

The reason is that when invoking a virtual method, there's no need to perform a null reference check explicitly—it is inherent in the method dispatch sequence (as we will see in Chapter 3). When the loop bodies are identical, so are the timing results.

Microbenchmarking Guidelines

For successful microbenchmarks you have to make sure that what you decided to measure adheres to the following guidelines:

- Your test code's environment is representative of the real environment for which it is being developed. For example, you should not run a method on in-memory data collections if it is designed to operate on database tables.

- Your test code's inputs are representative of the real input for which it is being developed. For example, you should not measure how a sorting method fares on three-element lists if it is designed to operate on collections with several million elements.

- The supporting code used to set up the environment should be negligible compared to the actual test code you are measuring. If this is impossible, then the setup should happen once and the test code should be repeated many times.

- The test code should run for sufficiently long so as to be considerable and reliable in the face of hardware and software fluctuations. For example, if you are testing the overhead of a boxing operation on value types, a single boxing operation is likely to be too fast to produce significant results, and will require many iterations of the same test to become substantial.

- The test code should not be optimized away by the language compiler or the JIT compiler. This happens often in Release mode when trying to measure simple operations. (We will return to this point later.)

When you have ascertained that your test code is sufficiently robust and measures the precise effect that you intended to measure, you should invest some time in setting up the benchmarking environment:

- When the benchmark is running, no other processes should be allowed to run on the target system. Networking, file I/O, and other types of external activity should be minimized (for example, by disabling the network card and shutting down unnecessary services).

- Benchmarks that allocate many objects should be wary of garbage collection effects. It's advisable to force a garbage collection before and after significant benchmark iterations to minimize their effects on each other.

- The hardware on the test system should be similar to the hardware to be used in the production environment. For example, benchmarks that involve intensive random disk seeks will run much faster on a solid state hard drive than a mechanical drive with a rotating head. (The same applies to graphics cards, specific processor features such as SIMD instructions, memory architecture, and other hardware traits.)

Finally, you should focus on the measurement itself. These are the things to keep in mind when designing benchmarking code:

- Discard the first measurement result—it is often influenced by the JIT compiler and other application startup costs. Moreover, during the first measurement data and instructions are unlikely to be in the processor's cache. (There are some benchmarks that measure cache effects, and should not heed this advice.)

- Repeat measurements many times and use more than just the average—the standard deviation (which represents the variance of the results) and the fluctuations between consecutive measurements are interesting as well.

- Subtract the measurement loop's overhead from the benchmarked code—this requires measuring the overhead of an empty loop, which isn't trivial because the JIT compiler is likely to optimize away empty loops. (Writing the loop by hand in assembly language is one way of countering this risk.)

- Subtract the time measurement overhead from the timing results, and use the least expensive and most accurate time measurement approach available—this is usually `System.Diagnostics.Stopwatch`.

- Know the resolution, precision, and accuracy of your measurement mechanism—for example, `Environment.TickCount`'s precision is usually only 10-15ms, although its resolution appears to be 1ms.

■ **Note**   Resolution is the fineness of the measurement mechanism. If it reports results in integer multiples of 100ns, then its resolution is 100ns. However, its precision might be far less—for a physical time interval of 500ns it might report 2×100ns on one occasion and 7×100ns on another. We might be able to place an upper bound on the precision at 300ns, in this case. Finally, accuracy is the degree of correctness of the measurement mechanism. If it reliably and repeatedly reports a 5000ns physical time interval as 5400ns with a precision of 100ns, we might say its accuracy is +8% of the truth.

The unfortunate example in the beginning of this section should not dissuade you from ever writing your own microbenchmarks. However, you should mind the advice given here and design meaningful benchmarks whose results you can trust. The worst performance optimization is one that is based on incorrect measurements; unfortunately, manual benchmarking often leads into this trap.

Summary

Performance measurement is no simple task, and one of the reasons is the large variety of metrics and tools, and the effect of the tools on the measurement accuracy and the application's behavior. We've seen a large number of tools in this chapter, and you might be feeling a little dizzy if asked to recite precisely which situations warrant the use of which tool. Table 2-3 summarizes the important characteristics of all the tools demonstrated in this chapter.

Table 2-3. *The Performance Measurement Tools Used in This Chapter*

Tool	Performance Metrics	Overhead	Special Pros/Cons
Visual Studio Sampling Profiler	CPU usage, cache misses, page faults, system calls	Low	--
Visual Studio Instrumentation Profiler	Running time	Medium	Can't attach to a running process
Visual Studio Allocation Profiler	Memory allocations	Medium	--
Visual Studio Concurrency Visualizer	Thread visualization, resource contention	Low	Visual thread progress information, contention details, unblocking stack
CLR Profiler	Memory allocations, GC statistics, object references	High	Visual heap graphs, allocation graphs, GC timeline visualization
Performance Monitor	Numeric performance metrics at the process or system level	None	Only numeric information, not method-level
BCL PerfMonitor	Running time, GC information, JIT information	Very low	Simple, almost no-overhead runtime profiling
PerfView	Running time, heap information, GC information, JIT information	Very low	Adds free heap analysis capabilities to PerfMonitor
Windows Performance Toolkit	ETW events from system- and application-level providers	Very low	--
Process Monitor	File, registry, and network I/O operations	Low	--
Entity Framework Profiler	Data access through the Entity Framework classes	Medium	--
ANTS Memory Profiler	Memory usage and heap information	Medium	Powerful filters and great visualization capabilities
.NET Memory Profiler	Memory usage and heap information	Medium	Can open memory dump files

Armed with these tools and general understanding of what performance metrics to expect from managed applications, we are ready now to dive into the internals of the CLR, and see what practical steps can be taken to improve the performance of managed applications.

CHAPTER 3

Type Internals

This chapter concerns the internals of .NET types, how value types and reference types are laid out in memory, what the JIT must do to invoke a virtual method, the intricacies of implementing a value type properly, and other details. Why would we trouble ourselves and spend a few dozen pages discussing these inner workings? How can these internal details affect our application's performance? It turns out that value types and reference types differ in layout, allocation, equality, assignment, storage, and numerous other parameters—which makes proper type selection of paramount importance to application performance.

An Example

Consider a simple type called Point2D that represents a point in a small two-dimensional space. Each of the two coordinates can be represented by a short, for a total of four bytes for the entire object. Now suppose that you want to store in memory an array of ten million points. How much space would be required for them? The answer to this question depends greatly on whether Point2D is a reference type or a value type. If it is a reference type, an array of ten million points would actually store ten million references. On a 32-bit system, these ten million references consume almost 40 MB of memory. The objects themselves would consume at least the same amount. In fact, as we will see shortly, each Point2D instance would occupy at least 12 bytes of memory, bringing the total memory usage for an array of ten million points to a whopping 160MB! On the other hand, if Point2D is a value type, an array of ten million points would store ten million points – not a single extra byte wasted, for a total of 40MB, four times less than the reference type approach (see Figure 3-1). This difference in *memory density* is a critical reason to prefer value types in certain settings.

Note   There is another disadvantage to storing references to points instead of the actual point instances. If you want to traverse this huge array of points sequentially, it is much easier for the compiler and the hardware to access a contiguous array of Point2D instances than it is to access through references the heap objects, which are not guaranteed to be contiguous in memory. As we shall see in Chapter 5, CPU cache considerations can affect the application's execution time up to an order of magnitude.

It is inevitable to conclude that understanding the details of how the CLR lays out objects in memory and how reference types differ from value types is crucial for the performance of our applications. We begin by reviewing the fundamental differences between value types and reference types at the language level and then dive into the internal implementation details.

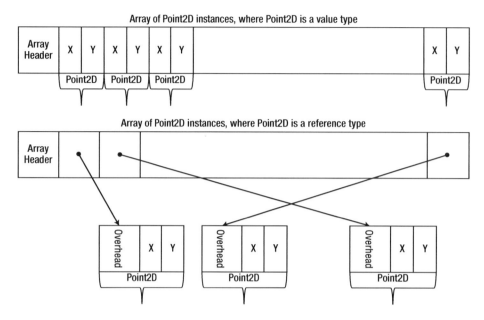

Figure 3-1. *An array of* Point2D *instances in the case* Point2D *is a reference type versus a value type*

Semantic Differences between Reference Types and Value Types

Reference types in .NET include classes, delegates, interfaces, and arrays. string (System.String), which is one of the most ubiquitous types in .NET, is a reference type as well. Value types in .NET include structs and enums. The primitive types, such as int, float, decimal, are value types – but .NET developers are free to define additional value types using the struct keyword.

On the language level, reference types enjoy *reference semantics,* where the identity of the object is considered before its content, while value types enjoy *value semantics,* where objects don't have an identity, are not accessed through references, and are treated according to their content. This affects several areas of the .NET languages, as Table 3-1 demonstrates.

Table 3-1. *Semantic Differences Between Value Types and Reference Types*

Criteria	Reference Types	Value Types
Passing an object to a method	Only the reference is passed; changes propagate to all other references	The object's contents are copied into the parameter (unless using the ref or out keywords); changes do not affect any code outside of the method
Assigning a variable to another variable	Only the reference is copied; two variables now contain references to the same object	The contents are copied; the two variables contain identical copies of unrelated data
Comparing two objects using operator==	The references are compared; two references are equal if they reference the same object	The contents are compared; two objects are equal if their content is identical on a field-by-field level

These semantic differences are fundamental to the way we write code in any .NET language. However, they are only the tip of the iceberg in terms of how reference types and value types and their purposes differ. First, let's consider the memory locations in which objects are stored, and how they are allocated and deallocated.

Storage, Allocation, and Deallocation

Reference types are allocated exclusively from the managed heap, an area of memory managed by the .NET garbage collector, which will be discussed in more detail in Chapter 4. Allocating an object from the managed heap involves incrementing a pointer, which is a fairly cheap operation in terms of performance. On a multi-processor system, if multiple processors are accessing the same heap, some synchronization is required, but the allocation is still extremely cheap compared to allocators in unmanaged environments, such as `malloc`.

The garbage collector reclaims memory in a non-deterministic fashion and makes no promises regarding its internal operation. As we shall see in Chapter 4, a full garbage collection process is extremely expensive, but the average garbage collection cost of a well-behaved application should be considerably smaller than that of a similar unmanaged counterpart.

■ **Note**   To be precise, there *is* an incarnation of reference types that can be allocated from the stack. Arrays of certain primitive types (such as arrays of integers) can be allocated from the stack using the `unsafe` context and the `stackalloc` keyword, or by embedding a fixed-size array into a custom struct, using the `fixed` keyword (discussed in Chapter 8). However, the objects created by the `stackalloc` and `fixed` keywords are not "real" arrays, and have a different memory layout than standard arrays allocated from the heap.

Stand-alone value types are usually allocated from the stack of the executing thread. However, value types can be embedded in reference types, in which case they are allocated on the heap, and can be boxed, transferring their storage to the heap (we will revisit boxing later in this chapter). Allocating a value type instance from the stack is a very cheap operation that involves modifying the stack pointer register (ESP on Intel x86), and has the additional advantage of allocating several objects at once. In fact, it is very common for a method's *prologue* code to use just a single CPU instruction to allocate stack storage for *all* the local variables present in its outermost block.

Reclaiming stack memory is very efficient as well, and requires a reverse modification of the stack pointer register. Due to the way methods are compiled to machine code, often enough the compiler is not required to keep track of the size of a method's local variables, and can destroy the entire stack frame in a standard set of three instructions, known as the function *epilogue*.

Below are the typical prologue and epilogue of a managed method compiled to 32-bit machine code (this is not actual production code produced by a JIT-compiler, which employs numerous optimizations discussed in Chapter 10). The method has four local variables, whose storage is allocated at once in the prologue and reclaimed at once in the epilogue:

```
int Calculation(int a, int b)
{
  int x = a + b;
  int y = a - b;
  int z = b - a;
  int w = 2 * b + 2 * a;
  return x + y + z + w;
}

; parameters are passed on the stack in [esp+4] and [esp+8]
push ebp
mov ebp, esp
```

```
add esp, 16 ; allocates storage for four local variables
mov eax, dword ptr [ebp+8]
add eax, dword ptr [ebp+12]
mov dword ptr [ebp-4], eax
; ...similar manipulations for y, z, w
mov eax, dword ptr [ebp-4]
add eax, dword ptr [ebp-8]
add eax, dword ptr [ebp-12]
add eax, dword ptr [ebp-16] ; eax contains the return value
mov esp, ebp ; restores the stack frame, thus reclaiming the local storage space
pop ebp
ret 8 ; reclaims the storage for the two parameters
```

■ **Note**   The new keyword does not imply heap allocation in C# and other managed languages. You can allocate a value type on the stack using the new keyword as well. For example, the following line allocates a DateTime instance from the stack, initialized with the New Year's Eve (System.DateTime is a value type): DateTime newYear = new DateTime(2011, 12, 31);

WHAT'S THE DIFFERENCE BETWEEN STACK AND HEAP?

Contrary to popular belief, there isn't that much of a difference between stacks and heaps in a .NET process. Stacks and heaps are nothing more than ranges of addresses in virtual memory, and there is no inherent advantage in the range of addresses reserved to the stack of a particular thread compared to the range of addresses reserved for the managed heap. Accessing a memory location on the heap is neither faster nor slower than accessing a memory location on the stack. There are several considerations that might, in certain cases, support the claim that memory access to stack locations is faster, overall, than memory access to heap locations. Among them:

- On the stack, temporal allocation locality (allocations made close together in time) implies spatial locality (storage that is close together in space). In turn, when temporal allocation locality implies temporal access locality (objects allocated together are accessed together), the sequential stack storage tends to perform better with respect to CPU caches and operating system paging systems.

- Memory density on the stack tends to be higher than on the heap because of the reference type overhead (discussed later in this chapter). Higher memory density often leads to better performance, e.g., because more objects fit in the CPU cache.

- Thread stacks tend to be fairly small – the default maximum stack size on Windows is 1MB, and most threads tend to actually use only a few stack pages. On modern systems, the stacks of all application threads can fit into the CPU cache, making typical stack object access extremely fast. (Entire heaps, on the other hand, rarely fit into CPU caches.)

With that said, you should not be moving all your allocations to the stack! Thread stacks on Windows are limited, and it is easy to exhaust the stack by applying injudicious recursion and large stack allocations.

Having examined the superficial differences between value types and reference types, it's time to turn to the underlying implementation details, which also explain the vast differences in memory density at which we hinted several times already. A small caveat before we begin: the details described below are internal implementation minutiae of the CLR, which are subject to change at any time without notice. We have done our best to ensure that this information is fresh and up to date with the .NET 4.5 release, but cannot guarantee that it will remain correct in the future.

Reference Type Internals

We begin with reference types, whose memory layout is fairly complex and has significant effect on their runtime performance. For the purpose of our discussion, let's consider a textbook example of an Employee reference type, which has several fields (instance and static), and a few methods as well:

```
public class Employee
{
  private int _id;
  private string _name;
  private static CompanyPolicy _policy;
  public virtual void Work() {
    Console.WriteLine("Zzzz...");
  }
  public void TakeVacation(int days) {
    Console.WriteLine("Zzzz...");
  }
  public static void SetCompanyPolicy(CompanyPolicy policy) {
    _policy = policy;
  }
}
```

Now consider an instance of the Employee reference type on the managed heap. Figure 3-2 describes the layout of the instance in a 32-bit .NET process:

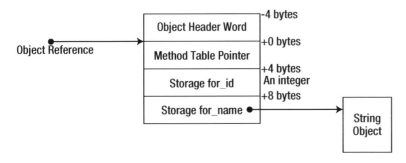

Figure 3-2. *The layout of an Employee instance on the managed heap, including the reference type overhead*

The order of the _id and _name fields inside the object is not guaranteed (although it can be controlled, as we will see in the "Value Type Internals" section, using the StructLayout attribute). However, the object's memory storage begins with a four byte field called *object header word* (or sync block index), followed by another four byte field called *method table pointer* (or type object pointer). These fields are not directly accessible from any .NET language – they serve the JIT and the CLR itself. The object reference (which, internally, is simply a memory address) points to the beginning of the method table pointer, so that the object header word is situated at a negative offset from the object's address.

■ **Note**   On 32-bit systems, objects in the heap are aligned to the nearest four byte multiple. This implies that an object with only a single `byte` member would still occupy 12 bytes in the heap, due to alignment (in fact, even a class with no instance fields will occupy 12 bytes when instantiated). There are several differences where 64-bit systems are introduced. First, the method table pointer field (a pointer that it is) occupies 8 bytes of memory, and the object header word takes 8 bytes as well. Second, objects in the heap are aligned to the nearest eight byte multiple. This implies that an object with only a single `byte` member in a 64-bit heap would occupy a whopping 24 bytes of memory. This only serves to demonstrate more strongly the memory density overhead of reference types, in particular where small objects are created in bulk.

The Method Table

The Method Table Pointer points to an internal CLR data structure called a method table (MT), which points in turn to another internal structure called EEClass (EE stands for Execution Engine). Together, the MT and EEClass contain the information required to dispatch virtual method calls, interface method calls, access static variables, determine the type of a runtime object, access the base type methods efficiently, and serve many additional purposes. The method table contains the frequently accessed information, which is required for the runtime operation of critical mechanisms such as virtual method dispatch, whereas the EEClass contains information that is less frequently accessed, but still used by some runtime mechanisms, such as Reflection. We can learn about the contents of both data structures using the `!DumpMT` and `!DumpClass` SOS commands and the Rotor (SSCLI) source code, bearing in mind that we are discussing internal implementation details that might differ significantly between CLR versions.

■ **Note**   SOS (Son of Strike) is a debugger extension DLL, which facilitates debugging managed applications using Windows debuggers. It is most commonly used with WinDbg, but can be loaded into Visual Studio using the Immediate Window. Its commands provide insight into CLR internals, which is why we are using it often in this chapter. For more information about SOS, consult the inline help (the `!help` command after loading the extension) and the MSDN documentation. An excellent treatment of SOS features in conjunction with debugging managed applications is in Mario Hewardt's book, "Advanced .NET Debugging" (Addison-Wesley, 2009).

The location of static fields is determined by the EEClass. Primitive fields (such as integers) are stored in dynamically allocated locations on the loader heap, while custom value types and reference types are stored as indirect references to a heap location (through an AppDomain-wide object array). To access a static field, it is not necessary to consult the method table or EEClass – the JIT compiler can hard-code the addresses of the static fields into the generated machine code. The array of references to static fields is pinned so that its address can't change during a garbage collection (discussed in more detail in Chapter 4), and the primitive static fields reside in the method table which is not touched by the garbage collector either. This ensures that hard-coded addresses can be used to access these fields:

```
public static void SetCompanyPolicy(CompanyPolicy policy)
{
    _policy = policy;
}
mov ecx, dword ptr [ebp+8]    ;copy parameter to ECX
mov dword ptr [0x3543320], ecx  ;copy ECX to the static field location in the global pinned array
```

The most obvious thing the method table contains is an array of code addresses, one for every method of the type, including any virtual methods inherited from its base types. For example, Figure 3-3 shows a possible method table layout for the Employee class above, assuming that it derives only from System.Object:

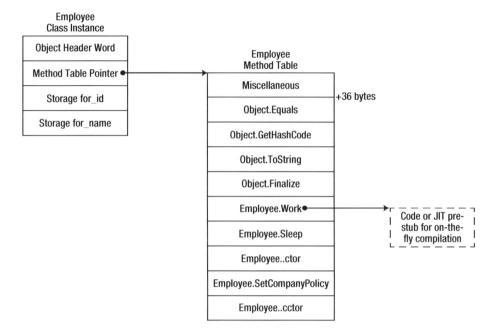

Figure 3-3. *The Employee class' method table (partial view)*

We can inspect method tables using the !DumpMT SOS command, given a method table pointer (which can be obtained from a live object reference by inspecting its first field, or by named lookup with the !Name2EE command). The -md switch will output the method descriptor table, containing the code addresses and method descriptors for each of the type's methods. (The JIT column can have one of three values: PreJIT, meaning that the method was compiled using NGEN; JIT, meaning that the method was JIT-compiled at runtime; or NONE, meaning that the method was not yet compiled.)

```
0:000> r esi
esi=02774ec8
0:000> !do esi
Name:        CompanyPolicy
MethodTable: 002a3828
EEClass:     002a1350
Size:        12(0xc) bytes
File:        D:\Development\...\App.exe
Fields:
None
0:000> dd esi L1
02774ec8 002a3828
0:000> !dumpmt -md 002a3828
EEClass:          002a1350
Module:           002a2e7c
```

```
Name:                CompanyPolicy
mdToken:             02000002
File:                D:\Development\...\App.exe
BaseSize:            0xc
ComponentSize:       0x0
Slots in VTable: 5
Number of IFaces in IFaceMap: 0
---------------------------------------
MethodDesc Table
    Entry MethodDe     JIT Name
5b625450 5b3c3524 PreJIT System.Object.ToString()
5b6106b0 5b3c352c PreJIT System.Object.Equals(System.Object)
5b610270 5b3c354c PreJIT System.Object.GetHashCode()
5b610230 5b3c3560 PreJIT System.Object.Finalize()
002ac058 002a3820   NONE CompanyPolicy..ctor()
```

> ■ **Note**   Unlike C++ virtual function pointer tables, CLR method tables contain code addresses for *all* methods, including non-virtual ones. The order in which methods are laid out by the method table creator is unspecified. Currently, they are arranged in the following order: inherited virtual methods (including any possible overrides – discussed later), newly introduced virtual methods, non-virtual instance methods, and static methods.

The code addresses stored in the method table are generated on the fly – the JIT compiler compiles methods when they are first called, unless NGEN was used (discussed in Chapter 10). However, users of the method table need not be aware of this step thanks to a fairly common compiler trick. When the method table is first created, it is populated with pointers to special pre-JIT stubs, which contain a single CALL instruction dispatching the caller to a JIT routine that compiles the relevant method on the fly. After compilation completes, the stub is overwritten with a JMP instruction that transfers control to the newly compiled method. The entire data structure which stores the pre-JIT stub and some additional information about the method is called a method descriptor (MD) and can be examined by the !DumpMD SOS command.

Before a method has been JIT-compiled, its method descriptor contains the following information:

```
0:000> !dumpmd 003737a8
Method Name:   Employee.Sleep()
Class:         003712fc
MethodTable:   003737c8
mdToken:       06000003
Module:        00372e7c
IsJitted:      no
CodeAddr:      ffffffff
Transparency: Critical
```

Here is an example of a pre-JIT stub that is responsible for updating the method descriptor:

```
0:000> !u 002ac035
Unmanaged code
002ac035 b002         mov     al,2
002ac037 eb08         jmp     002ac041
002ac039 b005         mov     al,5
002ac03b eb04         jmp     002ac041
```

```
002ac03d b008          mov    al,8
002ac03f eb00          jmp    002ac041
002ac041 0fb6c0        movzx  eax,al
002ac044 c1e002        shl    eax,2
002ac047 05a0372a00    add    eax,2A37A0h
002ac04c e98270ca66    jmp    clr!ThePreStub (66f530d3)
```

After the method was JIT-compiled, its method descriptor changes to the following:

```
0:007> !dumpmd 003737a8
Method Name:   Employee.Sleep()
Class:         003712fc
MethodTable:   003737c8
mdToken:       06000003
Module:        00372e7c
IsJitted:      yes
CodeAddr:      00490140
Transparency:  Critical
```

A real method table contains more information that we have previously disclosed. Understanding some of the additional fields is critical to the details of method dispatch discussed next; this is why we must take a longer look at the method table structure for an Employee instance. We assume additionally that the Employee class implements three interfaces: IComparable, IDisposable, and ICloneable.

In Figure 3-4, there are several additions to our previous understanding of method table layout. First, the method table header contains several interesting flags that allow dynamic discovery of its layout, such as

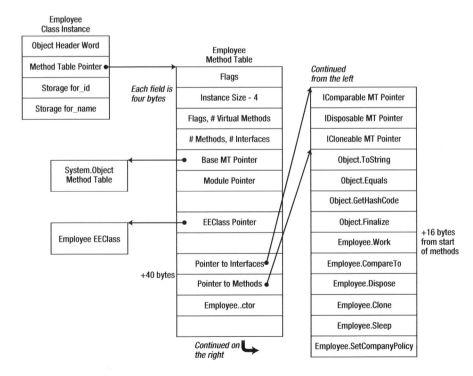

Figure 3-4. *Detailed view of the Employee method table, including internal pointers to interface list and method list used for virtual method invocation*

the number of virtual methods and the number of interfaces the type implements. Second, the method table contains a pointer to its base class's method table, a pointer to its module, and a pointer to its EEClass (which contains a back-reference to the method table). Third, the actual methods are preceded by a list of interface method tables that the type implements. This is why there is a pointer to the method list within the method table, at a constant offset of 40 bytes from the method table start.

■ **Note**   The additional dereference step required to reach the table of code addresses for the type's methods allows this table to be stored separately from the method table object, in a different memory location. For example, if you inspect the method table for System.Object, you may find that its method code addresses are stored in a separate location. Furthermore, classes with many virtual methods will have several first-level table pointers, allowing partial reuse of method tables in derived classes.

Invoking Methods on Reference Type Instances

Clearly, the method table can be used to invoke methods on arbitrary object instances. Suppose that the stack location EBP-64 contains the address of an Employee object with a method table layout as in the previous diagram. Then we can call the Work virtual method by using the following instruction sequence:

```
mov ecx, dword ptr [ebp-64]
mov eax, dword ptr [ecx]      ; the method table pointer
mov eax, dword ptr [eax+40]   ; the pointer to the actual methods inside the method table
call dword ptr [eax+16]       ; Work is the fifth slot (fourth if zero-based)
```

The first instruction copies the reference from the stack to the ECX register, the second instruction dereferences the ECX register to obtain the object's method table pointer, the third instruction fetches the internal pointer to the list of methods inside the method table (which is located at the constant offset of 40 bytes), and the fourth instruction dereferences the internal method table at offset 16 to obtain the code address of the Work method and calls it. To understand why it is necessary to use the method table for virtual method dispatching, we need to consider how runtime binding works – i.e., how polymorphism can be implemented through virtual methods.

Suppose that an additional class, Manager, were to derive from Employee and override its Work virtual method, as well as implement yet another interface:

```
public class Manager : Employee, ISerializable
{
  private List<Employee> _reports;
  public override void Work() ...
  //...implementation of ISerializable omitted for brevity
}
```

The compiler might be required to dispatch a call to the Manager.Work method through an object reference that has only the Employee static type, as in the following code listing:

```
Employee employee = new Manager(...);
employee.Work();
```

In this particular case, the compiler might be able to deduce – using static flow analysis – that the Manager. Work method should be invoked (this doesn't happen in the current C# and CLR implementations). In the general case, however, when presented with a statically typed Employee reference, the compiler needs to defer binding to runtime. In fact, the only way to bind to the right method is to determine at runtime the actual type of the object referenced by the employee variable, and dispatch the virtual method based on that type information. This is exactly what the method table enables the JIT compiler to do.

As depicted in Figure 3-5, the method table layout for the Manager class has the Work slot overridden with a different code address, and the method dispatch sequence would remain the same. Note that the offset of the overridden slot from the beginning of the method table is different because the Manager class implements an additional interface; however, the "Pointer to Methods" field is still at the same offset, and accommodates for this difference:

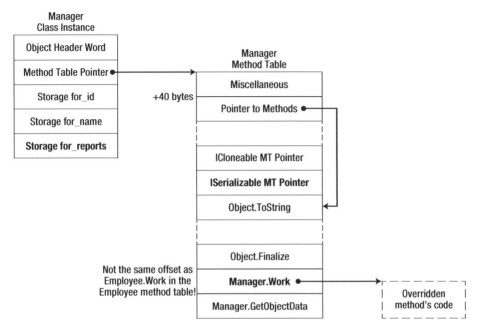

Figure 3-5. *Method table layout for the Manager method table.This method table contains an additional interface MT slot, which makes the "Pointer to Methods" offset larger*

```
mov ecx, dword ptr [ebp-64]
mov eax, dword ptr [ecx]
mov eax, dword ptr [ecx+40]  ;this accommodates for the Work method having a different
call dword ptr [eax+16]      ;absolute offset from the beginning of the MT
```

■ **Note**   The object layout in which an overridden method's offset from the beginning of the method table is not guaranteed to be the same in derived classes is new in CLR 4.0. Prior to CLR 4.0, the list of interfaces implemented by the type was stored at the end of the method table, after the code addresses; this meant that the offset of the Object.Equals address (and the rest of the code addresses) was constant in all derived classes. In turn, this meant that the virtual method dispatch sequence consisted of only three instructions instead of four (the third instruction in the sequence above was not necessary). Older articles and books may still reference the previous invocation sequence and object layout, serving as an additional demonstration for how internal CLR details can change between versions without any notice.

Dispatching Non-Virtual Methods

We can use a similar dispatch sequence to call non-virtual methods as well. However, for non-virtual methods, there is no need to use the method table for method dispatch: the code address of the invoked method (or at least its pre-JIT stub) is known when the JIT compiles the method dispatch. For example, if the stack location EBP-64 contains the address of an Employee object, as before, then the following instruction sequence will call the TakeVacation method with the parameter 5:

```
mov edx, 5                  ;parameter passing through register – custom calling convention
mov ecx, dword ptr [ebp-64] ;still required because ECX contains 'this' by convention
call dword ptr [0x004a1260]
```

It is still required to load the object's address into the ECX register – all instance methods expect to receive in ECX the implicit this parameter. However, there's no longer any need to dereference the method table pointer and obtain the address from the method table. The JIT compiler still needs to be able to update the call site after performing the call; this is obtained by performing an indirect call through a memory location (0x004a1260 in this example) that initially points to the pre-JIT stub and is updated by the JIT compiler as soon as the method is compiled.

Unfortunately, the method dispatch sequence above suffers from a significant problem. It allows method calls on null object references to be dispatched successfully and possibly remain undetected until the instance method attempts to access an instance field or a virtual method, which would cause an access violation. In fact, this is the behavior for C++ instance method calls – the following code would execute unharmed in most C++ environments, but would certainly make C# developers shift uneasily in their chairs:

```
class Employee {
public: void Work() { } //empty non-virtual method
};
Employee* pEmployee = NULL;
pEmployee->Work();      //runs to completion
```

If you inspect the actual sequence used by the JIT compiler to invoke non-virtual instance methods, it would contain an additional instruction:

```
mov edx, 5                  ;parameter passing through register – custom calling convention
mov ecx, dword ptr [ebp-64] ;still required because ECX contains 'this' by convention
cmp ecx, dword ptr [ecx]
call dword ptr [0x004a1260]
```

Recall that the CMP instruction subtracts its second operand from the first and sets CPU flags according to the result of the operation. The code above does not use the comparison result stored in the CPU flags, so how would the CMP instruction help prevent calling a method using a null object reference? Well, the CMP instruction attempts to access the memory address in the ECX register, which contains the object reference. If the object reference is null, this memory access would fail with an access violation, because accessing the address 0 is always illegal in Windows processes. This access violation is converted by the CLR to a NullReferenceException which is thrown at the invocation point; a much better choice than emitting a null check inside the method after it has already been called. Furthermore, the CMP instruction occupies only two bytes in memory, and has the advantage of being able to check for invalid addresses other than null.

■ **Note**   There is no need for a similar CMP instruction when invoking virtual methods; the null check is implicit because the standard virtual method invocation flow accesses the method table pointer, which makes sure the object pointer is valid. Even for virtual method calls you might not always see the CMP instruction being emitted; in recent CLR versions, the JIT compiler is smart enough to avoid redundant checks. For example, if the program flow has just returned from a virtual method invocation on an object — which contains the null check implicitly — then the JIT compiler might not emit the CMP instruction.

The reason we are so concerned with the precise implementation details of invoking virtual methods versus non-virtual methods is not the additional memory access or extra instruction that might or might not be required. The primary optimization precluded by virtual methods is *method inlining*, which is critical for modern high-performance applications. Inlining is a fairly simple compiler trick that trades code size for speed, whereby method calls to small or simple methods are replaced by the method's body. For example, in the code below, it makes perfect sense to replace the call to the Add method by the single operation performed inside it:

```
int Add(int a, int b)
{
  return a + b;
}
int c = Add(10, 12);
//assume that c is used later in the code
```

The non-optimized call sequence will have almost 10 instructions: three to set up parameters and dispatch the method, two to set up the method frame, one to add the numbers together, two to tear down the method frame, and one to return from the method. The optimized call sequence will have only *one* instruction – can you guess which one? One option is the ADD instruction, but in fact another optimization called constant-folding can be used to calculate at compile-time the result of the addition operation, and assign to the variable c the constant value 22.

The performance difference between inlined and non-inlined method calls can be vast, especially when the methods are as simple as the one above. Properties, for instance, make a great candidate for inlining, and compiler-generated automatic properties even more so because they don't contain any logic other than directly accessing a field. However, virtual methods prevent inlining because inlining can occur only when the compiler knows at compile-time (in the case of the JIT compiler, at JIT-time) which method is about to be invoked. When the method to be invoked is determined at runtime by the type information embedded into the object, there is no way to generate correctly inlined code for a virtual method dispatch. If all methods were virtual by default, properties would have been virtual as well, and the accumulated cost from indirect method dispatches where inlining was otherwise possible would have been overwhelming.

You might be wondering about the effects of the sealed keyword on method dispatch, in light of how important inlining may be. For example, if the Manager class declares the Work method as sealed, invocations of Work on object references that have the Manager static type can proceed as a non-virtual instance method invocation:

```
public class Manager : Employee
{
  public override sealed void Work() ...
}
Manager manager = ...; //could be an instance of Manager, could be a derived type
manager.Work();        //direct dispatch should be possible!
```

Nonetheless, at the time of writing, the sealed keyword has no effect on method dispatch on all the CLR versions we tested, even though knowledge that a class or method is sealed can be used to effectively remove the need for virtual method dispatch.

Dispatching Static and Interface Methods

For completeness, there are two additional types of methods we need to consider: static methods and interface methods. Dispatching static methods is fairly easy: there is no need to load an object reference, and simply calling the method (or its pre-JIT stub) would suffice. Because the invocation does not proceed through a method table, the JIT compiler uses the same trick as for non-virtual instance method: the method dispatch is indirect through a special memory location which is updated after the method is JIT compiled.

Interface methods, however, are a wholly different matter. It might appear that dispatching an interface method is not different from dispatching a virtual instance method. Indeed, interfaces enable a form of polymorphism reminiscent of classical virtual methods. Unfortunately, there is no guarantee that the interface implementations of a particular interface across several classes end up in the same slots in the method table. Consider the following code, where two classes implement the IComparable interface:

```
class Manager : Employee, IComparable {
  public override void Work() ...
  public void TakeVacation(int days) ...
  public static void SetCompanyPolicy(...) ...
  public int CompareTo(object other) ...
}
class BigNumber : IComparable {
  public long Part1, Part2;
  public int CompareTo(object other) ...
}
```

Clearly, the method table layout for these classes will be very different, and the slot number where the CompareTo method ends up will be different as well. Complex object hierarchies and multiple interface implementations make it evident that an additional dispatch step is required to identify where in the method table the interface methods were placed.

In prior CLR versions, this information was stored in a global (AppDomain-level) table indexed by an interface ID, generated when the interface is first loaded. The method table had a special entry (at offset 12) pointing into the proper location in the global interface table, and the global interface table entries pointed back into the method table, to the sub-table within it where the interface method pointers were stored. This allowed multi-step method dispatch, along the following lines:

```
mov ecx, dword ptr [ebp-64] ; object reference
mov eax, dword ptr [ecx]    ; method table pointer
mov eax, dword ptr [eax+12] ; interface map pointer
mov eax, dword ptr [eax+48] ; compile time offset for this interface in the map
call dword ptr [eax]        ; first method at EAX, second method at EAX+4, etc.
```

This looks complicated – and expensive! There are four memory accesses required to fetch the code address of the interface implementation and dispatch it, and for some interfaces this may be too high a cost. This is why you will never see the sequence above used by the production JIT compiler, even without optimizations enabled. The JIT uses several tricks to effectively inline interface methods, at least for the common case.

Hot-path analysis — when the JIT detects that the same interface implementation is often used, it replaces the specific call site with optimized code that may even inline the commonly used interface implementation:

```
mov ecx, dword ptr [ebp-64]
cmp dword ptr [ecx], 00385670 ; expected method table pointer
jne 00a188c0                  ; cold path, shown below in pseudo-code
jmp 00a19548                  ; hot path, could be inlined body here
```

```
cold path:
if (--wrongGuessesRemaining < 0) { ;starts at 100
  back patch the call site to the code discussed below
} else {
  standard interface dispatch as discussed above
}
```

Frequency analysis — when the JIT detects that its choice of hot path is no longer accurate for a particular call site (across a series of several dispatches), it replaces the former hot path guess with the new hot path, and continues to alternate between them every time it gets the guess wrong:

```
start: if (obj->MTP == expectedMTP) {
  direct jump to expected implementation
} else {
  expectedMTP = obj->MTP;
  goto start;
}
```

For more details on interface method dispatch, consider reading Sasha Goldshtein's article "JIT Optimizations" (http://www.codeproject.com/Articles/25801/JIT-Optimizations) and Vance Morrison's blog post (http://blogs.msdn.com/b/vancem/archive/2006/03/13/550529.aspx). Interface method dispatch is a moving target and a ripe ground for optimization; future CLR versions might introduce further optimizations not discussed here.

Sync Blocks And The lock Keyword

The second header field embedded in each reference type instance is the object header word (or sync block index). Unlike the method table pointer, this field is used for a variety of purposes, including synchronization, GC book-keeping, finalization, and hash code storage. Several bits of this field determine exactly which information is stored in it at any instant in time.

The most complex purpose for which the object header word is used is synchronization using the CLR monitor mechanism, exposed to C# through the lock keyword. The gist is as follows: several threads may attempt to enter a region of code protected by the lock statement, but only one thread at a time may enter the region, achieving mutual exclusion:

```
class Counter
{
  private int _i;
  private object _syncObject = new object();
  public int Increment()
  {
    lock (_syncObject)
    {
      return ++_i; //only one thread at a time can execute this statement
    }
  }
}
```

The lock keyword, however, is merely syntactic sugar that wraps the following construct, using the Monitor. Enter and Monitor.Exit methods:

```
class Counter
{
  private int _i;
  private object _syncObject = new object();
  public int Increment()
  {
    bool acquired = false;
    try
    {
      Monitor.Enter(_syncObject, ref acquired);
      return ++_i;
    }
    finally
    {
      if (acquired) Monitor.Exit(_syncObject);
    }
  }
}
```

To ensure this mutual exclusion, a synchronization mechanism can be associated with every object. Because it is expensive to create a synchronization mechanism for every object on the outset, this association occurs lazily, when the object is used for synchronization for the first time. When required, the CLR allocates a structure called a *sync block* from a global array called the *sync block table*. The sync block contains a backwards reference to its owning object (although this is a weak reference that does not prevent the object from being collected), and, among other things, a synchronization mechanism called monitor, which is implemented internally using a Win32 event. The numeric index of the allocated sync block is stored in the object's header word. Subsequent attempts to use the object for synchronization recognize the existing sync block index and use the associated monitor object for synchronization.

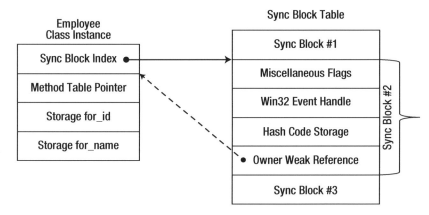

Figure 3-6. *A sync block associated with an object instance. The sync block index fields stores only the index into the sync block table, allowing the CLR to resize and move the table in memory without modifying the sync block index*

After a sync block has been unused for a long period of time, the garbage collector reclaims it and detaches its owning object from it, setting the sync block index to an invalid index. Following this reclamation, the sync block can be associated with another object, which conserves expensive operating system resources required for synchronization mechanisms.

The !SyncBlk SOS command can be used to inspect sync blocks that are currently contended, i.e., sync blocks which are owned by a thread and waited for by another thread (possibly more than one waiter). As of CLR 2.0, there is an optimization that may lazily create a sync block only when there is contention for it. While there is no sync block, the CLR may use a *thin lock* to manage synchronization state. Below we explore some examples of this.

First, let's take a look at the object header word of an object that hasn't been used for synchronization yet, but whose hash code has already been accessed (later in this chapter we will discuss hash code storage in reference types). In the following example, EAX points to an Employee object whose hash code is 46104728:

```
0:000> dd eax-4 L2
023d438c  0ebf8098 002a3860
0:000> ? 0n46104728
Evaluate expression: 46104728 = 02bf8098
0:000> .formats 0ebf8098
Evaluate expression:
  Hex:     0ebf8098
  Binary:  00001110 10111111 10000000 10011000
0:000> .formats 02bf8098
Evaluate expression:
  Hex:     02bf8098
  Binary:  00000010 10111111 10000000 10011000
```

There is no sync block index here; only the hash code and two bits set to 1, one of them probably indicating that the object header word now stores the hash code. Next, we issue a Monitor.Enter call for the object from one thread to lock it, and inspect the object header word:

```
0:004> dd 02444390-4 L2
0244438c  08000001 00173868
0:000> .formats 08000001
Evaluate    expression:
  Hex:      08000001
  Binary:   00001000 00000000 00000000 00000001
0:004> !syncblk
Index   SyncBlock   MonitorHeld   Recursion   Owning   Thread   Info   SyncBlock   Owner
    1   0097db4c             3           1   0092c698     1790      0   02444390   Employee
```

The object was assigned the sync block #1, which is evident from the !SyncBlk command output (for more information about the columns in the command's output, consult the SOS documentation). When another thread attempts to enter the lock statement with the same object, it enters a standard Win32 wait (albeit with message pumping if it's a GUI thread). Below is the bottom of the stack of a thread waiting for a monitor:

```
0:004> kb
ChildEBP RetAddr  Args to Child
04c0f404 75120bdd 00000001 04c0f454 00000001 ntdll!NtWaitForMultipleObjects+0x15
04c0f4a0 76c61a2c 04c0f454 04c0f4c8 00000000 KERNELBASE!WaitForMultipleObjectsEx+0x100
04c0f4e8 670f5579 00000001 7efde000 00000000 KERNEL32!WaitForMultipleObjectsExImplementation+0xe0
04c0f538 670f52b3 00000000 ffffffff 00000001 clr!WaitForMultipleObjectsEx_SO_TOLERANT+0x3c
04c0f5cc 670f53a5 00000001 0097db60 00000000 clr!Thread::DoAppropriateWaitWorker+0x22f
04c0f638 670f544b 00000001 0097db60 00000000 clr!Thread::DoAppropriateWait+0x65
04c0f684 66f5c28a ffffffff 00000001 00000000 clr!CLREventBase::WaitEx+0x128
04c0f698 670fd055 ffffffff 00000001 00000000 clr!CLREventBase::Wait+0x1a
04c0f724 670fd154 00939428 ffffffff f2e05698 clr!AwareLock::EnterEpilogHelper+0xac
04c0f764 670fd24f 00939428 00939428 00050172 clr!AwareLock::EnterEpilog+0x48
```

```
04c0f77c 670fce93 f2e05674 04c0f8b4 0097db4c clr!AwareLock::Enter+0x4a
04c0f7ec 670fd580 ffffffff f2e05968 04c0f8b4 clr!AwareLock::Contention+0x221
04c0f894 002e0259 02444390 00000000 00000000 clr!JITutil_MonReliableContention+0x8a
```

The synchronization object used is 25c, which is a handle to an event:

```
0:004> dd 04c0f454 L1
04c0f454  0000025c
0:004> !handle 25c f
Handle 25c
 Type             Event
 Attributes       0
 GrantedAccess    0x1f0003:
       Delete,ReadControl,WriteDac,WriteOwner,Synch
       QueryState,ModifyState
 HandleCount      2
 PointerCount     4
 Name             <none>
 Object Specific Information
   Event Type Auto Reset
   Event is Waiting
```

And finally, if we inspect the raw sync block memory assigned to this object, the hash code and synchronization mechanism handle are clearly visible:

```
0:004> dd 0097db4c
0097db4c  00000003 00000001 0092c698 00000001
0097db5c  80000001 0000025c 0000000d 00000000
0097db6c  00000000 00000000 00000000 02bf8098
0097db7c  00000000 00000003 00000000 00000001
```

A final subtlety worth mentioning is that in the previous example, we forced the subsequent creation of a sync block by calling GetHashCode before locking the object. As of CLR 2.0, there is a special optimization aimed to conserve time and memory that does not create a sync block if the object has not been associated with a sync block before. Instead, the CLR uses a mechanism called *thin lock*. When an object is locked for the first time and there is no contention yet (i.e., no other thread has attempted to lock the object), the CLR stores in the object header word the managed thread ID of the object's current owning thread. For example, here is the object header word of an object locked by the application's main thread before there is any contention for the lock:

```
0:004> dd 02384390-4
0238438c  00000001 00423870 00000000 00000000
```

Here, the thread with managed thread ID 1 is the application's main thread, as is evident from the output of the !Threads command:

```
0:004> !Threads
ThreadCount:      2
UnstartedThread:  0
BackgroundThread: 1
PendingThread:    0
DeadThread:       0
Hosted Runtime:   no
```

									Lock		
ID	OSID	ThreadOBJ	State	GC Mode	GC Alloc Context		Domain	Count	Apt	Exception
0	1	12f0	0033ce80	2a020	Preemptive	02385114:00000000	00334850	2	MTA	
2	2	23bc	00348eb8	2b220	Preemptive	00000000:00000000	00334850	0	MTA (Finalizer)

Thin locks are also reported by the SOS !DumpObj command, which indicates the owner thread for an object whose header contains a thin lock. Similarly, the !DumpHeap -thinlock command can output all the thin locks currently present in the managed heap:

```
0:004> !dumpheap -thinlock
 Address        MT    Size
02384390 00423870      12 ThinLock owner 1 (0033ce80) Recursive 0
02384758 5b70f98c      16 ThinLock owner 1 (0033ce80) Recursive 0
Found 2 objects.
0:004> !DumpObj 02384390
Name:        Employee
MethodTable: 00423870
EEClass:     004213d4
Size:        12(0xc) bytes
File:        D:\Development\...\App.exe
Fields:
      MT    Field   Offset        Type VT    Attr     Value Name
00423970    4000001       4  CompanyPolicy  0   static 00000000 _policy
ThinLock owner 1 (0033ce80), Recursive 0
```

When another thread attempts to lock the object, it will spin for a short time waiting for the thin lock to be released (i.e., the owner thread information to disappear from the object header word). If, after a certain time threshold, the lock is not released, it is converted to a sync block, the sync block index is stored within the object header word, and from that point on, the threads block on the Win32 synchronization mechanism as usual.

Value Type Internals

Now that we have an idea how reference types are laid out in memory and what purpose the object header fields serve, it's time to discuss value types. Value types have a much simpler memory layout, but it introduces limitations and boxing, an expensive process that compensates for the incompatibility of using a value type where a reference is required. The primary reason for using value types, as we have seen, is their excellent memory density and lack of overhead; every bit of performance matters when you develop your own value types.

For the purpose of our discussion, let's commit to a simple value type we discussed at the onset of this chapter, Point2D, representing a point in two-dimensional space:

```
public struct Point2D
{
  public int X;
  public int Y;
}
```

The memory layout of a Point2D instance initialized with X=5, Y=7 is simply the following, with no additional "overhead" fields clutter:

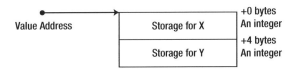

Figure 3-7. Memory layout for a Point2D value type instance

In some rare cases, it may be desired to customize value type layout – one example is for interoperability purposes, when your value type instance is passed unchanged to unmanaged code. This customization is possible through the use of two attributes, StructLayout and FieldOffset. The StructLayout attribute can be used to specify that the object's fields are to be laid out sequentially according to the type's definition (this is the default), or explicitly according to the instructions provided by the FieldOffset attribute. This enables the creation of C-style unions, where fields may overlap. A crude example of this is the following value type, which can "convert" a floating-point number to the four bytes used by its representation:

```
[StructLayout(LayoutKind.Explicit)]
public struct FloatingPointExplorer
{
  [FieldOffset(0)] public float F;
  [FieldOffset(0)] public byte B1;
  [FieldOffset(1)] public byte B2;
  [FieldOffset(2)] public byte B3;
  [FieldOffset(3)] public byte B4;
}
```

When you assign a floating-point value to the object's F field, it concurrently modifies the values of B1-B4, and vice versa. Effectively, the F field and the B1-B4 fields overlap in memory, as demonstrated by Figure 3-8:

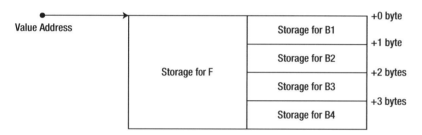

Figure 3-8. *Memory layout for a FloatingPointExplorer instance. Blocks aligned horizontally overlap in memory*

Because value type instances do not have an object header word and a method table pointer, they cannot allow the same richness of semantics offered by reference types. We will now look at the limitations their simpler layout introduces, and what happens when developers attempt to use value types in settings intended for reference types.

Value Type Limitations

First, consider the object header word. If a program attempts to use a value type instance for synchronization, it is most often a bug in the program (as we will see shortly), but should the runtime make it illegal and throw an exception? In the following code example, what should happen when the Increment method of the same Counter class instance is executed by two different threads?

```
class Counter
{
  private int _i;
  public int Increment()
  {
    lock (_i)
    {
```

```
      return ++_i;
    }
  }
}
```

As we attempt to verify what happens, we stumble upon an unexpected obstacle: the C# compiler would not allow using value types with the lock keyword. However, we are now seasoned in the inner workings of what the lock keyword does, and can attempt to code a workaround:

```
class Counter
{
  private int _i;
  public int Increment()
  {
    bool acquired=false;
    try
    {
      Monitor.Enter(_i, ref acquired);
      return ++_i;
    }
    finally
    {
      if (acquired) Monitor.Exit(_i);
    }
  }
}
```

By doing so, we introduced a bug into our program – it turns out that multiple threads will be able to enter the lock and modify _i at once, and furthermore the Monitor.Exit call will throw an exception (to understand the proper ways of synchronizing access to an integer variable, refer to Chapter 6). The problem is that the Monitor.Enter method accepts a System.Object parameter, which is a reference, and we are passing to it a value type – by value. Even if it were possible to pass the value unmodified where a reference is expected, the value passed to the Monitor.Enter method does not have the same *identity* as the value passed to the Monitor.Exit method; similarly, the value passed to the Monitor.Enter method on one thread does not have the same *identity* as the value passed to the Monitor.Enter method on another thread. If we pass around values (by value!) where references are expected, there is no way to obtain the correct locking semantics.

Another example of why value type semantics are not a good fit for object references arises when returning a value type from a method. Consider the following code:

```
object GetInt()
{
  int i = 42;
  return i;
}
object obj = GetInt();
```

The GetInt method returns a value type – which would typically be returned by value. However, the caller expects, from the method, to return an object reference. The method could return a direct pointer to the stack location where i is stored during the method's execution. Unfortunately, it would be a reference to an invalid memory location, because the stack frame for the method is cleaned up before it returns. This demonstrates that the copy-by-value semantics value types have by default are not a good fit for when an object reference (into the managed heap) is expected.

Virtual Methods on Value Types

We haven't considered the method table pointer yet, and already we have insurmountable problems when attempting to treat value types as first-class citizens. Now we turn to virtual methods and interface implementations. The CLR forbids inheritance relationships between value types, making it impossible to define new virtual methods on value types. This is fortunate, because if it were possible to define virtual methods on value types, invoking these methods would require a method table pointer which is not part of a value type instance. This is not a substantial limitation, because the copy-by-value semantics of reference types make them ill suited for polymorphism, which requires object references.

However, value types come equipped with virtual methods inherited from System.Object. There are several of them: Equals, GetHashCode, ToString, and Finalize. We will discuss only the first two here, but much of the discussion applies to the other virtual methods as well. Let's start by inspecting their signatures:

```
public class Object
{
  public virtual bool Equals(object obj) ...
  public virtual int GetHashCode() ...
}
```

These virtual methods are implemented by every .NET type, including value types. It means that given an instance of a value type, we should be able to dispatch the virtual method successfully, even though it doesn't have a method table pointer! This third example of how the value type memory layout affects our ability to do even simple operations with value type instances demands a mechanism that can "turn" value type instances into something that can more plausibly stand for an "authentic" object.

Boxing

Whenever the language compiler detects a situation that requires treating a value type instance as a reference type, it emits the box IL instruction. The JIT compiler, in turn, interprets this instruction and emits a call to a method that allocates heap storage, copies the content of the value type instance to the heap, and wraps the value type contents with an object header – object header word and method table pointer. It is this "box" that is used whenever an object reference is required. Note that the box is detached from the original value type instance – changes made to one do not affect the other.

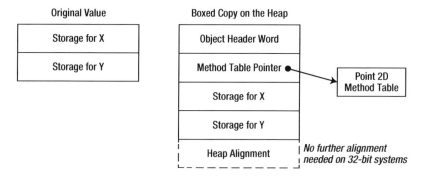

Figure 3-9. *Original value and boxed copy on the heap. The boxed copy has the standard reference type "overhead" (object header word and method table pointer), and may require further heap alignment*

```
.method private hidebysig static object GetInt() cil managed
{
    .maxstack 8
    L_0000: ldc.i4.s 0x2a
    L_0002: box int32
    L_0007: ret
}
```

Boxing is an expensive operation – it involves a memory allocation, a memory copy, and subsequently creates pressure on the garbage collector when it struggles to reclaim the temporary boxes. With the introduction of generics in CLR 2.0, there is hardly any need for boxing outside Reflection and other obscure scenarios. Nonetheless, boxing remains a significant performance problem in many applications; as we will see, "getting value types right" to prevent all kinds of boxing is not trivial without some further understanding of how method dispatch on value types operates.

Setting the performance problems aside, boxing provides a remedy to some of the problems we encountered earlier. For example, the GetInt method returns a reference to box on the heap which contains the value 42. This box will survive as long as there are references to it, and is not affected by the lifetime of local variables on the method's stack. Similarly, when the Monitor.Enter method expects an object reference, it receives at runtime a reference to a box on the heap and uses that box for synchronization. Unfortunately, boxes created from the same value type instance at different points in code are not considered identical, so the box passed to Monitor. Exit is not the same box passed to Monitor.Enter, and the box passed to Monitor.Enter on one thread is not the same box passed to Monitor.Enter on another thread. This means that any use of value types for monitor-based synchronization is inherently wrong, regardless of the partial cure afforded by boxing.

The crux of the matter remains the virtual methods inherited from System.Object. As it turns out, value types do not derive from System.Object directly; instead, they derive from an intermediate type called System. ValueType.

▓ **Note**   Confusingly, System.ValueType is a reference type – the CLR tells value types and reference types apart based on the following criterion: value types are types derived from System.ValueType. According to this criterion, System.ValueType is a reference type.

System.ValueType overrides the Equals and GetHashCode virtual methods inherited from System.Object, and does it for a good reason: value types have different default equality semantics from reference types and these defaults must be implemented somewhere. For example, the overridden Equals method in System. ValueType ensures that value types are compared based on their content, whereas the original Equals method in System.Object compares only the object references (identity).

Regardless of how System.ValueType implements these overridden virtual methods, consider the following scenario. You embed ten million Point2D objects in a List<Point2D> , and proceed to look up a single Point2D object in the list using the Contains method. In turn, Contains has no better alternative than to perform a linear search through ten million objects and compare them individually to the one you provided.

```
List<Point2D> polygon = new List<Point2D>();
//insert ten million points into the list
Point2D point = new Point2D { X = 5, Y = 7 };
bool contains = polygon.Contains(point);
```

Traversing a list of ten million points and comparing them one-by-one to another point takes a while, but it's a relatively quick operation. The number of bytes accessed is approximately 80,000,000 (eight bytes for each Point2D object), and the comparison operations are very quick. Regrettably, comparing two Point2D objects requires calling the Equals virtual method:

```
Point2D a = ..., b = ...;
a.Equals(b);
```

There are two issues at stake here. First, Equals – even when overridden by System.ValueType – accepts a System.Object reference as its parameter. Treating a Point2D object as an object reference requires boxing, as we have already seen, so b would have to be boxed. Moreover, dispatching the Equals method call requires boxing a to obtain the method table pointer!

▓ **Note**   The JIT compiler has a short-circuit behavior that could permit a direct method call to Equals, because value types are sealed and the virtual dispatch target is determined at compile-time by whether Point2D overrides Equals or not (this is enabled by the constrained IL prefix). Nevertheless, because System.ValueType is a reference type, the Equals method is free to treat its this implicit parameter as a reference type as well, whereas we are using a value type instance (Point2D a) to call Equals – and this requires boxing.

To summarize, we have two boxing operations for each Equals call on Point2D instances. For the 10,000,000 Equals calls performed by the code above, we have 20,000,000 boxing operations, each allocating (on a 32-bit system) 16 bytes, for a total of 320,000,000 bytes of allocations and 160,000,000 bytes of memory copied into the heap. The cost of these allocations surpasses by far the time required to actually compare points in two-dimensional space.

Avoiding Boxing on Value Types with the Equals Method

What can we do to get rid of these boxing operations entirely? One idea is to override the Equals method and provide an implementation suitable for our value type:

```
public struct Point2D
{
  public int X;
  public int Y;
  public override bool Equals(object obj)
  {
    if (!(obj is Point2D)) return false;
    Point2D other = (Point2D)obj;
    return X == other.X && Y == other.Y;
  }
}
```

Using the JIT-compiler's short-circuit behavior discussed previously, a.Equals(b) still requires boxing for b, because the method accepts an object reference, but no longer requires boxing for a. To get rid of the second boxing operation, we need to think outside the box (pun intended) and provide an *overload* of the Equals method:

```
public struct Point2D
{
  public int X;
  public int Y;
  public override bool Equals(object obj) ... //as before
  public bool Equals(Point2D other)
  {
```

```
            return X == other.X && Y == other.Y;
    }
}
```

Whenever the compiler encounters a.Equals(b), it will definitely prefer the second overload to the first, because its parameter type matches more closely the argument type provided. While we're at it, there are some more methods to overload – often enough, we compare objects using the == and != operators:

```
public struct Point2D
{
  public int X;
  public int Y;
  public override bool Equals(object obj) ... // as before
  public bool Equals(Point2D other) ... //as before
  public static bool operator==(Point2D a, Point2D b)
  {
    return a.Equals(b);
  }
  public static bool operator!= (Point2D a, Point2D b)
  {
    return !(a == b);
  }
}
```

This is almost enough. There is an edge case that has to do with the way the CLR implements generics, which still causes boxing when List<Point2D> calls Equals on two Point2D instances, with Point2D as a realization of its generic type parameter (T). We will discuss the exact details in Chapter 5; for now it suffices to say that Point2D needs to implement IEquatable<Point2D> , which allows clever behavior in List<T> and EqualityComparer<T> to dispatch the method call to the *overloaded* Equals method through the interface (at the cost of a virtual method call to the EqualityComparer<T>.Equals abstract method). The result is a 10-fold improvement in execution time and complete elimination of all memory allocations (introduced by boxing) when searching a list of 10,000,000 Point2D instances for a specific one!

```
public struct Point2D : IEquatable<Point2D>
{
  public int X;
  public int Y;
  public bool Equals(Point2D other) ... //as before
}
```

This is a good time to reflect upon the subject of interface implementations on value types. As we have seen, a typical interface method dispatch requires the object's method table pointer, which would solicit boxing where value types are concerned. Indeed, a conversion from a value type instance to an interface type variable requires boxing, because interface references can be treated as object references for all intents and purposes:

```
Point2D point = ...;
IEquatable<Point2D> equatable = point; //boxing occurs here
```

However, when making an interface call through a statically typed value type variable, no boxing will occur (this is the same short-circuiting enabled by the constrained IL prefix, discussed above):

```
Point2D point = ..., anotherPoint = ...;
point.Equals(anotherPoint); //no boxing occurs here, Point2D.Equals(Point2D) is invoked
```

Using value types through interfaces raises a potential concern if the value types are mutable, such as the Point2D we are churning through in this chapter. As always, modifying the boxed copy will not affect the original, which can lead to unexpected behavior:

```
Point2D point = new Point2D { X = 5, Y = 7 };
Point2D anotherPoint = new Point2D { X = 6, Y = 7 };
IEquatable<Point2D> equatable = point; //boxing occurs here
equatable.Equals(anotherPoint); //returns false
point.X = 6;
point.Equals(anotherPoint);      //returns true
equatable.Equals(anotherPoint); //returns false, the box was not modified!
```

This is one ground for the common recommendation to make value types immutable, and allow modification only by making more copies. (Consider the System.DateTime API for an example of a well-designed immutable value type.)

The final nail in the coffin of ValueType.Equals is its actual implementation. Comparing two arbitrary value type instances according to their content is not trivial. Disassembling the method offers the following picture (slightly edited for brevity):

```
public override bool Equals(object obj)
{
  if (obj == null) return false;
  RuntimeType type = (RuntimeType) base.GetType();
  RuntimeType type2 = (RuntimeType) obj.GetType();
  if (type2 != type) return false;

  object a = this;
  if (CanCompareBits(this))
  {
    return FastEqualsCheck(a, obj);
  }
  FieldInfo[] fields = type.GetFields(BindingFlags.NonPublic | ↵
                               BindingFlags.Public | BindingFlags.Instance);
  for (int i = 0; i < fields.Length; i++)
  {
    object obj3 = ((RtFieldInfo) fields[i]).InternalGetValue(a, false);
    object obj4 = ((RtFieldInfo) fields[i]).InternalGetValue(obj, false);
    if (obj3 == null && obj4 != null)
      return false;
    else if (!obj3.Equals(obj4))
      return false;
  }
  return true;
}
```

In brief, if CanCompareBits returns true, the FastEqualsCheck is responsible for checking equality; otherwise, the method enters a Reflection-based loop where fields are fetched using the FieldInfo class and compared recursively by invoking Equals. Needless to say, the Reflection-based loop is where the performance battle is conceded completely; Reflection is an extremely expensive mechanism, and everything else pales compared to it. The definition of CanCompareBits and FastEqualsCheck is deferred to the CLR – they are "internal calls", not implemented in IL – so we can't disassemble them easily. However, from experimentation we discovered that CanCompareBits returns true if either of the following conditions hold:

1. The value type contains only primitive types and does not override Equals

2. The value type contains only value types for which (1) holds and does not override Equals

3.   The value type contains only value types for which (2) holds and does not override
     Equals

The FastEqualsCheck method is similarly a mystery, but effectively it executes a memcmp operation – comparing the memory of both value type instances (byte-by-byte). Unfortunately, both of these methods remain an internal implementation detail, and relying on them as a high-performance way to compare instances of your value types is an extremely bad idea.

The GetHashCode Method

The final method that remains and is important to override is GetHashCode. Before we can show a suitable implementation, let's brush up our knowledge on what it is used for. Hash codes are used most often in conjunction with hash tables, a data structure that (under certain conditions) allows constant-time ($O(1)$) insertion, lookup, and deletion operations on arbitrary data. The common hash table classes in the .NET Framework include Dictionary<TKey,TValue>, Hashtable, and HashSet<T>. A typical hash table implementation consists of a dynamic-length array of buckets, each bucket containing a linked list of items. To place an item in the hash table, it first calculates a numeric value (by using the GetHashCode method), and then applies to it a hash function that specifies to which bucket the item is mapped. The item is inserted into its bucket's linked list.

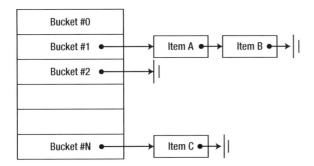

Figure 3-10. *A hash table, consisting of an array of linked lists (buckets) in which items are stored. Some buckets may be empty; other buckets may contain a considerable number of items*

The performance guarantees of hash tables rely strongly upon the hash function used by the hash table implementation, but require also several properties from the GetHashCode method:

1.   If two objects are equal, their hash codes are equal.

2.   If two objects are not equal, it should be unlikely that their hash codes are equal.

3.   GetHashCode should be fast (although often it is linear in the size of the object).

4.   An object's hash code should not change.

■ **Caution**   Property (2) cannot state "if two objects are not equal, their hash codes are not equal" because of the pigeonhole principle: there can be types of which there are many more objects than there are integers, so unavoidably there will be many objects with the same hash code. Consider `longs`, for example; there are 2^{64} different `longs`, but only 2^{32} different integers, so there will be at least one integer value which is the hash code of 2^{32} different `longs`!

Formally, property (2) can be stated as follows to require a uniform distribution of hash codes: set an object A, and let S(A) be the set of all the objects B such that:

- B is not equal to A;
- The hash code of B is equal to the hash code of A.

Property (2) requires that the size of S(A) is roughly the same for every object A. (This assumes that the probability to see every object is the same – which is not necessarily true for actual types.)

Properties (1) and (2) emphasize the relationship between object equality and hash code equality. If we went to the trouble of overriding and overloading the virtual `Equals` method, there is no choice but to make sure that the `GetHashCode` implementation is aligned with it as well. It would seem that a typical implementation of `GetHashCode` would rely somehow on the object's fields. For example, a good implementation of `GetHashCode` for an `int` is simply to return the integer's value. For a `Point2D` object, we might consider some linear combination of the two coordinates, or combine some of the bits of the first coordinate with some other bits of the second coordinate. Designing a good hash code in general is a very difficult undertaking, which is beyond the scope of this book.

Lastly, consider property (4). The reasoning behind it is as follows: suppose you have the point (5, 5) and embed it in a hash table, and further suppose that its hash code was 10. If you modify the point to (6, 6) – and its hash code is also modified to 12 – then you will not be able to find in the hash table the point you inserted to it. But this is not a concern with value types, because you *cannot* modify the object you inserted into the hash table – the hash table stores a *copy* of it, which is inaccessible to your code.

What of reference types? With reference types, content-based equality becomes a concern. Suppose that we had the following implementation of `Employee.GetHashCode`:

```
public class Employee
{
  public string Name { get; set; }
  public override int GetHashCode()
  {
    return Name.GetHashCode();
  }
}
```

This seems like a good idea; the hash code is based on the object's contents, and we are utilizing `String.GetHashCode` so that we don't have to implement a good hash code function for strings. However, consider what happens when we use an `Employee` object and change its name after it was inserted into the hash table:

```
HashSet<Employee> employees = new HashSet<Employee>();
Employee kate = new Employee { Name = "Kate Jones" };
employees.Add(kate);
kate.Name = "Kate Jones-Smith";
employees.Contains(kate); //returns false!
```

The object's hash code has changed because its contents have changed, and we can no longer find the object in the hash table. This is somewhat expected, perhaps, but the problem is that now we can't *remove* Kate from the hash table at all, even though we have access to the original object!

The CLR provides a default GetHashCode implementation for reference types that rely on the object's identity as their equality criterion. If two object references are equal if and only if they reference the same object, it would make sense to store the hash code somewhere in the object itself, such that it is never modified and is easily accessible. Indeed, when a reference type instance is created, the CLR can embed its hash code in the object heard word (as an optimization, this is done only the first time the hash code is accessed; after all, many objects are never used as hash table keys). To calculate the hash code, there's no need to rely on a random number generation or consider the object's contents; a simple counter would do.

■ **Note** How can the hash code coexist in the object header word alongside the sync block index? As you recall, most objects never use their object header word to store a sync block index, because they are not used for synchronization. In the rare case that an object is linked to a sync block through the object header word storing its index, the hash code is copied to the sync block and stored there until the sync block is detached from the object. To determine whether the hash code or the sync block index is currently stored in the object header word, one of the field's bits is used as a marker.

Reference types using the default Equals and GetHashCode implementation need not concern themselves with any of the four properties stressed above – they get them for free. However, if your reference type should choose to override the default equality behavior (this is what System.String does, for example), then you should consider making your reference type immutable if you use it as a key in a hash table.

Best Practices for Using Value Types

Below are some best practices that should guide you in the right direction when considering using a value type for a certain task:

- Use value types if your objects are small and you intend to create a great many of them.

- Use value types if you require high-density memory collections.

- Override Equals, overload Equals, implement IEquatable<T>, overload operator ==, and overload operator != on your value types.

- Override GetHashCode on your value types.

- Consider making your value types immutable.

Summary

In this chapter, we have unveiled the implementation details of reference types and value types, and how these details affect application performance. Value types exhibit superb memory density, which makes them a great candidate for large collections, but are not equipped with features required of objects such as polymorphism, synchronization support, and reference semantics. The CLR introduces two categories of types to provide a high-performance alternative to object orientation where it is required, but still demands a formidable effort from developers to implement value types correctly.

CHAPTER 4

Garbage Collection

In this chapter, we will examine the .NET garbage collector (GC), one of the primary mechanisms affecting the performance of .NET applications. While freeing developers from worrying about memory deallocation, the GC introduces new challenges for constructing deterministically well-behaving programs in which performance is paramount. First, we will review the types of GC available in the CLR, and see how adapting an application to the GC can be very beneficial in terms of overall GC performance and pause times. Next, we'll see how generations affect GC performance and how to tune applications accordingly. Toward the end of the chapter we will examine the APIs available for controlling the GC directly, as well as the subtleties involved in correctly using non-deterministic finalization.

Many of the examples in this chapter are based on the authors' personal experience with real-world systems. Where possible, we tried to point you to case studies and even sample applications that you can work on while reading this chapter, illustrating the primary performance pain points. The "Best Practices" section toward the end of the chapter is full of such case studies and examples. However, you should be aware that some of these points are difficult to demonstrate with short code snippets or even a sample program because the situations where performance differences arise are typically within large projects that have thousands of types and millions of objects in memory.

Why Garbage Collection?

Garbage collection is a high-level abstraction that absolves developers of the need to care about managing memory deallocation. In a garbage-collected environment, memory allocation is tied to the creation of objects, and when these objects are no longer referenced by the application, the memory can be freed. A garbage collector also provides a finalization interface for unmanaged resources that do not reside on the managed heap, so that custom cleanup code can be executed when these resources are no longer needed. The two primary design goals of the .NET garbage collector are:

- Remove the burden of memory management bugs and pitfalls
- Provide memory management performance that matches or exceeds the performance of manual native allocators

Existing programming languages and frameworks use several different memory management strategies. We will briefly examine two of them: free list management (that can be found in the C standard allocator) and reference counting garbage collection. This will provide us with a point of reference when looking at the internals of the .NET garbage collector.

Free List Management

Free list management is the underlying memory management mechanism in the C run-time library, which is also used by default by the C++ memory management APIs such as new and delete. This is a deterministic memory manager that relies on developers allocating and freeing memory as they deem fit. Free blocks of memory are stored in a linked list, from which allocations are satisfied (see Figure 4-1). Deallocated blocks of memory are returned to the free list.

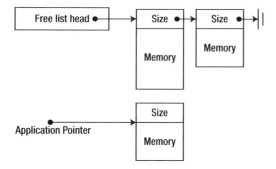

Figure 4-1. *The free list manager manages a list of unused memory blocks and satisfies allocation and deallocation requests. The application is handed out blocks of memory that usually contain the block size*

Free list management is not free of strategic and tactical decisions which affect the performance of an application using the allocator. Among these decisions:

- An application using free list management starts up with a small pool of free blocks of memory organized in a *free list*. This list can be organized by size, by the time of usage, by the arena of allocation determined by the application, and so forth.

- When an allocation request arrives from the application, a matching block is located in the free list. The matching block can be located by selecting the first-fit, the best-fit, or using more complex alternative strategies.

- When the free list is exhausted, the memory manager asks the operating system for another set of free blocks that are added to the free list. When a deallocation request arrives from the application, the freed memory block is added to the free list. Optimizations at this phase include joining adjacent free blocks together, defragmenting and trimming the list, and so on.

The primary issues associated with a free-list memory manager are the following:

- *Allocation cost*: Finding an appropriate block to satisfy an allocation request is time consuming, even if a first-fit approach is used. Additionally, blocks are often broken into multiple parts to satisfy allocation requests. In the case of multiple processors, contention on the free list and synchronization of allocation requests are inevitable, unless multiple lists are used. Multiple lists, on the other hand, deteriorate the fragmentation of the list.

- *Deallocation cost*: Returning a free block of memory to the free list is time consuming, and again suffers from the need of multi-processor synchronization of multiple deallocation requests.

- *Management cost*: Defragmenting and trimming the free lists is necessary to avoid memory exhaustion scenarios, but this work has to take place in a separate thread and acquire locks on the free lists, hindering allocation and deallocation performance. Fragmentation can be minimized by using fixed-size allocation buckets to maintain multiple free-lists, but this requires even more management and adds a small cost to every allocation and deallocation request.

Reference-Counting Garbage Collection

A reference-counting garbage collector associates each object with an integer variable—its *reference count*. When the object is created, its reference count is initialized to 1. When the application creates a new reference to the object, its reference count is incremented by 1 (see Figure 4-2). When the application removes an existing reference to the object, its reference count is decremented by 1. When the object's reference count reaches 0, the object can be deterministically destroyed and its memory can be reclaimed.

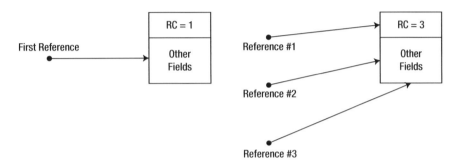

Figure 4-2. *Every object contains a reference count*

One example of reference-counting garbage collection in the Windows ecosystem is COM (Component Object Model). COM objects are associated with a reference count that affects their lifetime. When a COM object's reference count reaches 0, it is typically the object's responsibility to reclaim its own memory. The burden of managing the reference count is mostly with the developer, through explicit AddRef and Release method calls, although most languages have automatic wrappers that call these methods automatically when references are created and destroyed.

The primary issues associated with reference-counting garbage collection are the following:

- *Management cost*: Whenever a reference to an object is created or destroyed, the object's reference count must be updated. This means that trivial operations such as assignment of references (a = b) or passing a reference by value to a function incur the cost of updating the reference count. On multi-processor systems, these updates introduce contention and synchronization around the reference count, and cause cache thrashing if multiple processors update the same object's reference count. (See Chapters 5 and 6 for more information about single- and multi-processor cache considerations.)

- *Memory usage*: The object's reference count must be stored in memory and associated with the object. Depending on the number of references expected for each object, this increases the object's size by several bytes, making reference counting not worthwhile for flyweight objects. (This is less of an issue for the CLR, where objects have an "overhead" of 8 or 16 bytes already, as we have seen in Chapter 3.)

- *Correctness*: Under reference counting garbage collection, disconnected cycles of objects cannot be reclaimed. If the application no longer has a reference to two objects, but each of the objects holds a reference to the other, a reference counting application will experience a memory leak (see Figure 4-3). COM documents this behavior and requires breaking cycles manually. Other platforms, such as the Python programming language, introduce an additional mechanism for detecting such cycles and eliminating them, incurring an additional non-deterministic collection cost.

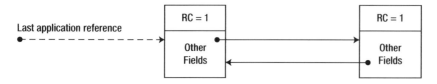

Figure 4-3. *When a cycle of objects is no longer referenced by the application, their internal reference counts remain 1 and they are not destroyed, producing a memory leak. (The dashed reference in the figure has been removed.)*

Tracing Garbage Collection

Tracing garbage collection is the garbage collection mechanism used by the .NET CLR, the Java VM and various other managed environments—these environments do not use reference counting garbage collection in any form. Developers do not need to issue explicit memory deallocation requests; this is taken care of by the garbage collector. A tracing GC does not associate an object with a reference count, and normally doesn't incur any deallocation cost until a memory usage threshold is reached.

When a garbage collection occurs, the collector begins with the *mark phase*, during which it resolves all objects that are still referenced by the application (live objects). After constructing the set of live objects, the collector moves to the *sweep phase*, at which time it reclaims the space occupied by unused objects. Finally, the collector concludes with the *compact phase*, in which it shifts live objects so that they remain consecutive in memory.

In this chapter, we will examine in detail the various issues associated with tracing garbage collection. A general outline of these issues, however, can be provided right now:

- *Allocation cost*: The allocation cost is comparable to a stack-based allocation, because there is no maintenance associated with free objects. An allocation consists of incrementing a pointer.

- *Deallocation cost*: Incurred whenever the GC cycle occurs instead of being uniformly distributed across the application's execution profile. This has its advantages and disadvantages (specifically for low-latency scenarios) that we will discuss later in this chapter.

- *Mark phase*: Locating referenced objects requires a great deal of discipline from the managed execution environment. References to objects can be stored in static variables, local variables on thread stacks, passed as pointers to unmanaged code, etc. Tracing every possible reference path to each accessible object is everything but trivial, and often incurs a run-time cost outside the collection cycle.

- *Sweep phase*: Moving objects around in memory costs time, and might not be applicable for large objects. On the other hand, eliminating unused space between objects facilitates locality of reference, because objects that were allocated together are positioned together in memory. Additionally, this removes the need for an additional defragmentation mechanism because objects are always stored consecutively. Finally, this means that the allocation code does not need to account for "holes" between objects when looking for free space; a simple pointer-based allocation strategy can be used instead.

In the subsequent sections, we will examine the .NET GC memory management paradigm, starting from understanding the GC mark and sweep phases and moving to more significant optimizations such as generations.

Mark Phase

In the *mark phase* of the tracing garbage collection cycle, the GC traverses the graph of all objects currently referenced by the application. To successfully traverse this graph and prevent *false positives* and *false negatives* (discussed later in this chapter), the GC needs a set of starting points from which reference traversal can ensue. These starting points are termed *roots*, and as their name implies, they form the roots of the directed reference graph that the GC builds.

After having established a set of roots, the garbage collector's work in the mark phase is relatively simple to understand. It considers each internal reference field in each root, and proceeds to traverse the graph until all referenced objects have been visited. Because reference cycles are allowed in .NET applications, the GC marks visited objects so that each object is visited once and only once—hence the name of the *mark* phase.

Local Roots

One of the most obvious types of roots is *local variables*; a single local variable can form the root of an entire object graph referenced by an application. For example, consider the following code fragment within the application's Main method that creates a System.Xml.XmlDocument object and proceeds to call its Load method:

```
static void Main(string[] args) {
    XmlDocument doc = new XmlDocument();
    doc.Load("Data.xml");
    Console.WriteLine(doc.OuterXml);
}
```

We do not exercise control over the garbage collector's timing, and therefore must assume that a garbage collection might occur during the Load method call. If that happens, we would not like the XmlDocument object to be reclaimed—the local reference in the Main method is the root of the document's object graph that must be considered by the garbage collector. Therefore, every local variable that can potentially hold a reference to an object (i.e., every local variable of a reference type) can appear to be an active root while its method is on the stack.

However, we do not need the reference to remain an active root until the *end* of its enclosing method. For example, after the document was loaded and displayed, we might want to introduce additional code within the same method that no longer requires the document to be kept in memory. This code might take a long time to complete, and if a garbage collection occurs in the meantime, we would like the document's memory to be reclaimed.

Does the .NET garbage collector provide this eager collection facility? Let's examine the following code fragment, which creates a System.Threading.Timer and initializes it with a callback that induces a garbage collection by calling GC.Collect (we will examine this API later in more detail):

```
using System;
using System.Threading;

class Program {
    static void Main(string[] args) {
        Timer timer = new Timer(OnTimer, null, 0, 1000);
        Console.ReadLine();
    }
```

```
static void OnTimer(object state) {
    Console.WriteLine(DateTime.Now.TimeOfDay);
    GC.Collect();
}
}
```

If you run the above code in Debug mode (if compiling from the command line, without the /optimize + compiler switch), you will see that the timer callback is called every second, as expected, implying that the timer is not garbage collected. However, if you run it in Release mode (with the /optimize + compiler switch), the timer callback is only called once! In other words, the timer is collected and stops invoking the callback. This is legal (and even desired) behavior because our local reference to the timer is no longer relevant as a root once we reach the Console.ReadLine method call. Because it's no longer relevant, the timer is collected, producing a rather unexpected result if you didn't follow the discussion on local roots earlier!

EAGER ROOT COLLECTION

This eager collection facility for local roots is actually provided by the .NET Just-In-Time Compiler (JIT). The garbage collector has no way of knowing on its own whether the local variable can still potentially be used by its enclosing method. This information is embedded into special tables by the JIT when it compiles the method. For each local variable, the JIT embeds into the table the addresses of the earliest and latest instruction pointers where the variable is still relevant as a root. The GC then uses these tables when it performs its stack walk. (Note that the local variables may be stored on the stack or in CPU registers; the JIT tables must indicate this.)

```
//Original C# code:
static void Main() {
  Widget a = new Widget();
  a.Use();
  //...additional code
  Widget b = new Widget();
  b.Use();
  //...additional code
  Foo(); //static method call
}


//Compiled x86 assembly code:
      ; prologue omitted for brevity
      call 0x0a890a30              ; Widget..ctor
+0x14 mov esi, eax                 ; esi now contains the object's reference
      mov ecx, esi
      mov eax, dword ptr [ecx]
      ; the rest of the function call sequence
+0x24 mov dword ptr [ebp-12], eax  ; ebp-12 now contains the object's reference
      mov ecx, dword ptr [ebp-12]
      mov eax, dword ptr [ecx]
      ; the rest of the function call sequence
+0x34 call 0x0a880480             ; Foo method call
      ; method epilogue omitted for brevity
```

```
//JIT-generated tables that the GC consults:
Register or stack          Begin offset          End offset
        ESI                  0x14                   0x24
     EBP - 12                0x24                   0x34
```

The above discussion implies that breaking your code into smaller methods and using less local variables is not just a good design measure or a software engineering technique. With the .NET garbage collector, it can provide a performance benefit as well because you have less local roots! It means less work for the JIT when compiling the method, less space to be occupied by the root IP tables, and less work for the GC when performing its stack walk.

What if we want to explicitly extend the lifetime of our timer until the end of its enclosing method? There are multiple ways of accomplishing this. We could use a static variable (which is a different type of root, to be discussed shortly). Alternatively, we could use the timer just before the method's terminating statement (e.g., call timer.Dispose()). But the cleanest way of accomplishing this is through the use of the GC.KeepAlive method, which guarantees that the reference to the object will be considered as a root.

How does GC.KeepAlive work? It might appear to be a magical method ascending from the internals of the CLR. However, it is fairly trivial—we could write it ourselves, and we will. If we pass the object reference to any method that can't be inlined (see Chapter 3 for a discussion of inlining), the JIT must automatically assume that the object is used. Therefore, the following method can stand in for GC.KeepAlive if we wanted to:

```
[MethodImpl(MethodImplOptions.NoInlining)]
static void MyKeepAlive(object obj) {
    //Intentionally left blank: the method doesn't have to do anything
}
```

Static Roots

Yet another category of roots is *static variables*. Static members of types are created when the type is loaded (we have seen this process in Chapter 3), and are considered to be potential roots throughout the entire lifetime of the application domain. For example, consider this short program which continuously creates objects which in turn register to a static event:

```
class Button {
  public void OnClick(object sender, EventArgs e) {
    //Implementation omitted
  }
}

class Program {
  static event EventHandler ButtonClick;

  static void Main(string[] args) {
    while (true) {
      Button button = new Button();
      ButtonClick += button.OnClick;
    }
  }
}
```

This turns out to be a memory leak, because the static event contains a list of delegates which in turn contain a reference to the objects we created. In fact, one of the most common .NET memory leaks is having a reference to your object from a static variable!

Other Roots

The two categories of roots just described are the most common ones, but additional categories exist. For example, *GC handles* (represented by the System.Runtime.InteropServices.GCHandle type) are also considered by the garbage collector as roots. The *f-reachable queue* is another example of a subtle type of root—objects waiting for finalization are still considered reachable by the GC. We will consider both root types later in this chapter; understanding the other categories of roots is important when debugging memory leaks in .NET applications, because oftentimes there are no trivial (read: static or local) roots referencing your object, but it still remains alive for some other reason.

INSPECTING ROOTS USING SOS.DLL

SOS.DLL, the debugger extension we have seen in Chapter 3, can be used to inspect the chain of roots that is responsible for keeping a particular object alive. Its !gcroot command provides succinct information of the root type and reference chain. Below are some examples of its output:

```
0:004> !gcroot 02512370
HandleTable:
    001513ec (pinned handle)
    -> 03513310 System.Object[]
    -> 0251237c System.EventHandler
    -> 02512370 Employee

0:004> !gcroot 0251239c
Thread 3068:
    003df31c 002900dc Program.Main(System.String[]) [d:\...\Ch04\Program.cs @ 38]
        esi:
            -> 0251239c Employee

0:004> !gcroot 0227239c
Finalizer Queue:
    0227239c
    -> 0227239c Employee
```

The first type of root in this output is likely a static field—although ascertaining this would involve some work. One way or another, it is a pinning GC handle (GC handles are discussed later in this chapter). The second type of root is the ESI register in thread 3068, which stores a local variable in the Main method. The last type of root is the f-reachable queue.

Performance Implications

The mark phase of the garbage collection cycle is an "almost read-only" phase, at which no objects are shifted in memory or deallocated from it. Nonetheless, there are significant performance implications that arise from the work done at the mark phase:

- During a full mark, the garbage collector must touch every single referenced object. This results in page faults if the memory is no longer in the working set, and results in cache misses and cache thrashing as objects are traversed.

- On a multi-processor system, since the collector marks objects by setting a bit in their header, this causes cache invalidation for other processors that have the object in their cache.

- Unreferenced objects are less costly in this phase, and therefore the performance of the mark phase is linear in the *collection efficiency factor*: the ratio between referenced and unreferenced objects in the collection space.

- The performance of the mark phase additionally depends on the number of objects in the graph, and not the memory consumed by these objects. Large objects that do not contain many references are easier to traverse and incur less overhead. This means that the performance of the mark phase is linear in the number of live objects in the graph.

Once all referenced objects have been marked, the garbage collector has a full graph of all referenced objects and their references (see Figure 4-4). It can now move on to the sweep phase.

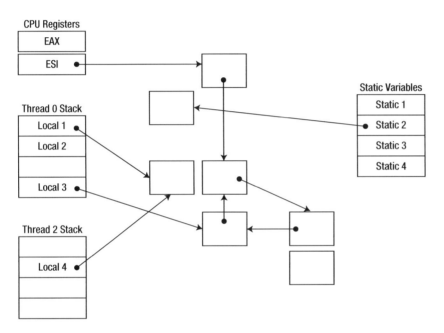

Figure 4-4. *An object graph with various types of roots. Cyclic references are permitted*

Sweep and Compact Phases

In the sweep and compact phases, the garbage collector reclaims memory, often by shifting live objects around so that they are placed consecutively on the heap. To understand the mechanics of shifting objects around, we must first examine the allocation mechanism which provides the motivation for the work performed in the sweep phase.

In the simple GC model we are currently examining, an allocation request from the application is satisfied by incrementing a single pointer, which always points to the next available slot of memory (see Figure 4-5). This pointer is called the *next object pointer* (or *new object pointer*), and it is initialized when the garbage-collected heap is constructed on application startup.

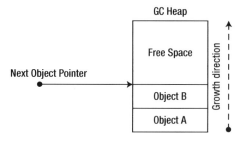

Figure 4-5. *GC heap and the next object pointer*

Satisfying an allocation request is extremely cheap in this model: it involves only the atomic increment of a single pointer. Multi-processor systems are likely to experience contention for this pointer (a concern that will be addressed later in this chapter).

If memory were infinite, allocation requests could be satisfied indefinitely by incrementing the new object pointer. However, at some point in time we reach a threshold that triggers a garbage collection. The thresholds are dynamic and configurable, and we will look into ways of controlling them later in this chapter.

During the compact phase, the garbage collector moves live objects in memory so that they occupy a consecutive area in space (see Figure 4-6). This aids locality of reference, because objects allocated together are also likely to be used together, so it is preferable to keep them close together in memory. On the other hand, moving objects around has at least two performance pain-points:

- Moving objects around means copying memory, which is an expensive operation for large objects. Even if the copy is optimized, copying several megabytes of memory in each garbage collection cycle results in unreasonable overhead. (This is why large objects are treated differently, as we shall see later.)

- When objects are moved, references to them must be updated to reflect their new location. For objects that are frequently referenced, this scattered memory access (when references are being updated) can be costly.

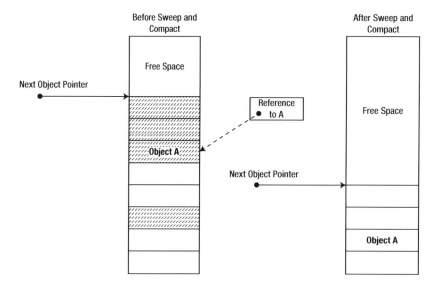

Figure 4-6. *The shaded objects on the left survive garbage collection and are shifted around in memory. This means that the reference to A (dashed line) has to be updated. (The updated reference is not shown in the diagram.)*

The general performance of the sweep phase is linear in the number of objects in the graph, and is especially sensitive to the collection efficiency factor. If most objects are discovered to be unreferenced, then the GC has to move only a few objects in memory. The same applies to the scenario where most objects are still referenced, as there are relatively few holes to fill. On the other hand, if every other object in the heap is unreferenced, the GC may have to move almost every live object to fill the holes.

■ **Note**   Contrary to popular belief, the garbage collector does not always move objects around (i.e., there are some sweep-only collections that do not proceed into the compact phase), even if they are not pinned (see below) and even if free space is available between objects. There is an implementation-defined heuristic which determines whether moving objects to fill free space is worthwhile during the sweep phase. For example, in one test suite executed on the author's 32-bit system, the garbage collector decided to move objects around if the free space is larger than 16 bytes, consists of more than one object, and more than 16KB of allocations have been made since the last garbage collection. You can't rely on these results being reproducible, but this does demonstrate the existence of the optimization.

The mark and sweep model described in the preceding sections is subject to one significant deficiency that we will address later in this chapter as we approach the generational GC model. Whenever a collection occurs, all objects in the heap are traversed even if they can be partitioned by likelihood of collection efficiency. If we had prior knowledge that some objects are more likely to die than others, we might be able to tune our collection algorithm accordingly and obtain a lower amortized collection cost.

Pinning

The garbage collection model presented above does not address a common use case for managed objects. This use case revolves around passing managed objects for consumption by unmanaged code. Two distinct approaches can be used for solving this problem:

- Every object that should be passed to unmanaged code is marshaled by value (copied) when it's passed to unmanaged code, and marshaled back when it's returned.

- Instead of copying the object, a pointer to it is passed to unmanaged code.

Copying memory around every time we need to interact with unmanaged code is an unrealistic proposition. Consider the case of soft real-time video processing software that needs to propagate high-resolution images from unmanaged code to managed code and vice versa at 30 frames per second. Copying multiple megabytes of memory every time a minor change is made will deteriorate performance to unacceptable levels.

The .NET memory management model provides the facilities for obtaining the memory address of a managed object. However, passing this address to unmanaged code in the presence of the garbage collector raises an important concern: What happens if the object is moved by the GC while the unmanaged code is still executing and using the pointer?

This scenario can have disastrous consequences—memory can easily become corrupted. One reliable solution to this problem is *turning off* the garbage collector while unmanaged code has a pointer to a managed object. However, this approach is not granular enough if objects are frequently passed between managed and unmanaged code. It also has the potential of deadlocks or memory exhaustion if a thread enters a long wait from within unmanaged code.

Instead of turning garbage collection off, every managed object whose address can be obtained must also be *pinned* in memory. Pinning an object prevents the garbage collector from moving it around during the sweep phase until it is *unpinned*.

The pinning operation itself is not very expensive—there are multiple mechanisms that perform it rather cheaply. The most explicit way to pin an object is to create a GC handle with the GCHandleType.Pinned flag. Creating a GC handle creates a new root in the process' *GC handle table*, which tells the GC that the object should be retained as well as pinned in memory. Other alternatives include the magic sauce used by the P/Invoke marshaler, and the pinned pointers mechanism exposed in C# through the fixed keyword (or pin_ptr<T> in C++/CLI), which relies on marking the pinning local variable in a special way for the GC to see. (Consult Chapter 8 for more details.)

However, the performance cost around pinning becomes apparent when we consider how pinning affects the garbage collection itself. When the garbage collector encounters a pinned object during the compact phase, it must work around that object to ensure that it is not moved in memory. This complicates the collection algorithm, but the direst effect is that *fragmentation* is introduced into the managed heap. A badly fragmented heap directly invalidates the assumptions which make garbage collection viable: It causes consecutive allocations to be fragmented in memory (and the loss of locality), introduces complexity into the allocation process, and causes a waste of memory as fragments cannot be filled.

■ **Note**   Pinning side-effects can be diagnosed with multiple tools, including the Microsoft CLR Profiler. The CLR profiler can display a graph of objects by address, showing free (fragmented) areas as unused white space. Alternatively, SOS.DLL (the managed debugging extension) can be used to display objects of type "Free", which are holes created due to fragmentation. Finally, the *# of Pinned Objects* performance counter (in the *.NET CLR Memory* performance counter category) can be used to determine how many objects were pinned in the last area examined by the GC.

Despite the above disadvantages, pinning is a necessity in many applications. Oftentimes we do not control pinning directly, when there is an abstraction layer (such as P/Invoke) that takes care of the fine details on our behalf. Later in this chapter, we will come up with a set of recommendations that will minimize the negative effects of pinning.

We have reviewed the basic steps the garbage collector undertakes during a collection cycle. We have also seen what happens to objects that must be passed to unmanaged code. Throughout the previous sections we have seen many areas where optimizations are in place. One thing that was mentioned frequently is that on multi-processor machines, contention and the need for synchronization might be a very significant factor for the performance of memory-intensive applications. In the subsequent sections, we will examine multiple optimizations including optimizations targeting multi-processor systems.

Garbage Collection Flavors

The .NET garbage collector comes in several flavors, even though it might appear to the outside as a large and monolithic piece of code with little room for customization. These flavors exist to differentiate multiple scenarios: Client-oriented applications, high-performance server applications, and so on. To understand how these various flavors are really different from each other, we must look at the garbage collector's interaction with the other application threads (often called *mutator threads*).

Pausing Threads for Garbage Collection

When a garbage collection occurs, application threads are normally executing. After all, the garbage collection request is typically a result of a new allocation being made in the application's code—so it's certainly willing to run. The work performed by the GC affects the memory locations of objects and the references to these objects. Moving objects in memory and changing their references while application code is using them is prone to be problematic.

On the other hand, in some scenarios executing the garbage collection process concurrently with other application threads is of paramount importance. For example, consider a classic GUI application. If the garbage collection process is triggered on a background thread, we want to be able to keep the UI responsive while the collection occurs. Even though the collection itself might take longer to complete (because the UI is competing for CPU resources with the GC), the user is going to be much happier because the application is more responsive.

There are two categories of problems that can arise if the garbage collector executes concurrently with other application threads:

- *False negatives*: An object is considered alive even though it is eligible for garbage collection. This is an undesired effect, but if the object is going to be collected in the next cycle, we can live with the consequences.

- *False positives*: An object is considered dead even though it is still referenced by the application. This is a debugging nightmare, and the garbage collector must do everything in its power to prevent this situation from happening.

Let's consider the two phases of garbage collection and see whether we can afford running application threads concurrently with the GC process. Note that whatever conclusions we might reach, there are still scenarios that will require pausing threads during the garbage collection process. For example, if the process truly runs out of memory, it will be necessary to suspend threads while memory is being reclaimed. However, we will review less exceptional scenarios, which amount for the majority of the cases.

SUSPENDING THREADS FOR GC

Suspending threads for garbage collection is performed at *safe points*. Not every set of two instructions can be interrupted to perform a collection. The JIT emits additional information so that the suspension occurs when it's safe to perform the collection, and the CLR tries to suspend threads gracefully—it will not resort to a blatant `SuspendThread` Win32 API call without verifying that the thread is safe after suspension.

In CLR 2.0, it was possible to come up with a scenario where a managed thread entangled in a very tight CPU-bound loop would pass around safe points for a long time, causing delays of up to 1500 milliseconds in GC startup (which, in turn, delayed any threads that were already blocked waiting for GC to complete). This problem was fixed in CLR 4.0; if you are curious about the details, read Sasha Goldshtein's blog post, "Garbage Collection Thread Suspension Delay" (`http://blog.sashag.net/archive/2009/07/31/garbage-collection-thread-suspension-delay-250ms-multiples.aspx`, 2009).

Note that unmanaged threads are not affected by thread suspension until they return to managed code—this is taken care of by the P/Invoke transition stub.

Pausing Threads during the Mark Phase

During the mark phase, the garbage collector's work is almost read-only. False negatives and false positives can occur nonetheless.

A newly created object can be considered dead by the collector even though it is referenced by the application. This is possible if the collector has already considered the part of the graph that is updated when the object is created (see Figure 4-7). This can be addressed by intercepting the creation of new references (and new objects) and making sure to mark them. It requires synchronization and increases the allocation cost, but allows other threads to execute concurrently with the collection process.

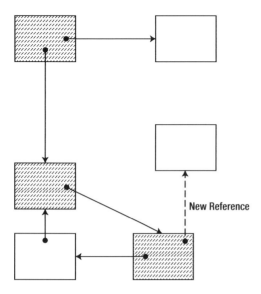

Figure 4-7. *An object is introduced into the graph after that part of the graph was already marked (dashed objects were already marked). This causes the object to be wrongly assumed unreachable*

An object that was already marked by the collector can be eligible for garbage collection if during the mark phase the last reference to it was removed (see Figure 4-8). This is not a severe problem that requires consideration; after all, if the object is really unreachable, it will be collected at the next GC cycle—there is no way for a dead object to become reachable again.

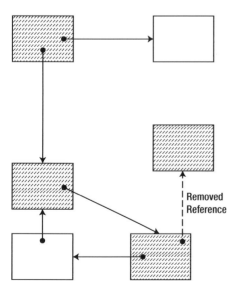

Figure 4-8. *An object is removed from the graph after that part of the graph was already marked (dashed objects were already marked). This causes the object to be wrongly assumed reachable*

Pausing Threads during the Sweep Phase

During the sweep phase, not only do references change, but objects move around in memory. This poses a new set of problems for application threads executing concurrently. Among these problems:

- Copying an object is not an atomic operation. This means that after part of the object has been copied, the original is still being modified by the application.

- Updating references to the object is not an atomic operation. This means that some parts of the application might be using the old object reference and some other parts might be using the new one.

Addressing these problems is possible (Azul Pauseless GC for JVM, `http://www.azulsystems.com/zing/pgc`, is one example), but has not been done in the CLR GC. It is simpler to declare that the sweep phase does not support application threads executing concurrently with the garbage collector.

■ **Tip** To determine whether concurrent GC can provide any benefit for your application, you must first determine how much time it normally spends performing garbage collection. If your application spends 50% of its time reclaiming memory, there remains plenty of room for optimization. On the other hand, if you only perform a collection once in a few minutes, you probably should stick to whatever works for you and pursue significant optimizations elsewhere. You can find out how much time you're spending performing garbage collection through the `% Time in GC` performance counter in the `.NET CLR Memory` performance category.

Now that we've reviewed how other application threads might behave while a garbage collection is in progress, we can examine the various GC flavors in greater detail.

Workstation GC

The first GC flavor we will look into is termed the *workstation GC*. It is further divided into two sub-flavors: *concurrent workstation GC* and *non-concurrent workstation GC*.

Under workstation GC, there is a single thread that performs the garbage collection—the garbage collection does not run in parallel. Note that there's a difference between running the collection process *itself* in parallel on multiple processors, and running the collection process concurrently with other application threads.

Concurrent Workstation GC

The *concurrent workstation* GC flavor is the *default* flavor. Under concurrent workstation GC, there is a separate, dedicated *GC thread* marked with `THREAD_PRIORITY_HIGHEST` that executes the garbage collection from start to finish. Moreover, the CLR can decide that it wants some phases of the garbage collection process to run concurrently with application threads (most of the mark phase can execute concurrently, as we have seen above). Note that the decision is still up to the CLR—as we will see later, some collections are fast enough to warrant full suspension, such as generation 0 collections. One way or another, when the sweep phase is performed, all application threads are suspended.

The responsiveness benefits of using the concurrent workstation GC can be trumped if the garbage collection is triggered by the UI thread. In that case, the application's background threads will be competing with the garbage collection, for which the UI is waiting. This can actually *lower* the UI responsiveness because the UI thread is blocked until GC completes, and there are other application threads competing for resources with the GC. (See Figure 4-9.)

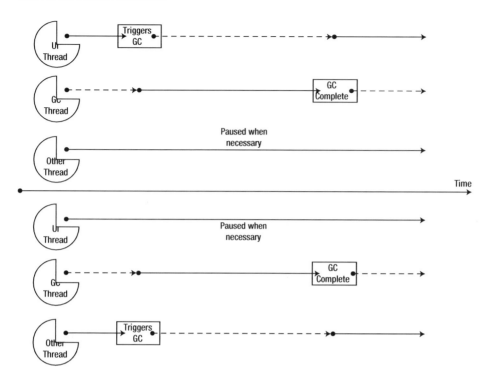

Figure 4-9. *The upper part shows concurrent GC when the UI thread triggers the collection. The lower part shows concurrent GC when one of the background threads triggers the collection. (Dashed lines represent blocked threads.)*

Therefore, UI applications using concurrent workstation GC should exercise great care to prevent garbage collections from occurring on the UI thread. This boils down to performing allocations on background threads, and refraining from explicitly calling GC.Collect on the UI thread.

The default GC flavor for all .NET applications (save ASP.NET applications), regardless of whether they run on a user's workstation or a powerful multiprocessor server is the concurrent workstation GC. This default is rarely appropriate for server applications, as we will see shortly. As we have just seen, this is not necessarily the appropriate default for UI applications either, if they tend to trigger garbage collections on the UI thread.

Non-Concurrent Workstation GC

The *non-concurrent workstation* GC flavor, as its name implies, suspends the application threads during both the mark and sweep phases. The primary usage scenario for non-concurrent workstation GC is the case mentioned in the previous section, when the UI thread tends to trigger garbage collections. In this case, non-concurrent GC might provide better responsiveness, because background threads won't be competing with the garbage collection for which the UI thread is waiting, thus releasing the UI thread more quickly. (See Figure 4-10.)

Figure 4-10. *The UI thread triggers a collection under non-concurrent GC. The other threads do not compete for resources during the collection*

Server GC

The *server* GC flavor is optimized for a completely different type of applications—server applications, as its name implies. Server applications in this context require high-throughput scenarios (often at the expense of latency for an individual operation). Server applications also require easy scaling to multiple processors – and memory management must be able to scale to multiple processors just as well.

An application that uses the server GC has the following characteristics:

- There is a separate managed heap for each processor in the affinity mask of the .NET process. Allocation requests by a thread on a specific processor are satisfied from the managed heap that belongs to that specific processor. The purpose of this separation is to minimize contention on the managed heap while allocations are made: most of the time, there is no contention on the next object pointer and multiple threads can perform allocations truly in parallel. This architecture requires dynamic adjustment of the heap sizes and GC thresholds to ensure fairness if the application creates manual worker threads and assigns them hard CPU affinity. In the case of typical server applications, which service requests off a thread pool worker thread, it is likely that all heaps will have approximately the same size.

- The garbage collection does not occur on the thread that triggered garbage collection. Instead, garbage collection occurs on a set of dedicated GC threads that are created during application startup and are marked THREAD_PRIORITY_HIGHEST. There is a GC thread for each processor that is in the affinity mask of the .NET process. This allows each thread to perform garbage collection in parallel on the managed heap assigned to its processor. Thanks to locality of reference, it is likely that each GC thread should perform the mark phase almost exclusively within its own heap, parts of which are guaranteed to be in that CPU's cache.

- During both phases of garbage collection, all application threads are suspended. This allows GC to complete in a timely fashion and allows application threads to continue processing requests as soon as possible. It maximizes throughput at the expense of latency: some requests might take longer to process while a garbage collection is in progress, but overall the application can process more requests because less context switching is introduced while GC is in progress.

When using server GC, the CLR attempts to balance object allocations across the processor heaps. Up to CLR 4.0, only the small object heap was balanced; as of CLR 4.5, the large object heap (discussed later) is balanced as well. As a result, the allocation rate, fill rate, and garbage collection frequency are kept similar for all heaps.

The only limitation imposed on using the server GC flavor is the number of physical processors on the machine. If there is just one physical processor on the machine, the only available GC flavor is the workstation GC. This is a reasonable choice, because if there is just a single processor available, there will be a single managed heap and a single GC thread, which hinders the effectiveness of the server GC architecture.

■ **Note**   Starting from NT 6.1 (Windows 7 and Windows Server 2008 R2), Windows supports more than 64 logical processors by using *processor groups*. As of CLR 4.5, the GC can use more than 64 logical processors as well. This requires placing the `<GCCpuGroup enabled="true" />` element in your application configuration file.

Server applications are likely to benefit from the server GC flavor. However, as we have seen before, the default GC flavor is the workstation concurrent GC. This is true for applications hosted under the default CLR host, in console applications, Windows applications and Windows services. Non-default CLR hosts can opt-in to a different GC flavor. This is what the IIS ASP.NET host does: it runs applications under the server GC flavor, because it's typical for IIS to be installed on a server machine (even though this behavior can still be customized through Web.config).

Controlling the GC flavor is the subject of the next section. It is an interesting experiment in performance testing, especially for memory-intensive applications. It's a good idea to test the behavior of such applications under the various GC flavors to see which one results in optimal performance under heavy memory load.

Switching Between GC Flavors

It is possible to control the GC flavor with CLR Hosting interfaces, discussed later in this chapter. However, for the default host, it is also possible to control the GC flavor selection using an application configuration file (App.config). The following XML application configuration file can be used to choose between the various GC flavors and sub-flavors:

```
<?xml version="1.0" encoding="utf-8" ?>
<configuration>
  <runtime>
    <gcServer enabled="true" />
    <gcConcurrent enabled="false" />
  </runtime>
</configuration>
```

The gcServer element controls the selection of server GC as opposed to workstation GC. The gcConcurrent element controls the selection of the workstation GC sub-flavor.

.NET 3.5 (including .NET 2.0 SP1 and .NET 3.0 SP1) added an additional API that can change the GC flavor at runtime. It is available as the System.Runtime.GCSettings class, which has two properties: IsServerGC and LatencyMode.

GCSettings.IsServerGC is a read-only property that specifies whether the application is running under the server GC. It can't be used to opt into server GC at runtime, and reflects only the state of the application's configuration or the CLR host's GC flavor definition.

The LatencyMode property, on the other hand, takes the values of the GCLatencyMode enumeration, which are: Batch, Interactive, LowLatency, and SustainedLowLatency. Batch corresponds to non-concurrent GC; Interactive corresponds to concurrent GC. The LatencyMode property can be used to switch between concurrent and non-concurrent GC at runtime.

The final, most interesting values of the GCLatencyMode enumeration are LowLatency and SustainedLowLatency. These values signal to the garbage collector that your code is currently in the middle of a time-sensitive operation where a garbage collection might be harmful. The LowLatency value was introduced in .NET 3.5, was supported only on concurrent workstation GC, and is designed for short time-sensitive regions. On the other hand, SustainedLowLatency was introduced in CLR 4.5, is supported on both server and workstation GC, and is designed for longer periods of time during which your application should not be paused for a full garbage collection. Low latency is not for the scenarios when you're about to execute missile-guiding code for reasons to be seen shortly. It is useful, however, if you're in the middle of performing a UI animation, and garbage collection will be disruptive for the user experience.

The low latency garbage collection mode instructs the garbage collector to refrain from performing full collections unless absolutely necessary—e.g., if the operating system is running low on physical memory (the effects of paging could be even worse than the effects of performing a full collection). Low latency does not mean the garbage collector is off; partial collections (which we will consider when discussing generations) will still be performed, but the garbage collector's share of the application's processing time will be significantly lower.

USING LOW LATENCY GC SAFELY

The only safe way of using the low latency GC mode is within a constrained execution region (CER). A CER delimits a section of code in which the CLR is constrained from throwing out-of-band exceptions (such as thread aborts) which would prevent the section of code from executing in its entirety. Code placed in a CER must call only code with strong reliability guarantees. Using a CER is the only way of guaranteeing that the latency mode will revert to its previous value. The following code demonstrates how this can be accomplished (you should import the System.Runtime.CompilerServices and System.Runtime namespaces to compile this code):

```
GCLatencyMode oldMode = GCSettings.LatencyMode;
RuntimeHelpers.PrepareConstrainedRegions();
try
{
    GCSettings.LatencyMode = GCLatencyMode.LowLatency;
    //Perform time-sensitive work here
}
finally
{
    GCSettings.LatencyMode = oldMode;
}
```

The amount of time you want to spend with a low latency GC mode must be kept to a minimum—the long-term effects once you exit the low latency mode and the GC aggressively begins to reclaim unused memory can hinder the application's performance. If you don't have full control of all allocations taking place within your process (e.g. if you're hosting plug-ins or have multiple background threads doing independent work), remember that switching to the low latency GC mode affects the entire process, and can cause undesired effects for other allocation paths.

Choosing the right GC flavor is not a trivial task, and most of the time we can only arrive at the appropriate mode through experimentation. However, for memory-intensive applications this experimentation is a must—we can't afford spending 50% of our precious CPU time performing garbage collections on a single processor while 15 others happily sit idle and wait for the collection to complete.

Some severe performance problems still plague us as we carefully examine the model laid out above. The following are the most significant problems:

- *Large Objects*: Copying large objects is an extremely expensive operation, and yet during the sweep phase large objects can be copied around all the time. In certain cases, copying memory might become the primary cost of performing a garbage collection. We arrive at the conclusion that objects must be differentiated by size during the sweep phase.

- *Collection Efficiency Factor*: Every collection is a full collection, which means that an application with a relatively stable set of objects will pay the heavy price of performing mark and sweep across the entire heap even though most of the objects are still referenced. To prevent a low collection efficiency factor, we must pursue an optimization which can differentiate objects by their *collection likelihood*: whether they are likely to be collected at the next GC cycle.

Most aspects of these problems can be addressed with the proper use of generations, which is the topic we cover in the next section. We will also touch on some additional performance issues that you need to consider when interacting with the .NET garbage collector.

Generations

The *generational model* of the .NET garbage collector optimizes collection performance by performing partial garbage collections. Partial garbage collections have a higher collection efficiency factor, and the objects traversed by the collector are those with optimal collection likelihood. The primary decision factor for partitioning objects by collection likelihood is their *age*—the model assumes that there is an inherent correlation between the object's age and its life expectancy.

Generational Model Assumptions

Contrary to the human and animal world, young .NET objects are expected to die quickly, whereas old .NET objects are expected to live longer. These two assumptions force the distribution of object life expectancies into the two corners of the graph in Figure 4-11.

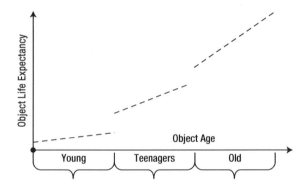

Figure 4-11. *Object life expectancy as a function of object age, partitioned into three areas*

■ **Note** The definitions of "young" and "old" depend on the frequency of garbage collections the application induces. An object that was created 5 seconds ago will be considered young if a garbage collection occurs once a minute. In another system, it will be considered old because the system is very memory-intensive and causes dozens of collections per second. Nevertheless, in most applications temporary objects (e.g. allocated locally as part of a method call) tend to die young, and objects allocated at application initialization tend to live longer.

Under the generational model, most new objects are expected to exhibit temporary behavior—allocated for a specific, short-lived purpose, and turned into garbage shortly afterwards. On the other hand, objects that have survived a long time (e.g. singleton or well-known objects allocated when the application was initialized) are expected to survive even longer.

Not every application obeys the assumptions imposed by the generational model. It is easy to envision a system in which temporary objects survive several garbage collections and then become unreferenced, and more temporary objects are created. This phenomenon, in which an object's life expectancy does not fall within the buckets predicted by the generational model, is informally termed *mid-life crisis*. Objects that exhibit this phenomenon outweigh the benefits of the performance optimization offered by the generational model. We will examine mid-life crisis later in this section.

.NET Implementation of Generations

In the generational model, the garbage collected heap is partitioned into three regions: generation 0, generation 1, and generation 2. These regions reflect on the projected life expectancy of the objects they contain: generation 0 contains the youngest objects, and generation 2 contains old objects that have survived for a while.

Generation 0

Generation 0 is the playground for all new objects (later in this section we will see that objects are also partitioned by size, which makes this statement only partially correct). It is very small, and cannot accommodate for all the memory usage of even the smallest of applications. Generation 0 usually starts with a budget between 256 KB-4 MB and might grow slightly if the need arises.

■ **Note**   Aside from OS bitness, L2 and L3 cache sizes also affect the size of generation 0, because the primary objective of this generation is to contain objects that are frequently accessed and are accessed together, for a short period of time. It is also controlled dynamically by the garbage collector at runtime, and can be controlled at application startup by a CLR host by setting the GC startup limits. The budget for both generation 0 and generation 1 together cannot exceed the size of a single segment (discussed later).

When a new allocation request cannot be satisfied from generation 0 because it is full, a garbage collection is initiated within generation 0. In this process, the garbage collector touches only those objects which belong in generation 0 during the mark and sweep phases. This is not trivial to achieve because there is no prior correlation between roots and generations, and there is always the possibility of an object outside generation 0 referencing an object inside generation 0. We will examine this difficulty shortly.

A garbage collection within generation 0 is a very cheap and efficient process for several reasons:

- Generation 0 is very small and therefore it does not contain many objects. Traversing such a small amount of memory takes very little time. On one of our test machines, performing a generation 0 collection with 2% of the objects surviving took approximately 70 μs (microseconds).

- Cache size affects the size of generation 0, which makes it more likely for all the objects in generation 0 to be found in cache. Traversing memory that is already in cache is significantly faster than accessing it from main memory or paging it in from disk, as we shall see in Chapter 5.

- Due to temporal locality, it is likely that objects allocated in generation 0 have references to other objects in generation 0. It is also likely that these objects are close to each other in space. This makes traversing the graph during the mark phase more efficient if cache misses are taken after all.

- Because new objects are expected to die quickly, the collection likelihood for each individual object encountered is extremely high. This in turn means that most of the objects in generation 0 do not have to be touched—they are just unused memory that can be reclaimed for other objects to use. This also means that we have not wasted time performing this garbage collection; most objects are actually unreferenced and their memory can be reused.

- When the garbage collection ends, the reclaimed memory will be used to satisfy new allocation requests. Because it has just been traversed, it is likely to be in the CPU cache, rendering allocations and subsequent object access somewhat faster.

As we have observed, almost all objects are expected to disappear from generation 0 when the collection completes. However, some objects might survive due to a variety of reasons:

- The application might be poorly-behaved and performs allocations of temporary objects that survive more than a single garbage collection.

- The application is at the initialization stage, when long-lived objects are being allocated.

- The application has created some temporary short-lived objects which happened to be in use when the garbage collection was triggered.

The objects that have survived a garbage collection in generation 0 are not swept to the beginning of generation 0. Instead, they are *promoted* to generation 1, to reflect the fact that their life expectancy is now longer. As part of this promotion, they are copied from the region of memory occupied by generation 0 to the region of memory occupied by generation 1 (see Figure 4-12). This copy might appear to be expensive, but it is a part of the sweep operation one way or another. Additionally, because the collection efficiency factor in generation 0 is very high, the amortized cost of this copy should be negligible compared to the performance gains from performing a partial collection instead of a full one.

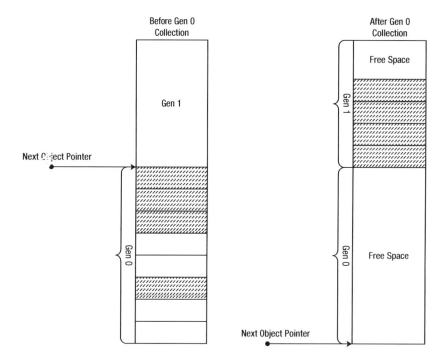

Figure 4-12. *Live (surviving) objects from generation 0 are promoted to generation 1 after a garbage collection completes*

MOVING PINNED OBJECTS ACROSS GENERATIONS

Pinning an object prevents it from being moved by the garbage collector. In the generational model, it prevents promotion of pinned objects between generations. This is especially significant in the younger generations, such as generation 0, because the size of generation 0 is very small. Pinned objects that cause fragmentation within generation 0 have the potential of causing more harm than it might appear from examining pinned before we introduced generations into the picture. Fortunately, the CLR has the ability to promote pinned objects using the following trick: if generation 0 becomes severely fragmented with pinned objects, the CLR can declare the entire space of generation 0 to be considered a higher generation, and allocate new objects from a new region of memory that will become generation 0. This is achieved by changing the ephemeral segment, which will be discussed later in this chapter.

The following code demonstrates that pinned objects can move across generations, by using the GC.GetGeneration method discussed later in this chapter:

```
static void Main(string[] args) {
    byte[] bytes = new byte[128];
    GCHandle gch = GCHandle.Alloc(bytes, GCHandleType.Pinned);

    GC.Collect();
    Console.WriteLine("Generation: " + GC.GetGeneration(bytes));

    gch.Free();
    GC.KeepAlive(bytes);
}
```

If we examine the GC heap before the garbage collection, the generations are aligned similarly to the following:

```
Generation 0 starts at 0x02791030
Generation 1 starts at 0x02791018
Generation 2 starts at 0x02791000
```

If we examine the GC heap after the garbage collection, the generations are re-aligned within the same segment similarly to the following:

```
Generation 0 starts at 0x02795df8
Generation 1 starts at 0x02791018
Generation 2 starts at 0x02791000
```

The object's address (in this case, 0x02791be0) hasn't changed because it is pinned, but by moving the generation boundaries the CLR maintains the illusion that the object was promoted between generations.

Generation 1

Generation 1 is the buffer between generation 0 and generation 2. It contains objects that have survived one garbage collection. It is slightly larger than generation 0, but still smaller by several orders of magnitude than the entire available memory space. A typical starting budget for generation 1 ranges from 512 KB-4 MB.

When generation 1 becomes full, a garbage collection is triggered in generation 1. This is still a partial garbage collection; only objects in generation 1 are marked and swept by the garbage collector. Note that the only natural trigger for a collection in generation 1 is a prior collection in generation 0, as objects are promoted from generation 0 to generation 1 (inducing a garbage collection manually is another trigger).

A garbage collection in generation 1 is still a relatively cheap process. A few megabytes of memory must be touched, at most, to perform a collection. The collection efficiency factor is still high, too, because most objects that reach generation 1 should be temporary short-lived objects—objects that weren't reclaimed in generation 0, but will not outlive another garbage collection. For example, short-lived objects with finalizers are guaranteed to reach generation 1. (We will discuss finalization later in this chapter.)

Surviving objects from generation 1 are promoted to generation 2. This promotion reflects the fact that they are now considered old objects. One of the primary risks in generational model is that temporary objects creep into generation 2 and die shortly afterwards; this is the mid-life crisis. It is extremely important to ensure that temporary objects do *not* reach generation 2. Later in this section we will examine the dire effects of the mid-life crisis phenomenon, and look into diagnostic and preventive measures.

Generation 2

Generation 2 is the ultimate region of memory for objects that have survived at least two garbage collections (and for large objects, as we will see later). In the generational model, these objects are considered old and, based on our assumptions, should not become eligible for garbage collection in the near future.

Generation 2 is not artificially limited in size. Its size can extend the entire memory space dedicated for the OS process, i.e., up to 2 GB of memory on a 32-bit system, or up to 8 TB of memory on a 64-bit system.

■ **Note** Despite its huge size, there are dynamic thresholds (watermarks) within generation 2 that cause a garbage collection to be triggered, because it does not make sense to wait until the entire memory space is full to perform a garbage collection. If every application on the system could run until the memory space is exhausted, and only then the GC would reclaim unused memory, paging effects will grind the system to a halt.

When a garbage collection occurs within generation 2, it is a full garbage collection. This is the most expensive kind of garbage collection, which can take the longest to complete. On one of our test machines, performing a full garbage collection of 100MB of referenced objects takes approximately 30ms (milliseconds)—several orders of magnitude slower than a collection of a younger generation.

Additionally, if the application behaves according to the generational model assumptions, a garbage collection in generation 2 is also likely to exhibit a very low collection efficiency factor, because most objects in generation 2 will outlive multiple garbage collection cycles. Because of this, a garbage collection in generation 2 should be a rare occasion—it is extremely slow compared to partial collections of the younger generations, and it is inefficient because most of the objects traversed are still referenced and there is hardly any memory to reclaim.

If all temporary objects allocated by the application die quickly, they do not get a chance to survive multiple garbage collections and reach generation 2. In this optimistic scenario, there will be no collections in generation 2, and the garbage collector's effect on application performance is minimized by several orders of magnitude.

Through the careful use of generations, we have managed to address one of our primary concerns with the naïve garbage collector outlined in the previous sections: partitioning objects by their collection likelihood. If we successfully predict the life expectancy of objects based on their current life span, we can perform cheap partial garbage collections and only rarely resort to expensive full collections. However, another concern remains unaddressed and even aggravated: large objects are copied during the sweep phase, which can be very expensive in terms of CPU and memory work. Additionally, in the generational model, it is unclear how generation 0 can contain an array of 10,000,000 integers, which is significantly larger than its size.

Large Object Heap

The *large object heap* (LOH) is a special area reserved for large objects. Large objects are objects that occupy more than 85KB of memory. This threshold applies to the object itself, and not to the size of the entire object graph rooted at the object, so that an array of 1,000 strings (each 100 characters in size) is not a large object because the array itself contains only 4-byte or 8-byte references to the strings, but an array of 50,000 integers is a large object.

Large objects are allocated from the LOH directly, and do not pass through generation 0, generation 1 or generation 2. This minimizes the cost of promoting them across generations, which would mean copying their memory around. However, when a garbage collection occurs within the LOH, the sweep phase might have to copy objects around, incurring the same performance hit. To avoid this performance cost, objects in the large object heap are not subject to the standard sweep algorithm.

Instead of sweeping large objects and copying them around, the garbage collector employs a different strategy when collecting the LOH. A linked list of all unused memory blocks is maintained, and allocation requests can be satisfied from this list. This strategy is very similar to the free list memory management strategy discussed in the beginning of this chapter, and comes with the same performance costs: allocation cost (finding an appropriate free block, breaking free blocks in parts), deallocation cost (returning the memory region into the free list) and management cost (joining adjacent blocks together). However, it is cheaper to use free list management than it is to copy large objects in memory—and this is a typical scenario where purity of implementation is compromised to achieve better performance.

■ **Caution**   Because objects in the LOH do not move, it might appear that pinning is unnecessary when taking the address in memory of a large object. This is wrong and relies on an implementation detail. You cannot assume that large objects retain the same memory location throughout their lifetime, and the threshold for a large object might change in the future without any notice! From a practical perspective, nonetheless, it is reasonable to assume that pinning large objects will incur less performance costs than pinning small young objects. In fact, in the case of pinned arrays, it is often advisable to allocate a large array, pin it in memory, and distribute chunks from the array instead of allocating a new small array for each operation that requires pinning.

The LOH is collected when the threshold for a collection in generation 2 is reached. Similarly, when a threshold for a collection in the LOH is reached, generation 2 is collected as well. Creating many large temporary objects, therefore, causes the same problems as the mid-life crisis phenomenon—full collections will be performed to reclaim these objects. Fragmentation in the large object heap is another potential problem, because holes between objects are not automatically removed by sweeping and defragmenting the heap.

The LOH model means application developers must take great care of large memory allocations, often bordering on manual memory management. One effective strategy is pooling large objects and reusing them instead of releasing them to the GC. The cost of maintaining the pool might be smaller than the cost of performing full collections. Another possible approach (if arrays of the same type are involved) is allocating a very large object and manually breaking it into chunks as they are needed (see Figure 4-13).

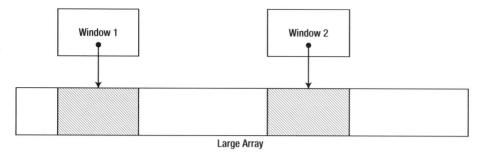

Figure 4-13. *Allocating a large object and manually breaking it into chunks that are exposed to clients through flyweight "window" objects*

References between Generations

When discussing the generational model, we dismissed a significant detail which can compromise the correctness and performance of the model. Recall that partial collections of the younger generations are cheap because only objects in the younger generations are traversed during the collection. How does the GC guarantee that it will only touch these younger objects?

Consider the mark phase during a collection of generation 0. During the mark phase, the GC determines the currently active roots, and begins constructing a graph of all objects referenced by the roots. In the process, we want to discard any objects that do not belong to generation 0. However, if we discard them after constructing the entire graph, then we have touched all referenced objects, making the mark phase as expensive as in a full collection. Alternatively, we could stop traversing the graph whenever we reach an object that is not in generation 0. The risk with this approach is that we will never reach objects from generation 0 that are referenced only by objects from a higher generation, as in Figure 4-14!

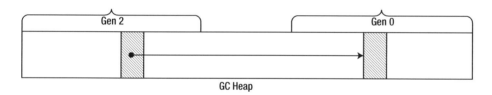

Figure 4-14. *References between generations might be missed if during the mark phase we stop following references once we reach an object in a higher generation*

This problem appears to require a compromise between correctness and performance. We can solve it by obtaining prior knowledge of the specific scenario when an object from an older generation has a reference to an object in a younger generation. If the GC had such knowledge prior to performing the mark phase, it could add these old objects into the set of roots when constructing the graph. This would enable the GC to stop traversing the graph when it encounters an object that does not belong to generation 0.

This prior knowledge can be obtained with assistance from the JIT compiler. The scenario in which an object from an older generation references an object from a younger generation can arise from only one category of statements: a non-null reference type assignment to a reference type's instance field (or an array element write).

```
class Customer {
    public Order LastOrder { get; set; }
}
```

```
class Order { }

class Program {
    static void Main(string[] args) {
        Customer customer = new Customer();
        GC.Collect();
        GC.Collect();
        //customer is now in generation 2
        customer.LastOrder = new Order();
    }
}
```

When the JIT compiles a statement of this form, it emits a *write barrier* which intercepts the reference write at run time and records auxiliary information in a data structure called a *card table*. The write barrier is a light-weight CLR function which checks whether the object being assigned to belongs to a generation older than generation 0. If that's the case, it updates a byte in the card table corresponding to the range of addresses 1024 bytes around the assignment target (see Figure 4-15).

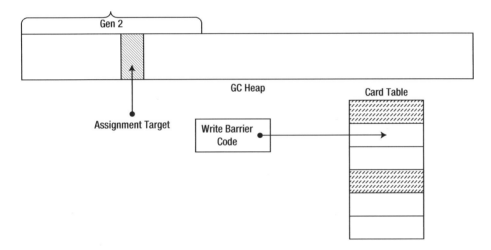

Figure 4-15. *An assignment to a reference field passes through a write barrier which updates the relevant bit in the card table, matching the region in which the reference was updated*

Tracing through the write-barrier code is fairly easy with a debugger. First, the actual assignment statement in Main was compiled by the JIT compiler to the following:

```
; ESI contains a pointer to 'customer', ESI+4 is 'LastOrder', EAX is 'new Order()'
lea edx, [esi+4]
call clr!JIT_WriteBarrierEAX
```

Inside the write barrier, a check is made to see whether the object being assigned to has an address lower than the start address of generation 1 (i.e., in generation 1 or 2). If that is the case, the card table is updated by assigning 0xFF to the byte at the offset obtained by shifting the object's address 10 bits to the right. (If the byte was set to 0xFF before, it is not set again, to prevent invalidations of other processor caches; see Chapter 6 for more details.)

```
mov dword ptr [edx], eax          ; the actual write
cmp eax, 0x272237C                ; start address of generation 1
jb NoNeedToUpdate
shr edx, 0xA                      ; shift 10 bits to the right
cmp byte ptr [edx+0x48639C], 0xFF ; 0x48639C is the start of the card table
jne NeedUpdate
NoNeedToUpdate:
ret
NeedUpdate:
mov byte ptr [edx+0x48639C], 0xFF ; update the card table
ret
```

The garbage collector uses this auxiliary information when performing the mark phase. It checks the card table to see which address ranges must be considered as roots when collecting the young generation. The collector traverses the objects within these address ranges and locates their references to objects in the younger generation. This enables the performance optimization mentioned above, in which the collector can stop traversing the graph whenever it encounters an object that does not belong to generation 0.

The card table can potentially grow to occupy a single byte for each KB of memory in the heap. This appears to waste ~0.1% of space, but provides a great performance boost when collecting the younger generations. Using an entry in the card table for each individual object reference would be faster (the GC would only have to consider that specific object and not a range of 1024 bytes), but storing additional information at run time for each object reference cannot be afforded. The existing card table approach perfectly reflects this trade-off between memory space and execution time.

░ **Note**   Although such micro-optimization is rarely worthwhile, we can actively minimize the cost associated with updating and traversing the card table. One possible approach is to pool objects and reuse them instead of creating them. This will minimize garbage collections in general. Another approach is to use value types whenever possible, and minimize the number of references in the graph. Value type assignments do not require a write barrier, because a value type on the heap is always a part of some reference type (or, in boxed form, it is trivially a part of itself).

Background GC

The workstation concurrent GC flavor introduced in CLR 1.0 has a major drawback. Although during a generation 2 concurrent GC application threads are allowed to continue allocating, they can only allocate as much memory as would fit into generations 0 and 1. As soon as this limit is encountered, application threads must block and wait for the collection to complete.

Background GC, introduced in CLR 4.0, enables the CLR to perform a garbage collection in generations 0 and 1 even though a full collection was underway. To allow this, the CLR creates *two* GC threads: a *foreground GC thread* and a *background GC thread*. The background GC thread executes generation 2 collections in the background, and periodically checks for requests to perform a quick collection in generations 0 and 1. When a request arrives (because the application has exhausted the younger generations), the background GC thread suspends itself and yields execution to the foreground GC thread, which performs the quick collection and unblocks the application threads.

In CLR 4.0, background GC was offered automatically for any application using the concurrent workstation GC. There was no way to opt-out of background GC or to use background GC with other GC flavors.

In CLR 4.5, background GC was expanded to the server GC flavor. Moreover, server GC was revamped to support concurrent collections as well. When using concurrent server GC in a process that is using *N* logical processors, the CLR creates *N* foreground GC threads and *N* background GC threads. The background GC threads take care of generation 2 collections, and allow the application code to execute concurrently in the foreground. The foreground GC threads are invoked whenever there's need to perform a blocking collection if the CLR deems fit, to perform compaction (the background GC threads do not compact), or perform a collection in the younger generations in the midst of a full collection on the background threads.To summarize, as of CLR 4.5, there are four distinct GC flavors that you can choose from using the application configuration file:

1. Concurrent workstation GC—the default flavor; has background GC.

2. Non-concurrent workstation GC—does not have background GC.

3. Non-concurrent server GC—does not have background GC.

4. Concurrent server GC—has background GC.

GC Segments and Virtual Memory

In our discussion of the basic GC model and the generational GC model, we have repeatedly assumed that a .NET process usurps the entire memory space available for its hosting process and uses this memory as the backing store for the garbage collected heap. This assumption is blatantly wrong, considering the fact that managed applications can't survive in isolation without using unmanaged code. The CLR itself is implemented in unmanaged code, the .NET base class library (BCL) often wraps Win32 and COM interfaces, and custom components developed in unmanaged code can be loaded into the otherwise "managed" process.

■ **Note**   Even if managed code could live in total isolation, it does not make sense for the garbage collector to immediately commit the entire available address space. Although committing memory without using it does not imply the backing store (RAM or disk space) for that memory is immediately required, it is not an operation that comes for free. It is generally advisable to allocate only slightly more than the amount of memory that you are likely to need. As we will see later, the CLR reserves significant memory regions in advance, but commits them only when necessary and makes a point of returning unused memory to Windows.

In view of the above, we must refine the garbage collector's interaction with the virtual memory manager. During CLR startup within a process, two blocks of memory called *GC segments* are allocated from virtual memory (more precisely, the CLR host is requested to provide this block of memory). The first segment is used for generation 0, generation 1 and generation 2 (called the *ephemeral segment*). The second segment is used for the large object heap. The size of the segment depends on the GC flavor and on GC startup limits if running under a CLR host. A typical segment size on 32-bit systems with workstation GC is 16MB, and for server GC it is in the 16-64MB range. On 64-bit systems the CLR uses 128MB-2 GB segments with server GC, and 128MB-256MB segments with workstation GC. (The CLR does not commit an entire segment at a time; it only reserves the address range and commits parts of the segment as the need arises.)

When the segment becomes full and more allocation requests arrive, the CLR allocates another segment. Only one segment can contain generation 0 and generation 1 at any given time. However, it does not have to be the same segment! We have previously observed that pinning objects in generation 0 or generation 1 for a long time is especially dangerous due to fragmentation effects in these small memory regions. The CLR handles these issues by declaring another segment as the ephemeral segment, which effectively promotes the objects previously in the younger generations straight into generation 2 (because there can be only one ephemeral segment).

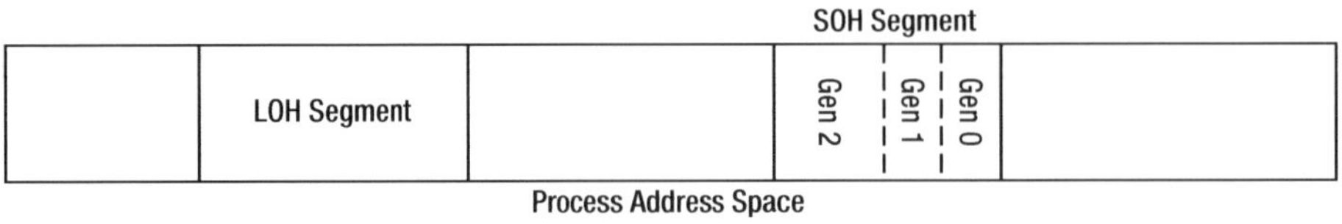

Figure 4-16. GC segments occupy the virtual address space of the process. The segment containing the young generations is called the ephemeral segment

When a segment becomes empty as the result of a garbage collection, the CLR usually releases the segment's memory and returns it to the operating system. This is the desired behavior for most applications, especially applications that exhibit infrequent large spikes in memory usage. However, it is possible to instruct the CLR to retain empty segments on a standby list without returning them to the operating system. This behavior is called *segment hoarding* or *VM hoarding*, and can be enabled through CLR hosting with the startup flags of the CorBindToRuntimeEx function. Segment hoarding can improve performance in applications which allocate and release segments very frequently (memory-intensive applications with frequent spikes in memory usage), and reduce out of memory exceptions due to virtual memory fragmentation (to be discussed shortly). It is used by default by ASP.NET applications. A custom CLR host can further customize this behavior by satisfying segment allocation requests from a memory pool or any other source by using the IHostMemoryManager interface.

The segmented model of managed memory space introduces an extremely serious problem which has to with external (virtual memory) fragmentation. Because segments are returned to the operating system when they are empty, an unmanaged allocation can occur in the middle of a memory region that was once a GC segment. This allocation causes fragmentation because segments must be consecutive in memory.

The most common causes of virtual memory fragmentation are late-loaded dynamic assemblies (such as XML serialization assemblies or ASP.NET debug compiled pages), dynamically loaded COM objects and unmanaged code performing scattered memory allocations. Virtual memory fragmentation can cause out of memory conditions even when the perceived memory usage of the process is nowhere near the 2 GB limit. Long-running processes such as web servers that perform memory-intensive work with frequent spikes in memory allocation tend to exhibit this behavior after several hours, days or weeks of execution. In non-critical scenarios where a failover is available (such as a load-balanced server farm), this is normally addressed by process recycling.

■ **Note**   Theoretically speaking, if the segment size is 64MB, the virtual memory allocation granularity is 4KB and the 32-bit process address space is 2GB (in which there is room for only 32 segments), it is possible to allocate only $4KB \times 32 = 128KB$ of unmanaged memory and still fragment the address space such that not a single consecutive segment can be allocated!

The Sysinternals VMMap utility can diagnose memory fragmentation scenarios quite easily. Not only does it report precisely which region of memory is used for which purposes, it has also a Fragmentation View option that displays a picture of the address space and makes it easy to visualize fragmentation problems. Figure 4-17 shows an example of an address space snapshot in which there are almost 500MB of free space, but no single free fragment large enough for a 16MB GC segment. In the screenshot, white areas are free memory regions.

Figure 4-17. *A badly fragmented address space snapshot. There are almost 500MB of available memory, but no chunk large enough to fit a GC segment*

EXPERIMENTING WITH VMMAP

You can try using VMMap with a sample application and see how quickly it points you in the right direction. Specifically, VMMap makes it very easy to determine whether the memory problems you're experiencing originate within the managed heap or elsewhere, and facilitates the diagnostics of fragmentation problems.

1. Download VMMap from Microsoft TechNet (`http://technet.microsoft.com/en-us/ sysinternals/dd535533.aspx`) and store it on your machine.

2. Run the OOM2.exe application from this chapter's sample code folder. The application quickly exhausts all available memory and crashes with an exception. When the Windows error reporting dialog appears, do not dismiss it—keep the application running.

3. Run VMMap and choose the OOM2.exe process to monitor. Note the amount of available memory (the "Free" row in the summary table). Open the Fragmentation View (from the View menu) to examine the address space visually. Inspect the detailed list of memory blocks for the "Free" type to see the largest free block in the application's address space.

4. As you can see, the application does not exhaust all the virtual address space, but there is not enough room to allocate a new GC segment—the largest available free block is smaller than 16 MB.

5. Repeat steps 2 and 3 with the OOM3.exe application from this chapter's sample code folder. The memory exhaustion is somewhat slower, and occurs for a different reason.

Whenever you stumble upon a memory-related problem in a Windows application, VMMap should always be ready on your toolbelt. It can point you to managed memory leaks, heap fragmentation, excessive assembly loading, and many other problems. It can even profile unmanaged allocations, helping to detect memory leaks: see Sasha Goldshtein's blog post on VMMap allocation profiling (`http://blog.sashag.net/ archive/2011/08/27/vmmap-allocation-profiling-and-leak-detection.aspx`).

There are two approaches for addressing the virtual memory fragmentation problem:

- Reducing the number of dynamic assemblies, reducing or pooling unmanaged memory allocations, pooling managed memory allocations or hoarding GC segments. This category of approaches typically extends the amount of time until the problem resurfaces, but does not eliminate it completely.

- Switching to a 64-bit operating system and running the code in a 64-bit process. A 64-bit process has 8TB of address space, which for all practical purposes eliminates the problem completely. Because the problem is not related to the amount of physical memory available, but rather strictly to the amount of virtual address space, switching to 64-bit is sufficient regardless of the amount of physical memory.

This concludes the examination of the segmented GC model, which defines the interaction between managed memory and its underlying virtual memory store. Most applications will never require customizing this interaction; should you be forced to do so in the specific scenarios outlined above, CLR hosting provides the most complete and customizable solution.

Finalization

This chapter so far addressed in sufficient detail the specifics of managing one type of resources, namely, managed memory. However, in the real world, many other types of resources exist, which can collectively be called *unmanaged resources* because they are not managed by the CLR or by the garbage collector (such as kernel object handles, database connections, unmanaged memory etc.). Their allocation and deallocation are not governed by GC rules, and the standard memory reclamation techniques outlined above do not suffice when they are concerned.

Freeing unmanaged resources requires an additional feature called *finalization*, which associates an object (representing an unmanaged resource) with code that must be executed when the object is no longer needed. Oftentimes, this code should be executed in a deterministic fashion when the resource becomes eligible for deallocation; at other times, it can be delayed for a later non-deterministic point in time.

Manual Deterministic Finalization

Consider a fictitious File class that serves as a wrapper for a Win32 file handle. The class has a member field of type System.IntPtr which holds the handle itself. When the file is no longer needed, the CloseHandle Win32 API must be called to close the handle and release the underlying resources.

The deterministic finalization approach requires adding a method to the File class that will close the underlying handle. It is then the client's responsibility to call this method, even in the face of exceptions, in order to deterministically close the handle and release the unmanaged resource.

```
class File {
    private IntPtr handle;

    public File(string fileName) {
        handle = CreateFile(...);     //P/Invoke call to Win32 CreateFile API
    }
```

```
  public void Close() {
    CloseHandle(handle);          //P/Invoke call to Win32 CloseHandle API
  }
}
```

This approach is simple enough and is proven to work in unmanaged environments such as C++, where it is the client's responsibility to release resources. However, .NET developers accustomed to the practice of automatic resource reclamation might find this model inconvenient. The CLR is expected to provide a mechanism for automatic finalization of unmanaged resources.

Automatic Non-Deterministic Finalization

The automatic mechanism cannot be deterministic because it must rely on the garbage collector to discover whether an object is referenced. The GC's non-deterministic nature, in turn, implies that finalization will be non-deterministic. At times, this non-deterministic behavior is a show-stopper, because temporary "resource leaks" or holding a shared resource locked for just slightly longer than necessary might be unacceptable behaviors. At other times, it is acceptable, and we try to focus on the scenarios where it is.

Any type can override the protected Finalize method defined by System.Object to indicate that it requires automatic finalization. The C# syntax for requesting automatic finalization on the File class is the ~File method. This method is called a *finalizer*, and it must be invoked when the object is destroyed.

■ **Note** Incidentally, only reference types (classes) can define a finalizer in C#, even though the CLR does not impose this limitation. However, it typically only makes sense for reference types to define a finalization behavior, because value types are eligible for garbage collection only when they are boxed (see Chapter 3 for a detailed treatment of boxing). When a value type is allocated on the stack, it is never added to the finalization queue. When the stack unfolds as part of returning from a method or terminating the frame because of an exception, value type finalizers are not called.

When an object with a finalizer is created, a reference to it is added to a special runtime-managed queue called the *finalization queue*. This queue is considered a root by the garbage collector, meaning that even if the application has no outstanding reference to the object, it is still kept alive by the finalization queue.

When the object becomes unreferenced by the application and a garbage collection occurs, the GC detects that the only reference to the object is the reference from the finalization queue. The GC consequently moves the object reference to another runtime-managed queue called the *f-reachable queue*. This queue is also considered a root, so at this point the object is still referenced and considered alive.

The object's finalizer is not run during garbage collection. Instead, a special thread called the *finalizer thread* is created during CLR initialization (there is one finalization thread per process, regardless of GC flavor, but it runs at THREAD_PRIORITY_HIGHEST). This thread repeatedly waits for the *finalization event* to become signaled. The GC signals this event after a garbage collection completes, if objects were moved to the f-reachable queue, and as a result the finalizer thread wakes up. The finalizer thread removes the object reference from the f-reachable queue and synchronously executes the finalizer method defined by the object. When the next garbage collection occurs, the object is no longer referenced and therefore the GC can reclaim its memory. Figure 4-18 contains all the moving parts:

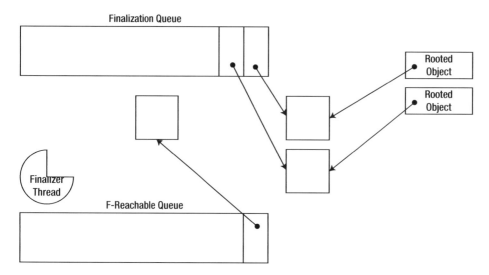

Figure 4-18. *The finalization queue holds references to objects that have a finalizer. When the application stops referencing them, the GC moves the object references to the f-reachable queue. The finalizer thread wakes up and executes the finalizers on these objects, and subsequently releases them*

Why doesn't the GC execute the object's finalizer instead of deferring the work to an asynchronous thread? The motivation for doing so is closing the loop without the f-reachable queue or an additional finalizer thread, which would appear to be cheaper. However, the primary risk associated with running finalizers during GC is that finalizers (which are user-defined by their nature) can take a long time to complete, thus blocking the garbage collection process, which in turn blocks all application threads. Additionally, handling exceptions that occur in the middle of GC is not trivial, and handling memory allocations that the finalizer might trigger in the middle of GC is not trivial either. To conclude, because of reliability reasons the GC does not execute finalization code, but defers this processing to a special dedicated thread.

Pitfalls of Non-Deterministic Finalization

The finalization model just described carries a set of performance penalties. Some of them are insignificant, but others warrant reconsideration of whether finalization is applicable for your resources.

- Objects with finalizers are guaranteed to reach at least generation 1, which makes them more susceptible to the mid-life crisis phenomenon. This increases the chances of performing many full collections.

- Objects with finalizers are slightly more expensive to allocate because they are added to the finalization queue. This introduces contention in multi-processor scenarios. Generally speaking, this cost is negligible compared to the other issues.

- Pressure on the finalizer thread (many objects requiring finalization) might cause memory leaks. If the application threads are allocating objects at a higher rate than the finalizer thread is able to finalize them, then the application will steadily leak memory from objects waiting for finalization.

The following code shows an application thread that allocates objects at a higher rate than they can be finalized, because of blocking code executing in the finalizer. This causes a steady memory leak.

```
class File2 {
    public File2() {
        Thread.Sleep(10);
    }
    ~File2() {
        Thread.Sleep(20);
    }
    //Data to leak:
    private byte[] data = new byte[1024];
}

class Program {
    static void Main(string[] args) {
        while (true) {
            File2 f = new File2();
        }
    }
}
```

EXPERIMENTING WITH A FINALIZATION-RELATED LEAK

In this experiment, you will run a sample application that exhibits a memory leak and perform partial diagnostics before consulting the source code. Without giving away the problem completely, the leak is related to improper use of finalization, and is similar in spirit to the code listing for the File2 class.

1. Run the MemoryLeak.exe application from this chapter's source code folder.

2. Run Performance Monitor and monitor the following performance counters from the .NET CLR Memory category for this application (for more information on Performance Monitor and how to run it, consult Chapter 2): # Bytes in All Heaps, # Gen 0 Collections, # Gen 1 Collections, # Gen 2 Collections, % Time in GC, Allocated Bytes/sec, Finalization Survivors, Promoted Finalization-Memory from Gen 0.

3. Monitor these counters for a couple of minutes until patterns emerge. For example, you should see the # Bytes in All Heaps counter gradually go up, although it sometimes drops slightly. Overall, the application's memory usage is going up, indicating a likely memory leak.

4. Note that application allocates memory at an average rate of 1MB/s. This is not a very high allocation rate, and indeed the fraction of time in GC is very low—this is not a case of the garbage collector struggling to keep up with the application.

5. Finally, note that the Finalization Survivors counter, whenever it is updated, is quite high. This counter represents the number of objects that survived a recent garbage collection only because they are registered for finalization, and their finalizer has not yet run (in other words, these objects are rooted by the f-reachable queue). The Promoted Finalization-Memory from Gen 0 counter points toward a considerable amount of memory that is being retained by these objects.

Adding these pieces of information together, you can deduce that it is likely that the application is leaking memory because it puts insurmountable pressure on the finalizer thread. For example, it might be creating (and releasing) finalizable resources at a faster rate than the finalizer thread is able to clean them. You can now inspect the application's source code (use .NET Reflector, ILSpy, or any other decompiler for this) and verify that the source of leak is related to finalization, specifically the Employee and Schedule classes.

Aside from performance issues, using automatic non-deterministic finalization is also the source of bugs which tend to be extremely difficult to find and resolve. These bugs occur because finalization is asynchronous by definition, and because the order of finalization between multiple objects is undefined.

Consider a finalizable object *A* that holds a reference to another finalizable object *B*. Because the order of finalization is undefined, *A* can't assume that when its finalizer is called, *B* is valid for use—its finalizer might have executed already. For example, an instance of the System.IO.StreamWriter class can hold a reference to an instance of the System.IO.FileStream class. Both instances have finalizable resources: the stream writer contains a buffer that must be flushed to the underlying stream, and the file stream has a file handle that must be closed. If the stream writer is finalized first, it will flush the buffer to the valid underlying stream, and when the file stream is finalized it will close the file handle. However, because finalization order is undefined, the opposite scenario might occur: the file stream is finalized first and closes the file handle, and when the stream writer is finalized it flushes the buffer to an invalid file stream that was previously closed. This is an irresolvable issue, and the "solution" adopted by the .NET Framework is that StreamWriter does not define a finalizer, and relies on deterministic finalization only. If the client forgets to close the stream writer, its internal buffer is lost.

■ **Tip** It *is* possible for resource pairs to define the finalization order among themselves if one of the resources derives from the System.Runtime.ConstrainedExecution.CriticalFinalizerObject abstract class, which defines its finalizer as a *critical finalizer*. This special base class guarantees that its finalizer will be called *after* all other non-critical finalizers have been called. It is used by resource pairs such as System.IO.FileStream with Microsoft.Win32.SafeHandles.SafeFileHandle and System.Threading.EventWaitHandle with Microsoft.Win32.SafeHandles.SafeWaitHandle.

Another problem has to do with the asynchronous nature of finalization which occurs in a dedicated thread. A finalizer might attempt to acquire a lock that is held by the application code, and the application might be waiting for finalization to complete by calling GC.WaitForPendingFinalizers(). The only way to resolve this issue is to acquire the lock with a timeout and fail gracefully if it can't be acquired.

Yet another scenario is caused by the garbage collector's eagerness to reclaim memory as soon as possible. Consider the following code which represents a naïve implementation of a File class with a finalizer that closes the file handle:

```
class File3 {
  Handle handle;
  public File3(string filename) {
    handle = new Handle(filename);
  }
  public byte[] Read(int bytes) {
    return Util.InternalRead(handle, bytes);
  }
  ~File3() {
    handle.Close();
  }
}
```

```
class Program {
  static void Main() {
    File3 file = new File3("File.txt");
    byte[] data = file.Read(100);
    Console.WriteLine(Encoding.ASCII.GetString(data));
  }
}
```

This innocent piece of code can break in a very nasty manner. The Read method can take a long time to complete, and it only uses the handle contained within the object, and not the object itself. The rules for determining when a local variable is considered an active root dictate that the local variable held by the client is no longer relevant after the call to Read has been dispatched. Therefore, the object is considered eligible for garbage collection and its finalizer might execute before the Read method returns! If this happens, we might be closing the handle while it is being used, or just before it is used.

THE FINALIZER MIGHT NEVER BE CALLED

Even though finalization is normally considered a bullet-proof feature that guarantees resource deallocation, the CLR doesn't actually provide a guarantee that a finalizer will be called under any possible set of circumstances.

One obvious scenario in which finalization will not occur is the case of a brutal process shutdown. If the user closes the process via Task Manager or an application calls the TerminateProcess Win32 API, finalizers do not get a chance to reclaim resources. Therefore, it is incorrect to blindly rely on finalizers for cleaning up resources that cross process boundaries (such as deleting files on disk or writing specific data to a database).

Less obvious is the case when the application encounters an out of memory condition and is on the verge of shutting down. Typically, we would expect finalizers to run even in the face of exceptions, but what if the finalizer for some class has never been called yet, and has to be JITted? The JIT requires a memory allocation to compile the finalizer, but there is no memory available. This can be addressed by using .NET pre-compilation (NGEN) or deriving from CriticalFinalizerObject which guarantees that the finalizer will be eagerly JITted when the type is loaded.

Finally, the CLR imposes time limitations on finalizers that run as part of process shutdown or AppDomain unload scenarios. In these cases (which can be detected through Environment.HasShutdownStarted or AppDomain.IsFinalizingForUnload()), each individual finalizer has (roughly) two seconds to complete its execution, and all finalizers combined have (roughly) 40 seconds to complete their execution. If these time limits are breached, finalizers might not execute. This scenario can be diagnosed at runtime using the BreakOnFinalizeTimeout registry value. See Sasha Goldshtein's blog post, "Debugging Shutdown Finalization Timeout" (http://blog.sashag.net/archive/2008/08/27/debugging-shutdown-finalization-timeout.aspx, 2008) for more details.

The Dispose Pattern

We have reviewed multiple problems and limitations with the implementation of non-deterministic finalization. It is now appropriate to reconsider the alternative—deterministic finalization—which was mentioned earlier.

The primary problem with deterministic finalization is that the *client* is responsible for using the object properly. This contradicts the object-orientation paradigm, in which the object is responsible for its own state and invariants. This problem cannot be addressed to a full extent because automatic finalization is always non-deterministic. However, we can introduce a contractual mechanism that will strive to ensure that deterministic finalization occurs, and that will make it easier to use from the client side. In exceptional scenarios, we will have to provide automatic finalization, despite all the costs mentioned in the previous section.

The conventional contract established by the .NET Framework dictates that an object which requires deterministic finalization must implement the IDisposable interface, with a single Dispose method. This method should perform deterministic finalization to release unmanaged resources.

Clients of an object implementing the IDisposable interface are responsible for calling Dispose when they have finished using it. In C#, this can be accomplished with a using block, which wraps object usage in a try...finally block and calls Dispose within the finally block.

This contractual model is fair enough if we trust our clients completely. However, often we can't trust our clients to call Dispose deterministically, and must provide a backup behavior to prevent a resource leak. This can be done using automatic finalization, but brings up a new problem: if the client calls Dispose and later the finalizer is invoked, we will release the resources twice. Additionally, the idea of implementing deterministic finalization was avoiding the pitfalls of automatic finalization!

What we need is a mechanism for instructing the garbage collector that the unmanaged resources have already been released and that automatic finalization is no longer required for a particular object. This can be done using the GC.SuppressFinalize method, which disables finalization by setting a bit in the object's header word (see Chapter 3 for more details about the object header). The object still remains in the finalization queue, but most of the finalization cost is not incurred because the object's memory is reclaimed immediately after the first collection, and it is never seen by the finalizer thread.

Finally, we might want a mechanism to alert our clients of the case when a finalizer was called, because it implies that they haven't used the (significantly more efficient, predictable and reliable) deterministic finalization mechanism. This can be done using System.Diagnostics.Debug.Assert or a logging framework of some sort.

The following code is a rough draft of a class wrapping an unmanaged resource that follows these guidelines (there are more details to consider if the class were to derive from another class that also manages unmanaged resources):

```
class File3 : IDisposable {
  Handle handle;
  public File3(string filename) {
    handle = new Handle(filename);
  }
  public byte[] Read(int bytes) {
    Util.InternalRead(handle, bytes);
  }
  ~File3() {
    Debug.Assert(false, "Do not rely on finalization! Use Dispose!");
    handle.Close();
  }
  public void Dispose() {
    handle.Close();
    GC.SuppressFinalize(this);
  }
}
```

▥ **Note** The finalization pattern described in this section is called the *Dispose pattern*, and covers additional areas such as the interaction between derived and base classes requiring finalization. For more information on the Dispose pattern, refer to the MSDN documentation. Incidentally, C++/CLI implements the Dispose pattern as part of its native syntax: !File is the C++/CLI finalizer and ~File is the C++/CLI IDisposable.Dispose implementation. The details of calling the base class and ensuring finalization is suppressed are taken care of automatically by the compiler.

Ensuring that your implementation of the Dispose pattern is correct is not as difficult as ensuring that clients using your class will use deterministic finalization instead of automatic finalization. The assertion approach outlined earlier is a brute-force option that works. Alternatively, static code analysis can be used to detect improper use of disposable resources.

Resurrection

Finalization provides an opportunity for an object to execute arbitrary code after it is no longer referenced by the application. This opportunity can be used to create a new reference from the application to the object, reviving the object after it was already considered dead. This ability is called *resurrection*.

Resurrection is useful in a handful of scenarios, and should be used with great care. The primary risk is that other objects referenced by your object might have an invalid state, because their finalizers might have run already. This problem can't be solved without reinitializing all objects referenced by your object. Another issue is that your object's finalizer will not run again unless you use the obscure GC.ReRegisterForFinalize method, passing a reference to your object (typically this) as a parameter.

One of the applicable scenarios for using resurrection is *object pooling*. Object pooling implies that objects are allocated from a pool and returned to the pool when they are no longer used, instead of being garbage collected and recreated. Returning the object to the pool can be performed deterministically or delayed to finalization time, which is a classic scenario for using resurrection.

Weak References

Weak references are a supplementary mechanism for handling references to managed objects. The typical object reference (also known as *strong reference*) is very deterministic: as long as you have a reference to the object, the object will stay alive. This is the correctness promise of the garbage collector.

However, in some scenarios, we would like to keep an invisible string attached to an object without interfering with the garbage collector's ability to reclaim that object's memory. If the GC reclaimed the memory, our string becomes unattached and we can detect this. If the GC hasn't touched the object yet, we can pull the string and retrieve a strong reference to the object to use it again.

This facility is useful for various scenarios, of which the following are the most common:

- Providing an external service without keeping the object alive. Services such as timers and events can be provided to objects without keeping them referenced, which can solve many typical memory leaks.

- Automatically managing a cache or pool strategy. A cache can keep weak references to the least recently used objects without preventing them from being collected; a pool can be partitioned into a minimum size which contains strong references and an optional size which contains weak references.

- Keeping a large object alive with the hope that it will not be collected. The application can hold a weak reference to a large object that took a long time to create and initialize. The object might be collected, in which case the application will reinitialize it; otherwise, it can be used the next time it is needed.

Weak references are exposed to application code through the System.WeakReference class, which is a special case of the System.Runtime.InteropServices.GCHandle type. A weak reference has the IsAlive Boolean property which indicates whether the underlying object hasn't been collected yet, and the Target property that can be used to retrieve the underlying object (if it has been collected, null is returned).

■ **Caution**   Note that the only safe way of obtaining a strong reference to the target of a weak reference is by using the Target property. If the IsAlive property returns true, it is possible that immediately afterwards the object will be collected. To defend against this race condition, you must use the Target property, assign the returned value to a strong reference (local variable, field etc.) and then check whether the returned value is null. Use the IsAlive property when you are interested only in the case that the object is dead; for example, to remove the weak reference from a cache.

The following code shows a draft implementation of an event based on weak references (see Figure 4-19). The event itself can't use a .NET delegate directly, because a delegate has a strong reference to its target and this is not customizable. However, it can store the delegate's target (as a weak reference) and its method. This prevents one of the most common .NET memory leaks—forgetting to unregister from an event!

```
public class Button {
  private class WeakDelegate {
    public WeakReference Target;
    public MethodInfo Method;
  }
  private List<WeakDelegate> clickSubscribers = new List<WeakDelegate>();

  public event EventHandler Click {
    add {
      clickSubscribers.Add(new WeakDelegate {
        Target = new WeakReference(value.Target),
        Method = value.Method
      });
    }
    remove {
      //...Implementation omitted for brevity
    }
  }
  public void FireClick() {
    List<WeakDelegate> toRemove = new List<WeakDelegate>();
    foreach (WeakDelegate subscriber in clickSubscribers) {
      object target = subscriber.Target.Target;
      if (target == null) {
        toRemove.Add(subscriber);
      } else {
        subscriber.Method.Invoke(target, new object[] { this, EventArgs.Empty });
      }
    }
    clickSubscribers.RemoveAll(toRemove);
  }
}
```

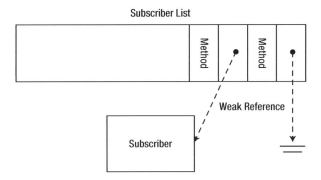

Figure 4-19. *The weak event has a weak reference to every subscriber. If the subscriber is unreachable by the application, the weak event can detect this because the weak reference is nulled out*

Weak references do not track object resurrection by default. To enable resurrection tracking, use the overloaded constructor that accepts a Boolean parameter and pass true to indicate that resurrection should be tracked. Weak references that track resurrection are called *long weak references*; weak references that do not track resurrection are called *short weak references*.

GC HANDLES

Weak references are a special case of *GC handles*. A GC handle is a special low-level value type that can provide several facilities for referencing objects:

- Keeping a standard (strong) reference to an object, preventing it from being collected. This is represented by the GCHandleType.Normal enumeration value.

- Keeping a short weak reference to an object. This is represented by the GCHandleType.Weak enumeration value.

- Keeping a long weak reference to an object. This is represented by the GCHandleType.WeakTrackResurrection enumeration value.

- Keeping a reference to an object, pinning it so that it cannot move in memory and obtaining its address if necessary. This is represented by the GCHandleType.Pinned enumeration value.

There is rarely any need to use GC handles directly, but they often come up in profiling results as another type of root that can retain managed objects.

Interacting with the Garbage Collector

So far, we viewed our application as a passive participant in the GC story. We delved into the implementation of the garbage collector, and reviewed significant optimizations, all performed automatically and requiring little or no involvement from our part. In this section, we will examine the available means of active interaction with the garbage collector in order to tune the performance of our applications and receive diagnostic information that is unavailable otherwise.

The System.GC Class

The System.GC class is the primary point of interaction with the .NET garbage collector from managed code. It contains a set of methods that control the garbage collector's behavior and obtain diagnostic information regarding its work so far.

Diagnostic Methods

The diagnostic methods of the System.GC class provide information on the garbage collector's work. They are meant for use in diagnostic or debugging scenarios; do not rely on them to make decisions at normal run time. The information set returned by some of these diagnostic methods is available as performance counters, under the *.NET CLR Memory* performance category.

- The GC.CollectionCount method returns the number of garbage collections of the specified generation since application startup. It can be used to determine whether a collection of the specified generation occurred between two points in time.

- The GC.GetTotalMemory method returns the total memory consumed by the garbage collected heap, in bytes. If its Boolean parameter is true, a full garbage collection is performed before returning the result, to ensure that only memory that could not be reclaimed is accounted for.

- The GC.GetGeneration method returns the generation to which a specific object belongs. Note that under the current CLR implementation, objects are not guaranteed to be promoted between generations when a garbage collection occurs.

Notifications

Introduced in .NET 3.5 SP1, the GC notifications API provides applications an opportunity to learn in advance that a full garbage collection is imminent. The API is available only when using non-concurrent GC, and is aimed at applications that have long GC pause times and want to redistribute work or notify their execution environment when they sense a pause approaching.

First, an application interested in GC notifications calls the GC.RegisterForFullGCNotification method, and passes to it two thresholds (numbers between 1 and 99). These thresholds indicate how early the application wants the notification based on thresholds in generation 2 and the large object heap. In a nutshell, larger thresholds make sure that you receive a notification but the actual collection may be delayed for a while, whereas smaller thresholds risk not receiving a notification at all because the collection was too close to the notification trigger.

Next, the application uses the GC.WaitForFullGCApproach method to synchronously block until the notification occurs, makes all the preparations for GC, and then calls GC.WaitForFullGCComplete to synchronously block until the GC completes. Because these APIs are synchronous, you might want to call them on a background thread and raise events to your main processing code, like so:

```
public class GCWatcher {
  private Thread watcherThread;

  public event EventHandler GCApproaches;
  public event EventHandler GCComplete;

  public void Watch() {
    GC.RegisterForFullGCNotification(50, 50);
    watcherThread = new Thread(() => {
      while (true) {
        GCNotificationStatus status = GC.WaitForFullGCApproach();
        //Omitted error handling code here
        if (GCApproaches != null) {
          GCApproaches(this, EventArgs.Empty);
        }
        status = GC.WaitForFullGCComplete();
        //Omitted error handling code here
        if (GCComplete != null) {
          GCComplete(this, EventArgs.Empty);
        }
      }
    });
    watcherThread.IsBackground = true;
    watcherThread.Start();
  }

  public void Cancel() {
    GC.CancelFullGCNotification();
    watcherThread.Join();
  }
}
```

For more information and a complete example using the GC notifications API to redistribute server load, consult the MSDN documentation at http://msdn.microsoft.com/en-us/library/cc713687.aspx.

Control Methods

The GC.Collect method instructs the garbage collector to perform a garbage collection of the specified generation (including all younger generations). Starting with .NET 3.5 (and also available in .NET 2.0 SP1 and .NET 3.0 SP1), the GC.Collect method is overloaded with a parameter of the enumerated type GCCollectionMode. This enumeration has the following possible values:

- When using GCCollectionMode.Forced, the garbage collector performs the collection immediately and synchronously with the current thread. When the method returns, it is guaranteed that the garbage collection completed.

- When using GCCollectionMode.Optimized, the garbage collector can decide whether a collection will be productive at this point in time or not. The ultimate decision whether a collection will be performed is delayed to run time, and is not guaranteed by the implementation. This the recommended mode to use if you are trying to assist the garbage collector by providing hints as to when a collection might be beneficial.

In diagnostic scenarios, or when you want to force a full garbage collection to reclaim specific objects that you are interested in, you should use GCCollectionMode.Forced instead.

- As of CLR 4.5, using GCCollectionMode.Default is equivalent to GCCollectionMode. Forced.

Forcing the garbage collector to perform a collection is not a common task. The optimizations described in this chapter are largely based on dynamic tuning and heuristics that have been thoroughly tested for various application scenarios. It is not recommended to force a garbage collection or even to recommend a garbage collection (using GCCollectionMode.Optimized) in non-exceptional circumstances. With that said, we can outline several scenarios that warrant the careful consideration of forcing a garbage collection:

- When an infrequent repeatable action that required a large amount of long-lived memory completes, this memory becomes eligible for garbage collection. If the application does not cause full garbage collections frequently, this memory might remain in generation 2 (or in the LOH) for a long time before being reclaimed. In this scenario, it makes sense to force a garbage collection when the memory is known to be unreferenced so that it does not occupy unnecessary space in the working set or in the page file.

- When using the low latency GC mode, it is advisable to force garbage collections at safe points when it is known that the time-sensitive work has idled and can afford pausing to perform a collection. Staying in low latency mode without performing a collection for a long period of time might result in out of memory conditions. Generally speaking, if the application is sensitive to garbage collection timing, it's reasonable to force a collection during idle times to influence a biased redistribution of garbage collection overhead into the idle run time regions.

- When non-deterministic finalization is used to reclaim unmanaged resources, it is often desirable to block until all such resources have been reclaimed. This can be accomplished by following a GC.Collect call with a GC.WaitForPendingFinalizers call. Deterministic finalization is always preferred in these scenarios, but often we do not have control over the internal classes that actually perform the finalization work.

▓ **Note** As of .NET 4.5, the GC.Collect method has an additional overload with a trailing Boolean parameter: GC.Collect(int generation, GCCollectionMode mode, **bool blocking**). This parameter controls whether a blocking garbage collection is required (the default) or whether the request can be satisfied asynchronously by launching a background garbage collection.

The other control methods are the following:

- The GC.AddMemoryPressure and GC.RemoveMemoryPressure methods can be used to notify the garbage collector about unmanaged memory allocations taking place in the current process. Adding memory pressure indicates to the garbage collector that the specified amount of unmanaged memory has been allocated. The garbage collector may use this information for tuning the aggressiveness and frequency of garbage collections, or ignore it altogether. When the unmanaged allocation is known to be reclaimed, notify the garbage collector that the memory pressure can be removed.

- The GC.WaitForPendingFinalizers method blocks the current thread until all finalizers have finished executing. This method should be used with caution because it might introduce deadlocks; for example, if the main thread blocks inside `GC.WaitForPendingFinalizers` while holding some lock, and one of the active finalizers requires that same lock, a deadlock occurs. Because `GC.WaitForPendingFinalizers` does not accept a timeout parameter, the locking code inside the finalizer must use timeouts for graceful error handling.

- The `GC.SuppressFinalize` and `GC.ReRegisterForFinalize` methods are used in conjunction with finalization and resurrection features. They are discussed in the finalization section of this chapter.

- Starting with .NET 3.5 (and also available in .NET 2.0 SP1 and .NET 3.0 SP1), another interface to the garbage collector is provided by the `GCSettings` class that was discussed earlier, for controlling the GC flavor and switching to low latency GC mode.

For other methods and properties of the `System.GC` class that were not mentioned in this section, refer to the MSDN documentation.

Interacting with the GC using CLR Hosting

In the preceding section, we have examined the diagnostic and control methods available for interacting with the garbage collector from managed code. However, the degree of control offered by these methods leaves much to be desired; additionally, there is no notification mechanism available to let the application know that a garbage collection occurs.

These deficiencies cannot be addressed by managed code alone, and require *CLR hosting* to further control the interaction with the garbage collector. CLR hosting offers multiple mechanisms for controlling .NET memory management:

- The `IHostMemoryManager` interface and its associated `IHostMalloc` interface provide callbacks which the CLR uses to allocate virtual memory for GC segments, to receive a notification when memory is low, to perform non-GC memory allocations (e.g. for JITted code) and to estimate the available amount of memory. For example, this interface can be used to ensure that all CLR memory allocation requests are satisfied from physical memory that cannot be paged out to disk. This is the essence of the Non-Paged CLR Host open source project (http://nonpagedclrhost.codeplex.com/, 2008).

- The `ICLRGCManager` interface provides methods to control the garbage collector and obtain statistics regarding its operation. It can be used to initiate a garbage collection from the host code, to retrieve statistics (that are also available as performance counters under the *.NET CLR Memory* performance category) and to initialize GC startup limits including the GC segment size and the maximum size of generation 0.

- The `IHostGCManager` interface provides methods to receive a notification when a garbage collection is starting or ending, and when a thread is suspended so that a garbage collection can proceed.

Below is a small code extract from the Non-Paged CLR Host open source project, which shows how the CLR host customizes segment allocations requested by the CLR and makes sure any committed pages are locked into physical memory:

```
HRESULT __stdcall HostControl::VirtualAlloc(
  void* pAddress, SIZE_T dwSize, DWORD flAllocationType,
  DWORD flProtect, EMemoryCriticalLevel dwCriticalLevel, void** ppMem) {
```

```
  *ppMem = VirtualAlloc(pAddress, dwSize, flAllocationType, flProtect);
  if (*ppMem == NULL) {
    return E_OUTOFMEMORY;
  }
  if (flAllocationType & MEM_COMMIT) {
    VirtualLock(*ppMem, dwSize);
    return S_OK;
  }
}

HRESULT __stdcall HostControl::VirtualFree(
  LPVOID lpAddress, SIZE_T dwSize, DWORD dwFreeType) {

  VirtualUnlock(lpAddress, dwSize);
  if (FALSE == VirtualFree(lpAddress, dwSize, dwFreeType)) {
    return E_FAIL;
  }
  return S_OK;
}
```

For information about additional GC-related CLR hosting interfaces, including IGCHost, IGCHostControl and IGCThreadControl, refer to the MSDN documentation.

GC Triggers

We have seen several reasons for the GC to fire, but never listed them all in one place. Below are the triggers used by the CLR to determine whether it's necessary to perform a GC, listed in order of likelihood:

1. Generation 0 fills. This happens all the time as the application allocates new objects in the small object heap.

2. The large object heap reaches a threshold. This happens as the application allocates large objects.

3. The application calls GC.Collect explicitly.

4. The operating system reports that it is low on memory. The CLR uses the memory resource notification Win32 APIs to monitor system memory utilization and be a good citizen in case resources are running low for the entire system.

5. An AppDomain is unloaded.

6. The process (or the CLR) is shutting down. This is a degenerate garbage collection—nothing is considered a root, objects are not promoted, and the heap is not compacted. The primary reason for this collection is to run finalizers.

Garbage Collection Performance Best Practices

In this section, we will provide a summary of best practices for interacting with the .NET garbage collector. We will examine multiple scenarios which demonstrate aspects of these best practices, and point out pitfalls that must be avoided.

Generational Model

We reviewed the generational model as the enabler of two significant performance optimizations to the naïve GC model discussed previously. The generational heap partitions managed objects by their life expectancy, enabling the GC to frequently collect objects that are short-lived and have high collection likelihood. Additionally, the separate large object heap solves the problem of copying large objects around by employing a free list management strategy for reclaimed large memory blocks.

We can now summarize the best practices for interacting with the generational model, and then review a few examples.

- Temporary objects should be short-lived. The greatest risk is temporary objects that creep into generation 2, because this causes frequent full collections.

- Large objects should be long-lived or pooled. A LOH collection is equivalent to a full collection.

- References between generations should be kept to a minimum.

The following case studies represent the risks of the mid-life crisis phenomenon. In a monitoring UI application implemented by one of our customers, 20,000 log records were constantly displayed on the application's main screen. Each individual record contained a severity level, a brief description message and additional (potentially large) contextual information. These 20,000 records were continuously replaced as new log records would flow into the system.

Because of the large amount of log records on display, most log records would survive two garbage collections and reach generation 2. However, the log records are not long-lived objects, and shortly afterwards they are replaced by new records which in turn creep into generation 2, exhibiting the mid-life crisis phenomenon. The net effect was that the application performed hundreds of full garbage collections per minute, spending nearly 50% of its time in GC code.

After an initial analysis phase, we had reached the conclusion that displaying 20,000 log records in the UI is unnecessary. We trimmed the display to show the 1,000 most recent records, and implemented pooling to reuse and reinitialize existing record objects instead of creating new ones. These measures minimized the memory footprint of the application, but, even more significantly, minimized the time in GC to 0.1%, with a full collection occurring only once in a few minutes.

Another example of mid-life crisis is a scenario encountered by one of our web servers. The web server system is partitioned to a set of front-end servers which receive web requests. These front-end servers use synchronous web service calls to a set of back-end servers in order to process the individual requests.

In the QA lab environment, the web service call between the front-end and back-end layers would return within several milliseconds. This caused the HTTP request to be dismissed shortly, so the request object and its associated object graph were truly short-lived.

In the production environment, the web service call would often take longer to execute, due to network conditions, back-end server load and other factors. The request still returned to the client within a fraction of a second, which was not worth optimizing because a human being cannot observe the difference. However, with many requests flowing into the system each second, the lifetime of each request object and its associated object graph was extended such that these objects survived multiple garbage collections and creep into generation 2.

It is important to observe that the server's ability to process requests was not harmed by the fact requests lived slightly longer: the memory load was still acceptable and the clients didn't feel a difference because the requests were still returned within a fraction of a second. However, the server's ability to scale was significantly harmed, because the front-end application spent 70% of its time in GC code.

Resolving this scenario requires switching to asynchronous web service calls or releasing most objects associated with the request as eagerly as possible (before performing the synchronous service call). A combination of the two brought time in GC down to 3%, improving the site's ability to scale by a factor of 3!

Finally, consider a design scenario for a simple 2D pixel-based graphics rendering system. In this kind of system, a drawing surface is a long-lived entity which constantly repaints itself by placing and replacing short-lived pixels of varying color and opacity.

If these pixels were represented by a reference type, then not only would we double or triple the memory footprint of the application; we would also create references between generations and create a gigantic object graph of all the pixels. The only practical approach is using value types to represent pixels, which can bring down the memory footprint by a factor of 2 or 3, and the time spent in GC by several orders of magnitude.

Pinning

We have previously discussed pinning as a correctness measure that must be employed to ensure that the address of a managed object can safely be passed to unmanaged code. Pinning an object keeps it in the same location in memory, thereby reducing the garbage collector's inherent ability to defragment the heap by sweeping objects around.

With this in mind, we can summarize the best practices for using pinning in applications that require it.

- Pin objects for the shortest possible time. Pinning is cheap if no garbage collection occurs while the object is pinned. If calling unmanaged code that requires a pinned object for an indefinite amount of time (such as an asynchronous call), consider copying or unmanaged memory allocation instead of pinning a managed object.

- Pin a few large buffers instead of many small ones, even if it means you have to manage the small buffer sizes yourself. Large objects do not move in memory, thus minimizing the fragmentation cost of pinning.

- Pin and re-use old objects that have been allocated in the application's startup path instead of allocating new buffers for pinning. Old objects rarely move, thus minimizing the fragmentation cost of pinning.

- Consider allocating unmanaged memory if the application relies heavily on pinning. Unmanaged memory can be directly manipulated by unmanaged code without pinning or incurring any garbage collection cost. Using unsafe code (C# pointers) it is possible to conveniently manipulate unmanaged memory blocks from managed code without copying the data to managed data structures. Allocating unmanaged memory from managed code is typically performed using the `System.Runtime.InteropServices.Marshal` class. (See Chapter 8 for more details.)

Finalization

The spirit of the finalization section makes it quite clear that the automatic non-deterministic finalization feature provided by .NET leaves much to be desired. The best piece of advice with regard to finalization is to make it deterministic whenever possible, and delegate the exceptional cases to the non-deterministic finalizer.

The following practices summarize the proper way to address finalization in your application:

- Prefer deterministic finalization and implement `IDisposable` to ensure that clients know what to expect from your class. Use `GC.SuppressFinalize` within your `Dispose` implementation to ensure that the finalizer isn't called if it isn't necessary.

- Provide a finalizer and use `Debug.Assert` or a logging statement to ensure that clients are aware of the fact they didn't use your class properly.

- When implementing a complex object, wrap the finalizable resource in a separate class (the `System.Runtime.InteropServices.SafeHandle` type is a canonical example). This will ensure that only this small type wrapping the unmanaged resource will survive an extra garbage collection, and the rest of your object can be destroyed when the object is no longer referenced.

Miscellaneous Tips and Best Practices

In this section, we will briefly examine assorted best practices and performance tips that do not belong to any other major section discussed in this chapter.

Value Types

When possible, prefer value types to reference types. We have examined the various traits of value types and reference types from a general perspective in Chapter 3. Additionally, value types have several characteristics that affect garbage collection cost in the application:

- Value types have the most negligible allocation cost when used as local stack variables. This allocation is associated with the extension of the stack frame, which is created whenever a method is entered.

- Value types used as local stack variables have no deallocation (garbage collection) cost—they are deallocated automatically when the method returns and its stack frame is destroyed.

- Value types embedded in reference types minimize the cost of both phases of garbage collections: if objects are larger, there are less objects to mark, and if objects are larger, the sweep phase copies more memory at each time, which reduces the overhead of copying many small objects around.

- Value types reduce the application's memory footprint because they occupy less memory. Additionally, when embedded inside a reference type, they do not require a reference in order to access them, thereby eliminating the need to store an additional reference. Finally, value types embedded in reference types exhibit locality of access—if the object is paged in and hot in cache, its embedded value type fields are also likely to be paged in and hot in cache.

- Value types reduce references between generations, because fewer references are introduced into the object graph.

Object Graphs

Reducing the size of the object graph directly affects the amount of work the garbage collector has to perform. A simple graph of large objects is faster to mark and sweep than a complex graph of many small objects. We have mentioned a specific scenario of this earlier.

Additionally, introducing fewer local variables of reference types reduces the size of the local root tables generated by the JIT, which improves compilation times and saves a small amount of memory.

Pooling Objects

Object pooling is a mechanism designed to manage memory and resources manually instead of relying on the facilities provided by the execution environment. When object pooling is in effect, allocating a new object means retrieving it from a pool of unused objects, and deallocating an object means returning it to the pool.

Pooling can provide a performance boost if the allocation and deallocation costs (not including initialization and uninitialization) are more expensive than managing the lifetime of the objects manually. For example, pooling large objects instead of allocating and freeing them using the garbage collector might provide a performance improvement, because freeing large objects that are frequently allocated requires a full garbage collection.

▧ **Note** Windows Communication Foundation (WCF) implements pooling of byte arrays used for storing and transmitting messages. The `System.ServiceModel.Channels.BufferManager` abstract class serves as the pool façade, providing the facilities for obtaining an array of bytes from the pool and for returning it to the pool. Two internal implementations of the abstract base operations provide a GC-based allocation and deallocation mechanism side-by-side with a mechanism which manages pool of buffers. The pooled implementation (as of the time of writing) manages multiple pools internally for varying sizes of buffers, and takes the allocating thread into account. A similar technique is used by the Windows Low-Fragmentation Heap, introduced in Windows XP.

Implementing an efficient pool requires taking at least the following factors into consideration:

- Synchronization around the allocation and deallocation operations must be kept to a minimum. For example, a lock-free (wait-free) data structure could be used to implement the pool (see Chapter 6 for a treatment of lock-free synchronization).

- The pool should not be allowed to grow indefinitely, implying that under certain circumstances objects will be returned to the mercy of the garbage collector.

- The pool should not be exhausted frequently, implying that a growth heuristic is needed to balance the pool size based on the frequency and amount of allocation requests.

Most pooling implementations will also benefit from implementing a least recently used (LRU) mechanism for retrieving objects from the pool, because the least recently used object is likely to be paged in and hot in CPU cache.

Implementing pooling in .NET requires hooking the allocation and deallocation requests for instances of the pooled type. There is no way to hook the allocation directly (the new operator cannot be overloaded), but an alternative API such as `Pool.GetInstance` can be used. Returning an object to the pool is best implemented using the Dispose pattern, with finalization as a backup.

An extremely simplified skeleton of a .NET pool implementation and a matching poolable object base is shown in the following code:

```
public class Pool<T> {
  private ConcurrentBag<T> pool = new ConcurrentBag<T>();
  private Func<T> objectFactory;
```

```
  public Pool(Func<T> factory) {
    objectFactory = factory;
  }
  public T GetInstance() {
    T result;
    if (!pool.TryTake(out result)) {
      result = objectFactory();
    }
    return result;
  }
  public void ReturnToPool(T instance) {
    pool.Add(instance);
  }
}

public class PoolableObjectBase<T> : IDisposable {
  private static Pool<T> pool = new Pool<T>();

  public void Dispose() {
    pool.ReturnToPool(this);
  }
  ~PoolableObjectBase() {
    GC.ReRegisterForFinalize(this);
    pool.ReturnToPool(this);
  }
}

public class MyPoolableObjectExample : PoolableObjectBase<MyPoolableObjectExample> {
  ...
}
```

Paging and Allocating Unmanaged Memory

The .NET garbage collector automatically reclaims unused memory. Therefore, by definition, it cannot provide a perfect solution for every memory management need that may arise in real-world applications.

In previous sections, we examined numerous scenarios in which the garbage collector behaves poorly and must be tuned to provide adequate performance. An additional example that can bring the application down to its knees involves using the garbage collector where physical memory is insufficient to contain all objects.

Consider an application that runs on a machine with 8GB of physical memory (RAM). Such machines are soon to become extinct, but the scenario easily scales to any amount of physical memory, as long as the application is capable of addressing it (on a 64-bit system, this is a lot of memory). The application allocates 12GB of memory, of which at most 8GB will reside in the working set (physical memory) and at least 4GB will be paged out to disk. The Windows working set manager will ensure that pages containing objects frequently accessed by the application will remain in physical memory, and pages containing objects rarely accessed by the application will be paged out to disk.

During normal operation, the application might not exhibit paging at all because it very rarely accesses the paged-out objects. However, when a full garbage collection occurs, the GC must traverse every reachable object to construct the graph in the mark phase. Traversing every reachable object means performing 4GB of reads from disk to access them. Because physical memory is full, this also implies that 4GB of writes to disk must be performed to free physical memory for the paged-out objects. Finally, after the garbage collection completes, the application will attempt accessing its frequently used objects, which might have been paged out to disk, inducing additional page faults.

Typical hard drives, at the time of writing, provide transfer rates of approximately 150MB/s for sequential reads and writes (even fast solid-state drivers don't exceed this by more than a factor of 2). Therefore, performing 8GB of transfers while paging in from and paging out to disk might take approximately 55 seconds. During this time, the application is waiting for the GC to complete (unless it is using concurrent GC); adding more processors (i.e. using server GC) would not help because the disk is the bottleneck. Other applications on the system will suffer a substantial decrease in performance because the physical disk will be saturated by paging requests.

The only way to address this scenario is by allocating unmanaged memory to store objects that are likely to be paged out to disk. Unmanaged memory is not subject to garbage collection, and will be accessed only when the application needs it.

Another example that has to do with controlling paging and working set management is locking pages into physical memory. Windows applications have a documented interface to the system requesting that specific regions of memory are not paged out to disk (disregarding exceptional circumstances). This mechanism can't be used directly in conjunction with the .NET garbage collector, because a managed application does not have direct control over the virtual memory allocations performed by the CLR. However, a custom CLR host can lock pages into memory as part of the virtual memory allocation request arriving from the CLR.

Static Code Analysis (FxCop) Rules

Static code analysis (FxCop) for Visual Studio has a set of rules targeting common performance and correctness problems related to garbage collection. We recommend using these rules because they often catch bugs during the coding phase, which are cheapest to identify and fix. For more information on managed code analysis with or without Visual Studio, consult the MSDN online documentation.

The GC-related rules that shipped with Visual Studio 11 are:

- Design Rules—*CA1001*—Types that own disposable fields should be disposable. This rule ensures deterministic finalization of type members by their aggregating type.

- Design Rules—*CA1049*—Types that own native resources should be disposable. This rule ensures that types providing access to native resources (such as `System.Runtime.InteropServices.HandleRef`) implement the Dispose pattern correctly.

- Design Rules—*CA1063*—Implement `IDisposable` correctly. This rule ensures that the Dispose pattern is correctly implemented by disposable types.

- Performance Rules—*CA1821*—Remove empty finalizers. This rule ensures that types do not have empty finalizers, which degrade performance and effect mid-life crisis.

- Reliability Rules—CA2000—Dispose objects before losing scope. This rule ensures that all local variables of an `IDisposable` type are disposed before they disappear out of scope.

- Reliability Rules—*CA2006*—Use `SafeHandle` to encapsulate native resources. This rule ensures that when possible, the `SafeHandle` class or one of its derived classes is used instead of a direct handle (such as `System.IntPtr`) to an unmanaged resource.

- Usage Rules—*CA1816*—Call `GC.SuppressFinalize` correctly. This rule ensures that disposable types call suppress finalization within their finalizer, and do not suppress finalization for unrelated objects.

- Usage Rules—*CA2213*—Disposable fields should be disposed. This rule ensures that types implementing `IDisposable` should in turn call `Dispose` on all their fields that implement `IDisposable`.

- Usage Rules—*CA2215*—Dispose methods should call base class dispose. This rule ensures that the Dispose pattern is implemented correctly by invoking the base class' Dispose method if it is also IDisposable.

- Usage Rules—*CA2216*—Disposable types should declare finalizer. This rule ensures that disposable types provide a finalizer as a backup for the scenario when the class user neglects to deterministically finalize the object.

Summary

Through the course of this chapter, we reviewed the motivation and implementation of the .NET garbage collector, the entity responsible for automatically reclaiming unused memory. We examined alternatives to tracing garbage collection, including reference counting garbage collection and manual free list management.

At the heart of the .NET garbage collector lie the following coordinating concepts, which we examined in detail:

- *Roots* provide the starting point for constructing a graph of all reachable objects.

- *Mark* is the stage at which the garbage collector constructs a graph of all reachable objects and marks them as used. The mark phase can be performed concurrently with application thread execution.

- *Sweep* is the stage at which the garbage collector shifts reachable objects around and updates references to these objects. The sweep phase requires stopping all application threads before proceeding.

- *Pinning* is a mechanism which locks an object in place so that the garbage collector can't move it. Used in conjunction with unmanaged code requiring a pointer to a managed object, and can cause fragmentation.

- *GC flavors* provide static tuning for the behavior of the garbage collector in a specific application to better suit its memory allocation and deallocation patterns.

- *The generational model* describes the life expectancy of an object based on its current age. Younger objects are expected to die fast; old objects are expected to live longer.

- *Generations* are conceptual regions of memory that partition objects by their life expectancy. Generations facilitate frequently performing cheap partial collections with higher collection likelihood, and rarely performing full collections which are expensive and less efficient.

- *Large object heap* is an area of memory reserved for large objects. The LOH can become fragmented, but objects do not move around, thereby reducing the cost of the sweep phase.

- *Segments* are regions of virtual memory allocated by the CLR. Virtual memory can become fragmented because segment size is fixed.

- *Finalization* is a backup mechanism for automatically releasing unmanaged resources in a non-deterministic fashion. Prefer deterministic finalization to automatic finalization whenever possible, but offer clients both alternatives.

The common pitfalls associated with garbage collection are often related to the virtues of its most powerful optimizations:

- The generational model provides performance benefits for well-behaved applications, but can exhibit the mid-life crisis phenomenon which direly affects performance.

- Pinning is a necessity whenever managed objects are passed by reference to unmanaged code, but can introduce internal fragmentation into the GC heap, including the lower generations.

- Segments ensure that virtual memory is allocated in large chunks, but can exhibit external fragmentation of virtual memory space.

- Automatic finalization provides convenient disposal of unmanaged resources, but is associated with a high performance cost and often leads to mid-life crisis, high-pressure memory leaks and race conditions.

The following is a list of some of the best practices for getting the most of the .NET garbage collector:

- Allocate temporary objects so that they die fast, but keep old objects alive for the entire lifetime of your application.

- Pin large arrays at application initialization, and break them into small buffers as needed.

- Manage memory using pooling or unmanaged allocation where the GC fails.

- Implement deterministic finalization and rely on automatic finalization as a backup strategy only.

- Tune your application using GC flavors to find which one works best on various types of hardware and software configurations.

Some of the tools that can be used to diagnose memory-related issues and to examine the behavior of your application from the memory management perspective are the following:

- *CLR Profiler* can be used to diagnose internal fragmentation, determine the heavy memory allocation paths in an application, see which objects are reclaimed at each garbage collection and obtain general statistics on the size and age of retained objects.

- *SOS.DLL* can be used to diagnose memory leaks, analyze external and internal fragmentation, obtain garbage collection timing, list the objects in the managed heap, inspect the finalization queue and view the status of the GC threads and the finalizer thread.

- *CLR performance counters* can be used to obtain general statistics on garbage collection, including the size of each generation, the allocation rate, finalization information, pinned object count and more.

- *CLR hosting* can be used as a diagnostic utility to analyze segment allocations, garbage collection frequencies, threads causing garbage collections and non-GC related memory allocation requests originating at the CLR.

Armed by the theory of garbage collection, the subtleties of all related mechanisms, common pitfalls and best performance practices, and diagnostic tools and scenarios, you are now ready to begin the quest to optimize memory management in your applications and to design them with a proper memory management strategy.

CHAPTER 5

Collections and Generics

There is scarcely even a code sample that doesn't use a collection such as a List<T> or a Dictionary<K,V>. Large applications may have hundreds of thousands of collection instances in concurrent use. Selecting the right collection type for your needs — or trying to do better by writing your own — can provide significant performance benefits to many applications. Because as of .NET 2.0, collections are intimately linked with the CLR implementation of generic types, we begin our discussion with generics.

Generics

Often enough the need arises to create a class or method that can work equally well with any data type. Polymorphism and inheritance can help only to a certain extent; a method that requires complete genericity of its parameters is forced to work with System.Object, which leads to the two primary problems of generic programming in .NET prior to .NET 2.0:

- *Type safety*: how to verify operations on generic data types at compile-time and explicitly prohibit anything that may fail at runtime?

- *No boxing*: how to avoid boxing value types when the method's parameters are System. Object references?

These are no small problems. To see why, consider the implementation of one of the simplest collections in .NET 1.1, the ArrayList. The following is a trivialized implementation that nonetheless exhibits the problems alluded above:

```
public class ArrayList : IEnumerable, ICollection, IList, ... {
  private object[] items;
  private int size;
  public ArrayList(int initialCapacity) {
    items = new object[initialCapacity];
  }
  public void Add(object item) {
    if (size < items.Length - 1) {
      items[size] = item;
      ++size;
    } else {
      //Allocate a larger array, copy the elements, then place 'item' in it
    }
  }
  public object this[int index] {
    get {
```

```
      if (index < 0 || index >= size) throw IndexOutOfBoundsException(index);
      return items[index];
    }
    set {
      if (index < 0 || index >= size) throw IndexOutOfBoundsException(index);
      items[index] = value;
    }
  }
  //Many more methods omitted for brevity
}
```

We have highlighted throughout the code all the occurrences of System.Object, which is the "generic" type on which the collection is based. Although this may appear to be a perfectly valid solution, actual usage is not quite so flawless:

```
ArrayList employees = new ArrayList(7);
employees.Add(new Employee("Kate"));
employees.Add(new Employee("Mike"));
Employee first = (Employee)employees[0];
```

This ugly downcast to Employee is required because the ArrayList does not retain any information about the type of elements in it. Furthermore, it does not constrain objects inserted into it to have any common traits. Consider:

```
employees.Add(42);                        //Compiles and works at runtime!
Employee third = (Employee)employees[2]; //Compiles and throws an exception at runtime...
```

Indeed, the number 42 does not belong in a collection of employees, but nowhere did we specify that the ArrayList is restricted to instances of a particular type. Although it is possible to create an ArrayList implementation that restricts its items to a particular type, this would still be a costly runtime operation and a statement like employees.Add(42) would not fail to compile.

This is the problem of *type safety*; "generic" collections based on System.Object cannot guarantee compile-time type safety and defer all checks (if any) to runtime. However, this could be the least of our concerns from a *performance* viewpoint — but it turns out that there is a serious performance problem where value types are involved. Examine the following code, which uses the Point2D struct from Chapter 3 (a simple value type with X and Y integer coordinates):

```
ArrayList line = new ArrayList(1000000);
for (int i = 0; i < 1000000; ++i) {
  line.Add(new Point2D(i, i));
}
```

Every instance of Point2D inserted to the ArrayList is boxed, because its Add method accepts a reference type parameter (System.Object). This incurs the cost of 1,000,000 heap allocations for boxed Point2D objects. As we have seen in Chapter 3, on a 32-bit heap 1,000,000 boxed Point2D objects would occupy 16,000,000 bytes of memory (compared to 8,000,000 bytes as plain value types). Additionally, the items reference array inside the ArrayList would have at least 1,000,000 references, which amounts to another 4,000,000 bytes — a total of 20,000,000 bytes (see Figure 5-1) where 8,000,000 would suffice. Indeed, this is the exact same problem which led us to abandon the idea of making Point2D a reference type; ArrayList forces upon us a collection that works well only with reference types!

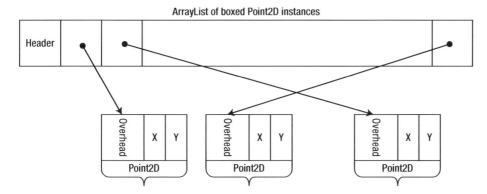

Figure 5-1. *An ArrayList that contains boxed Point2D objects stores references which occupy extra memory and forces the Point2D objects to be boxed on the heap, which adds overhead to them as well*

Is there any room for improvement? Indeed, we could write a specialized collection for two-dimensional points, as follows (although we would also have to come up with specialized IEnumerable, ICollection, and IList interfaces for points...). It is exactly identical to the "generic" ArrayList, but has Point2D wherever we previously had object:

```
public class Point2DArrayList : IPoint2DEnumerable, IPoint2DCollection, IPoint2DList, ... {
  private Point2D[] items;
  private int size;
  public ArrayList(int initialCapacity) {
    items = new Point2D[initialCapacity];
  }
  public void Add(Point2D item) {
    if (size < items.Length - 1) {
      items[size] = item;
      ++size;
    } else {
      //Allocate a larger array, copy the elements, then place 'item' in it
    }
  }
  public Point2D this[int index] {
    get {
      if (index < 0 || index >= size) throw IndexOutOfBoundsException(index);
      return items[index];
    }
    set {
      if (index < 0 || index >= size) throw IndexOutOfBoundsException(index);
      items[index] = value;
    }
  }
  //Many more methods omitted for brevity
}
```

A similar specialized collection for Employee objects would address the type safety problem we have considered earlier. Unfortunately, it is hardly practical to develop a specialized collection for every data type. This is precisely the role of the language compiler as of .NET 2.0 — to allow generic data types in classes and methods while achieving type safety and doing away with boxing.

.NET Generics

Generic classes and methods allow *real* generic code, which does not fall back to System.Object on the one hand and does not require specialization for each data type on the other hand. The following is a sketch of a generic type, List<T>, which replaces our previous ArrayList experiment and addresses both the type safety and boxing concerns:

```
public class List<T> : IEnumerable<T>, ICollection<T>, IList<T>, ... {
  private T[] items;
  private int size;
  public List(int initialCapacity) {
    items = new T[initialCapacity];
  }
  public void Add(T item) {
    if (size < items.Length - 1) {
      items[size] = item;
      ++size;
    } else {
      //Allocate a larger array, copy the elements, then place 'item' in it
    }
  }
  public T this[int index] {
    get {
      if (index < 0 || index >= size) throw IndexOutOfBoundsException(index);
      return items[index];
    }
    set {
      if (index < 0 || index >= size) throw IndexOutOfBoundsException(index);
      items[index] = value;
    }
  }
  //Many more methods omitted for brevity
}
```

■ **Note** If you are not familiar at all with the syntax of C# generics, Jon Skeet's "C# in Depth" (Manning, 2010) is a good textbook. Through the rest of this chapter we assume you have written a generic class or at least consumed generic classes, such as the .NET Framework's collections.

If you have ever written a generic class or method, you know how easy it is to convert pseudo-generic code based on System.Object instances to truly generic code, with one or more *generic type parameters*. It is also exceptionally easy to use generic classes and methods by substituting *generic type arguments* where necessary:

```
List<Employee> employees = new List<Employee>(7);
employees.Add(new Employee("Kate"));
Employee first = employees[0];        //No downcast required, completely type-safe
employees.Add(42);                    //Does not compile!

List<Point2D> line = new List<Point2D>(1000000);
for (int i = 0; i < 1000000; ++i) {
  line.Add(new Point2D(i, i));        //No boxing, no references stored
}
```

Almost magically, the generic collection is type safe (in that it does not allow inappropriate elements to be stored in it) and requires no boxing for value types. Even the internal storage — the items array — adapts itself accordingly to the generic type argument: when T is Point2D, the items array is a Point2D[], which stores *values* and not references. We will unfold some of this magic later, but for now we have an effective language-level solution for the basic problems of generic programming.

This solution alone appears to be insufficient when we require some additional capabilities from the generic parameters. Consider a method that performs a binary search in a sorted array. A completely generic version of it would not be capable of doing the search, because System.Object is not equipped with any comparison-related facilities:

```
public static int BinarySearch<T>(T[] array, T element) {
  //At some point in the algorithm, we need to compare:
  if (array[x] < array[y]) {
    ...
  }
}
```

System.Object does not have a static operator <, which is why this method simply fails to compile! Indeed, we have to prove to the compiler that for every generic type argument we provide to the method, it will be able to resolve all method calls (including operators) on it. This is where generic constraints enter the picture.

Generic Constraints

Generic constraints indicate to the compiler that only *some* types are allowed as generic type arguments when using a generic type. There are five types of constraints:

```
//T must implement an interface:
public int Format(T instance) where T : IFormattable {
  return instance.ToString("N", CultureInfo.CurrentUICulture);
  //OK, T must have IFormattable.ToString(string, IFormatProvider)
}

//T must derive from a base class:
public void Display<T>(T widget) where T : Widget {
  widget.Display(0, 0);
  //OK, T derives from Widget which has the Display(int, int) method
}

//T must have a parameterless constructor:
public T Create<T>() where T : new() {
  return new T();
  //OK, T has a parameterless constructor
  //The C# compiler compiles 'new T()' to a call to Activator.CreateInstance<T>(),
  //which is sub-optimal, but there is no IL equivalent for this constraint
}

//T must be a reference type:
public void ReferencesOnly<T>(T reference) where T : class

//T must be a value type:
public void ValuesOnly<T>(T value) where T : struct
```

If we revisit the binary search example, the interface constraint proves to be very useful (and indeed, it is the most often used kind of constraint). Specifically, we can require T to implement IComparable, and compare array elements using the IComparable.CompareTo method. However, IComparable is not a generic interface, and its CompareTo method accepts a System.Object parameter, incurring a boxing cost for value types. It stands to reason that there should be a generic version of IComparable, IComparable<T>, which serves here perfectly:

```
//From the .NET Framework:
public interface IComparable<T> {
  int CompareTo(T other);
}

public static int BinarySearch<T>(T[] array, T element) where T : IComparable<T> {
  //At some point in the algorithm, we need to compare:
  if (array[x].CompareTo(array[y]) < 0) {
  ...
  }
}
```

This binary search version does not incur boxing when comparing value type instances, works with any type that implements IComparable<T> (including all the built-in primitive types, strings, and many others), and is completely type safe in that it does not require runtime discovery of comparison capabilities.

INTERFACE CONSTRAINTS AND IEQUATABLE<T>

In Chapter 3 we have seen that a critical performance optimization for value types is to override the Equals method and implement the IEquatable<T> interface. Why is this interface so important? Consider the following code:

```
public static void CallEquals<T>(T instance) {
  instance.Equals(instance);
}
```

The Equals call inside the method defers to a virtual call to Object.Equals, which accepts a System.Object parameter and causes boxing on value types. This is the only alternative that the C# compiler considers guaranteed to be present on every T we use. If we want to convince the compiler that T has an Equals method that accepts T, we need to use an explicit constraint:

```
//From the .NET Framework:
public interface IEquatable<T> {
  bool Equals(T other);
}

public static void CallEquals<T>(T instance) where T : IEquatable<T> {
  instance.Equals(instance);
}
```

Finally, you might want to allow callers to use any type as T, but defer to the IEquatable<T> implementation if T provides it, because it does not require boxing and is more efficient. What List<T> does in this regard is fairly interesting. If List<T> required an IEquatable<T> constraint on its generic type parameter, it wouldn't be useful for types that don't implement that interface. Therefore, List<T> does not have an IEquatable<T> constraint. To implement the Contains method (and other methods that require comparing objects for equality), List<T> relies on an *equality comparer*—a concrete implementation of the abstract EqualityComparer<T> class (which, incidentally, implements the IEqualityComparer<T> interface, used directly by some collections, including HashSet<T> and Dictionary<K,V>).

When `List<T>.Contains` needs to invoke `Equals` on two elements of the collection, it uses the `EqualityComparer<T>.Default` static property to retrieve an equality comparer implementation suitable for comparing instances of `T`, and calls its `Equals(T, T)` virtual method. It's the `EqualityComparer<T>.CreateComparer` private static method that creates the appropriate equality comparer the first time it's requested and subsequently caches it in a static field. When `CreateComparer` sees that `T` implements `IEquatable<T>`, it returns an instance of `GenericEqualityComparer<T>`, which has an `IEquatable<T>` constraint and invokes `Equals` through the interface. Otherwise, `CreateComparer` resorts to the `ObjectEqualityComparer<T>` class, which has no constraints on `T` and invokes the `Equals` virtual method provided by `Object`.

This trick employed by `List<T>` for equality checking can be useful for other purposes as well. When a constraint is available, your generic class or method can use a potentially more efficient implementation that does not resort to runtime type checking.

▓ **Tip**   As you see, there are no generic constraints to express mathematical operators, such as addition or multiplication. This means that you can't write a generic method that uses an expression such as a+b on generic parameters. The standard solution for writing generic numeric algorithms is to use a helper struct that implements an `IMath<T>` interface with the required arithmetic operations, and instantiate this struct in the generic method. For more details, see Rüdiger Klaehn's CodeProject article, "Using generics for calculations," available at `http://www.codeproject.com/Articles/8531/Using-generics-for-calculations`).

Having examined most syntactic features of generics in C#, we turn to their runtime implementation. Before we can concern ourselves with this matter, it's paramount to ask whether there *is* a runtime representation of generics — as we will see shortly, C++ templates, a similar mechanism, have no runtime representation to speak of. This question is easily answered if you look at the wonders Reflection can do with generic types *at runtime*:

```
Type openList = typeof(List<>);
Type listOfInt = openList.MakeGenericType(typeof(int));
IEnumerable<int> ints = (IEnumerable<int>)Activator.CreateInstance(listOfInt);

Dictionary<string, int> frequencies = new Dictionary<string, int>();
Type openDictionary = frequencies.GetType().GetGenericTypeDefinition();
Type dictStringToDouble = openDictionary.MakeGenericType(typeof(string), typeof(double));
```

As you see, we can dynamically create generic types from an existing generic type and parameterize an "open" generic type to create an instance of a "closed" generic type. This demonstrates that generics are first-class citizens and have a runtime representation, which we now survey.

Implementation of CLR Generics

The syntactic features of CLR generics are fairly similar to Java generics and even slightly resemble C++ templates. However, it turns out that their internal implementation and the limitations imposed upon programs using them are very different from Java and C++. To understand these differences we should briefly review Java generics and C++ templates.

Java Generics

A generic class in Java can have generic type parameters, and there is even a constraint mechanism quite similar to what .NET has to offer (bounded type parameters and wildcards). For example, here's a first attempt to convert our List<T> to Java:

```java
public class List<E> {
  private E[] items;
  private int size;
  public List(int initialCapacity) {
    items = new E[initialCapacity];
  }
  public void Add(E item) {
    if (size < items.Length - 1) {
      items[size] = item;
      ++size;
    } else {
      //Allocate a larger array, copy the elements, then place 'item' in it
    }
  }
  public E getAt(int index) {
    if (index < 0 || index >= size) throw IndexOutOfBoundsException(index);
    return items[index];
  }
  //Many more methods omitted for brevity
}
```

Unfortunately, this code does not compile. Specifically, the expression new E[initialCapacity] is not legal in Java. The reason has to do with the way Java compiles generic code. The Java compiler removes any mentions of the generic type parameter and replaces them with java.lang.Object, a process called *type erasure*. As a result, there is only one type at runtime — List, the *raw* type — and any information about the generic type argument provided is lost. (To be fair, by using type erasure Java retains binary compatibility with libraries and applications that were created before generics — something that .NET 2.0 does not offer for .NET 1.1 code.)

Not all is lost, though. By using an Object array instead, we can reconcile the compiler and still have a type-safe generic class that works well at compilation time:

```java
public class List<E> {
  private Object[] items;
  private int size;
  public void List(int initialCapacity) {
    items = new Object[initialCapacity];
  }
  //The rest of the code is unmodified
}

List<Employee> employees = new List<Employee>(7);
employees.Add(new Employee("Kate"));
employees.Add(42);  //Does not compile!
```

However, adopting this approach in the CLR voices a concern: what is to become of value types? One of the two reasons for introducing generics was that we wanted to avoid boxing at any cost. Inserting a value type to an array of objects requires boxing and is not acceptable.

C++ Templates

Compared to Java generics, C++ templates may appear enticing. (They are also extremely powerful: you may have heard that the template resolution mechanism in itself is Turing-complete.) The C++ compiler does not perform type erasure — quite the opposite — and there's no need for constraints, because the compiler is happy to compile whatever you throw in its way. Let's start with the list example, and then consider what happens with constraints:

```
template <typename T>
class list {
private:
  T* items;
  int size;
  int capacity;
public:
  list(int initialCapacity) : size(0), capacity(initialCapacity) {
    items = new T[initialCapacity];
  }
  void add(const T& item) {
    if (size < capacity) {
      items[size] = item;
      ++size;
    } else {
      //Allocate a larger array, copy the elements, then place 'item' in it
    }
  }
  const T& operator[](int index) const {
    if (index < 0 || index >= size) throw exception("Index out of bounds");
    return items[index];
  }
  //Many more methods omitted for brevity
};
```

The list template class is completely type-safe: *every* instantiation of the template creates a new class that uses the template definition as a... template. Although this happens under the hood, here is an example of what it *could* look like:

```
//Original C++ code:
list<int> listOfInts(14);

//Expanded by the compiler to:
class __list__int {
private:
  int* items;
  int size;
  int capacity;
public:
  __list__int(int initialCapacity) : size(0), capacity(initialCapacity) {
    items = new int[initialCapacity];
  }
};
__list__int listOfInts(14);
```

Note that the add and `operator[]` methods were not expanded — the calling code did not use them, and the compiler generates only the parts of the template definition that are used for the particular instantiation. Also note that the compiler does not generate *anything* from the template definition; it waits for a specific instantiation before it produces any code.

This is why there is no need for constraints in C++ templates. Returning to our binary search example, the following is a perfectly reasonable implementation:

```
template <typename T>
int BinarySearch(T* array, int size, const T& element) {
  //At some point in the algorithm, we need to compare:
  if (array[x] < array[y]) {
    ...
  }
}
```

There's no need to prove anything to the C++ compiler. After all, the template definition is meaningless; the compiler waits carefully for any instantiations:

```
int numbers[10];
BinarySearch(numbers, 10, 42); //Compiles, int has an operator <
class empty {};
empty empties[10];
BinarySearch(empties, 10, empty()); //Does not compile, empty does not have an operator <
```

Although this design is extremely tempting, C++ templates have unattractive costs and limitations, which are undesirable for CLR generics:

- Because the template expansion occurs at compile-time, there is no way to share template instantiations between different binaries. For example, two DLLs loaded into the same process may have separate compiled versions of list<int>. This consumes a large amount of memory and causes long compilation times, by which C++ is renowned.

- For the same reason, template instantiations in two different binaries are considered incompatible. There is no clean and supported mechanism for exporting template instantiations from DLLs (such as an exported function that returns list<int>).

- There is no way to produce a binary library that contains template definitions. Template definitions exist only in source form, as header files that can be #included into a C++ file.

Generics Internals

After giving ample consideration to the design of Java generics C++ templates, we can understand better the implementation choice for CLR generics. CLR generics are implemented as follows. Generic types — even open ones, like List<> — are first-class runtime citizens. There is a method table and an EEClass (see Chapter 3) for each generic type and a System.Type instance can be produced as well. Generic types can be exported from assemblies and only a single definition of the generic type exists at compile-time. Generic types are not expanded at compile-time, but as we have seen the compiler makes sure that any operation attempted on generic type parameter instances is compatible with the specified generic constraints.

When the CLR needs to create an instance of a closed generic type, such as List<int>, it creates a method table and EEClass based on the open type. As always, the method table contains method pointers, which are compiled on the fly by the JIT compiler. However, there is a crucial optimization here: compiled method bodies on closed generic types that have reference type parameters can be shared. To digest this, let's consider the List<T>.Add method and try to compile it to x86 instructions when T is a reference type:

```
//C# code:
public void Add(T item) {
  if (size < items.Length - 1) {
    items[size] = item;
    ++size;
  } else {
    AllocateAndAddSlow(item);
  }
}

; x86 assembly when T is a reference type
; Assuming that ECX contains 'this' and EDX contains 'item', prologue and epilogue omitted
mov eax, dword ptr [ecx+4]        ; items
mov eax, dword ptr [eax+4]        ; items.Length
dec eax
cmp dword ptr [ecx+8], eax        ; size < items.Length - 1
jge AllocateAndAddSlow
mov eax, dword ptr [ecx+4]
mov ebx, dword ptr [ecx+8]
mov dword ptr [eax+4*ebx+4], edx  ; items[size] = item
inc dword ptr [eax+8]             ; ++size
```

It's clear that the method's code does not depend on T in any way, and will work exactly as well for any reference type. This observation allows the JIT compiler to conserve resources (time and memory) and share the method table pointers for List<T>.Add in all method tables where T is a reference type.

■ **Note**   This idea requires some further refinement, which we will not carry out. For example, if the method's body contained a new T[10] expression, it would require a separate code path for each T, or at least a way of obtaining T at runtime (e.g., through an additional hidden parameter passed to the method). Additionally, we haven't considered how constraints affect the code generation — but you should be convinced by now that invoking interface methods or virtual methods through base classes requires the same code regardless of the type.

The same idea does not work for value types. For example, when T is long, the assignment statement items[size]=item requires a different instruction, because 8 bytes must be copied instead of 4. Even larger value types may even require more than one instruction; and so on.

To demonstrate Figure 5-2 in a simple setting, we can inspect using SOS the method tables of closed generic types that are all realizations of the same open generic type. For example, consider a BasicStack<T> class with only Push and Pop methods, as follows:

```
class BasicStack<T> {
    private T[] items;
    private int topIndex;

    public BasicStack(int capacity = 42) {
        items = new T[capacity];
    }
    public void Push(T item) {
        items[topIndex++] = item;
    }
    public T Pop() {
```

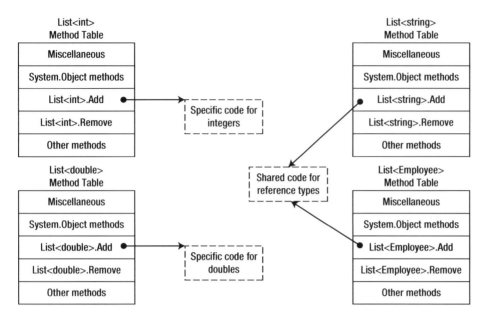

Figure 5-2. *The Add method table entries for reference type realizations of* List<T> *have shared pointers to a single method implementation, whereas the entries for value type realizations have separate versions of the code*

```
        return items[--topIndex];
    }
}
```

The method tables for BasicStack<string>, BasicStack<int[]>, BasicStack<int>, and BasicStack<double> are listed below. Note that the method table entries (i.e. code addresses) for the closed types with a reference type generic type argument are shared, and for the value types are not:

```
0:004> !dumpheap –stat
...
00173b40        1       16 BasicStack`1[[System.Double, mscorlib]]
00173a98        1       16 BasicStack`1[[System.Int32, mscorlib]]
00173a04        1       16 BasicStack`1[[System.Int32[], mscorlib]]
001739b0        1       16 BasicStack`1[[System.String, mscorlib]]
...

0:004> !dumpmt -md 001739b0
EEClass:        001714e0
Module:         00172e7c
Name:           BasicStack`1[[System.String, mscorlib]]
...
MethodDesc Table
   Entry MethodDe  JIT Name
...
00260360 00173924  JIT BasicStack`1[[System.__Canon, mscorlib]].Push(System.__Canon)
00260390 0017392c  JIT BasicStack`1[[System.__Canon, mscorlib]].Pop()

0:004> !dumpmt -md 00173a04
EEClass:        001714e0
Module:         00172e7c
```

```
Name:       BasicStack`1[[System.Int32[], mscorlib]]
...
MethodDesc Table
   Entry MethodDe  JIT Name
...
00260360 00173924  JIT BasicStack`1[[System.__Canon, mscorlib]].Push(System.__Canon)
00260390 0017392c  JIT BasicStack`1[[System.__Canon, mscorlib]].Pop()

0:004> !dumpmt -md 00173a98
EEClass:        0017158c
Module:         00172e7c
Name:           BasicStack`1[[System.Int32, mscorlib]]
...
MethodDesc Table
   Entry MethodDe  JIT Name
...
002603c0 00173a7c  JIT BasicStack`1[[System.Int32, mscorlib]].Push(Int32)
002603f0 00173a84  JIT BasicStack`1[[System.Int32, mscorlib]].Pop()

0:004> !dumpmt -md 00173b40
EEClass:        001715ec
Module:         00172e7c
Name:           BasicStack`1[[System.Double, mscorlib]]
...
MethodDesc Table
   Entry MethodDe  JIT Name
...
00260420 00173b24  JIT BasicStack`1[[System.Double, mscorlib]].Push(Double)
00260458 00173b2c  JIT BasicStack`1[[System.Double, mscorlib]].Pop()
```

Finally, if we inspect the actual method bodies, it becomes evident that the reference type versions do not depend at all on the actual type (all they do is move references around), and the value type versions *do* depend on the type. Copying an integer, after all, is different from copying a double floating-point number. Below are the disassembled versions of the Push method, with the line that actually moves the data around highlighted:

```
0:004> !u 00260360
Normal JIT generated code
BasicStack`1[[System.__Canon, mscorlib]].Push(System.__Canon)
00260360 57             push    edi
00260361 56             push    esi
00260362 8b7104         mov     esi,dword ptr [ecx+4]
00260365 8b7908         mov     edi,dword ptr [ecx+8]
00260368 8d4701         lea     eax,[edi+1]
0026036b 894108         mov     dword ptr [ecx+8],eax
0026036e 52             push    edx
0026036f 8bce           mov     ecx,esi
00260371 8bd7           mov     edx,edi
00260373 e8f4cb3870     call    clr!JIT_Stelem_Ref (705ecf6c)
00260378 5e             pop     esi
00260379 5f             pop     edi
0026037a c3             ret

0:004> !u 002603c0
Normal JIT generated code
```

```
BasicStack`1[[System.Int32, mscorlib]].Push(Int32)
002603c0 57              push    edi
002603c1 56              push    esi
002603c2 8b7104          mov     esi,dword ptr [ecx+4]
002603c5 8b7908          mov     edi,dword ptr [ecx+8]
002603c8 8d4701          lea     eax,[edi+1]
002603cb 894108          mov     dword ptr [ecx+8],eax
002603ce 3b7e04          cmp     edi,dword ptr [esi+4]
002603d1 7307            jae     002603da
002603d3 8954be08        mov     dword ptr [esi+edi*4+8],edx
002603d7 5e              pop     esi
002603d8 5f              pop     edi
002603d9 c3              ret
002603da e877446170      call    clr!JIT_RngChkFail (70874856)
002603df cc              int     3

0:004> !u 00260420
Normal JIT generated code
BasicStack`1[[System.Double, mscorlib]].Push(Double)
00260420 56              push    esi
00260421 8b5104          mov     edx,dword ptr [ecx+4]
00260424 8b7108          mov     esi,dword ptr [ecx+8]
00260427 8d4601          lea     eax,[esi+1]
0026042a 894108          mov     dword ptr [ecx+8],eax
0026042d 3b7204          cmp     esi,dword ptr [edx+4]
00260430 730c            jae     0026043e
00260432 dd442408        fld     qword ptr [esp+8]
00260436 dd5cf208        fstp    qword ptr [edx+esi*8+8]
0026043a 5e              pop     esi
0026043b c20800          ret     8
0026043e e813446170      call    clr!JIT_RngChkFail (70874856)
00260443 cc              int     3
```

We have already seen that the .NET generics implementation is fully type-safe at compile-time. It only remains to ascertain that there is no boxing cost incurred when using value types with generic collections. Indeed, because the JIT compiler compiles a separate method body for each closed generic type where the generic type arguments are value types, there is no need for boxing.

To summarize, .NET generics offer significant advantages when contrasted with Java generics or C++ templates. The generic constraints mechanism is somewhat limited compared to the Wild West that C++ affords, but the flexibility gains from sharing generic types across assemblies and the performance benefits from generating code on demand (and sharing it) are overwhelming.

Collections

The .NET Framework ships with a large number of collections, and it is not the purpose of this chapter to review every one of them — this is a task best left to the MSDN documentation. However, there are some non-trivial considerations that need to be taken into account when choosing a collection, especially for performance-sensitive code. It is these considerations that we will explore throughout this section.

■ **Note** Some developers are wary of using any collection classes but built-in arrays. Arrays are highly inflexible, non-resizable, and make it difficult to implement some operations efficiently, but they are known for having the most minimal overhead of any other collection implementation. You should not be afraid of using built-in collections as long as you are equipped with good measurement tools, such as those we considered in Chapter 2. The internal implementation details of the .NET collections, discussed in this section, will also facilitate good decisions. One example of trivia: iterating a List<T> in a foreach loop takes slightly longer than in a for loop, because foreach-enumeration must verify that the underlying collection hasn't been changed throughout the loop.

First, recall the collection classes shipped with .NET 4.5 — excluding the concurrent collections, which we discuss separately — and their runtime performance characteristics. Comparing the insertion, deletion, and lookup performance of collections is a reasonable way to arrive at the best candidate for your needs. The following table lists only the generic collections (the non-generic counterparts were retired in .NET 2.0):

Table 5-1. *Collections in the .NET Framework*

Collection	Details	Insertion Time	Deletion Time	Lookup Time	Sorted	Index Access
List<T>	Automatically resizable array	Amortized $O(1)$*	$O(n)$	$O(n)$	No	Yes
LinkedList<T>	Doubly-linked list	$O(1)$	$O(1)$	$O(n)$	No	No
Dictionary<K,V>	Hash table	$O(1)$	$O(1)$	$O(1)$	No	No
HashSet<T>	Hash table	$O(1)$	$O(1)$	$O(1)$	No	No
Queue<T>	Automatically resizable cyclic array	Amortized $O(1)$	$O(1)$	--	No	No
Stack<T>	Automatically resizable array	Amortized $O(1)$	$O(1)$	--	No	No
SortedDictionary<K,V>	Red-black tree	$O(\log n)$	$O(\log n)$	$O(\log n)$	Yes (keys)	No
SortedList<K,V>	Sorted resizable array	$O(n)$**	$O(n)$	$O(\log n)$	Yes (keys)	Yes
SortedSet<T>	Red-black tree	$O(\log n)$	$O(\log n)$	$O(\log n)$	Yes	No

* By "amortized" in this case we mean that there are operations that may take $O(n)$ time, but most operations will take $O(1)$ time, such that the average time across n operations is $O(1)$.
** Unless the data are inserted in sort order, in which case $O(1)$.

There are several lessons to be learned from collection design, the choice of collections that made the cut to be included in the .NET Framework, and the implementation details of some collections:

- The storage requirements of different collections vary significantly. Later in this chapter we will see how internal collection layout affects cache performance with List<T> and LinkedList<T>. Another example is the SortedSet<T> and List<T> classes; the former is implemented in terms of a binary search tree with n nodes for n elements, and the latter in terms of a contiguous array of n elements. On a 32-bit system, storing n value types of size s in a sorted set requires $(20+s)n$ bytes of storage, whereas the list requires only sn bytes.

- Some collections have additional requirements of their elements to achieve satisfactory performance. For example, as we have seen in Chapter 3, any implementation of a hash table requires access to a good hash code for the hash table's elements.

- Amortized $O(1)$ cost collections, when executed well, are hardly distinguishable from true $O(1)$ cost collections. After all, few programmers (and programs!) are wary of the fact that List<T>.Add may sometimes incur a significant memory allocation cost and run for a duration of time that is linear in the number of list elements. Amortized time analysis is a useful tool; it has been used to prove optimality bounds on numerous algorithms and collections.

- The ubiquitous space-time tradeoff is present in collection design and even the choice of which collections to include in the .NET Framework. SortedList<K,V> offers very compact and sequential storage of elements at the expense of linear time insertion and deletion, whereas SortedDictionary<K,V> occupies more space and is non-sequential, but offers logarithmic bounds on all operations.

▓ **Note**   There's no better opportunity to mention strings, which are also a simple collection type — a collection of characters. Internally, the System.String class is implemented as an immutable, non-resizable array of characters. All operations on strings result in the creation of a new object. This is why creating long strings by concatenating thousands of smaller strings together is extremely inefficient. The System.Text.StringBuilder class addresses these problems as its implementation is similar to List<T>, and doubles its internal storage when it's mutated. Whenever you need to construct a string from a large (or unknown) number of smaller strings, use a StringBuilder for the intermediate operations.

This richness of collection classes may seem overwhelming, but there are cases when none of the built-in collections is a good fit. We will consider a few examples later. Until .NET 4.0, a common cause of complaint with respect to the built-in collections was the lack of thread safety: none of the collections in Table 5-1 is safe for concurrent access from multiple threads. In .NET 4.0 the System.Collections.Concurrent namespace introduces several new collections designed from the ground up for concurrent programming environments.

Concurrent Collections

With the advent of the Task Parallel Library in .NET 4.0, the need for thread-safe collections became more acute. In Chapter 6 we will see several motivating examples for accessing a data source or an output buffer concurrently from multiple threads. For now, we focus on the available concurrent collections and their performance characteristics in the same spirit of the standard (non-thread-safe) collections we examined earlier.

Table 5-2. Concurrent Collections in the .NET Framework

Collection	Most Similar To	Details	Synchronization
ConcurrentStack<T>	Stack<T>	Singly linked list[1]	Lock-free (CAS), exponential backoff when spinning
ConcurrentQueue<T>	Queue<T>	Linked list of array segments (32 elements each)[2]	Lock-free (CAS), brief spinning when dequeueing an item that was just enqueued
ConcurrentBag<T>	--	Thread-local lists, work stealing[3]	Usually none for local lists, Monitor for work stealing
Concurrent Dictionary<K,V>	Dictionary<K,V>	Hash table: buckets and linked lists[4]	For updates: Monitor per group of hash table buckets (independent of other buckets)
			For reads: none

Notes on the "Details" column:

1. In Chapter 6 we will see a sketch implementation of a lock-free stack using CAS, and discuss the CAS atomic primitive on its own merit.

2. The ConcurrentQueue<T> class manages a linked list of array segments, which allows it to emulate an unbounded queue with a bounded amount of memory. Enqueuing or dequeuing items involves only incrementing pointers into array segments. Synchronization is required in several locations, e.g., to ensure that items are not dequeued before the enqueuing thread has completed the enqueue operation. However, all synchronization is CAS-based.

3. The ConcurrentBag<T> class manages a list of items in no specific order. Items are stored in thread-local lists; adding or removing items to a thread-local list is done at the head of the list and usually requires no synchronization. When threads have to steal items from other threads' lists, they steal from the tail of the list, which causes contention only when there are fewer than three items in the list.

4. ConcurrentDictionary<K,V> uses a classic hash table implementation with chaining (linked lists hanging off each bucket; for a general description of a hash table's structure, see also Chapter 3). Locking is managed at the bucket level—all operations on a certain bucket require a lock, of which there is a limited amount determined by the constructor's concurrencyLevel parameter. Operations on buckets that are associated with different locks can proceed concurrently with no contention. Finally, all read operations do not require any locks, because all mutating operations are atomic (e.g., inserting a new item into the list hanging off its bucket).

Although most concurrent collections are quite similar to their non-thread-safe counterparts, they have slightly different APIs that are affected by their concurrent nature. For example, the ConcurrentDictionary<K,V> class has helper methods that can greatly minimize the amount of locks required and address subtle race conditions that can arise when carelessly accessing the dictionary:

```
//This code is prone to a race condition between the ContainsKey and Add method calls:
Dictionary<string, int> expenses = ...;
if (!expenses.ContainsKey("ParisExpenses")) {
  expenses.Add("ParisExpenses", currentAmount);
} else {
  //This code is prone to a race condition if multiple threads execute it:
  expenses["ParisExpenses"] += currentAmount;
}

//The following code uses the AddOrUpdate method to ensure proper synchronization when
//adding an item or updating an existing item:
```

```
ConcurrentDictionary<string, int> expenses = ...;
expenses.AddOrUpdate("ParisExpenses", currentAmount, (key, amount) => amount + currentAmount);
```

The AddOrUpdate method guarantees the necessary synchronization around the composite "add or update" operation; there is a similar GetOrAdd helper method that can either retrieve an existing value or add it to the dictionary if it doesn't exist and then return it.

Cache Considerations

Choosing the right collection is not only about its performance considerations. The way data are laid out in memory is often more critical to CPU-bound applications than any other criterion, and collections affect this layout greatly. The main factor behind carefully examining data layout in memory is the CPU cache.

Modern systems ship with large main memories. Eight GB of memory is fairly standard on a mid-range workstation or a gaming laptop. Fast DDR3 SDRAM memory units are capable of ~ 15 ns memory access latencies, and theoretical transfer rates of ~ 15 GB/s. Fast processors, on the other hand, can issue billions of instructions per second; theoretically speaking, stalling for 15 ns while waiting for memory access can prevent the execution of dozens (and sometimes hundreds) of CPU instructions. Stalling for memory access is the phenomenon known as *hitting the memory wall*.

To distance applications from this wall, modern processors are equipped with several levels of *cache memory*, which has different internal characteristics than main memory and tends to be very expensive and relatively small. For example, one of the author's Intel i7-860 processor ships with three cache levels (see Figure 5-3):

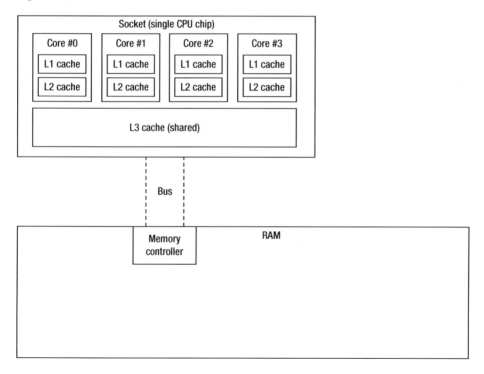

Figure 5-3. *Intel i7-860 schematic of cache, core, and memory relationships*

- Level 1 cache for program instructions, 32 KB, one for each core (total of 4 caches).

- Level 1 cache for data, 32 KB, one for each core (total of 4 caches).

- Level 2 cache for data, 256 KB, one for each core (total of 4 caches).

- Level 3 cache for data, 8 MB, shared (total of 1 cache).

When the processor attempts to access a memory address, it begins by checking whether the data is already in its L1 cache. If it is, the memory access is satisfied from the cache, which takes ~ 5 CPU cycles (this is called a *cache hit*). If it isn't, the L2 cache is checked; satisfying the access from the L2 cache takes ~ 10 cycles. Similarly, satisfying the access from L3 cache takes ~ 40 cycles. Finally, if the data isn't in any of the cache levels, the processor will stall for the system's main memory (this is called a *cache miss*). When the processor accesses main memory, it reads from it not a single byte or word, but a *cache line*, which on modern systems consists of 32 or 64 bytes. Accessing any word on the same cache line will not involve another cache miss until the line is evicted from the cache.

Although this description does not do justice to the true hardware complexities of how SRAM caches and DRAM memories operate, it provides enough food for thought and discussion of how our high-level software algorithms can be affected by data layout in memory. We now consider a simple example that involves a single core's cache; in Chapter 6 we will see that multiprocessor programs can afflict additional performance loss by improperly utilizing the caches of multiple cores.

Suppose the task at hand is traversing a large collection of integers and performing some aggregation on them, such as finding their sum or average. Below are two alternatives; one accesses the data from a LinkedList< int > and the other from an array of integers (int[ ]), two of the built-in .NET collections.

```
LinkedList<int> numbers = new LinkedList<int>(Enumerable.Range(0, 20000000));
int sum = 0;
for (LinkedListNode<int> curr = numbers.First; curr != null; curr = curr.Next) {
  sum += curr.Value;
}

int[] numbers = Enumerable.Range(0, 20000000).ToArray();
int sum = 0;
for (int curr = 0; curr < numbers.Length; ++curr) {
  sum += numbers[curr];
}
```

The second version of the code runs *2× faster* than the first on the system mentioned above. This is a non-negligible difference, and if you only consider the number of CPU instructions issued, you might not be convinced that there should be a difference at all. After all, traversing a linked list involves moving from one node to the next, and traversing an array involves incrementing an index into the array. (In fact, without JIT optimizations, accessing an array element would require also a range check to make sure that the index is within the array's bounds.)

```
; x86 assembly for the first loop, assume 'sum' is in EAX and 'numbers' is in ECX
xor eax, eax
mov ecx, dword ptr [ecx+4]        ; curr = numbers.First
test ecx, ecx
jz LOOP_END
LOOP_BEGIN:
add eax, dword ptr [ecx+10]       ; sum += curr.Value
mov ecx, dword ptr [ecx+8]        ; curr = curr.Next
test ecx, ecx
jnz LOOP_BEGIN                     ; total of 4 instructions per iteration
LOOP_END:
...
```

```
; x86 assembly for the second loop, assume 'sum' is in EAX and 'numbers' is in ECX
mov edi, dword ptr [ecx+4]        ; numbers.Length
test edi, edi
jz LOOP_END
xor edx, edx                      ; loop index
LOOP_BEGIN:
add eax, dword ptr [ecx+edx*4+8]  ; sum += numbers[i], no bounds check
inc edx
cmp esi, edx
jg LOOP_BEGIN                      ; total of 4 instructions per iteration
LOOP_END:
...
```

Given this code generation for both loops (and barring optimizations such as using SIMD instructions to traverse the array, which is contiguous in memory), it is hard to explain the significant performance difference by inspecting only the instructions executed. Indeed, we must analyze the memory access patterns of this code to reach any acceptable conclusions.

In both loops, each integer is accessed only once, and it would seem that cache considerations are not as critical because there is no reusable data to benefit from cache hits. Still, the way the data is laid out in memory affects greatly the performance of this program — not because the data is reused, but because of the way it is brought into memory. When accessing the array elements, a cache miss at the beginning of a cache line brings into the cache 16 consecutive integers (cache line = 64 bytes = 16 integers). Because array access is sequential, the next 15 integers are now in the cache and can be accessed without a cache miss. This is an almost-ideal scenario, with a 1:16 cache miss ratio. On the other hand, when accessing linked list elements, a cache miss at the beginning of a cache line can bring into cache *at most* 3 consecutive linked list nodes, a 1:4 cache miss ratio! (A node consists of a back pointer, forward pointer, and integer datum, which occupy 12 bytes on a 32-bit system; the reference type header brings the tally to 20 bytes per node.)

The much higher cache miss ratio is the reason for most of the performance difference between the two pieces of code we tested above. Furthermore, we are assuming the ideal scenario in which all linked list nodes are positioned sequentially in memory, which would be the case only if they were allocated simultaneously with no other allocations taking place, and is fairly unlikely. Had the linked list nodes been distributed less ideally in memory, the cache miss ratio would have been even higher, and the performance even poorer.

A concluding example that shows another aspect of cache-related effects is the known algorithm for matrix multiplication by blocking. Matrix multiplication (which we revisit again in Chapter 6 when discussing C++ AMP) is a fairly simple algorithm that can benefit greatly from CPU caches because elements are reused several times. Below is the naïve algorithm implementation:

```
public static int[,] MultiplyNaive(int[,] A, int[,] B) {
  int[,] C = new int[N, N];
  for (int i = 0; i < N; ++i)
    for (int j = 0; j < N; ++j)
      for (int k = 0; k < N; ++k)
        C[i, j] += A[i, k] * B[k, j];
  return C;
}
```

In the heart of the inner loop there is a scalar product of the i-th row in the first matrix with the j-th column of the second matrix; the entire i-th row and j-th column are traversed. The potential for reuse by caching stems from the fact that the entire i-th row in the output matrix is calculated by repeatedly traversing the i-th row of the first matrix. The same elements are reused many times. The first matrix is traversed in a very cache-friendly fashion: its first row is iterated completely N times, then its second row is iterated completely N times, and so on. This does not help, though, because after the outer loop is done with iteration i, the method it does not the i-th row again. Unfortunately, the second matrix is iterated in a very cache-unfriendly fashion: its first *column* is iterated completely *N* times, then its second *column*, and so on. (The reason this is cache-unfriendly is that the matrix, an int[,], is stored in memory in row-major order, as Figure 5-4 illustrates.)

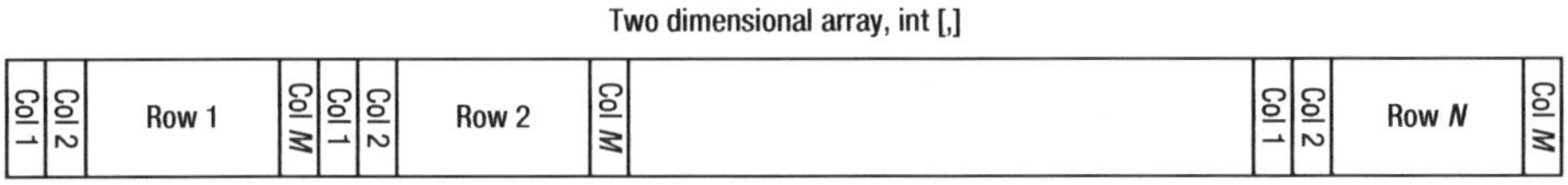

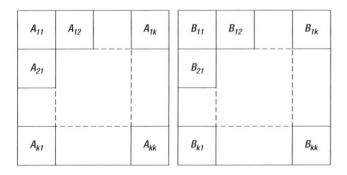

Two dimensional array, int [,]

Figure 5-4. *The memory layout of a two dimensional array (int[,]). Rows are consecutive in memory, columns are not*

If the cache was big enough to fit the entire second matrix, then after a single iteration of the outer loop the entire second matrix would be in the cache, and subsequent accesses to it in column-major order would still be satisfied from cache. However, if the second matrix does not fit in the cache, cache misses will occur very frequently: a cache miss for the element *(i,j)* would produce a cache line that contains elements from row *i* but no additional elements from column *j*, which means a cache miss for every access!

Matrix multiplication by blocking introduces the following idea. Multiplying two matrices can be performed by the naïve algorithm above, or by splitting them into smaller matrices (blocks), multiplying the blocks together, and then performing some additional arithmetic on the results.

Specifically, if the matrices *A* and *B* are given in block form, as in Figure 5-5, then the matrix $C=AB$ can be calculated in blocks, such that $C_{ij}=A_{i1}B_{1j}+A_{i2}B_{2j}+...+A_{ik}B_{kj}$. In practice, this leads to the following code:

Figure 5-5. *Matrices A and B given in block form, k × k blocks each*

```
public static int[,] MultiplyBlocked(int[,] A, int[,] B, int bs) {
  int[,] C = new int[N, N];
  for (int ii = 0; ii < N; ii += bs)
    for (int jj = 0; jj < N; jj += bs)
      for (int kk = 0; kk < N; kk += bs)
        for (int i = ii; i < ii + bs; ++i)
          for (int j = jj; j < jj + bs; ++j)
```

```
        for (int k = kk; k < kk + bs; ++k)
          C[i, j] += A[i, k] * B[k, j];
    return C;
}
```

The apparently complex *six* nested loops are quite simple—the three innermost loops perform naïve matrix multiplication of two blocks, the three outermost loops iterate over the blocks. To test the blocking multiplication algorithm, we used the same machine from the previous examples (which has an 8 MB L3 cache) and multiplied 2048×2048 matrices of integers. The total size of both matrices is $2048 \times 2048 \times 4 \times 2 = 32$ MB, which does not fit in the cache. The results for different block sizes are shown in Table 5-3. In Table 5-3 you can see that blocking helps considerably, and that finding the best block size can have a significant secondary effect on performance:

Table 5-3. *Timing results of blocking multiplication for varying block sizes*

	Naïve (no blocks)	bs=4	bs=8	bs=16	bs=32	bs=64	bs=512	bs=1024
Time (s)	178	92	81	81	79	106	117	147

There are many additional examples where cache considerations are paramount, even outside the arena of algorithm design and collection optimization. There are also some even more refined aspects of cache and memory-related considerations: the relationships between caches at different levels, effects of cache associativity, memory access dependencies and ordering, and many others. For more examples, consider reading the concise article by Igor Ostrovsky, "Gallery of Processor Cache Effects" (http://igoro.com/archive/gallery-of-processor-cache-effects/, 2010).

Custom Collections

There are a great many collections well known in the computer science literature, which haven't made the cut for being included in the .NET Framework. Some of them are fairly common and your applications may benefit from using them instead of the built-in ones. Furthermore, most of them offer sufficiently simple algorithms that can be implemented in a reasonable time. Although it is not our intent to explore the large variety of collections, below are two examples that differ greatly from the existing .NET collections and offer insight into situations where custom collections may be useful.

Disjoint-Set (Union-Find)

The *disjoint-set* data structure (often called *union-find*) is a collection in which partitions of elements into disjoint subsets are stored. It differs from all .NET collections because you do not store elements in it. Instead, there is a domain of elements in which each element forms a single set, and consecutive operations on the data structure join sets together to form larger sets. The data structure is designed to perform two operations efficiently:

- *Union*: Join two subsets together to form a single subset.

- *Find*: Determine to which subset a particular element belongs. (Most commonly used to determine whether two elements belong to the same subset.)

Typically, sets are manipulated as representative elements, with a single representative for each set. The union and find operations, then, receive and return representatives instead of entire sets.

A naïve implementation of union-find involves using a collection to represent each set, and merging the collections together when necessary. For example, when using a linked list to store each set, the merge takes linear time and the find operation may be implemented in constant time if each element has a pointer to the set representative.

The Galler-Fischer implementation has *much* better runtime complexity. The sets are stored in a forest (set of trees); in each tree, every node contains a pointer to its parent node, and the root of the tree is the set representative. To make sure that the resulting trees are balanced, when trees are merged, the smaller tree is always attached to the root of the larger tree (this requires tracking the tree's depth). Additionally, when the find operation executes, it compresses the path from the desired element to its representative. Below is a sketch implementation:

```
public class Set<T> {
  public Set Parent;
  public int Rank;
  public T Data;
  public Set(T data) {
    Parent = this;
    Data = data;
  }

  public static Set Find(Set x) {
    if (x.Parent != x) {
      x.Parent = Find(x.Parent);
    }
    return x.Parent;
  }

  public static void Union(Set x, Set y) {
    Set xRep = Find(x);
    Set yRep = Find(y);
    if (xRep == yRep) return; //It's the same set

    if (xRep.Rank < yRep.Rank)      xRep.Parent = yRep;
    else if (xRep.Rank > yRep.Rank) yRep.Parent = xRep;
    else {
      yRep.Parent = xRep;
      ++xRep.Rank; //Merged two trees of equal rank, so rank increases
    }
  }
}
```

Accurate runtime analysis of this data structure is quite complex; a simple upper bound is that the amortized time per operation in a forest with n elements is $O(\log^* n)$, where $\log^* n$ (the iterated logarithm of n) is the number of times the logarithm function must be applied to get a result that is smaller than 1, i.e. the minimal number of times "log" must appear in the inequality log log log ... log $n \le 1$. For practical values of n, e.g., $n \le 10^{50}$, this is no more than 5, which is "effectively constant."

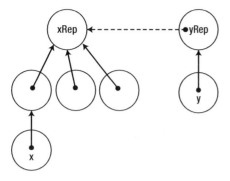

Figure 5-6. *Merge of two sets x and y where y's set is smaller. The dashed arrow is the result of the merge*

Skip List

A *skip list* is a data structure that stores a sorted linked list of elements and allows lookup in $O(\log n)$ time, comparable to a binary search in an array or lookup in a balanced binary tree. Clearly, the major problem with performing a binary search in a linked list is that linked lists do not allow random access by index. Skip lists address this limitation by using a hierarchy of increasingly sparse linked lists: the first linked list links together all the nodes; the second linked list links together nodes 0, 2, 4, ...; the third linked list links together nodes 0, 4, 8, ...; the fourth linked list links together nodes 0, 8, 16, ...; and so forth.

To perform a lookup for an element in the skip list, the procedure iterates the sparsest list first. When an element is encountered that is greater than or equal to the desired element, the procedure returns to the previous element and drops to the next list in the hierarchy. This repeats until the element is found. By using $O(\log n)$ lists in the hierarchy, $O(\log n)$ lookup time can be guaranteed.

Unfortunately, maintaining the skip list elements is not at all trivial. If the entire linked list hierarchy must be reallocated when elements are added or removed, it would offer no advantages over a trivial data structure such as SortedList<T>, which simply maintains a sorted array. A common approach is to randomize the hierarchy of lists (see Figure 5-7), which results in expected logarithmic time for insertion, deletion, and lookup of elements. The precise details of how to maintain a skip list can be found in William Pugh's paper, "Skip lists: a probabilistic alternative to balanced trees" (ACM, 1990).

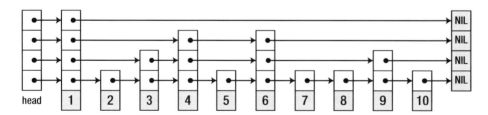

Figure 5-7. *Skip list structure with four randomized lists in the hierarchy (Image from Wikipedia: http://upload. wikimedia.org/wikipedia/commons/8/86/Skip_list.svg, released into the public domain.)*

One-Shot Collections

It may also be the case that you have a unique situation which warrants the use of a completely custom collection. We call these *one-shot collections*, because they might be an undeniably new invention tailored to your specific domain. As time goes by you may find that some of the one-shot collections you implemented are in fact quite reusable; in this subsection we will take a look at one example.

Consider the following application. You are running a candy exchange system, which keeps candy traders up to date with prices for various candy types. Your main data table is stored in memory and contains a row for each type of candy, listing its current price. Table 5-4 is an example of the data at a certain instant in time:

Table 5-4. *Example of data table for the candy exchange system*

Type of Candy	Price ($)
Twix	0.93
Mars	0.88
Snickers	1.02
Kisses	0.66

There are two types of clients in your system:

- Candy traders are connected to your system through a TCP socket and periodically ask you for up-to-date information on a certain type of candy. A typical request from a trader is "What's the price of Twix?" and your response is "$0.93". There are tens of thousands of these requests per second.

- Candy suppliers are connected to your system through a UDP socket and periodically send you candy price updates. There are two subtypes of requests:

    - "Update the price of Mars to $0.91". No response is necessary. There are thousands of these requests per second.

    - "Add a new candy, Snowflakes, with a starting price of $0.49". No response is necessary. There are no more than a few dozens of these requests per day.

It is also known that 99.9 % of operations read or update the price of candy types that existed at the beginning of the trade; only 0.1 % of operations access candy types that were added by the add operation.

Armed with this information, you set out to design a data structure — a collection — to store the data table in memory. This data structure must be thread-safe, because hundreds of threads may be competing for access to it at a given time. You need not concern yourself with copying the data to persistent storage; we are inspecting only its in-memory performance characteristics.

The shape of the data and the types of requests our system serves suggest strongly that we should use a hash table to store the candy prices. Synchronizing access to a hash table is a task best left to ConcurrentDictionary<K,V>. Reads from a concurrent dictionary can be satisfied without any synchronization, whereas update and add operations require synchronization at a fairly fine-grained level. Although this may be an adequate solution, we set ourselves a higher bar: we would like reads and updates to proceed without any synchronization in the 99.9 % of operations on pre-existing candy types.

A possible solution to this problem is a *safe-unsafe cache*. This collection is a set of two hash tables, the *safe table* and the *unsafe table*. The safe table is prepopulated with the candy types available at the beginning of the trade; the unsafe table starts out empty. Operations on the safe table are satisfied without any locks because it is not mutated; new candy types are added to the unsafe table. Below is a possible implementation using Dictionary<K,V> and ConcurrentDictionary<K,V>:

```
//Assumes that writes of TValue can be satisfied atomically, i.e. it must be a reference
//type or a sufficiently small value type (4 bytes on 32-bit systems).
public class SafeUnsafeCache<TKey, TValue> {
  private Dictionary<TKey, TValue> safeTable;
  private ConcurrentDictionary<TKey, TValue> unsafeTable;

  public SafeUnsafeCache(IDictionary<TKey, TValue> initialData) {
    safeTable = new Dictionary<TKey, TValue>(initialData);
    unsafeTable = new ConcurrentDictionary<TKey, TValue>();
  }
  public bool Get(TKey key, out TValue value) {
    return safeTable.TryGetValue(key, out value) || unsafeTable.TryGetValue(key, out value);
  }
  public void AddOrUpdate(TKey key, TValue value) {
    if (safeTable.ContainsKey(key)) {
      safeTable[key] = value;
    } else {
      unsafeTable.AddOrUpdate(key, value, (k, v) => value);
    }
  }
}
```

A further refinement would be to periodically stop all trade operations and merge the unsafe table into the safe table. This would further improve the expected synchronization required for operations on the candy data.

IMPLEMENTING IENUMERABLE<T>AND OTHER INTERFACES

Almost any collection will eventually implement IEnumerable<T> and possibly other collection-related interfaces. The advantages of complying with these interfaces are numerous, and as of .NET 3.5 have to do with LINQ as much as anything. After all, any class that implements IEnumerable<T> is *automatically* furnished with the variety of extension methods offered by System.Linq and can participate in C# 3.0 LINQ expressions on equal terms with the built-in collections.

Unfortunately, naïvely implementing IEnumerable<T> on your collection sentences your callers to pay the price of interface method invocation when they enumerate it. Consider the following code snippet, which enumerates a List<int>:

```
List<int> list = ...;
IEnumerator<int> enumerator = list.GetEnumerator();
long product = 1;
while (enumerator.MoveNext()) {
  product *= enumerator.Current;
}
```

There are two interface method invocations per iteration here, which is an unreasonable overhead for traversing a list and finding the product of its elements. As you may recall from Chapter 3, inlining interface method invocations is not trivial, and if the JIT fails to inline them successfully, the price is steep.

There are several approaches that can help avoid the cost of interface method invocation. Interface methods, when invoked directly on a value type variable, can be dispatched directly. Therefore, if the enumerator variable in the above example had been a value type (and not IEnumerator<T>), the interface dispatch cost would have been prevented. This can only work if the collection implementation could return a value type directly from its GetEnumerator method, and the caller would use that value type instead of the interface.

To achieve this, List<T> has an explicit interface implementation of IEnumerable<T>.GetEnumerator, which returns IEnumerator<T>, and another public method called GetEnumerator, which returns List<T>. Enumerator— an inner value type:

```
public class List<T> : IEnumerable<T>, ... {
  public Enumerator GetEnumerator() {
    return new Enumerator(this);
  }
  IEnumerator<T> IEnumerable<T>.GetEnumerator() {
    return new Enumerator(this);
  }
  ...
  public struct Enumerator { ... }
}
```

This enables the following calling code, which gets rid of the interface method invocations entirely:

```
List<int> list = ...;
List.Enumerator<int> enumerator = list.GetEnumerator();
long product = 1;
while (enumerator.MoveNext()) {
  product *= enumerator.Current;
}
```

An alternative would be to make the enumerator a reference type, but repeat the same explicit interface implementation trick on its MoveNext method and Current property. This would also allow callers using the class directly to avoid interface invocation costs.

Summary

Throughout this chapter we have seen more than a dozen collection implementations and compared them from the memory density, runtime complexity, space requirements, and thread-safety perspectives. You should now have a better intuition for choosing collections and proving the optimality of your choices, and shouldn't fear to steer away from what the .NET Framework has to offer and implement a one-shot collection or use an idea from the computer science literature.

CHAPTER 6

■ ■ ■

Concurrency and Parallelism

For many years, the processing power of computer systems increased exponentially. Processors have been getting faster with every model, and programs designed to challenge the hardware resources of an expensive workstation were being ported to laptops and handheld devices. This era came to an end several years ago, and today processors are not exponentially increasing in *speed*; they are exponentially increasing in *number*. Writing programs to take advantage of multiple processing cores hasn't been easy when multi-processor systems were rare and expensive, and it hasn't turned easy today, when even smartphones ship with dual- and quad-core processors.

In this chapter, we shall embark on a whirlwind tour through the world of modern parallel programming in .NET. Although this modest chapter cannot begin to describe all the APIs, frameworks, tools, pitfalls, design patterns, and architectural models that parallel programming is today, no book on performance optimization would be complete without discussing one of the apparently cheapest ways to improve application performance—namely, scaling to multiple processors.

Challenges and Gains

Another challenge of harnessing parallelism is the rising heterogeneity of multi-processor systems. CPU manufacturers take pride in delivering reasonably priced consumer-oriented systems with four or eight processing cores, and high-end server systems with dozens of cores. However, nowadays a mid-range workstation or a high-end laptop often comes equipped with a powerful graphics processing unit (GPU), with support for *hundreds* of concurrent threads. As if the two kinds of parallelism were not enough, Infrastructure-as-a-Service (IaaS) price drops sprout weekly, making thousand-core clouds accessible in a blink of an eye.

■ **Note** Herb Sutter gives an excellent overview of the heterogeneous world that awaits parallelism frameworks in his article "Welcome to the Jungle" (2011). In another article from 2005, "The Free Lunch Is Over," he shaped the resurgence of interest in concurrency and parallelism frameworks in everyday programming. If you should find yourself hungry for more information on parallel programming than this single chapter can provide, we can recommend the following excellent books on the subject of parallel programming in general and .NET parallelism frameworks in particular: Joe Duffy, "Concurrent Programming on Windows" (Addison-Wesley, 2008); Joseph Albahari, "Threading in C#" (online, 2011). To understand in more detail the operating system's inner workings around thread scheduling and synchronization mechanisms, Mark Russinovich's, David Solomon's, and Alex Ionescu's "Windows Internals, 5th Edition" (Microsoft Press, 2009) is an excellent text. Finally, the MSDN is a good source of information on the APIs we will see in this chapter, such as the Task Parallel Library.

The performance gains from parallelism are not to be dismissed lightly. I/O-bound applications can benefit greatly from offloading I/O to separate thread, performing asynchronous I/O to provide higher responsiveness, and scaling by issuing multiple I/O operations. CPU-bound applications with algorithms that yield themselves to parallelization can scale by an order of magnitude on typical consumer hardware by utilizing all available CPU cores or by two orders of magnitude by utilizing all available GPU cores. Later in this chapter you will see how a simple algorithm that performs matrix multiplication is sped up 130-fold by only changing a few lines of code to run on the GPU.

As always, the road to parallelism is laden with pitfalls—deadlocks, race conditions, starvation, and memory corruptions await at every step. Recent parallelism frameworks, including the Task Parallel Library (.NET 4.0) and C++ AMP that we will be using in this chapter, aim to reduce somewhat the complexity of writing parallel applications and harvesting the ripe performance profits.

Why Concurrency and Parallelism?

There are many reasons to introduce multiple threads of control into your applications. This book is dedicated to improving application performance, and indeed most reasons for concurrency and parallelism lie in the performance realm. Here are some examples:

- Issuing asynchronous I/O operations can improve application responsiveness. Most GUI applications have a single thread of control responsible for all UI updates; this thread must never be occupied for a long period of time, lest the UI become unresponsive to user actions.

- Parallelizing work across multiple threads can drive better utilization of system resources. Modern systems, equipped with multiple CPU cores and even more GPU cores can gain an order-of-magnitude increase in performance through parallelization of simple CPU-bound algorithms.

- Performing several I/O operations at once (for example, retrieving prices from multiple travel websites simultaneously, or updating files in several distributed Web repositories) can help drive better overall throughput, because most of the time is spent waiting for I/O operations to complete, and can be used to issue additional I/O operations or perform result processing on operations that have already completed.

From Threads to Thread Pool to Tasks

In the beginning there were threads. Threads are the most rudimentary means of parallelizing applications and distributing asynchronous work; they are the most low-level abstraction available to user-mode programs. Threads offer little in the way of structure and control, and programming threads directly resembles strongly the long-gone days of unstructured programming, before subroutines and objects and agents have gained in popularity.

Consider the following simple task: you are given a large range of natural numbers, and are required to find all the prime numbers in the range and store them in a collection. This is a purely CPU-bound job, and has the appearance of an easily parallelizable one. First, let's write a naïve version of the code that runs on a single CPU thread:

```
//Returns all the prime numbers in the range [start, end)
public static IEnumerable<uint> PrimesInRange(uint start, uint end) {
  List<uint> primes = new List<uint>();
  for (uint number = start; number < end; ++number) {
```

```
    if (IsPrime(number)) {
      primes.Add(number);
    }
  }
  return primes;
}
private static bool IsPrime(uint number) {
  //This is a very inefficient O(n) algorithm, but it will do for our expository purposes
  if (number == 2) return true;
  if (number % 2 == 0) return false;
  for (uint divisor = 3; divisor<number; divisor += 2) {
    if (number % divisor == 0) return false;
  }
  return true;
}
```

Is there anything to improve here? Mayhap the algorithm is so quick that there is nothing to gain by trying to optimize it? Well, for a reasonably large range, such as [100, 200000), the code above runs for several seconds on a modern processor, leaving ample room for optimization.

You may have significant reservations about the efficiency of the algorithm (e.g., there is a trivial optimization that makes it run in $O(\sqrt{n})$ time instead of linear time), but regardless of algorithmic optimality, it seems very likely to yield well to parallelization. After all, discovering whether 4977 is prime is independent of discovering whether 3221 is prime, so an apparently easy way to parallelize the above code is by dividing the range into a number of chunks and creating a separate thread to deal with each chunk (as illustrated in Figure 6-1). Clearly, we will have to synchronize access to the collection of primes to protect it against corruption by multiple threads. A naïve approach is along the following lines:

```
public static IEnumerable<uint> PrimesInRange(uint start, uint end) {
  List<uint> primes = new List<uint>();
  uint range = end - start;
  uint numThreads = (uint)Environment.ProcessorCount; //is this a good idea?
  uint chunk = range / numThreads; //hopefully, there is no remainder
  Thread[] threads = new Thread[numThreads];
  for (uint i = 0; i<numThreads; ++i) {
    uint chunkStart = start+i*chunk;
    uint chunkEnd = chunkStart+chunk;
    threads[i] = new Thread(() => {
      for (uint number = chunkStart; number < chunkEnd; ++number) {
        if (IsPrime(number)) {
          lock(primes) {
            primes.Add(number);
          }
        }
      }
    });
    threads[i].Start();
  }
```

```
  foreach (Thread thread in threads) {
    thread.Join();
  }
  return primes;
}
```

The range of numbers divided across the multiple threads			
1 - 25,000	25,001 - 50,000	50,001 - 75,000	75,001 - 100,000
Thread 1	Thread 2	Thread 3	Thread 4

Figure 6-1. *Dividing the range of prime numbers across multiple threads*

On an Intel i7 system, the sequential code took ~ 2950 ms on average to traverse the range [100, 200000), and the parallelized version took ~ 950 ms on average to do the same. From a system with 8 CPU cores you expect better results, but this particular strain of i7 processors uses HyperThreading, which means there are only 4 physical cores (each physical core hosts two logical cores). A 4× speedup is more reasonable to expect, and we gained a 3× speedup, which is still non-negligible. However, as the Concurrency Profiler's report in Figures 6-2 and 6-3 shows, some threads finish faster than others, bringing the overall CPU utilization to much lower than 100% (to run the Concurrency Profiler on your applications, consult Chapter 2).

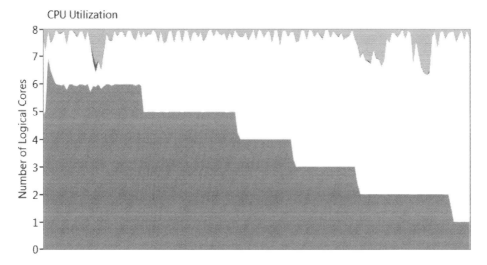

Figure 6-2. *Overall CPU utilization rose to almost 8 logical cores (100%) and then dropped to only one logical core at the end of the run*

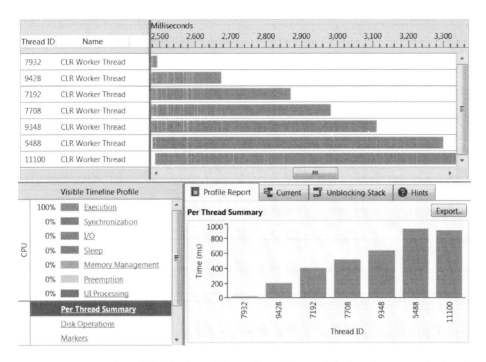

Figure 6-3. *Some threads finished much faster than others. While thread 9428 ran for less than 200ms, thread 5488 ran for more than 800ms*

Indeed, this program might run faster than the sequential version (although will *not* scale linearly), especially if you throw a lot of cores into the mix. This begets several questions, however:

- How many threads are optimal? If the system has eight CPU cores, should we create eight threads?

- How do we make sure that we don't monopolize system resources or create oversubscription? For example, what if there is another thread in our process that needs to calculate prime numbers, and tries to run the same parallelized algorithm as we do?

- How do the threads synchronize access to the resulting collection? Accessing a List < uint > from multiple threads is unsafe, and will result in data corruption, as we shall see in a subsequent section. However, taking a lock every time we add a prime number to the collection (which is what the naïve solution above does) will prove to be extremely expensive and throttle our ability to scale the algorithm to a further increasing number of processing cores.

- For a small range of numbers, is it worthwhile to spawn several new threads, or perhaps it would be a better idea to execute the entire operation synchronously on a single thread? (Creating and destroying a thread is cheap on Windows, but not as cheap as finding out whether 20 small numbers are prime or composite.)

- How do we make sure that all the threads have an equal amount of work? Some threads might finish more quickly than others, especially those that operate on smaller numbers. For the range [100, 100000) divided into four equal parts, the thread responsible for the range [100, 25075) will finish more than twice as fast as the thread responsible for the range [75025, 100000), because our primality testing algorithm becomes increasingly slower as it encounters large prime numbers.

- How should we deal with exceptions that might arise from the other threads? In this particular case, it would appear that there are no possible errors to come out of the IsPrime method, but in real-world examples the parallelized work could be ridden with potential pitfalls and exceptional conditions. (The CLR's default behavior is to terminate the entire process when a thread fails with an unhandled exception, which is generally a good idea—fail-fast semantics—but won't allow the caller of PrimesInRange to deal with the exception at all.)

Good answers to these questions are far from trivial, and developing a framework that allows concurrent work execution without spawning too many threads, that avoids oversubscription and makes sure work is evenly distributed across all threads, that reports errors and results reliably, and that cooperates with other sources of parallelism within the process was precisely the task for the designers of the Task Parallel Library, which we shall deal with next.

From manual thread management, the natural first step was towards thread pools. A thread pool is a component that manages a bunch of threads available for work item execution. Instead of creating a thread to perform a certain task, you queue that task to the thread pool, which selects an available thread and dispatches that task for execution. Thread pools help address some of the problems highlighted above—they mitigate the costs of creating and destroying threads for extremely short tasks, help avoid monopolization of resources and oversubscription by throttling the total number of threads used by the application, and automate decisions pertaining to the optimal number of threads for a given task.

In our particular case, we may decide to break the number range into a significantly larger number of chunks (at the extreme, a chunk per loop iteration) and queue them to the thread pool. An example of this approach for a chunk size of 100 is below:

```
public static IEnumerable<uint> PrimesInRange(uint start, uint end) {
  List<uint> primes = new List<uint>();
  const uint ChunkSize = 100;
  int completed = 0;
  ManualResetEvent allDone = new ManualResetEvent(initialState: false);
  uint chunks = (end - start) / ChunkSize; //again, this should divide evenly
  for (uint i = 0; i<chunks; ++i) {
    uint chunkStart = start+i*ChunkSize;
    uint chunkEnd = chunkStart+ChunkSize;
    ThreadPool.QueueUserWorkItem(_ =>{
      for (uint number = chunkStart; number<chunkEnd; ++number) {
        if (IsPrime(number)) {
          lock(primes) {
            primes.Add(number);
          }
        }
      }
      if (Interlocked.Increment(ref completed) == chunks) {
        allDone.Set();
      }
    });
  }
  allDone.WaitOne();
  return primes;
}
```

This version of the code is significantly more scalable, and executes faster than the previous versions we have considered. It improves upon the ~ 950 ms (for the range [100, 300000)) required for the unsophisticated thread-based version and completes within ~ 800 ms on average (which is almost a 4× speedup compared to the sequential version). What's more, CPU usage is at a consistent level of close to 100%, as the Concurrency Profiler report in Figure 6-4 indicates.

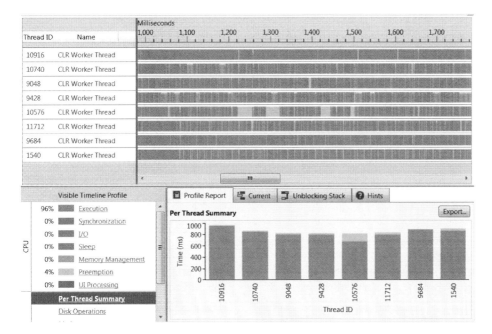

Figure 6-4. *The CLR thread pool used 8 threads (one per logical core) during the program's execution. Each thread ran for almost the entire duration*

As of CLR 4.0, the CLR thread pool consists of several cooperating components. When a thread that doesn't belong to the thread pool (such as the application's main thread) dispatches work items to the thread pool, they are enqueued into a global FIFO (first-in-first-out) queue. Each thread pool thread has a local LIFO (last-in-first-out) queue, to which it will enqueue work items created on that thread (see Figure 6-5). When a thread pool thread is looking for work, it begins by consulting its own LIFO queue, and executes work items from it as long as they are available. If a thread's LIFO queue is exhausted, it will attempt *work stealing*—consulting the local queues of other threads and taking work items from them, in FIFO order. Finally, if all the local queues are empty, threads will consult the global (FIFO) queue and execute work items from there.

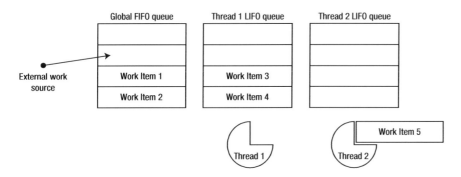

Figure 6-5. *Thread #2 is currently executing work item #5; after completing its execution, it will borrow work from the global FIFO queue. Thread #1 will drain its local queue before tending to any other work*

THREAD POOL FIFO AND LIFO SEMANTICS

The reason behind the apparently eccentric FIFO and LIFO queue semantics is the following: when work is enqueued to the global queue, no particular thread has any preference to executing that work, and fairness is the only criterion by which work is selected for execution. This is why FIFO semantics are suitable for the global queue. However, when a thread pool thread queues a work item for execution, it is likely to use the same data and the same instructions as the currently executing work item; that's why it makes sense to enqueue it in a LIFO queue that belongs to the same thread—it will be executed shortly after the currently executing work item, and take advantage of the CPU data and instruction caches.

Furthermore, accessing work items on the thread's local queue requires less synchronization and is less likely to encounter contention from other threads than when accessing the global queue. Similarly, when a thread steals work from another thread's queue, it steals it in FIFO order, so that the LIFO optimization with respect to CPU caches on the original thread's processor is maintained. This thread pool structure is very friendly towards work item hierarchies, where a single work item enqueued into the global queue will spawn off dozens of additional work items and provide work for several thread pool threads.

As with any abstraction, thread pools take some of the granular control over thread lifetime and work item scheduling away from the application developer. Although the CLR thread pool has some control APIs, such as `ThreadPool.SetMinThreads` and `SetMaxThreads` that control the number of threads, it does not have built-in APIs to control the *priority* of its threads or tasks. More often than not, however, this loss of control is more than compensated by the application's ability to scale automatically on more powerful systems, and the performance gain from not having to create and destroy threads for short-lived tasks.

Work items queued to the thread pool are extremely inept; they do not have state, can't carry exception information, don't have support for asynchronous continuations and cancellation, and don't feature any mechanism for obtaining a result from a task that has completed. The Task Parallel Library in .NET 4.0 introduces *tasks*, which are a powerful abstraction on top of thread pool work items. Tasks are the structured alternative to threads and thread pool work items, much in the same way that objects and subroutines were the structured alternative to `goto`-based assembly language programming.

Task Parallelism

Task parallelism is a paradigm and set of APIs for breaking down a large task into a set of smaller ones, and executing them on multiple threads. The Task Parallel Library (TPL) has first-class APIs for managing millions of tasks simultaneously (through the CLR thread pool). At the heart of the TPL is the `System.Threading.Tasks.Task` class, which represents a task. The `Task` class provides the following capabilities:

- Scheduling work for independent execution on an unspecified thread. (The specific thread to execute a given task is determined by a *task scheduler*; the default task scheduler enqueues tasks to the CLR thread pool, but there are schedulers that send tasks to a particular thread, such as the UI thread.)

- Waiting for a task to complete and obtaining the result of its execution.

- Providing a continuation that should run as soon as the task completes. (This is often called a callback, but we shall use the term *continuation* throughout this chapter.)

- Handling exceptions that arise in a single task or even a hierarchy of tasks on the original thread that scheduled them for execution, or any other thread that is interested in the task results.

- Canceling tasks that haven't started yet, and communicating cancellation requests to tasks that are in the middle of executing.

Because we can think of tasks as a higher-level abstraction on top of threads, we could rewrite the code we had for prime number calculation to use tasks instead of threads. Indeed, it would make the code shorter—at the very least, we wouldn't need the completed task counter and the ManualResetEvent object to keep track of task execution. However, as we shall see in the next section, the data parallelism APIs provided by the TPL are even more suitable for parallelizing a loop that finds all prime numbers in a range. Instead, we shall consider a different problem.

There is a well-known recursive comparison-based sorting algorithm called QuickSort that yields itself quite easily to parallelization (and has an average case runtime complexity of $O(n\log(n))$), which is optimal—although scarcely any large framework uses QuickSort to sort anything these days). The QuickSort algorithm proceeds as follows:

```csharp
public static void QuickSort<T>(T[] items) where T : IComparable<T>{
  QuickSort(items, 0, items.Length);
}
private static void QuickSort<T>(T[] items, int left, int right) where T : IComparable<T>{
  if (left == right) return;
  int pivot = Partition(items, left, right);
  QuickSort(items, left, pivot);
  QuickSort(items, pivot+1, right);
}
private static int Partition<T>(T[] items, int left, int right) where T : IComparable<T>{
  int pivotPos = ...; //often a random index between left and right is used
  T pivotValue = items[pivotPos];
  Swap(ref items[right-1], ref items[pivotPos]);
  int store = left;
  for (int i = left; i<right - 1; ++i) {
    if (items[i].CompareTo(pivotValue)<0) {
      Swap(ref items[i], ref items[store]);
      ++store;
    }
  }
  Swap(ref items[right-1], ref items[store]);
  return store;
}
private static void Swap<T>(ref T a, ref T b) {
  T temp = a;
  a = b;
  b = temp;
}
```

Figure 6-6 is an illustration of a single step of the Partition method. The fourth element (whose value is 5) is chosen as the pivot. First, it's moved to the far right of the array. Next, all elements larger than the pivot are propagated towards the right side of the array. Finally, the pivot is positioned such that all elements to its right are strictly larger than it, and all elements to its left are either smaller than or equal to it.

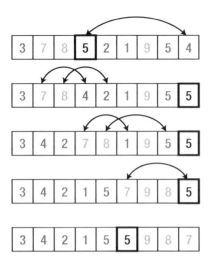

Figure 6-6. *Illustration of a single invocation of the* `Partition` *method.*

The recursive calls taken by QuickSort at every step must set the parallelization alarm. Sorting the left and right parts of the array are independent tasks, which require no synchronization among them, and the Task class is ideal for expressing this. Below is a first attempt at parallelizing QuickSort using Tasks:

```
public static void QuickSort<T>(T[] items) where T : IComparable<T> {
  QuickSort(items, 0, items.Length);
}
private static void QuickSort<T>(T[] items, int left, int right) where T : IComparable<T> {
  if (right - left<2) return;
  int pivot = Partition(items, left, right);
  Task leftTask  = Task.Run(() => QuickSort(items, left, pivot));
  Task rightTask = Task.Run(() => QuickSort(items, pivot+1, right));
  Task.WaitAll(leftTask, rightTask);
}
private static int Partition<T>(T[] items, int left, int right) where T : IComparable<T> {
  //Implementation omitted for brevity
}
```

The `Task.Run` method creates a new task (equivalent to calling `new Task()`) and schedules it for execution (equivalent to the newly created task's `Start` method). The `Task.WaitAll` static method waits for both tasks to complete and then returns. Note that we don't have to deal with specifying how to wait for tasks to complete, nor when to create threads and when to destroy them.

There is a helpful utility method called `Parallel.Invoke`, which executes a set of tasks provided to it and returns when all the tasks have completed. This would allow us to rewrite the core of the QuickSort method body with the following:

```
Parallel.Invoke(
    () => QuickSort(items, left, pivot),
    () => QuickSort(items, pivot+1, right)
);
```

Regardless of whether we use `Parallel.Invoke` or create tasks manually, if we try to compare this version with the straightforward sequential one, we will find that it runs significantly *slower*, even though it seems to take advantage of all the available processor resources. Indeed, using an array of 1,000,000 random integers, the sequential version ran (on our test system) for ~ 250 ms and the parallelized version took nearly ~ 650 ms to complete on average!

The problem is that parallelism needs to be sufficiently coarse-grained; attempting to parallelize the sorting of a three-element array is futile, because the overhead introduced by creating Task objects, scheduling work items to the thread pool, and waiting for them to complete execution overwhelms completely the handful of comparison operations required.

Throttling Parallelism in Recursive Algorithms

How do you propose to throttle the parallelism to prevent this overhead from diminishing any returns from our optimization? There are several viable approaches:

- Use the parallel version as long as the size of the array to be sorted is bigger than a certain threshold (say, 500 items), and switch to the sequential version as soon as it is smaller.

- Use the parallel version as long as the recursion depth is smaller than a certain threshold, and switch to the sequential version as soon as the recursion is very deep. (This option is somewhat inferior to the previous one, unless the pivot is always positioned exactly in the middle of the array.)

- Use the parallel version as long as the number of outstanding tasks (which the method would have to maintain manually) is smaller than a certain threshold, and switch to the sequential version otherwise. (This is the only option when there are no other criteria for limiting parallelism, such as recursion depth or input size.)

Indeed, in the case above, limiting the parallelization for arrays larger than 500 elements produces excellent results on the author's Intel i7 processor, yielding a 4× improvement in execution time compared to the sequential version. The code changes are quite simple, although the threshold should not be hardcoded in a production-quality implementation:

```
private static void QuickSort<T>(T[] items, int left, int right) where T : IComparable<T> {
  if (right - left<2) return;
  int pivot = Partition(items, left, right);
  if (right - left>500) {
    Parallel.Invoke(
      () => QuickSort(items, left, pivot),
      () => QuickSort(items, pivot+1, right)
    );
  } else {
    QuickSort(items, left, pivot);
    QuickSort(items, pivot+1, right);
  }
}
```

More Examples of Recursive Decomposition

There are many additional algorithms that can be parallelized by applying similar recursive decomposition. In fact, almost all recursive algorithms that split their input into several parts are *designed* to execute independently on each part and combine the results afterwards. Later in this chapter we shall consider examples that do not succumb so easily for parallelization, but first let's take a look at a few that do:

- Strassen's algorithm for matrix multiplication (see
  http://en.wikipedia.org/wiki/Strassen_algorithm for an overview). This algorithm
  for matrix multiplication offers better performance than the naïve cubic algorithm we
  shall see later in this chapter. Strassen's algorithm recursively decomposes a matrix of
  size $2^n \times 2^n$ into four equal block matrices of size $2^{n-1} \times 2^{n-1}$, and uses a clever trick that relies
  on *seven* multiplications instead of eight to obtain asymptotic running time of $\sim O(n^{2.807})$.
  As in the QuickSort example, practical implementations of Strassen's algorithm often
  fall back to the standard cubic algorithm for small-enough matrices; when parallelizing
  Strassen's algorithm using its recursive decomposition, it is even more important to put a
  threshold on parallelization for smaller matrices.

- Fast Fourier Transform (Cooley-Tukey algorithm, see
  http://en.wikipedia.org/wiki/Cooley%E2%80%93Tukey_FFT_algorithm). This
  algorithm computes the DFT (Discrete Fourier Transform) of a vector of length 2^n using
  a recursive decomposition of the vector into two vectors of size 2^{n-1}. Parallelizing this
  computation is fairly easy, but it is again important to be wary of placing a threshold to
  the parallelization for sufficiently small vectors.

- Graph traversal (Depth-First Search or Breadth-First Search). As we have seen in Chapter
  4, the CLR garbage collector traverses a graph in which objects are vertices and references
  between objects are edges. Graph traversal using DFS or BFS can benefit greatly from
  parallelization as well as other recursive algorithms we have considered; however,
  unlike QuickSort or FFT, when parallelizing branches of the graph traversal it is difficult
  to estimate in advance the amount of work a recursive call represents. This difficulty
  requires heuristics to decide how the search space should be partitioned to multiple
  threads: we have seen that the server GC flavor performs this partitioning rather crudely,
  based on the separate heaps from which each processor allocates objects.

If you are looking for more examples to practice your parallel programming skills, consider also Karatsuba's
multiplication algorithm that relies on recursive decomposition to multiply n-digit numbers in $\sim O(n^{1.585})$
operations; merge sort that relies on recursive decomposition for sorting, similarly to QuickSort; and numerous
dynamic programming algorithms, which often require advanced tricks to employ memoization in different
branches of the parallel computation (we will examine one example later).

Exceptions and Cancellation

We haven't tapped into the full power of the Task class yet. Suppose we wanted to handle exceptions that could
arise from the recursive invocations of QuickSort down the line, and provide support for canceling the entire sort
operation if it hasn't completed yet.

The task execution environment provides the infrastructure for marshaling exceptions that arise within the
task back to any thread deemed appropriate to receive it. Suppose that one of the recursive invocations of the
QuickSort tasks encountered an exception, perhaps because we didn't consider the array bounds carefully and
introduced an off-by-one error to either side of the array. This exception would arise on a thread pool thread, a
thread that is not under our explicit control and that does not allow any overarching exception handling behavior.
Fortunately, the TPL will catch the exception and store it within the Task object for later propagation.

The exception that arose within a task will be rethrown (wrapped in an AggregateException object) when
the program attempts to wait for the task to complete (using the Task.Wait instance method) or to retrieve
its result (using the Task.Result property). This allows automatic and centralized exception handling within
the code that created the task, and does not require manual propagation of errors to a central location and
synchronization of error-reporting activities. The following minimal code example demonstrates the exception-
handling paradigm in the TPL:

```
int i = 0;
Task<int> divideTask = Task.Run(() =>{ return 5/i; });
try {
  Console.WriteLine(divideTask.Result); //accessing the Result property eventually throws
} catch (AggregateException ex) {
  foreach (Exception inner in ex.InnerExceptions) {
    Console.WriteLine(inner.Message);
  }
}
```

▓ **Note** When creating a task from within the body of an existing task, the `TaskCreationOptions.Attached-ToParent` enumeration value establishes a relationship between the new child task and its parent task in which it was created. We will see later in this chapter that parent–child relationships between tasks affect cancellation, continuations, and debugging aspects of task execution. As far as exception handling is concerned, however, waiting for the parent task to complete implies waiting for all the child tasks to complete, and any exceptions from the child tasks are propagated to the parent task as well. This is why the TPL throws an `AggregateException` instance, which contains a hierarchy of exceptions that may have arisen from a hierarchy of tasks.

Cancellation of existing work is another matter to consider. Suppose that we have a hierarchy of tasks, such as the hierarchy created by QuickSort if we used the `TaskCreationOptions.AttachedToParent` enumeration value. Even though there may be hundreds of tasks running simultaneously, we might want to provide the user with cancellation semantics, e.g. if the sorted data is no longer required. In other scenarios, cancellation of outstanding work might be an integral part of the task execution. For example, consider a parallelized algorithm that looks up a node in a graph using DFS or BFS. When the desired node is found, the entire hierarchy of tasks performing the lookup should be recalled.

Canceling tasks involves the `CancellationTokenSource` and `CancellationToken` types, and is performed cooperatively. In other words, if a task's execution is already underway, it cannot be brutally terminated using TPL's cancellation mechanisms. Cancellation of already executing work requires cooperation from the code executing that work. However, tasks that have not begun executing yet can be cancelled completely without any malignant consequences.

The following code demonstrates a binary tree lookup where each node contains a potentially long array of elements that needs to be linearly traversed; the entire lookup can be cancelled by the caller using the TPL's cancellation mechanisms. On the one hand, unstarted tasks will be cancelled automatically by the TPL; on the other hand, tasks that have already started will periodically monitor their cancellation token for cancellation instructions and stop cooperatively when required.

```
public class TreeNode<T> {
  public TreeNode<T> Left, Right;
  public T[] Data;
}
public static void TreeLookup<T>(
  TreeNode<T> root, Predicate<T> condition, CancellationTokenSource cts) {
  if (root == null) {
    return;
  }
  //Start the recursive tasks, passing to them the cancellation token so that they are
  //cancelled automatically if they haven't started yet and cancellation is requested
  Task.Run(() => TreeLookup(root.Left, condition, cts), cts.Token);
```

```
    Task.Run(() => TreeLookup(root.Right, condition, cts), cts.Token);
    foreach (T element in root.Data) {
      if (cts.IsCancellationRequested) break; //abort cooperatively
      if (condition(element)) {
        cts.Cancel(); //cancels all outstanding work
        //Do something with the interesting element
      }
    }
  }
}

//Example of calling code:
CancellationTokenSource cts = new CancellationTokenSource();
Task.Run(() => TreeLookup(treeRoot, i =>i % 77 == 0, cts));
//After a while, e.g. if the user is no longer interested in the operation:
cts.Cancel();
```

Inevitably, there will be examples of algorithms where an easier way of expressing parallelism should be desirable. Consider the primality testing example with which we started. We could break the range manually into chunks, create a task for each chunk, and wait for all the tasks to complete. In fact, there is an entire family of algorithms in which there is a range of data to which a certain operation is applied. These algorithms mandate a higher-level abstraction than task parallelism. We now turn to this abstraction.

Data Parallelism

Whilst task parallelism dealt primarily with tasks, data parallelism aims to remove tasks from direct view and replace them by a higher-level abstraction—parallel loops. In other words, the source of parallelism is not the algorithm's *code*, but rather the *data* on which it operates. The Task Parallel Library offers several APIs providing data parallelism.

Parallel.For and Parallel.ForEach

for and foreach loops are often excellent candidates for parallelization. Indeed, since the dawn of parallel computing, there have been attempts to parallelize such loops automatically. Some attempts have gone the way of language changes or language extensions, such as the OpenMP standard (which introduced directives such as #pragma omp parallel for to parallelize for loops). The Task Parallel Library provides loop parallelism through explicit APIs, which are nonetheless very close to their language counterparts. These APIs are Parallel.For and Parallel.ForEach, matching as closely as possible the behavior of for and foreach loops in the language.

Returning to the example of parallelizing primality testing, we had a loop iterating over a large range of numbers, checking each one for primality and inserting it into a collection, as follows:

```
for (int number = start; number< end; ++number) {
  if (IsPrime(number)) {
    primes.Add(number);
  }
}
```

Converting this code to use Parallel.For is almost a mechanical task, although synchronizing access to the collection of primes warrants some caution (and there exist much better approaches, such as aggregation, that we consider later):

```
Parallel.For(start, end, number => {
  if (IsPrime(number)) {
```

```
    lock(primes) {
      primes.Add(number);
    }
  }
});
```

By replacing the language-level loop with an API call we gain automatic parallelization of the loop's iterations. Moreover, the `Parallel.For` API is not a straightforward loop that generates a task per iteration, or a task for each hard-coded chunk-sized part of the range. Instead, `Parallel.For` adapts slowly to the execution pace of individual iterations, takes into account the number of tasks currently executing, and prevents too-granular behavior by dividing the iteration range dynamically. Implementing these optimizations manually is not trivial, but you can apply specific customizations (such as controlling the maximum number of concurrently executing tasks) using another overload of `Parallel.For` that takes a `ParallelOptions` object or using a custom partitioner to determine how the iteration ranges should be divided across different tasks.

A similar API works with `foreach` loops, where the data source may not be fully enumerated when the loop begins, and in fact may not be finite. Suppose that we need to download from the Web a set of RSS feeds, specified as an `IEnumerable<string>`. The skeleton of the loop would have the following shape:

```
IEnumerable<string> rssFeeds = ...;
WebClient webClient = new WebClient();
foreach (string url in rssFeeds) {
  Process(webClient.DownloadString(url));
}
```

This loop can be parallelized by the mechanical transformation where the `foreach` loop is replaced by an API call to `Parallel.ForEach`. Note that the data source (the `rssFeeds` collection) need not be thread-safe, because `Parallel.ForEach` will use synchronization when accessing it from several threads.

```
IEnumerable<string> rssFeeds = ...; //The data source need not be thread-safe
WebClient webClient = new WebClient();
Parallel.ForEach(rssFeeds, url => {
  Process(webClient.DownloadString(url));
});
```

▓ **Note** You can voice a concern about performing an operation on an infinite data source. It turns out, however, that it is quite convenient to begin such an operation and expect to terminate it early when some condition is satisfied. For example, consider an infinite data source such as all the natural numbers (specified in code by a method that returns `IEnumerable<BigInteger>`). We can write and parallelize a loop that looks for a number whose digit sum is 477 but is not divisible by 133. Hopefully, there is such a number, and our loop will terminate.

Parallelizing loops it not as simple as it may seem from the above discussion. There are several "missing" features we need to consider before we fasten this tool assuredly to our belt. For starters, C# loops have the `break` keyword, which can terminate a loop early. How can we terminate a loop that has been parallelized across multiple threads, where we don't even know which iteration is currently executing on threads other than our own?

The `ParallelLoopState` class represents the state of a parallel loop's execution, and allows breaking early from a loop. Here is a simple example:

```
int invitedToParty = 0;
Parallel.ForEach(customers, (customer, loopState) => {
  if (customer.Orders.Count > 10 && customer.City == "Portland") {
```

```
    if (Interlocked.Increment(ref invitedToParty) >= 25) {
      loopState.Stop(); //no attempt will be made to execute any additional iterations
    }
  }
}
});
```

Note that the Stop method does not guarantee that the last iteration to execute is the one that called it—iterations that have already started executing will run to completion (unless they poll the ParallelLoopState.ShouldExitCurrentIteration property). However, no additional iterations that have been queued will begin to execute.

One of the drawbacks of ParallelLoopState.Stop is that it does not guarantee that all iterations up to a certain one have executed. For example, if there are 1,000 customers, it is possible that customers 1–100 have been processed completely, customers 101–110 have not been processed at all, and customer 111 was the last to be processed before Stop was called. If you would like to guarantee that all iterations before a certain iteration will have executed (even if they haven't started yet!), you should use the ParallelLoopState.Break method instead.

Parallel LINQ (PLINQ)

Possibly the highest level of abstraction for parallel computation is that where you declare: "I want this code to run in parallel", and leave the rest for the framework to implement. This is what Parallel LINQ is about. But first, a short refresher on LINQ is due. LINQ (Language INtegrated Query) is a framework and a set of language extensions introduced in C# 3.0 and .NET 3.5, blurring the line between imperative and declarative programming where iterating over data is concerned. For example, the following LINQ query retrieves from a data source called customers—which might be an in-memory collection, a database table, or a more exotic origin—the names and ages of the Washington-based customers who have made at least three over $10 purchases over the last ten months, and prints them to the console:

```
var results = from customer in customers
              where customer.State == "WA"
              let custOrders = (from order in orders
                                where customer.ID == order.ID
                                select new { order.Date, order.Amount })
              where custOrders.Count(co => co.Amount >= 10 &&
                                      co.Date >= DateTime.Now.AddMonths(-10)) >= 3
              select new { customer.Name, customer.Age };
foreach (var result in results) {
  Console.WriteLine("{0} {1}", result.Name, result.Age);
}
```

The primary thing to note here is that most of the query is specified declaratively—quite like an SQL query. It doesn't use loops to filter out objects or to group together objects from different data sources. Often enough, you shouldn't worry about synchronizing different iterations of the query, because most LINQ queries are purely functional and have no side effects—they convert one collection (IEnumerable<T>) to another without modifying any additional objects in the process.

To parallelize the execution of the above query, the only code change required is to modify the source collection from a general IEnumerable<T> to a ParallelQuery<T>. The AsParallel extension method takes care of this, and allows the following elegant syntax:

```
var results = from customer in customers.AsParallel()
              where customer.State == "WA"
              let custOrders = (from order in orders
                                where customer.ID == order.ID
```

```
                        select new { order.Date, order.Amount })
            where custOrders.Count(co => co.Amount >= 10 &&
                            co.Date >= DateTime.Now.AddMonths(-10)) >= 3
            select new { customer.Name, customer.Age };
foreach (var result in results) {
  Console.WriteLine("{0} {1}", result.Name, result.Age);
}
```

PLINQ uses a three-stage processing pipeline to execute parallel queries, as illustrated in Figure 6-7. First, PLINQ decides how many threads should be used to parallelize the query's execution. Next, the worker threads retrieve chunks of work from the source collection, ensuring that it is accessed under a lock. Each thread proceeds to execute its work items independently, and the results are queued locally within each thread. Finally, all the local results are buffered into a single result collection, which is polled by a foreach loop in the above example.

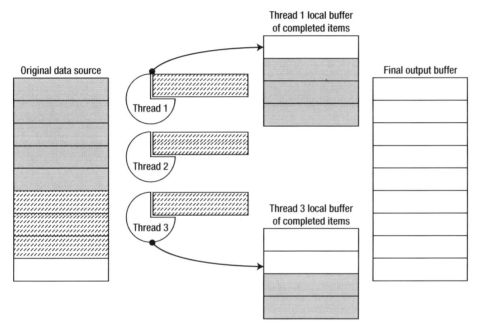

Figure 6-7. *Work item execution in PLINQ. Solid grey work items have been completed and placed in thread-local buffers, from which they are subsequently moved to the final output buffer available to the caller. Dashed work items are currently being executed*

The primary advantage of PLINQ compared to Parallel.ForEach stems from the fact that PLINQ automatically handles aggregation of temporary processing results locally within each thread that executes the query. When using Parallel.ForEach to find prime numbers, we had to access a global collection of prime numbers to aggregate the results (and later in this chapter we will consider an optimization that uses aggregation). This global access required continuous synchronization and introduced a significant overhead. We could accomplish the same result by using PLINQ, as follows:

```
List<int> primes = (from n in Enumerable.Range(3, 200000).AsParallel()
                where IsPrime(n)
                select n).ToList();
//Could have used ParallelEnumerable.Range instead of Enumerable.Range(...).AsParallel()
```

189

CUSTOMIZING PARALLEL LOOPS AND PLINQ

Parallel loops (`Parallel.For` and `Parallel.ForEach`) and PLINQ have several customization APIs, which make them extremely flexible and close in richness and expressiveness to the explicit task parallelism APIs we have considered previously. The parallel loop APIs accept a `ParallelOptions` object with various properties, whereas PLINQ relies on additional methods of `ParallelQuery<T>`. These options include:

- Limiting the degree of parallelism (the number of tasks that would be allowed to execute concurrently)

- Providing a cancellation token for canceling the parallel execution

- Forcing output ordering of a parallel query

- Controlling output buffering (merge mode) of a parallel query

With parallel loops, it is most common to limit the degree of parallelism using the `ParallelOptions` class, whereas with PLINQ, you would often customize the query's merge mode and ordering semantics. For more information on these customization options, consult the MSDN documentation.

C# 5 Async Methods

So far, we considered rich APIs that allow a variety of parallelism solutions to be expressed using the classes and methods of the Task Parallel Library. However, other parallel programming environments sometimes rely on language extensions to obtain even better expressiveness where APIs are clumsy or insufficiently concise. In this section we will see how C# 5 adapts to the challenges of the concurrent programming world by providing a language extension to express continuations more easily. But first, we must consider continuations in the asynchronous programming world.

Often enough, you would want to associate a *continuation* (or callback) with a specific task; the continuation should be executed when the task completes. If you have control of the task—i.e., you schedule it for execution—you can embed the callback in the task itself, but if you receive the task from another method, an explicit continuation API is desirable. The TPL offers the `ContinueWith` instance method and `ContinueWhenAll`/`ContinueWhenAny` static methods (self-explanatory) to control continuations in several settings. The continuation may be scheduled only in specific circumstances (e.g., only when the task ran to completion or only when the task has encountered an exception), and may be scheduled on a particular thread or thread group using the `TaskScheduler` API. Below are some examples of the various APIs:

```
Task<string> weatherTask = DownloadWeatherInfoAsync(...);
weatherTask.ContinueWith(_ => DisplayWeather(weatherTask.Result), TaskScheduler.Current);
Task left  = ProcessLeftPart(...);
Task right = ProcessRightPart(...);
TaskFactory.ContinueWhenAll(
  new Task[] { left, right },
  CleanupResources
);
TaskFactory.ContinueWhenAny(
  new Task[] { left, right },
  HandleError,
  TaskContinuationOptions.OnlyOnFaulted
);
```

Continuations are a reasonable way to program asynchronous applications, and are very valuable when performing asynchronous I/O in a GUI setting. For example, to ensure that Windows 8 Metro-style applications maintain a responsive user interface, the WinRT (Windows Runtime) APIs in Windows 8 offer only asynchronous versions of all operations that might run for longer than 50 milliseconds. With multiple asynchronous calls chained together, nested continuations become somewhat clumsy, as the following example may demonstrate:

```
//Synchronous version:
private void updateButton_Clicked(...) {
  using (LocationService location = new LocationService())
  using (WeatherService weather   = new WeatherService()) {
    Location loc       = location.GetCurrentLocation();
    Forecast forecast = weather.GetForecast(loc.City);
    MessageDialog msg = new MessageDialog(forecast.Summary);
    msg.Display();
  }
}

//Asynchronous version:
private void updateButton_Clicked(...) {
  TaskScheduler uiScheduler = TaskScheduler.Current;
  LocationService location = new LocationService();
  Task<Location> locTask = location.GetCurrentLocationAsync();
  locTask.ContinueWith(_ => {
    WeatherService weather = new WeatherService();
    Task<Forecast> forTask = weather.GetForecastAsync(locTask.Result.City);
    forTask.ContinueWith(__ => {
      MessageDialog message = new MessageDialog(forTask.Result.Summary);
      Task msgTask = message.DisplayAsync();
      msgTask.ContinueWith(___ => {
        weather.Dispose();
        location.Dispose();
      });
    }, uiScheduler);
  });
}
```

This deep nesting is not the only peril of explicit continuation-based programming. Consider the following synchronous loop that requires conversion to an asynchronous version:

```
//Synchronous version:
private Forecast[] GetForecastForAllCities(City[] cities) {
  Forecast[] forecasts = new Forecast[cities.Length];
  using (WeatherService weather = new WeatherService()) {
    for (int i = 0; i<cities.Length; ++i) {
      forecasts[i] = weather.GetForecast(cities[i]);
    }
  }
  return forecasts;
}
```

```
//Asynchronous version:
private Task<Forecast[]>GetForecastsForAllCitiesAsync(City[] cities) {
  if (cities.Length == 0) {
    return Task.Run(() =>new Forecast[0]);
  }
  WeatherService weather = new WeatherService();
  Forecast[] forecasts = new Forecast[cities.Length];
  return GetForecastHelper(weather, 0, cities, forecasts).ContinueWith(_ => forecasts);
}
private Task GetForecastHelper(
  WeatherService weather, int i, City[] cities, Forecast[] forecasts) {
  if (i>= cities.Length) return Task.Run(() => { });
  Task<Forecast> forecast = weather.GetForecastAsync(cities[i]);
  forecast.ContinueWith(task => {
    forecasts[i] = task.Result;
    GetForecastHelper(weather, i+1, cities, forecasts);
  });
  return forecast;
}
```

Converting this loop requires completely rewriting the original method and scheduling a continuation that essentially executes the next iteration in a fairly unintuitive and recursive manner. This is something the C# 5 designers have chosen to address on the language level by introducing two new keywords, async and await.

An async method must be marked with the async keyword and may return void, Task, or Task<T>. Within an async method, the await operator can be used to express a continuation without using the ContinueWith API. Consider the following example:

```
private async void updateButton_Clicked(...) {
  using (LocationService location = new LocationService()) {
    Task<Location> locTask = location.GetCurrentLocationAsync();
    Location loc = await locTask;
    cityTextBox.Text = loc.City.Name;
  }
}
```

In this example, the await locTask expression provides a continuation to the task returned by GetCurrentLocationAsync. The continuation's body is the rest of the method (starting from the assignment to the loc variable), and the await expression evaluates to what the task returns, in this case—a Location object. Moreover, the continuation is implicitly scheduled on the UI thread, which is something we had to explicitly take care of earlier using the TaskScheduler API.

The C# compiler takes care of all the relevant syntactic features associated with the method's body. For example, in the method we just wrote, there is a try...finally block hidden behind the using statement. The compiler rewrites the continuation such that the Dispose method on the location variable is invoked regardless of whether the task completed successfully or an exception occurred.

This smart rewriting allows almost trivial conversion of synchronous API calls to their asynchronous counterparts. The compiler supports exception handling, complex loops, recursive method invocation—language constructs that are *hard* to combine with the explicit continuation-passing APIs. For example, here is the asynchronous version of the forecast-retrieval loop that caused us trouble earlier:

```
private async Task<Forecast[]> GetForecastForAllCitiesAsync(City[] cities) {
  Forecast[] forecasts = new Forecast[cities.Length];
  using (WeatherService weather = new WeatherService()) {
    for (int i = 0; i<cities.Length; ++i) {
```

```
    forecasts[i] = await weather.GetForecastAsync(cities[i]);
    }
  }
  return forecasts;
}
```

Note that the changes are minimal, and the compiler handles the details of taking the forecasts variable (of type Forecast[]) our method returns and creating the Task<Forecast[]> scaffold around it.

With only two simple language features (whose implementation is everything but simple!), C# 5 dramatically decreases the barrier of entry for asynchronous programming, and makes it easier to work with APIs that return and manipulate tasks. Furthermore, the language implementation of the await operator is not wed to the Task Parallel Library; native WinRT APIs in Windows 8 return IAsyncOperation<T> and not Task instances (which are a managed concept), but can still be awaited, as in the following example, which uses a real WinRT API:

```
using Windows.Devices.Geolocation;
...
private async void updateButton_Clicked(...) {
  Geolocator locator = new Geolocator();
  Geoposition position = await locator.GetGeopositionAsync();
  statusTextBox.Text = position.CivicAddress.ToString();
}
```

Advanced Patterns in the TPL

So far in this chapter, we have considered fairly simple examples of algorithms that were subjected to parallelization. In this section, we will briefly inspect a few advanced tricks that you may find useful when dealing with real-world problems; in several cases we may be able to extract a performance gain from very surprising places.

The first optimization to consider when parallelizing loops with shared state is *aggregation* (sometimes called *reduction*). When using shared state in a parallel loop, scalability is often lost because of synchronization on the shared state access; the more CPU cores are added to the mix, the smaller the gains because of the synchronization (this phenomenon is a direct corollary of Amdahl's Law, and is often called *The Law of Diminishing Returns*). A big performance boost is often available from aggregating local state within each thread or task that executes the parallel loop, and combining the local states to obtain the eventual result at the end of the loop's execution. TPL APIs that deal with loop execution come equipped with overloads to handle this kind of local aggregation.

For example, consider the prime number computation we implemented earlier. One of the primary hindrances to scalability was the need to insert newly discovered prime numbers into a shared list, which required synchronization. Instead, we can use a local list in each thread, and aggregate the lists together when the loop completes:

```
List<int> primes = new List<int>();
Parallel.For(3, 200000,
  () => new List<int>(),        //initialize the local copy
  (i, pls, localPrimes) => {    //single computation step, returns new local state
    if (IsPrime(i)) {
      localPrimes.Add(i);       //no synchronization necessary, thread-local state
    }
    return localPrimes;
  },
  localPrimes => {              //combine the local lists to the global one
    lock(primes) {             //synchronization is required
      primes.AddRange(localPrimes);
    }
  }
);
```

In the example above, the number of locks taken is significantly smaller than earlier—we only need to take a lock once per thread that executes the parallel loop, instead of having to take it per each prime number we discovered. We *did* introduce an additional cost of combining the lists together, but this cost is negligible compared to the scalability gained by local aggregation.

Another source of optimization is loop iterations that are too small to be parallelized effectively. Even though the data parallelism APIs chunk multiple iterations together, there may be loop bodies that are so quick to complete that they are dominated by the delegate invocation required to call the loop body for each iteration. In this case, the `Partitioner` API can be used to extract manually chunks of iterations, minimizing the number of delegate invocations:

```
Parallel.For(Partitioner.Create(3, 200000), range => { //range is a Tuple<int,int>
  for (int i = range.Item1; i<range.Item2; ++i) ...   //loop body with no delegate invocation
});
```

For more information on custom partitioning, which is as well an important optimization available to data-parallel programs, consult the MSDN article "Custom Partitioners for PLINQ and TPL", at `http://msdn.microsoft.com/en-us/library/dd997411.aspx`.

Finally, there are applications which can benefit from custom task schedulers. Some examples include scheduling work on the UI thread (something we have already done using `TaskScheduler.Current` to queue continuations to the UI thread), prioritizing tasks by scheduling them to a higher-priority scheduler, and affinitizing tasks to a particular CPU by scheduling them to a scheduler that uses threads with a specific CPU affinity. The `TaskScheduler` class can be extended to create custom task schedulers. For an example of a custom task scheduler, consult the MSDN article "How to: Create a Task Scheduler That Limits the Degree of Concurrency", at `http://msdn.microsoft.com/en-us/library/ee789351.aspx`.

Synchronization

A treatment of parallel programming warrants at least a cursory mention of the vast topic of synchronization. In the simple examples considered throughout this text, we have seen numerous cases of multiple threads accessing a shared memory location, be it a complex collection or a single integer. Aside from read-only data, every access to a shared memory location requires synchronization, but not all synchronization mechanisms have the same performance and scalability costs.

Before we begin, let's revisit the need for synchronization when accessing small amounts of data. Modern CPUs can issue atomic reads and writes to memory; for example, a write of a 32 bit integer always executes atomically. This means that if one processor writes the value 0xDEADBEEF to a memory location previously initialized with the value 0, another processor will not observe the memory location with a partial update, such as 0xDEAD0000 or 0x0000BEEF. Unfortunately, the same thing is not true of larger memory locations; for example, even on a 64 bit processor, writing 20 bytes into memory is not an atomic operation and cannot be performed atomically.

However, even when accessing a 32 bit memory location but issuing multiple operations, synchronization problems arise immediately. For example, the operation ++i (where i is a stack variable of type int) is typically translated to a sequence of three machine instructions:

```
mov eax, dword ptr [ebp-64] ;copy from stack to register
inc eax                     ;increment value in register
mov dword ptr [ebp-64], eax ;copy from register to stack
```

Each of these instructions executes atomically, but without additional synchronization it is possible for two processors to execute parts of the instruction sequence concurrently, resulting in *lost updates*. Suppose that the variable's initial value was 100, and examine the following execution history:

Processor #1
```
mov eax, dword ptr [ebp-64]


inc eax
mov dword ptr [ebp-64], eax
```

Processor #2
```

mov eax, dword ptr [ebp-64]
inc eax


mov dword ptr [ebp-64], eax
```

In this case, the variable's eventual value will be 101, even though *two* processors have executed the increment operation and should have brought it to 102. This race condition—which is hopefully obvious and easily detectable—is a representative example of the situations that warrant careful synchronization.

OTHER DIRECTIONS

Many researchers and programming language designers do not believe that the situation governing shared memory synchronization can be addressed without changing completely the semantics of programming languages, parallelism frameworks, or processor memory models. There are several interesting directions in this area:

- Transactional memory in hardware or software suggests an explicit or implicit isolation model around memory operations and rollback semantics for series of memory operations. Currently, the performance cost of such approaches impedes their wide adoption in mainstream programming languages and frameworks.

- Agent-based languages bake a concurrency model deep into the language and require explicit communication between agents (objects) in terms of message-passing instead of shared memory access.

- Message-passing processor and memory architectures organize the system using a private-memory paradigm, where access to a shared memory location must be explicit through message-passing at the hardware level.

Throughout the rest of this section, we shall assume a more pragmatic view and attempt to reconcile the problems of shared memory synchronization by offering a set of synchronization mechanisms and patterns. However, the authors firmly believe that synchronization is more difficult than it should be; our shared experience demonstrates that a large majority of difficult bugs in software today stem from the simplicity of corrupting shared state by improperly synchronizing parallel programs. We hope that in a few years—or decades—the computing community will come up with somewhat better alternatives.

Lock-Free Code

One approach to synchronization places the burden on the operating system. After all, the operating system provides the facilities for creating and managing threads, and assumes full responsibility for scheduling their execution. It is then natural to expect from it to provide a set of synchronization primitives. Although we will discuss Windows synchronization mechanisms shortly, this approach begs the question of how the operating system *implements* these synchronization mechanisms. Surely Windows itself is in need of synchronizing access to its internal data structures—even the data structures representing other synchronization mechanisms—and it cannot implement synchronization mechanisms by deferring to them recursively. It also turns out that Windows synchronization mechanisms often require a system call (user-mode to kernel-mode transition) and thread context switch to ensure synchronization, which is relatively expensive if the operations that require synchronization are very cheap (such as incrementing a number or inserting an item into a linked list).

All the processor families on which Windows can run implement a *hardware* synchronization primitive called Compare-And-Swap (CAS). CAS has the following semantics (in pseudo-code), and executes *atomically*:

```
WORD CAS(WORD* location, WORD value, WORD comparand) {
  WORD old = *location;
  if (old == comparand) {
    *location = value;
  }
  return old;
}
```

Simply put, CAS compares a memory location with a provided value. If the memory location contains the provided value, it is replaced by another value; otherwise, it is unchanged. In any case, the content of the memory location prior to the operation is returned.

For example, on Intel x86 processors, the LOCK CMPXCHG instruction implements this primitive. Translating a CAS(&a,b,c) call to LOCK CMPXCHG is a simple mechanical process, which is why we will be content with using CAS throughout the rest of this section. In the .NET Framework, CAS is implemented using a set of overloads called Interlocked.CompareExchange.

```
//C# code:
int n = ...;
if (Interlocked.CompareExchange(ref n, 1, 0) == 0) { //attempt to replace 0 with 1
  //...do something
}


//x86 assembly instructions:
mov eax, 0                            ;the comparand
mov edx, 1                            ;the new value
lock cmpxchg dword ptr [ebp-64], edx  ;assume that n is in [ebp-64]
test eax, eax                         ;if eax = 0, the replace took place
jnz not_taken
;...do something
not_taken:
```

A single CAS operation is often not enough to ensure any useful synchronization, unless the desirable semantics are to perform a one-time check-and-replace operation. However, when combined with a looping construct, CAS can be used for a non-negligible variety of synchronization tasks. First, we consider a simple example of in-place multiplication. We want to execute the operation x *= y atomically, where x is a shared memory location that may be written to simultaneously by other threads, and y is a constant value that is not modified by other threads. The following CAS-based C# method performs this task:

```
public static void InterlockedMultiplyInPlace(ref int x, int y) {
  int temp, mult;
  do {
    temp = x;
    mult = temp * y;
  } while(Interlocked.CompareExchange(ref x, mult, temp) ! = temp);
}
```

Each loop iteration begins by reading the value of x to a temporary stack variable, which cannot be modified by another thread. Next, we find the multiplication result, ready to be placed into x. Finally, the loop terminates if and only if CompareExchange reports that it successfully replaced the value of x with the multiplication result, granted that the original value was not modified. We cannot guarantee that the loop will terminate in a bounded number of iterations; however, it is highly unlikely that—even under pressure from other processors—a single processor will be skipped more than a few times when trying to replace x with its new value. Nonetheless, the loop must be prepared to face this case (and try again). Consider the following execution history with x = 3, y = 5 on two processors:

Processor #1	Processor #2
`temp = x; (3)`	
	`temp = x; (3)`
`mult = temp * y; (15)`	
	`mult = temp * y; (15)`
	`CAS(ref x, mult, temp) == 3 (== temp)`
`CAS(ref x, mult, temp) == 15 (!=temp)`	

Even this extremely simple example is very easy to get wrong. For example, the following loop may cause lost updates:

```
public static void InterlockedMultiplyInPlace(ref int x, int y) {
  int temp, mult;
  do {
    temp = x;
    mult = x * y;
  } while(Interlocked.CompareExchange(ref x, mult, temp) ! = temp);
}
```

Why? Reading the value of x twice in rapid succession does not guarantee that we see the same value! The following execution history demonstrates how an incorrect result can be produced, with x = 3, y = 5 on two processors—at the end of the execution x = 60!

Processor #1	Processor #2
`temp = x; (3)`	
	`x = 12;`
`mult = x * y; (60!)`	
	`x = 3;`
`CAS(ref x, mult, temp) == 3 (== temp)`	

We can generalize this result to any algorithm that needs to read only a single mutating memory location and replace it with a new value, no matter how complex. The most general version would be the following:

```
public static void DoWithCAS<T>(ref T location, Func<T,T>generator) where T : class {
  T temp, replace;
  do {
    temp = location;
    replace = generator(temp);
  } while (Interlocked.CompareExchange(ref location, replace, temp) ! = temp);
}
```

Expressing the multiplication method in terms of this general version is very easy:

```
public static void InterlockedMultiplyInPlace(ref int x, int y) {
  DoWithCAS(ref x, t => t * y);
}
```

Specifically, there is a simple synchronization mechanism called *spinlock* that can be implemented using CAS. The idea here is as follows: to acquire a lock is to make sure that any other thread that attempts to acquire it will fail and try again. A spinlock, then, is a lock that allows a single thread to acquire it and all other threads to *spin* ("waste" CPU cycles) while trying to acquire it:

```
public class SpinLock {
  private volatile int locked;
  public void Acquire() {
    while (Interlocked.CompareExchange(ref locked, 1, 0) ! = 0);
  }
  public void Release() {
    locked = 0;
  }
}
```

MEMORY MODELS AND VOLATILE VARIABLES

A complete treatment of synchronization would include a discussion of memory models and the need for volatile variables. However, we lack the space to cover this subject adequately, and offer only a brief account. Joe Duffy's book "Concurrent Programming on Windows" (Addison-Wesley, 2008) offers an in-depth detailed description.

Generally speaking, a memory model for a particular language/environment describes how the compiler and the processor hardware may reorder operations on memory performed by different threads—the interaction of threads through shared memory. Although most memory models agree that read and write operations on the *same* memory location may not be reordered, there is scarce agreement on the semantics of read and write operations on *different* memory locations. For example, the following program may output 13 when starting from the state $f = 0$, $x = 13$:

Processor #1	**Processor #2**
while (f == 0);	x = 42;
print(x);	f = 1;

The reason for this unintuitive result is that the compiler and processor are free to reorder the instructions on processor #2 such that the write to f completes before the write to x, and to reorder the instructions on processor #1 such that the read of x completes before the read of f. Failing to take into account the details of a particular memory model may lead to extremely difficult bugs.

There are several remedies available to C# developers when dealing with memory reordering issues. First is the volatile keyword, which prevents compiler reorderings and most processor reorderings around operations on a particular variable. Second is the set of Interlocked APIs and Thread.MemoryBarrier, which introduce a fence which cannot be crossed in one or both directions as far as reorderings are concerned. Fortunately, the Windows synchronization mechanisms (which involve a system call) as well as any lock-free synchronization primitives in the TPL issue a memory barrier when necessary. However, if you attempt the already-risky task of implementing your own low-level synchronization, you should invest a significant amount of time understanding the details of your target environment's memory model.

We cannot stress this harder: if you choose to deal with memory ordering directly, it is *absolutely crucial* that you understand the memory model of every language and hardware combination you use for programming your multithreaded applications. There will be no framework to guard your steps.

In our spinlock implementation, 0 represents a free lock and 1 represents a lock that is taken. Our implementation attempts to replace its internal value with 1, provided that its current value is 0—i.e., acquire the lock, provided that it is not currently acquired. Because there is no guarantee that the owning thread will release the lock quickly, using a spinlock means that you may devote a set of threads to spinning around, wasting CPU cycles, waiting for a lock to become available. This makes spinlocks inapplicable for protecting operations such as database access, writing out a large file to disk, sending a packet over the network, and similar long-running operations. However, spinlocks are very useful when the guarded code section is very quick—modifying a bunch of fields on an object, incrementing several variables in a row, or inserting an item into a simple collection.

Indeed, the Windows kernel itself uses spinlocks extensively to implement internal synchronization. Kernel data structures such as the scheduler database, file system cache block list, memory page frame number database and others are protected by one or more spinlocks. Moreover, the Windows kernel introduces additional optimizations to the simple spinlock implementation described above, which suffers from two problems:

1. The spinlock is not *fair*, in terms of FIFO semantics. A processor may be the last of ten processors to call the Acquire method and spin inside it, but may be the first to actually acquire it after it has been released by its owner.

2. When the spinlock owner releases the spinlock, it invalidates the cache of all the processors currently spinning in the Acquire method, although only one processor will actually acquire it. (We will revisit cache invalidation later in this chapter.)

The Windows kernel uses *in-stack queued spinlocks*; an in-stack queued spinlock maintains a queue of processors waiting for a lock, and every processor waiting for the lock spins around a separate memory location, which is not in the cache of other processors. When the spinlock's owner releases the lock, it finds the first processor in the queue and signals the bit on which this particular processor is waiting. This guarantees FIFO semantics and prevents cache invalidations on all processors but the one that successfully acquires the lock.

■ **Note** Production-grade implementations of spinlocks can be more robust in face of failures, avoid spinning for more than a reasonable threshold (by converting spinning to a blocking wait), track the owning thread to make sure spinlocks are correctly acquired and released, allow recursive acquisition of locks, and provide additional facilities. The SpinLock type in the Task Parallel Library is one recommended implementation.

Armed with the CAS synchronization primitive, we now reach an incredible feat of engineering—a lock-free stack. In Chapter 5 we have considered some concurrent collections, and will not repeat this discussion, but the implementation of ConcurrentStack<T> remained somewhat of a mystery. Almost magically, ConcurrentStack<T> allows multiple threads to push and pop items from it, but never requires a blocking synchronization mechanism (that we consider next) to do so.

We shall implement a lock-free stack by using a singly linked list. The stack's top element is the head of the list; pushing an item onto the stack or popping an item from the stack means replacing the head of the list. To do this in a synchronized fashion, we rely on the CAS primitive; in fact, we can use the DoWithCAS<T> helper introduced previously:

```
public class LockFreeStack<T> {
  private class Node {
    public T Data;
    public Node Next;
  }
  private Node head;
  public void Push(T element) {
    Node node = new Node { Data = element };
    DoWithCAS(ref head, h => {
      node.Next = h;
      return node;
    });
  }
}
```

```
public bool TryPop(out T element) {
  //DoWithCAS does not work here because we need early termination semantics
  Node node;
  do {
    node = head;
    if (node == null) {
      element = default(T);
      return false; //bail out - nothing to return
    }
  } while (Interlocked.CompareExchange(ref head, node.Next, node) ! = node);
  element = node.Data;
  return true;
  }
}
```

The Push method attempts to replace the list head with a new node, whose Next pointer points to the current list head. Similarly, the TryPop method attempts to replace the list head with the node to which the current head's Next pointer points, as illustrated in Figure 6-8.

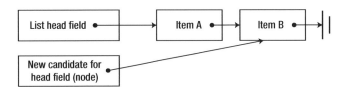

Figure 6-8. *The TryPop operation attempts to replace the current list head with a new one*

You may be tempted to think that every data structure in the world can be implemented using CAS and similar lock-free primitives. Indeed, there are some additional examples of lock-free collections in wide use today:

- Lock-free doubly linked list
- Lock-free queue (with a head and tail)
- Lock-free simple priority queue

However, there is a great variety of collections that cannot be easily implemented using lock-free code, and still rely on blocking synchronization mechanisms. Furthermore, there is a considerable amount of code that requires synchronization but cannot use CAS because it takes too long to execute. We now turn to discuss "real" synchronization mechanisms, which involve blocking, implemented by the operating system.

Windows Synchronization Mechanisms

Windows offers numerous synchronization mechanisms to user-mode programs, such as events, semaphores, mutexes, and condition variables. Our programs can access these synchronization mechanisms through handles and Win32 API calls, which issue the corresponding system calls on our behalf. The .NET Framework wraps most Windows synchronization mechanisms in thin object-oriented packages, such as ManualResetEvent, Mutex, Semaphore, and others. On top of the existing synchronization mechanisms, .NET offers several new ones, such as ReaderWriterLockSlim and Monitor. We will not examine exhaustively every synchronization mechanism in minute detail, which is a task best left to API documentation; it is important, however, to understand their general performance characteristics.

The Windows kernel implements the synchronization mechanisms we are now discussing by blocking a thread that attempts to acquire the lock when the lock is not available. Blocking a thread involves removing it from the CPU, marking it as waiting, and scheduling another thread for execution. This operation involves a system call, which is a user-mode to kernel-mode transition, a context switch between two threads, and a small set of data structure updates (see Figure 6-9) performed in the kernel to mark the thread as waiting and associate it with the synchronization mechanism for which it's waiting.

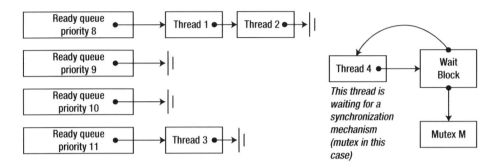

Figure 6-9. *The data maintained by the operating system scheduler. Threads ready for execution are placed in FIFO queues, sorted by priority. Blocked threads reference their synchronization mechanism through an internal structure called a wait block*

Overall, there are potentially thousands of CPU cycles spent to block a thread, and a similar number of cycles is required to unblock it when the synchronization mechanism becomes available. It is clear, then, that if a kernel synchronization mechanism is used to protect a long-running operation, such as writing a large buffer to a file or performing a network round-trip, this overhead is negligible, but if a kernel synchronization mechanism is used to protect an operation like ++i, this overhead introduces an inexcusable slowdown.

The synchronization mechanisms Windows and .NET make available to applications differ primarily in terms of their acquire and release semantics, also known as their signal state. When a synchronization mechanism becomes signaled, it wakes up a thread (or a group of threads) waiting for it to become available. Below are the signal state semantics for some of the synchronization mechanisms currently accessible to .NET applications:

Table 6-1. *Signal State Semantics of Some Synchronization Mechanisms*

Synchronization Mechanism	When Does It Become Signaled?	Which Threads Are Woken?
Mutex	When a thread calls `Mutex.ReleaseMutex`	One of the threads that are waiting for the mutex
Semaphore	When a thread calls `Semaphore.Release`	One of the threads that are waiting for the semaphore
ManualResetEvent	When a thread calls `ManualResetEvent.Set`	All of the threads that are waiting for the event
AutoResetEvent	When a thread calls `AutoResetEvent.Set`	One of the threads that are waiting for the event
Monitor	When a thread calls `Monitor.Exit`	One of the threads that are waiting for the Monitor

(continued)

Table 6-1. (*continued*)

Synchronization Mechanism	When Does It Become Signaled?	Which Threads Are Woken?
Barrier	When all the participating threads have called Barrier.SignalAndWait	All of the threads that are waiting for the barrier
ReaderWriterLock—for reading	When there are no writer threads, or the last writer thread has released the lock for writing	All of the threads that are waiting to enter the lock for reading
ReaderWriterLock—for writing	When there are no reader threads or writer threads	One of the threads that are waiting to enter the lock for writing

Other than the signal state semantics, some synchronization mechanisms differ also in terms of their internal implementation. For example, the Win32 critical section and the CLR Monitor implement an optimization for locks that are currently available. With that optimization, a thread attempting to acquire an available lock can grab it directly without performing a system call. On a different front, the reader-writer lock family of synchronization mechanisms distinguishes between readers and writers accessing a certain object, which permits better scalability when the data is most often accessed for reading.

Choosing the appropriate synchronization mechanism from the list of what Windows and .NET have to offer is often difficult, and there are times when a custom synchronization mechanism may offer better performance characteristics or more convenient semantics than the existing ones. We will not consider synchronization mechanisms any further; it is your responsibility when programming concurrent applications to choose responsibly between lock-free synchronization primitives and blocking synchronization mechanisms, and to determine the best combination of synchronization mechanisms to use.

▓ **Note** No discussion of synchronization could be complete without highlighting data structures (collections) designed from the ground up for concurrency. Such collections are thread-safe—they allow safe access from multiple threads—as well as scalable without introducing unreasonable performance degradation due to locking. For a discussion of concurrent collections, as well as designing concurrent collections, consult Chapter 5.

Cache Considerations

We have previously paid a visit to the subject of processor caches in the context of collection implementation and memory density. In parallel programs it is similarly important to regard cache size and hit rates on a single processor, but it is even more important to consider how the caches of multiple processors interact. We will now consider a single representative example, which demonstrates the important of cache-oriented optimization, and emphasizes the value of good tools when it concerns performance optimization in general.

First, examine the following sequential method. It performs the rudimentary task of summing all the elements in a two-dimensional array of integers and returns the result.

```
public static int MatrixSumSequential(int[,] matrix) {
  int sum = 0;
  int rows = matrix.GetUpperBound(0);
  int cols = matrix.GetUpperBound(1);
```

```
  for (int i = 0; i<rows; ++i) {
    for (int j = 0; j<cols; ++j) {
      sum+= matrix[i,j];
    }
  }
  return sum;
}
```

We have in our arsenal a large set of tools for parallelizing programs of this sort. However, imagine for a moment that we don't have the TPL at our disposal, and choose to work directly with threads instead. The following attempt at parallelization may appear sufficiently reasonable to harvest the fruits of multi-core execution, and even implements a crude aggregation to avoid synchronization on the shared sum variable:

```
public static int MatrixSumParallel(int[,] matrix) {
  int sum = 0;
  int rows = matrix.GetUpperBound(0);
  int cols = matrix.GetUpperBound(1);
  const int THREADS = 4;
  int chunk = rows/THREADS; //should divide evenly
  int[] localSums = new int[THREADS];
  Thread[] threads = new Thread[THREADS];
  for (int i = 0; i<THREADS; ++i) {
    int start = chunk*i;
    int end = chunk*(i+1);
    int threadNum = i; //prevent the compiler from hoisting the variable in the lambda capture
    threads[i] = new Thread(() => {
      for (int row = start; row<end; ++row) {
        for (int col = 0; col<cols; ++col) {
          localSums[threadNum]+= matrix[row,col];
        }
      }
    });
    threads[i].Start();
  }
  foreach (Thread thread in threads) {
    thread.Join();
  }
  sum = localSums.Sum();
  return sum;
}
```

Executing each of the two methods 25 times on an Intel i7 processor produced the following results for a 2,000 × 2,000 matrix of integers: the sequential method completed within 325ms on average, whereas the parallelized method took a whopping 935ms on average, thrice as slow as the sequential version!

This is clearly unacceptable, but why? This is not another example of too fine-grained parallelism, because the number of threads is only 4. If you accept the premise that the problem is somehow cache-related (because this example appears in the "Cache Considerations" section), it would make sense to measure the number of cache misses introduced by the two methods. The Visual Studio profiler (when sampling at each 2,000 cache misses) reported 963 exclusive samples in the parallel version and only 659 exclusive samples in the sequential version; the vast majority of samples were on the inner loop line that reads from the matrix.

Again, why? Why would the line of code writing to the localSums array introduce so many more cache misses than the line writing to the sum local variable? The simple answer is that the writes to the shared array *invalidate cache lines at other processors*, causing every += operation on the array to be a cache miss.

As you recall from Chapter 5, processor caches are organized in cache lines, and adjacent memory locations share the same cache line. When one processor writes to a memory location that is in the cache of another processor, the hardware causes a cache invalidation that marks the cache line in the other processor's cache as invalid. Accessing an invalid cache line causes a cache miss. In our example above, it is very likely that the entire localSums array fits in a single cache line, and resides simultaneously in the caches of *all* four processors on which the application's threads are executing. Every write performed to any element of the array on any of the processors invalidates the cache line on all other processors, causing a constant ping-pong of cache invalidations (see Figure 6-10).

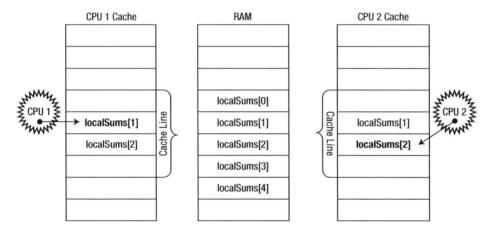

Figure 6-10. *CPU 1 writes to* localSums[1] *while CPU 2 writes to* localSums[2]. *Because both array elements are adjacent and fit into the same cache line in both processor caches, each such write causes a cache invalidation on the other processor*

To make sure that the problem is completely related to cache invalidations, it is possible to make the array strides sufficiently larger such that cache invalidation does not occur, or to replace the direct writes to the array with writes to a local variable in each thread that is eventually flushed to the array when the thread completes. Either of these optimizations restores sanity to the world, and makes the parallel version faster than the sequential one on a sufficiently large number of cores.

Cache invalidation (or cache collision) is a nasty problem that is exceptionally difficult to detect in a real application, even when aided by powerful profilers. Taking it into consideration upfront when designing CPU-bound algorithms will save you a lot of time and aggravation later.

■ **Note**   The authors encountered a similar case of cache invalidation in a production scenario with a shared work item queue between two threads executing on two different processors. When a certain minor change was made to the internal structure of the queue class' fields, significant performance degradation (approximately 20%) was detected in subsequent builds. Upon very long and detailed examination, it became apparent that reordering fields in the queue class was responsible for the performance degradation; two fields that were being written to by different threads have become too close together and were placed on the same cache line. Adding padding betwee the fields restored the queue's performance to acceptable levels.

General Purpose GPU Computing

So far, our coverage of parallel programming has been partial to CPU cores. Indeed, we have several skills at our disposal to parallelize programs across multiple cores, synchronize access to shared resources, and use high-speed CPU primitives for lock-free synchronization. As we noted at the outset of this chapter, there is another source of parallelism available to our programs—the GPU, which on modern hardware offers considerably many cores than even high-end CPUs. GPU cores are very suitable for data-parallel algorithms, and their sheer number makes up for the clumsiness often associated with running programs on them. In this section we examine one way of running programs on the GPU, using a set of C++ language extensions called C++ AMP.

■ **Note** C++ AMP is based on C++, which is why this section will use C++ code examples. However, by applying a moderate amount of .NET Interoperability, you can use C++ AMP algorithms in your .NET applications as well. We will return to this subject at the end of the section.

Introduction to C++ AMP

At its essence, a GPU is a processor like any other, with a specific instruction set, numerous cores, and a memory access protocol. However, there are significant differences between modern GPUs and CPUs, and understanding them is central for writing efficient GPU-based programs:

- There is only a small subset of instructions available to modern CPUs that are available on the GPU. This implies some limitations: there are no function calls, data types are limited, library functions are missing, and others. Other operations, such as branching, may introduce a performance cost unparalleled to that on the CPU. Clearly, this makes porting massive amounts of code from the CPU to the GPU a considerable effort.

- There is a considerably larger number of cores on a mid-range graphics card than on a mid-range CPU socket. There will be work units that are too small or cannot be broken into sufficiently many pieces to benefit properly from parallelization on the GPU.

- There is scarce support for synchronization between GPU cores executing a task, and no support for synchronization between GPU cores executing different tasks. This requires the synchronization and orchestration of GPU work to be performed on the CPU.

WHAT TASKS ARE SUITABLE FOR EXECUTION ON THE GPU?

Not every algorithm is suitable for execution on the GPU. For example, GPUs do not have access to other I/O devices, so you can scarcely improve the performance of a program that fetches RSS feeds from the Web by using a GPU. However, many CPU-bound data-parallel algorithms can be ported to the GPU and procure from it massive parallelization. Here are some examples (the list is by no means exhaustive):

- Image blur, sharpen, and other transformations

- Fast Fourier Transform

- Matrix transpose and multiplication

- Number sorting

- Brute-force hash reversal

A good source of additional examples is the Microsoft Native Concurrency team blog (`http://blogs.msdn.com/b/nativeconcurrency/`), which has sample code and explanations for a variety of algorithms that have been ported to C++ AMP.

C++ AMP is a framework that ships with Visual Studio 2012 and provides C++ developers with simple means to run computations on the GPU, and requires only a DirectX 11 driver to run. Microsoft has released C++ AMP as an open specification (available online at the time of writing at `http://blogs.msdn.com/b/nativeconcurrency/archive/2012/02/03/c-amp-open-spec-published.aspx`), which any compiler vendor can implement. In C++ AMP, code can execute on *accelerators*, which represent computational devices. C++ AMP discovers dynamically all the accelerators with a DirectX 11 driver. Out of the box, C++ AMP also ships with a reference accelerator that performs software emulation, and a CPU-based accelerator, WARP, which is a reasonable fallback on machines without a GPU or with a GPU that doesn't have a DirectX 11 driver, and uses multi-core and SIMD instructions.

With no further ado, let us consider an algorithm that can be easily parallelized on the GPU. The algorithm below takes two vectors of the same length and calculates a pointwise result. There's hardly anything that could be more straightforward:

```
void VectorAddExpPointwise(float* first, float* second, float* result, int length) {
  for (int i = 0; i < length; ++i) {
    result[i] = first[i] + exp(second[i]);
  }
}
```

Parallelizing this algorithm on the *CPU* requires splitting the iteration range into several chunks and creating a thread to handle each part. Indeed, we have devoted quite some time to doing just that with our primality testing example—we have seen how to parallelize it by manually creating threads, by issuing work items to the thread pool, and by using the `Parallel.For` automatic parallelization capabilities. Also, recall that when parallelizing similar algorithms on the CPU we have taken great care to avoid work items that were too granular (e.g., a work item per iteration wouldn't do).

On the *GPU*, no such caution is necessary. The GPU is equipped with many cores that can execute threads very rapidly, and the cost of a context switch is significantly lower than on the CPU. Below is the code required using C++ AMP's `parallel_foreach` API:

```
#include < amp.h>
#include < amp_math.h>
using namespace concurrency;

void VectorAddExpPointwise(float* first, float* second, float* result, int length) {
  array_view< const float,1> avFirst (length, first);
  array_view< const float,1> avSecond(length, second);
  array_view< float,1>       avResult(length, result);
  avResult.discard_data();
  parallel_for_each(avResult.extent, [=](index< 1> i) restrict(amp) {
    avResult[i] = avFirst[i] + fast_math::exp(avSecond[i]);
  });
  avResult.synchronize();
}
```

We now examine each part of the code individually. First, the general shape of the main loop has been maintained, although the original for loop has been replaced with an API call to `parallel_foreach`. Indeed, the principle of converting a loop to an API call is not new—we have seen the same with TPL's `Parallel.For` and `Parallel.ForEach` APIs.

Next, the original data passed to the method (the `first`, `second`, and `result` parameters) has been wrapped in `array_view` instances. The `array_view` class wraps data that must be moved to an accelerator (GPU). Its template parameters are the type of the data and its dimensionality. If we want the GPU to execute instructions that access data that was originally on the CPU, some entity must take care of copying the data to the GPU, because most of today's GPUs are discrete devices with their own memory. This is the task of the `array_view` instances—they make sure data is copied on demand, and only when it is required.

When the work on the GPU is done, the data is copied back to its original location. By creating `array_view` instances with a `const` template type argument, we make sure that `first` and `second` are copied only *to* the GPU but don't have to be copied back *from* the GPU. Similarly, by calling the `discard_data` method, we make sure that `result` is not copied from the CPU to the GPU, but only from the GPU to the CPU when there is a result worth copying.

The `parallel_foreach` API takes an *extent*, which is the shape of the data we are working on, and a function to execute for each of the elements in the extent. We used a lambda function in the code above, which is a welcome addition to C++ as of the 2011 ISO C++ standard (C++11). The `restrict(amp)` keyword instructs the compiler to verify that the body of the function can execute on the GPU, forbidding most of the C++ syntax—syntax that cannot be compiled to GPU instructions.

The lambda function's parameter is an `index<1>` object, which represents a one-dimensional index. This must match the extent we used—should we declare a two-dimensional extent (such as the data shape of a matrix), the index would have to be two-dimensional as well. We will see an example of this shortly.

Finally, the `synchronize` method call at the end of the method makes sure that by the time `VectorAdd` returns, the changes made on the CPU to the `avResult` `array_view` are copied back into its original container, the `result` array.

This concludes our first foray into the world of C++ AMP, and we are ready for a closer examination of what is going on—as well as a better example, which will yield benefits from GPU parallelization. Vector addition is not the most exciting of algorithms, and does not make a good candidate for offloading to the GPU because the memory transfer outweights the computation's parallelization. In the following subsection we look at two examples that should be more interesting.

Matrix Multiplication

The first "real-world" example we shall consider is matrix multiplication. We will optimize the naïve cubic time algorithm for matrix multiplication and not Strassen's algorithm, which runs in sub-cubic time. Given two matrices of suitable dimensions, A that is m-by-w and B that is w-by-n, the following sequential program produces their product, a matrix C that is m-by-n:

```
void MatrixMultiply(int* A, int m, int w, int* B, int n, int* C) {
  for (int i = 0; i<m; ++i) {
    for (int j = 0; j<n; ++j) {
      int sum = 0;
      for (int k = 0; k<w; ++k) {
        sum+= A[i*w+k] * B[k*w+j];
      }
      C[i*n+j] = sum;
    }
  }
}
```

There are several sources for parallelism here, and if you were willing to parallelize this code on the CPU, you might be right in suggesting that we parallelize the outer loop and be done with it. On the GPU, however, there are sufficiently many cores that if we parallelize only the outer loop we might not create enough work for all the cores. Therefore, it makes sense to parallelize the two outer loops, still leaving a meaty algorithm for the inner loop:

```
void MatrixMultiply(int* A, int m, int w, int* B, int n, int* C) {
  array_view<const int,2> avA(m, w, A);
  array_view<const int,2> avB(w, n, B);
```

```
array_view<int,2>        avC(m, n, C);
avC.discard_data();
parallel_for_each(avC.extent, [=](index<2> idx) restrict(amp) {
  int sum = 0;
  for (int k = 0; k<w; ++k) {
    sum += avA(idx[0]*w, k) * avB(k*w, idx[1]);
  }
  avC[idx] = sum;
});
}
```

Everything is still very similar to sequential multiplication and the vector addition example we have seen earlier—with the exception of the index, which is two-dimensional, and accessed by the inner loop using the [ ] operator. How does this version fare compared to the sequential CPU alternative? To multiply two 1024 × 1024 matrices (of integers), the CPU version required 7350 ms on average, whereas the GPU version—hold tight—took 50 ms on average, a *147-fold improvement*!

N-Body Simulation

The examples we have seen so far had very trivial code in the inner loop that was scheduled on the GPU. Clearly, this must not always be the case. One of the examples on the Native Concurrency team blog we referred to demonstrates an N-body simulation, which simulates the interactions between particles where the force of gravity is applied. The simulation consists of an infinite number of steps; in each step, it has to determine the updated acceleration vector of each particle and then determine its new location. The parallelizable component here is the vector of particles—with sufficiently many particles (a few thousands or more) there is ample work for all GPU cores to do at once.

The kernel that determines the result of an interaction between two bodies is the following code, which can be ported very easily to the GPU:

```
//float4 here is a four-component vector with pointwise operations
void bodybody_interaction(
  float4& acceleration, const float4 p1, const float4 p2) restrict(amp) {
  float4 dist = p2 - p1;
  float absDist = dist.x*dist.x+dist.y*dist.y+dist.z*dist.z; //w is unused here
  float invDist = 1.0f / sqrt(absDist);
  float invDistCube = invDist*invDist*invDist;
  acceleration+= dist*PARTICLE_MASS*invDistCube;
}
```

Each simulation step takes an array of particle positions and velocities, and generates a new array of particle positions and velocities based on the results of the simulation:

```
struct particle {
  float4 position, velocity;
  //ctor, copy ctor, and operator = with restrict(amp) omitted for brevity
};
void simulation_step(array<particle,1>& previous, array<particle,1>& next, int bodies) {
  extent<1>ext(bodies);
  parallel_for_each(ext, [&](index<1>idx) restrict(amp) {
    particle p = previous[idx];
    float4 acceleration(0, 0, 0, 0);
    for (int body = 0; body<bodies; ++body) {
      bodybody_interaction(acceleration, p.position, previous[body].position);
    }
```

```
    p.velocity+= acceleration*DELTA_TIME;
    p.position+= p.velocity*DELTA_TIME;
    next[idx] = p;
  });
}
```

With an appropriate GUI, this simulation is very entertaining. The full sample provided by the C++ AMP team is available on the Native Concurrency blog. On the author's system, an Intel i7 processor with an ATI Radeon HD 5800 graphics card, a simulation with 10,000 particles yielded ~ 2.5 frames per second (steps) from the sequential CPU version and 160 frames per second (steps) from the optimized GPU version (see Figure 6-11), an incredible improvement.

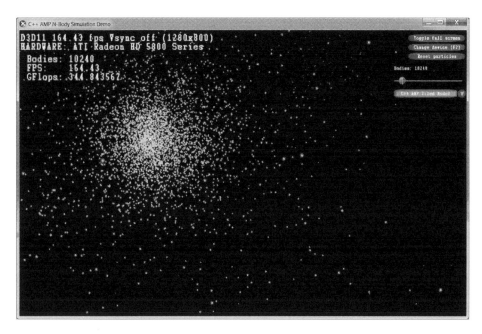

Figure 6-11. *N-body simulation UI demo, showing >160 frames per second (simulation steps) when using the optimized C++ AMP implementation with 10,240 simulated particles*

Tiles and Shared Memory

Before we conclude this section, there is a very important optimization surfaced by C++ AMP that can improve even more the performance of our GPU code. GPUs offer a programmable data cache (often called *shared memory*). Values stored in it are shared across all threads in the same *tile*. By using tiled memory, C++ AMP programs can read data from the GPU's main memory once into the shared tile memory, and then access it quickly from *multiple* threads in the same tile without refetching it from the GPU's main memory. Accessing shared tile memory can be around 10 times faster than accessing the GPU's main memory—in other words, you have a reason to keep reading.

To execute a tiled version of a parallel loop, the `parallel_for_each` method accepts a `tiled_extent` domain, which subdivides a multi-dimensional extent into multi-dimensional tiles, and a `tiled_index` lambda parameter, which specifies both the global thread ID within the extent, and the local thread ID within the tile. For example, a 16 × 16 matrix can be subdivided into 2 × 2 tiles (see Figure 6-12) and then passed into `parallel_for_each`:

```
extent<2> matrix(16,16);
tiled_extent<2,2> tiledMatrix = matrix.tile<2,2>();
parallel_for_each(tiledMatrix, [=](tiled_index<2,2> idx) restrict(amp) { ... });
```

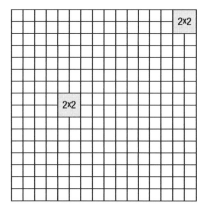

Figure 6-12. *A 16×16 matrix is divided into tiles of 2×2 each. Every four threads that belong in the same tile can share data between them*

Within the GPU kernel, idx.global can be used in place of the standard index<2> we have seen earlier when performing operations on matrices. However, clever use of the local tile memory and local tile indices can reap significant performance benefits. To declare tile-specific memory that is shared across all threads in the same tile, the tile_static storage specifier can be applied to local variables inside the kernel. It is common to declare a shared memory location and have each thread in the tile initialize a small part of it:

```
parallel_for_each(tiledMatrix, [=](tiled_index<2,2> idx) restrict(amp) {
  tile_static int local[2][2];         //32 bytes shared between all threads in the tile
  local[idx.local[0]][idx.local[1]] = 42; //assign to this thread's location in the array
});
```

Clearly, procuring any benefits from memory shared with other threads in the same tile is only possible if all the threads can synchronize their access to the shared memory; i.e., they shouldn't attempt to access shared memory locations before their tile neighboring threads have initialized them. tile_barrier objects synchronize the execution of all the threads in a tile—they can proceed executing after calling tile_barrier.wait only after all the threads in the tile have called tile_barrier.wait as well (this is similar to the TPL's Barrier class). For example:

```
parallel_for_each(tiledMatrix, [](tiled_index<2,2> idx) restrict(amp) {
  tile_static int local[2][2];         //32 bytes shared between all threads in the tile
  local[idx.local[0]][idx.local[1]] = 42; //assign to this thread's location in the array
  idx.barrier.wait();                  //idx.barrier is a tile_barrier instance
  //Now this thread can access "local" at other threads' indices!
});
```

It is now time to apply all this knowledge to a concrete example. We will revisit the matrix multiplication algorithm previously implemented without tiling, and introduce a tiling-based optimization into it. Let's assume that the matrix dimensions are divisible by 256—this allows us to work with 16×16 thread tiles. Matrix multiplication contains inherent blocking, which can be used to our advantage (in fact, one of the most common optimizations of extremely large matrix multiplication on the CPU is by using blocking to obtain better cache behavior). The primary observation boils down to the following. To find $C_{i,j}$ (the element at row i and column j in the result matrix), we have to find the scalar product between $A_{i,*}$ (the entire i-th row of the first matrix) and $B_{*,j}$ (the entire j-th row of the second matrix). However, this is equivalent to finding the scalar products of partial rows and partial columns and summing the results together. We can use this to translate our matrix multiplication algorithm to the tiled version:

```
void MatrixMultiply(int* A, int m, int w, int* B, int n, int* C) {
  array_view<const int,2> avA(m, w, A);
  array_view<const int,2> avB(w, n, B);
  array_view<int,2>       avC(m, n, C);
  avC.discard_data();
  parallel_for_each(avC.extent.tile<16,16>(), [=](tiled_index<16,16> idx) restrict(amp) {
    int sum = 0;
    int localRow = idx.local[0], localCol = idx.local[1];
    for (int k = 0; k<w; k += 16) {
      tile_static int localA[16][16], localB[16][16];
      localA[localRow][localCol] = avA(idx.global[0], localCol+k);
      localB[localRow][localCol] = avB(localRow+k, idx.global[1]);
      idx.barrier.wait();
      for (int t = 0; t<16; ++t) {
        sum+= localA[localRow][t]*localB[t][localCol];
      }
      idx.barrier.wait(); //to avoid having the next iteration overwrite the shared memory
    }
    avC[idx.global] = sum;
  });
}
```

The essence of the tiled optimization is that each thread in the tile (there are 256 threads, the tile is 16×16) initializes its own element in the 16×16 local copies of sub-blocks from the A and B input matrices (see Figure 6-13). Each thread in the tile needs only one row and one column of these sub-blocks, but all the threads together will access every row 16 times and every column 16 times, reducing significantly the number of main memory accesses.

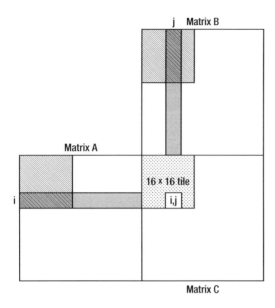

Figure 6-13. *To find the element (i,j) in the result matrix, the algorithm requires the entire i-th row of the first matrix and j-th column of the second matrix. When the threads in the 16 × 16 tile shown in the diagram execute and k = 0, the shaded areas in the first and second matrices will eventually be read into shared memory. The thread responsible for the (i,j)-th element in the result matrix will then have the partial scalar product of the first k elements from the i-th row with the first k elements from the j-th row*

In this case, tiling is a worthwhile optimization. The tiled version of matrix multiplication executes significantly faster than the simple one, and takes 17 ms on average to complete (using the same 1024 × 1024 matrices). This concludes a *430-fold speed increase* compared to the CPU version!

Before we part with C++ AMP, it's worthwhile to mention the development tools (Visual Studio) available to C++ AMP developers. Visual Studio 2012 features a GPU debugger, which you can use to place breakpoints in GPU kernels, inspect simulated call stacks, read and modify local variables (some accelerators support GPU debugging; with others, Visual Studio uses a software emulator), and a profiler that can be used to gauge what your application has gained from using GPU parallelization. For more information on the Visual Studio GPU debugging experience, consult the MSDN article "Walkthrough: Debugging a C++ AMP Application", at `http://msdn.microsoft.com/en-us/library/hh368280(v=VS.110).aspx`.

.NET ALTERNATIVES FOR GPGPU COMPUTING

Although so far this entire section has dealt exclusively with C++, there are several options for harnessing the power of the GPU from managed applications. One option is to use managed-native interoperability (discussed in Chapter 8), deferring to a native C++ component to implement the GPU kernels. This is a reasonable option if you like C++ AMP, or have a reusable C++ AMP component that is used in managed applications as well as native ones.

Another option is to use a library that works with the GPU directly from managed code. There are several such libraries available, for example GPU.NET and CUDAfy.NET (both commercial offerings). Here is an example from GPU.NET GitHub repository, demonstrating a scalar product of two vectors:

```
[Kernel]
public static void MultiplyAddGpu(double[] a, double[] b, double[] c) {
  int ThreadId = BlockDimension.X * BlockIndex.X+ThreadIndex.X;
  int TotalThreads = BlockDimension.X * GridDimension.X;
  for (int ElementIdx = ThreadId; ElementIdx<a.Length; ElementIdx+= TotalThreads) {
    c[ElementIdx] = a[ElementIdx] * b[ElementIdx];
  }
}
```

In the authors' opinion, language extensions (the C++ AMP approach) are more effective and easier to learn than attempts to bridge the gap purely at the library level, or by introducing significant IL rewriting.

This section hardly scratches the surface of the possibilities offered by C++ AMP. We have only taken a look at some of the APIs and parallelized an algorithm or two. If you are interested in more details about C++ AMP, we strongly recommend Kate Gregory's and Ade Miller's book, "C++ AMP: Accelerated Massive Parallelism with Microsoft Visual C++" (Microsoft Press, 2012).

Summary

Through the course of this chapter, it has become evident that parallelization is a crucial tool to have for performance optimization work. On many servers and workstations around the world, CPUs and GPUs idle and waste precious hardware resources because applications fail to tap into the machine's full computing power. With the Task Parallel Library at our disposal, taking advantage of all available CPU cores is easier than before, although synchronization problems, oversubscription, and unequal work distribution leave some interesting issues and pitfalls to deal with. On the GPU front, C++ AMP and other libraries for general-purpose GPU computing are flourishing with algorithms and APIs to parallelize your code on hundreds of GPU cores. Finally, unexploited in this chapter, remain the performance gains harvestable from distributed computing—*the cloud*—which is the biggest trend in IT today.

■ ■ ■

CHAPTER 7

Networking, I/O, and Serialization

Most of this book focuses on optimizing computational aspects of application performance. We have seen numerous examples, such as tuning garbage collection, parallelizing loops and recursive algorithms, and even by coming up with better algorithms to reduce runtime costs.

For some applications, optimizing only the computational aspect results in limited performance gains, because the performance bottleneck lies in I/O work, such as network transfers or disk accesses. In our experience, a considerable portion of performance problems encountered in the field is not caused by an unoptimized algorithm or excessive CPU utilization, but is due to an inefficient utilization of the system's I/O devices. Let us consider two scenarios in which optimizing I/O can result in performance gains:

- An application might incur a significant computational (CPU) overhead due to inefficient use of I/O, which comes at the expense of useful work. Worse, this overhead might be so high that it becomes the limiting factor to realizing the full potential capacity of the I/O device.

- The I/O device might be under-utilized or its capacity is wasted because of inefficient usage patterns, such as making many small I/O transfers or by failing to keep the channel fully utilized.

This chapter discusses strategies for improving I/O performance in general and network I/O performance in particular. In addition, we cover serialization performance and compare several serializers.

General I/O Concepts

This section explores I/O concepts and provides performance guidelines pertaining to I/O of any kind. This advice is applicable to networking applications, heavy disk-accessing processes, and even software designed to access a custom high-bandwidth hardware device.

Synchronous and Asynchronous I/O

With synchronous I/O, the I/O transfer function (e.g. `ReadFile`, `WriteFile,` or `DeviceIoControl` Win32 API functions) blocks until the I/O operation completes. Although this model is convenient to use, it is not very efficient. During the time between issuing successive I/O requests, the device may be idle and, therefore, is potentially under-utilized. Another problem with synchronous I/O is that a thread is "wasted" for each concurrently pending I/O request. For example, in a server application servicing many clients concurrently, you may end up creating a thread per session. These threads, which are essentially mostly idle, are wasting memory and may create a situation called *thread thrashing* in which many threads wake up when I/O completes and compete with each other for CPU time, resulting in many context switches and poor scalability.

The Windows I/O subsystem (including device drivers) is internally asynchronous – execution of program flow can continue while an I/O operation is in progress. Almost all modern hardware is asynchronous in nature as well and does not need polling to transfer data or to determine if an I/O operation is complete. Most devices instead rely on Direct Memory Access (DMA) controllers to transfer data between the device and the computer RAM, without requiring the CPU's attention during the transfer, and then raise an interrupt to signal completion the data transfer. It is only at the application level that Windows allows synchronous I/O that is actually asynchronous internally.

In Win32, asynchronous I/O is called *overlapped I/O* (see Figure 7-1 comparing synchronous and overlapped I/O). Once an application issues an overlapped I/O, Windows either completes the I/O operation immediately or returns a status code indicating the I/O operation is still pending. The thread can then issue more I/O operations, or it can do some computational work. The programmer has several options for receiving a notification about the I/O operation's completion:

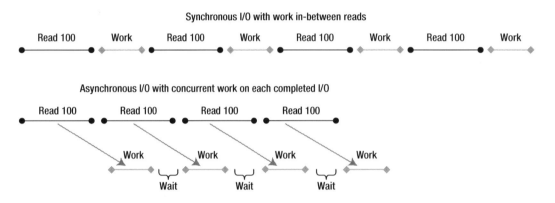

Figure 7-1. *Comparison between synchronous and overlapped I/O*

- Signaling of a Win32 event: A wait operation on this event will complete when the I/O completes.

- Invocation of a user callback routine via the Asynchronous Procedure Call (APC) mechanism: The issuing thread must be in a state of *alertable wait* to allow APCs.

- Notification via I/O Completion Ports: This is usually the most efficient mechanism. We explore I/O completion ports in detail later in this chapter.

▨ **Note**   Some I/O devices (e.g. a file opened in unbuffered mode) benefit (by increasing device utilization) if an application can keep a small amount of I/O requests pending. A recommended strategy is to pre-issue a certain number of I/O requests and, for each request that completes, re-issue another. This ensures the device driver can initiate the next I/O as quickly as possible, without waiting for the application to issue the next I/O in response. However, do not exaggerate with the amount of pending data, since it can consume limited kernel memory resources.

I/O Completion Ports

Windows provides an efficient asynchronous I/O completion notification mechanism called the *I/O Completion Port* (IOCP). It is exposed through the .NET ThreadPool.BindHandle method. Several .NET types dealing with I/O utilize this functionality internally: FileStream, Socket, SerialPort, HttpListener, PipeStream, and some .NET Remoting channels.

An IOCP (see Figure 7-2) is associated with zero or more I/O handles (sockets, files, and specialized device driver objects) opened in overlapped mode and with user-created threads. Once an I/O operation of an associated I/O handle completes, Windows enqueues the completion notification to the appropriate IOCP and an associated thread handles the completion notification. By having a thread pool that services completions and by intelligently controlling thread wakeup, context switches are reduced and multi-processor concurrency is maximized. It is no surprise that high-performance servers, such as Microsoft SQL Server, use I/O completion ports.

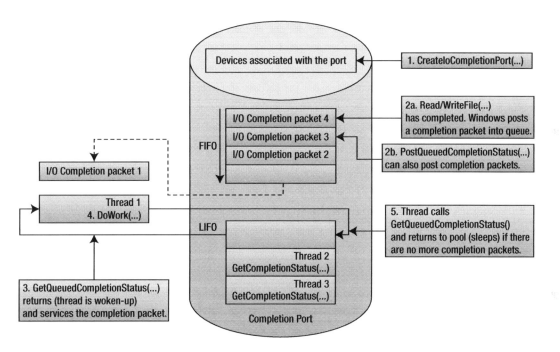

Figure 7-2. *Structure and operation of an I/O Completion Port*

A completion port is created by calling the CreateIoCompletionPort Win32 API function, passing a maximum concurrency value, a completion key and optionally associating it with an I/O-capable handle. A completion key is a user-specified value that serves to distinguish between different I/O handles at completion. More I/O handles can be associated with the same or a different IOCP by again calling CreateIoCompletionPort and specifying the existing completion port handle.

User-created threads then call GetCompletionStatus to become bound to the specified IOCP and to wait for completion. A thread can only be bound to one IOCP at a time. GetQueuedCompletionStatus blocks until there is an I/O completion notification available (or a timeout period has elapsed), at which point it returns with the I/O operation details, such as the number of number of bytes transferred, the completion key, and the overlapped structure passed during I/O. If another I/O completes while all associated threads are busy (i.e., not blocked on GetQueuedCompletionStatus), the IOCP wakes another thread in LIFO order, up to the maximum concurrency value. If a thread calls GetQueuedCompletionStatus and the notification queue is not empty, the call returns immediately, without the thread blocking in the OS kernel.

■ **Note** The IOCP is aware if one of the "busy" threads is actually doing a synchronous I/O or wait and will wake additional associated threads (if any), potentially exceeding the concurrency value. A completion notification can also be posted manually without involving I/O by calling `PostQueuedCompletionStatus`.

The following code listing shows an example of using `ThreadPool.BindHandle` on a Win32 file handle. Start by looking at the `TestIOCP` method. Here, we call `CreateFile`, which is a P/Invoke'd Win32 function used to open or create files or devices. We must specify the `EFileAttributes.Overlapped` flag in the call to use any kind of asynchronous I/O. `CreateFile` returns a Win32 file handle if it succeeds, which we then bind to .NET's I/O completion port by calling `ThreadPool.BindHandle`. We create an auto-reset event, which is used to temporarily block the thread issuing I/O operations if there are too many such operations in progress (the limit is set by the `MaxPendingIos` constant).

We then begin a loop of asynchronous write operations. At each iteration, we allocate a buffer that contains the data to be written. We also allocate an `Overlapped` structure that contains the file offset (here, we always write to offset 0), an event handle signaled when I/O completes (not used in I/O Completion Ports) and an optional user-created `IAsyncResult` object that can be used to carry state to the completion function. We then call `Overlapped` structure's `Pack` method, which takes the completion function and data buffer as parameters. It allocates an equivalent native overlapped structure from unmanaged memory and pins the data buffer. The native structure has to be manually freed to release the unmanaged memory it occupies and to unpin the managed buffer.

If there are not too many I/O operations in progress, we call `WriteFile`, while specifying the native overlapped structure. Otherwise, we wait until the event becomes signaled, which indicates the pending I/O operations count has dropped below the limit.

The I/O completion function `WriteComplete` is invoked by .NET I/O Completion thread pool threads when I/O completes. It receives a pointer to the native overlapped structure, which can be unpacked to convert it back to the managed `Overlapped` structure.

```
using System;
using System.Threading;
using Microsoft.Win32.SafeHandles;
using System.Runtime.InteropServices;

[DllImport("kernel32.dll", SetLastError=true, CharSet=CharSet.Auto)]
internal static extern SafeFileHandle CreateFile(
    string lpFileName,
    EFileAccess dwDesiredAccess,
    EFileShare dwShareMode,
    IntPtr lpSecurityAttributes,
    ECreationDisposition dwCreationDisposition,
    EFileAttributes dwFlagsAndAttributes,
    IntPtr hTemplateFile);

[DllImport("kernel32.dll", SetLastError=true)]
[return: MarshalAs(UnmanagedType.Bool)]
static unsafe extern bool WriteFile(SafeFileHandle hFile, byte[] lpBuffer,
    uint nNumberOfBytesToWrite, out uint lpNumberOfBytesWritten,
    System.Threading.NativeOverlapped *lpOverlapped);

[Flags]
enum EFileShare : uint {
```

```
    None = 0x00000000,
    Read = 0x00000001,
    Write = 0x00000002,
    Delete = 0x00000004
}

enum ECreationDisposition : uint {
    New = 1,
    CreateAlways = 2,
    OpenExisting = 3,
    OpenAlways = 4,
    TruncateExisting = 5
}

[Flags]
enum EFileAttributes : uint {
    //Some flags not present for brevity
    Normal = 0x00000080,
    Overlapped = 0x40000000,
    NoBuffering = 0x20000000,
}

[Flags]
enum EFileAccess : uint {
    //Some flags not present for brevity
    GenericRead = 0x80000000,
    GenericWrite = 0x40000000,
}

static long _numBytesWritten;
static AutoResetEvent _waterMarkFullEvent; // throttles writer thread
static int _pendingIosCount;

const int MaxPendingIos = 10;

//Completion routine called by .NET ThreadPool I/O completion threads
static unsafe void WriteComplete(uint errorCode, uint numBytes, NativeOverlapped* pOVERLAP) {
    _numBytesWritten += numBytes;
    Overlapped ovl = Overlapped.Unpack(pOVERLAP);

    Overlapped.Free(pOVERLAP);
    //Notify writer thread that pending I/O count fell below watermark
    if (Interlocked.Decrement(ref _pendingIosCount) < MaxPendingIos)
        _waterMarkFullEvent.Set();
}

static unsafe void TestIOCP() {
    //Open file in overlapped mode
    var handle = CreateFile(@"F:\largefile.bin",
        EFileAccess.GenericRead | EFileAccess.GenericWrite,
        EFileShare.Read | EFileShare.Write,
```

```
    IntPtr.Zero, ECreationDisposition.CreateAlways,
    EFileAttributes.Normal | EFileAttributes.Overlapped, IntPtr.Zero);

  _waterMarkFullEvent = new AutoResetEvent(false);
  ThreadPool.BindHandle(handle);

  for (int k = 0; k < 1000000; k++) {
    byte[] fbuffer = new byte[4096];

    //Args: file offset low & high, event handle, IAsyncResult object
    Overlapped ovl = new Overlapped(0, 0, IntPtr.Zero, null);
    //The CLR takes care to pin the buffer
    NativeOverlapped* pNativeOVL = ovl.Pack(WriteComplete, fbuffer);
    uint numBytesWritten;

    //Check if too many I/O requests are pending
    if (Interlocked.Increment(ref _pendingIosCount) < MaxPendingIos) {
      if (WriteFile(handle, fbuffer, (uint)fbuffer.Length, out numBytesWritten,
                    pNativeOVL)) {
        //I/O completed synchronously
        _numBytesWritten += numBytesWritten;
        Interlocked.Decrement(ref _pendingIosCount);
      } else {
        if (Marshal.GetLastWin32Error() != ERROR_IO_PENDING) {
          return; //Handle error
        }
      }
    } else {
      Interlocked.Decrement(ref _pendingIosCount);
      while (_pendingIosCount >= MaxPendingIos) {
        _waterMarkFullEvent.WaitOne();
      }
    }
  }
}
```

To summarize, when working with high-throughput I/O devices, use overlapped I/O with completion ports, either by directly creating and using your own completion port in the unmanaged library or by associating a Win32 handle with .NET's completion port through ThreadPool.BindHandle.

NET Thread Pool

The .NET Thread Pool is used for many purposes, each served by a different kind of thread. Chapter 6 showed the thread pool APIs that we used to tap into the thread pool's ability to parallelize a CPU-bound computation. However, there are numerous kinds of work for which the thread pool is suited:

- *Worker threads* handle asynchronous invocation of user delegates (e.g. BeginInvoke or ThreadPool.QueueUserWorkItem).

- *I/O completion threads* handle completions for the global IOCP.

- *Wait threads* handle registered wait. A registered wait saves threads by combining several waits into one wait (using WaitForMultipleObjects), up to the Windows limit (MAXIMUM_WAIT_OBJECTS = 64). Registered wait is used for overlapped I/O that is not using I/O completion ports.

- *Timer thread* combines waiting on multiple timers.

- *Gate thread* monitors CPU usage of thread pool threads, as well as grows or shrinks the thread counts (within preset limits) for best performance.

■ **Note** You can issue an I/O operation that may appear asynchronous, although it really is not. For example, calling `ThreadPool.QueueUserWorkItem` on a delegate and then doing a synchronous I/O operation does not make it truly asynchronous and is no better than doing so on a regular thread.

Copying Memory

Commonly, a data buffer received from a hardware device is copied over and over until the application finishes processing it. Copying can become a significant source of CPU overhead and, thus, should be avoided for high throughput I/O code paths. We now survey some scenarios in which you copy data and how to avoid it.

Unmanaged Memory

In .NET, an unmanaged memory buffer is more cumbersome to work with than a managed `byte[]`, so programmers often take the easy way out and just copy the buffer to managed memory.

If your API or library lets you specify your own memory buffer or has a user-defined allocator callback, allocate a managed buffer and pin it so that it can be accessed through both a pointer and as a managed reference. If the buffer is so large (>85,000 bytes) it is allocated in the Large Object Heap, try to re-use the buffer. If re-using is non-trivial because of indeterminate object lifetime, use memory pooling, as described in Chapter 8.

In other cases, the API or library insists on allocating its own (unmanaged) memory buffer. You can access it directly with a pointer (requires unsafe code) or by using wrapper classes, such as `UnmanagedMemoryStream` or `UnmanagedMemoryAccessor`. However, if you need to pass the buffer to some code that only works with `byte[]` or `string` objects, copying may be unavoidable.

Even if you cannot avoid copying memory, if some or most of your data is filtered early on (e.g. network packets), it is possible to avoid unnecessary memory copying by first checking if the data is useful without copying it.

Exposing Part of a Buffer

As Chapter 8 explains, programmers sometime assume that a `byte[]` contains only the desired data and that it spans from the beginning until the end, forcing the caller to splice the buffer (allocate a new `byte[]` and copy only the desired portion). This scenario often comes up in parsing a protocol stack. In contrast, equivalent unmanaged code would take a pointer, will have no knowledge whether it points to the beginning of the allocation or not, and will have to take a length parameter to tell it where the data ends.

To avoid unnecessary memory copying, take an offset and length parameters wherever you take a `byte[]` parameter. The length parameter is used instead of the array's `Length` property, and the offset value is added to the index.

Scatter–Gather I/O

Scatter–gather is a Windows I/O capability that enables I/O transfers to or from a set of non-contiguous memory locations as if they were contiguous. Win32 exposes this capability through `ReadFileScatter` and `WriteFileGather` functions. The Windows Sockets library also supports scatter–gather through its own functions: `WSASend`, `WSARecv,` as well as others.

Scatter–gather is useful in the following scenarios:

- You have a fixed header prepended to the payload of each packet. This saves you from copying the header each time to make a contiguous buffer.

- You want to save on system call overhead by performing I/O to multiple buffers in one system call.

Although `ReadFileScatter` and `WriteFileGather` are limiting because each buffer must be exactly of system page size and the functions require that the handle be opened as overlapped and unbuffered (which imposes even more constraints), socket-based scatter–gather is more practical, because it does not have these limitations. The .NET Framework exposes socket scatter–gather through overloads of Socket's `Send` and `Receive` methods, but the generic scatter/gather functions are not exposed.

An example of scatter–gather usage is by `HttpWebRequest`. It combines an HTTP header with the payload without constructing a contiguous buffer to hold both.

File I/O

Normally, file I/O goes through the filesystem cache, which has some performance benefits: caching of recently accessed data, read-ahead (speculative pre-fetching data from disk), write-behind (asynchronously writing data to disk), and combining of small writes. By hinting Windows about your expected file access pattern, you can gain a bit more performance. If your application does overlapped I/O and can intelligently handle buffers facing some complexities, then bypassing caching entirely can be more efficient.

Cache Hinting

When creating or opening a file, you specify flags and attributes to the `CreateFile` Win32 API function, some of which influence caching behavior:

- `FILE_FLAG_SEQUENTIAL_SCAN` hints to the Cache Manager that the file is accessed sequentially, possibly skipping some parts, but is seldom accessed randomly. The cache will read further ahead.

- `FILE_FLAG_RANDOM_ACCESS` hints that the file is accessed in random order, so the Cache Manager reads less ahead, since it is unlikely that this data will actually be requested by the application.

- `FILE_ATTRIBUTE_TEMPORARY` hints that the file is temporary, so flushing writes to disk (to prevent data loss) can be delayed.

NET exposes these options (except the last one) through a `FileStream` constructor overload that accepts a `FileOptions` enumeration parameter.

■ **Caution** Random access is bad for performance, especially on disk media since the read/write head has to physically move. Historically, disk throughput has improved with increasing aereal storage density, but latency has not. Modern disks can intelligently (taking disk rotation into account) re-order random-access I/O so that the total time the head spends travelling is minimized. This is called Native Command Queuing (NCQ). For this to work effectively, the disk controller must be aware of several I/O requests ahead. In other words, if possible, you should have several asynchronous I/O requests pending.

Unbuffered I/O

Unbuffered I/O bypasses the Windows cache entirely. This has both benefits and drawbacks. Like with cache hinting, unbuffered I/O is enabled through the "flags and attributes" parameter during file creation, but .NET does not expose this functionality:

- `FILE_FLAG_NO_BUFFERING` prevents the data read or written from being cached but has no effect on hardware caching by the disk controller. This avoids a memory copy (from user buffer to cache) and prevents cache pollution (filling the cache with useless data at the expense of more important data). However, reads and writes must obey alignment requirements. The following parameters must be aligned to or have a size that is an integer multiple of the disk sector size: I/O transfer size, file offset, and memory buffer address. Typically, the sector size is 512 bytes long. Recent high-capacity disk drives have 4,096 byte sectors (known as "Advanced Format"), but they can run in a compatibility mode that emulates 512 byte sectors (at the expense of performance).

- `FILE_FLAG_WRITE_THROUGH` instructs the Cache Manager to flush cached writes (if `FILE_FLAG_NO_BUFFERING` is not specified) and instructs the disk controller to commit writes to physical media immediately, rather than storing them in the hardware cache.

Read-ahead improves performance by keeping the disk utilized, even if the application makes synchronous reads, and has delays between reads. This depends on Windows correctly predicting what part of the file the application will request next. By disabling buffering, you also disable read-ahead and should keep the disk busy by having multiple overlapped I/O operations pending.

Write-behind also improves performance for applications making synchronous writes by giving the illusion that disk-writes finish very quickly. The application can better utilize the CPU, because it blocks for less time. When you disable buffering, writes complete in the actual amount of time it takes to write them to disk. Therefore, doing asynchronous I/O becomes even more important when using unbuffered I/O.

Networking

Network access is a fundamental capability in most modern applications. Server applications that process client requests strive to maximize scalability and their throughput capacity to serve clients faster and to serve more clients per server, whereas clients aim to minimize network access latencies or to mitigate its effects. This section provides advice and tips for maximizing networking performance.

Network Protocols

The way an applicative network protocol (OSI Layer 7) is constructed can have a profound influence on performance. This section explores some optimization techniques to better utilize the available network capacity and to minimize overhead.

Pipelining

In a non-pipelined protocol, a client sends a request to server and then waits for the response to arrive before it can send the next request. With such a protocol, network capacity is under-utilized, because, during the network round-trip time (i.e. time it takes network packets to reach the server and back), the network is idle. Conversely, in a pipelined connection, the client can continue to send more requests, even before the server has processed the previous requests. Better yet, the server can decide to respond to requests out of order, responding to trivial requests first, while deferring processing of more computationally-demanding requests.

Pipelining is increasingly important, because, while Internet bandwidth continues to increase worldwide, latency improves at a much slower rate because it is capped to physical limits imposed by the speed of light.

An example of pipelining in a real-world protocol is HTTP 1.1, but it is often disabled by default on most servers and web browsers because of compatibility issues. Google SPDY, an experimental HTTP-like protocol supported by Chrome and Firefox web browsers, as well as some HTTP servers, and the upcoming HTTP 2.0 protocol mandate pipelining support.

Streaming

Streaming is not just for video and audio, but can be used for messaging. With streaming, the application begins sending data over the network even before it is complete. Streaming reduces latency and improves network channel utilization.

For example, if a server application fetches data from a database in response to a request, it can either read it in one chunk into a DataSet (which can consume large amounts of memory) or it can use a DataReader to retrieve records one at a time. In the former approach, the server has to wait until the entire dataset has arrived before it can begin sending a response to the client, whereas in the latter approach, the server can begin sending a response to the client as soon as the first DB record arrives.

Message Chunking

Sending small chunks of data at a time over the network is wasteful. Ethernet, IP, and TCP/UDP headers are no smaller, because the payload is smaller, so although bandwidth utilization can still be high, you end up wasting it on headers, not actual data. Additionally, Windows itself has per-call overhead that is independent or weakly dependent on data chunk size. A protocol can mitigate this by allowing several requests to be combined. For example, the Domain Name Service (DNS) protocol allows a client to resolve multiple domain names in one request.

Chatty Protocols

Sometimes, the client cannot pipeline requests, even if the protocol allows this, because the next requests depend on the content of the previous replies.

Consider an example of a chatty protocol session. When you browse to a web page, the browser connects to the web server via TCP, sends an HTTP GET request for the URL you are trying to visit, and receives an HTML page as a response. The browser then parses the HTML to figure out which JavaScript, CSS, and image resources it has to retrieve and downloads them individually. The JavaScript script is then executed, and it can fetch further content. In summary, the client does not immediately know all the content it has to retrieve to render the page. Instead, it has to iteratively fetch content until it discovers and downloads all content.

To mitigate this problem, the server might hint to the client which URLs it will need to retrieve to render the page and might even send content without the client requesting it.

Message Encoding and Redundancy

Network bandwidth is often a constrained resource, and having a wasteful messaging format does not help performance. Here are a few tips to optimize messaging format:

- Do not transmit the same thing over and over, and keep headers small.

- Use smart encoding or representation for data. For example, strings can be encoded in UTF-8, instead of UTF-16. A binary protocol can be many times more compact than a human-readable protocol. If possible, avoid encapsulations, such as Base64 encoding.

- Use compression for highly compressible data, such as text. Avoid it for uncompressible data, such as already-compressed video, images, and audio.

Network Sockets

The sockets API is the standard way for applications to work with network protocols, such as TCP and UDP. Originally, the sockets API was introduced in the BSD UNIX operating system and since became standard in virtually all operating systems, sometimes with proprietary extensions, such as Microsoft's WinSock. There are a number of ways for doing socket I/O in Windows: blocking, non-blocking with polling, and asynchronous. Using the right I/O model and socket parameters enables higher throughput, lower latency, and better scalability. This section outlines performance optimization pertaining to Windows Sockets.

Asynchronous Sockets

.NET supports asynchronous I/O through the Socket class. However, there are two families of asynchronous APIs: BeginXXX and XXXAsync, where XXX stands for Accept, Connect, Receive, Send, and other operations. The former use the .NET Thread Pool's registered wait capability to await overlapped I/O completion, whereas the latter use .NET Thread Pool's I/O Completion Port mechanism, which is more performant and scalable. The latter APIs were introduced in .NET Framework 2.0 SP1.

Socket Buffers

Socket objects expose two settable buffer sizes: ReceiveBufferSize and SendBufferSize, which specify buffer sizes allocated by the TCP/IP stack (in OS memory space). Both are set to 8,192 bytes by default. The receive buffer is used to hold received data not yet read by the application. The send buffer is used to hold data that has been sent by the application but that has not yet been acknowledged by the receiver. Should the need to retransmit arise, data from the send buffer is retransmitted.

When the application reads from the socket, it unfills the receive buffer by the amount read. When the receive buffer becomes empty, the call either blocks or becomes pending, depending if synchronous or asynchronous I/O is used.

When the application writes to the socket, it can write data without blocking until the send buffer is full and cannot accommodate the data or until the receiver's receive buffer becomes full. The receiver advertises how full its receive buffer size is with each acknowledgement.

For high-bandwidth, high latency connections, such as satellite links, the default buffer sizes may be too small. The sending end quickly fills up its send buffer and has to wait for acknowledgement, which is slow to arrive because of high latency. While waiting, the pipe is not kept full and the endpoints only utilize a fraction of the available bandwidth.

In a perfectly reliable network, the ideal buffer size is the product of the bandwidth and latency. For example, in a 100Mbps connection with a 5 ms round-trip time, an ideal buffer window size would be $(100,000,000 / 8) \times 0.005 = 62,500$ bytes. Packet loss reduces this value.

Nagle's Algorithm

As mentioned before, small packets are wasteful, because packet headers may be large compared to the payload. Nagle's algorithm improves performance of TCP sockets by coalescing multiple writes by the application into up to a whole packet's worth of data. However, this service does not come for free as it introduces delay before data is sent. A latency sensitive application should disable Nagle's algorithm by setting the Socket.NoDelay property to true. A well-written application would send large buffers at a time and would not benefit from Nagle's algorithm.

Registered I/O

Registered I/O (RIO) is a new extension of WinSock available in Windows Server 2012 that provides a very efficient buffer registration and notification mechanism. RIO eliminates the most significant inefficiencies in Windows I/O:

- User buffer probing (checking for page access permissions), locking and unlocking (ensuring the buffers are resident in RAM).

- Handle lookups (translating a Win32 HANDLE to a kernel object pointer).

- System calls made (e.g. to dequeue I/O completion notifications).

These are "taxes" paid to isolate the application from the operating system and from other applications, to the end of ensuring security and reliability. Without RIO, you pay these taxes per call, which, at high I/O rates, becomes significant. Conversely, with RIO, you incur the costs of the "taxes" only once, during initialization.

RIO requires registration of buffers, which locks them in physical memory until they are de-registered (when the application or subsystem uninitializes). Since the buffers remain allocated and resident in memory, Windows can skip probing, locking, and unlocking per call.

RIO request and completion queues reside in the process' memory space and are accessible to it, meaning a system call is no longer required to poll the queue or dequeue completion notifications.

RIO supports three notification mechanisms:

- Polling: This has the lowest latency but means a logical processor is dedicated to polling the network buffers.

- I/O Completion Ports.

- Signaling a Windows event.

At the time of writing, RIO was not exposed by the .NET Framework, but it is accessible through the standard .NET interoperability mechanisms (discussed in Chapter 8).

Data Serialization and Deserialization

Serialization is the act of representing an object in a format that can be written to disk or sent via a network. De-serialization is the act of reconstructing an object from the serialized representation. For example, a hash table can be serialized to an array of key-value records.

Serializer Benchmarks

The .NET Framework comes with several generic serializers that can serialize and de-serialize user-defined types. This section weighs the advantages and disadvantages of each, benchmark serializers in terms serialization throughput and serialized message size.

First, we review the available serializers:

- `System.Xml.Serialization.XmlSerializer`

  - Serializes to XML, either text or binary.

  - Works on child objects, but does not support circular references.

  - Works only on public fields and properties, except those that are explicitly excluded.

  - Uses Reflection only once to code-generate a serialization assembly, for efficient operation. You can use the sgen.exe tool to pre-create the serialization assembly.

- • Allows customization of XML schema.

- • Requires knowing all types that participate in serialization a priori: It infers this information automatically, except when inherited types are used.

- • `System.Runtime.Serialization.Formatters.Binary.BinaryFormatter`

  - • Serializes to a proprietary binary format, consumable only by .NET BinaryFormatter.

  - • Is used by .NET Remoting, but can also be used stand-alone for general serialization.

  - • Works in both public and non-public fields.

  - • Handles circular references.

  - • Does not require a priori knowledge of types to be serialized.

  - • Requires types to be marked as serializable by applying the `[Serializable]` attribute.

- • `System.Runtime.Serialization.Formatters.Soap.SoapFormatter`

  - • Is similar in capabilities to `BinaryFormatter`, but serializes to a SOAP XML format, which is more interoperable but less compact.

  - • Does not support generics and generic collections, and therefore deprecated in recent versions of the .NET Framework.

- • `System.Runtime.Serialization.DataContractSerializer`

  - • Serializes to XML, either text or binary.

  - • Is used by WCF but can also be used stand-alone for general serialization.

  - • Serializes types and fields as an opt-in through the use of `[DataContract]` and `[DataMember]` attributes: If a class is marked by the `[Serializable]` attribute, all fields get serialized.

  - • Requires knowing all types that participate in serialization a priori: It infers this information automatically, except when inherited types are used.

- • `System.Runtime.Serialization.NetDataContractSerializer`

  - • Is similar to DataContractSerializer, except it embeds .NET-specific type information in the serialized data.

  - • Does not require foreknowledge of types that participate in serialization.

  - • Requires sharing assemblies containing serialized types.

- • `System.Runtime.Serialization.DataContractJsonSerializer`

  - • Is similar to `DataContractSerializer,` but serializes to JSON format instead of XML format.

Figure 7-3 presents benchmark results for the previously listed serializers. Some serializers are tested twice for both text XML output and binary XML output. The benchmark involves the serialization and de-serialization of a high-complexity object graph, consisting of 3,600 instances of five types with a tree-like referencing pattern. Each type consists of `string` and `double` fields and arrays thereof. No circular references were present, because not all serializers support them; however, those serializers that support circular references ran significantly

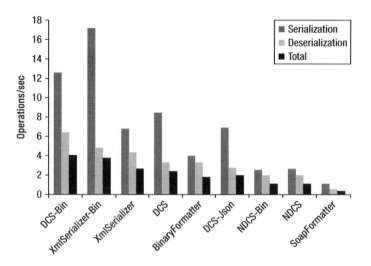

Figure 7-3. *Serializer throughput benchmark results, in operations/sec*

slower in their presence. The benchmark results presented here were run on .NET Framework 4.5 RC, which has slightly improved results over .NET Framework 3.5 for tests using binary XML, but otherwise there is no significant difference.

The benchmark results show that DataContractSerializer and XmlSerializer, when working with binary XML format, are fastest overall.

Next, we compare the serialized data size of the serializers (see Figure 7-4). There are several serializers that are very close to one another in this metric. This is likely because the object tree has most of its data in the form of strings, which is represented the same way across all serializers.

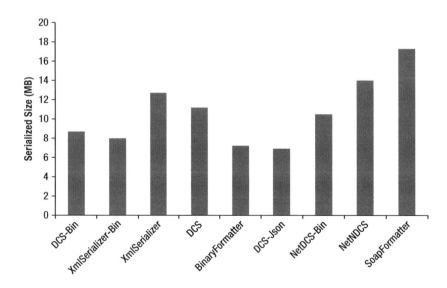

Figure 7-4. *Comparison of serialized data size*

The most compact serialized representation is produced by the `DataContractJsonSerializer`, closely followed by `XmlSerializer` and `DataContractSerializer` when used with a binary XML writer. Perhaps surprisingly, `BinaryFormatter` was outperformed by most other serializers.

DataSet Serialization

A `DataSet` is an in-memory cache for data retrieved from a database through a `DataAdapter`. It contains a collection of `DataTable` objects, which contain the database schema and data rows, each containing a collection of serialized objects. `DataSet` objects are complex, consume a large amount of memory, and are computationally intensive to serialize. Nevertheless, many applications pass them between tiers of the application. Tips to somewhat reduce the serialization overhead include:

- Call `DataSet.ApplyChanges` method before serializing the `DataSet`. The `DataSet` stores both the original values and the changed values. If you do not need to serialize the old values, call `ApplyChanges` to discard them.

- Serialize only the `DataTables` you need. If the `DataSet` contains other tables you do not need, consider copying only the required tables to a new `DataSet` object and serializing it instead.

- Use column name aliasing (As keyword) to give shorter names and reduce serialized length. For example, consider this SQL statement:
  `SELECT EmployeeID As I, Name As N, Age As A`

Windows Communication Foundation

Windows Communication Foundation (WCF), released in .NET 3.0, is quickly becoming the de-facto standard for most networking needs in .NET applications. It offers an unparalleled choice of network protocols and customizations and is continuously being extended with new .NET releases. This section covers WCF performance optimizations.

Throttling

WCF, especially before .NET Framework 4.0, has conservative throttling values by default. These are designed to protect against Denial of Service (DoS) attacks, but, unfortunately in the real world, they are often set too low to be useful.

Throttling settings can be modified by editing the `system.serviceModel` section in either app.config (for desktop applications) or web.config for ASP.NET applications:

```
<system.serviceModel>
  <behaviors>
    <serviceBehaviors>
      <behavior>
        <serviceThrottling>
          <serviceThrottling maxConcurrentCalls="16"
            maxConcurrentSessions="10" maxConcurrentInstances="26" />
```

Another way to change these parameters is by setting properties on a `ServiceThrottling` object during service creation time:

```
Uri baseAddress=new Uri("http://localhost:8001/Simple");
ServiceHost serviceHost=new ServiceHost(typeof(CalculatorService), baseAddress);
```

```
serviceHost.AddServiceEndpoint(
    typeof(ICalculator),
    new WSHttpBinding(),
    "CalculatorServiceObject");

serviceHost.Open();

IChannelListener icl=serviceHost.ChannelDispatchers[0].Listener;
ChannelDispatcher dispatcher=new ChannelDispatcher(icl);
ServiceThrottle throttle=dispatcher.ServiceThrottle;
throttle.MaxConcurrentSessions=10;
throttle.MaxConcurrentCalls=16;
throttle.MaxConcurrentInstances=26;
```

Let us understand what these parameters mean.

- maxConcurrentSessions limits the number of messages that currently process across a ServiceHost. Calls in excess of the limit are queued.
  Default value is 10 for .NET 3.5 and 100 times the number of processors in .NET 4.

- maxConcurrentCalls limits the number of InstanceContext objects that execute at one time across a ServiceHost. Requests to create additional instances are queued and complete when a slot below the limit becomes available.
  Default value is 16 for .NET 3.5 and 16 times the number of processors in .NET 4.

- maxConcurrentInstances limits the number of sessions a ServiceHost object can accept. The service accepts connections in excess of the limit, but only the channels below the limit are active (messages are read from the channel).
  Default value is 26 for .NET 3.5 and 116 times the number of processors in .NET 4.

Another important limit is the number of concurrent connections an application is allowed per host, which is two by default. If your ASP.NET application calls an external WCF service, this limit may be a significant bottleneck. This is a configuration example that sets these limits:

```
<system.net>
  <connectionManagement>
    <add address="*" maxconnection="100" />
  </connectionManagement>
</system.net>
```

Process Model

When writing a WCF service, you need to determine its activation and concurrency model. This is controlled by ServiceBehavior attribute's InstanceContextMode and ConcurrencyMode properties, respectively. The meaning of InstanceContextMode values is as follows:

- PerCall – A service object instance is created for each call.

- PerSession (default) – A service object instance is created for each session. If the channel does not support sessions, this behaves like PerCall.

- Single – A single service instance is re-used for all calls.

The meaning of ConcurrencyMode values is as follows:

- Single (default) – The service object is single-threaded and does not support re-entrancy. If InstanceContextMode is set to Single and it already services a request, then additional requests have to wait for their turn.

- Reentrant – The service object is single-threaded but is re-entrant. If the service calls another service, it may be re-entered. It is your responsibility to ensure object state is left in a consistent state prior to the invocation of another service.

- Multiple – No synchronization guarantees are made, and the service must handle synchronization on its own to ensure consistency of state.

Do not use Single or Reentrant ConcurrencyMode in conjunction with Single InstanceContextMode. If you use Multiple ConcurrencyMode, use fine-grained locking so that better concurrency is achieved.

WCF invokes your service objects from .NET thread pool I/O completion threads, previously described within this chapter. If during servicing you perform synchronous I/O or do waits, you may need to increase the number of thread pool threads allowed by editing the system.web configuration section for an ASP.NET application (see below) or by calling ThreadPool.SetMinThreads and ThreadPool.SetMaxThreads in a desktop application.

```
<system.web>
   <processModel
   ...
   enable = "true"
   autoConfig = "false"
   maxWorkerThreads = "80"
   maxIoThreads = "80"
   minWorkerThreads = "40"
   minIoThreads = "40"
   />
```

Caching

WCF does not ship with built-in support for caching. Even if you are hosting your WCF service in IIS, it still cannot use its cache by default. To enable caching, mark your WCF service with the AspNetCompatibilityRequirements attribute.

```
[AspNetCompatibilityRequirements(RequirementsMode = AspNetCompatibilityRequirementsMode.Allowed)]
```

In addition, enable ASP.NET compatibility by editing web.config and adding the following element under the system.serviceModel section:

```
<serviceHostingEnvironment aspNetCompatibilityEnabled = "true" />
```

Starting with .NET Framework 4.0, you can use the new System.Runtime.Caching types to implement caching. It is not dependent on the System.Web assembly, so it is not limited to ASP.NET.

Asynchronous WCF Clients and Servers

WCF lets you issue asynchronous operation on both the client and server side. Each side can independently decide whether it operates synchronously or asynchronously.

On the client side, there are two ways to invoke a service asynchronously: event-based and .NET async pattern based. The event-based model is not compatible with channels created with ChannelFactory. To use the event-based model, generate a service proxy by using the svcutil.exe tool with both the /async and /tcv:Version35 switches:

```
svcutil /n:http://Microsoft.ServiceModel.Samples,Microsoft.ServiceModel.Samples
http://localhost:8000/servicemodelsamples/service/mex /async /tcv:Version35
```

The generated proxy can then be used as follows:

```
// Asynchronous callbacks for displaying results.
static void AddCallback(object sender, AddCompletedEventArgs e) {
  Console.WriteLine("Add Result: {0}", e.Result);
}

static void Main(String[] args) {
  CalculatorClient client=new CalculatorClient();
  client.AddCompleted+=new EventHandler<AddCompletedEventArgs>(AddCallback);
  client.AddAsync(100.0, 200.0);
}
```

In the IAsyncResult-based model, you use svcutil to create a proxy specifying the /async switch but without also specifying the /tcv:Version35 switch. You then call the BeginXXX methods on the proxy and provide a completion callback as follows:

```
static void AddCallback(IAsyncResult ar) {
  double result=((CalculatorClient)ar.AsyncState).EndAdd(ar);
  Console.WriteLine("Add Result: {0}", result);
}

static void Main(String[] args) {
  ChannelFactory<ICalculatorChannel> factory=new ChannelFactory<ICalculatorChannel>();
  ICalculatorChannel channelClient=factory.CreateChannel();
  IAsyncResult arAdd=channelClient.BeginAdd(100.0, 200.0, AddCallback, channelClient);
}
```

On the server, asynchrony is implemented by creating BeginXX and EndXX versions of your contract operations. You should not have another operation named the same but without the Begin/End prefix, because WCF will invoke it instead. Follow these naming conventions, because WCF requires it.

The BeginXX method should take input parameters and return IAsyncResult with little processing; I/O should be done asynchronously. The BeginXX method (and it alone) should have the OperationContract attribute applied with the AsyncPattern parameter set to true.

The EndXX method should take an IAsyncResult, have the desired return value, and have the desired output parameters. The IAsyncResult object (returned from BeginXX) should contain all the necessary information to return the result.

Additionally, WCF 4.5 supports the new Task-based async/await pattern in both server and client code. For example:

```
//Task-based asynchronous service
public class StockQuoteService : IStockQuoteService {
  async public Task<double> GetStockPrice(string stockSymbol) {
    double price=await FetchStockPriceFromDB();
    return price;
  }
}
```

```
//Task-based asynchronous client
public class TestServiceClient : ClientBase<IStockQuoteService>, IStockQuoteService {
  public Task<double> GetStockPriceAsync(string stockSymbol) {
    return Channel.GetStockPriceAsync();
  }
}
```

Bindings

When designing your WCF service, it is important to select the right binding. Each binding has its own features and performance characteristics. Choose the simplest binding, and use the smallest number of binding features that will serve your needs. Features, such as reliability, security, and authentication, add a great deal of overhead, so use them only when necessary.

For communication between processes on the same machine, the Named Pipe binding offers the best performance. For cross-machine two-way communication, the Net TCP binding offers the best performance. However, it is not interoperable and can only work with WCF clients. It is also not load-balancer-friendly, as the session becomes affine to a particular server address.

You can use a custom binary HTTP binding to get most of the performance benefits of TCP binding, while remaining compatible with load balancers. Below is an example of configuring such a binding:

```
<bindings>
  <customBinding>
    <binding name="NetHttpBinding">
      <reliableSession />
      <compositeDuplex />
      <oneWay />
      <binaryMessageEncoding />
      <httpTransport />
    </binding>
  </customBinding>
  <basicHttpBinding>
    <binding name="BasicMtom" messageEncoding="Mtom" />
  </basicHttpBinding>
  <wsHttpBinding>
    <binding name="NoSecurityBinding">
      <security mode="None" />
    </binding>
  </wsHttpBinding>
</bindings>
<services>
  <service name="MyServices.CalculatorService">
    <endpoint address=" " binding="customBinding" bindingConfiguration="NetHttpBinding"
              contract="MyServices.ICalculator" />
  </service>
</services>
```

Finally, choose the basic HTTP binding over the WS-compatible one. The latter has a significantly more verbose messaging format.

Summary

As you have seen throughout this chapter, by improving your application's I/O performance, you can make a vast difference and refrain from any computation-related optimizations. This chapter:

- Examined the difference between synchronous and asynchronous I/O.

- Explored various I/O completion notification mechanisms.

- Gave general tips about I/O, such as minimizing memory buffer copying.

- Discussed file-I/O-specific optimizations.

- Examined socket-specific optimizations.

- Showed how to optimize network protocol to fully exploit available network capacity.

- Compared and benchmarked various serializers built into the .NET Framework.

- Covered WCF optimizations.

■ ■ ■

CHAPTER 8

Unsafe Code
and Interoperability

Few real-world applications are composed strictly of managed code. Instead, they frequently make use of in-house or 3rd party libraries implemented in native code. The .NET Framework offers several mechanisms to interoperate with native code that is implemented in a number of widespread technologies:

- P/Invoke: enables interoperability with DLLs exporting C-style functions.

- COM Interop: enables consumption of COM objects by managed code as well as exposing .NET classes as COM objects to be consumed by native code.

- C++/CLI language: enables interoperability with C and C++ via a hybrid programming language.

In fact, the Base Class Library (BCL), which is the set of DLLs shipped with the .NET Framework (mscorlib.dll being the main one) that contain .NET Framework's built-in types, uses all of the aforementioned mechanisms. It can therefore be argued that any non-trivial managed application is actually a hybrid application under the covers, in the sense that it calls native libraries.

While these mechanisms are very useful, it is important to understand the performance implications associated with each interop mechanism, and how to minimise their impact.

Unsafe Code

Managed code offers type safety, memory safety, and security guarantees, which eliminate some of the most difficult to diagnose bugs and security vulnerabilities prevalent in native code, such as heap corruptions and buffer overflows. This is made possible by prohibiting direct memory access with pointers, instead working with strongly-typed references, checking array access boundaries and ensuring only legal casting of objects.

However, in some cases these constraints may complicate otherwise simple tasks and reduce performance by forcing you to use a safe alternative. For example, one might read data from a file into a byte[ ] but would like to interpret this data as an array of double values. In C/C++, you would simply cast the char pointer to a double pointer. In contrast, in a safe .NET code, one could wrap the buffer with a MemoryStream object and use a BinaryReader object on top of the former to read each memory location as double values; another option is to use the BitConverter class. These solutions would work, but they're slower than doing this in unmanaged code. Fortunately, C# and the CLR support unsafe memory access with pointers and pointer casting. Other unsafe features are stack memory allocation and embedded arrays within structures. The downside of unsafe code is compromised safety, which can lead to memory corruptions and security vulnerabilities, so you should be very careful when writing unsafe code.

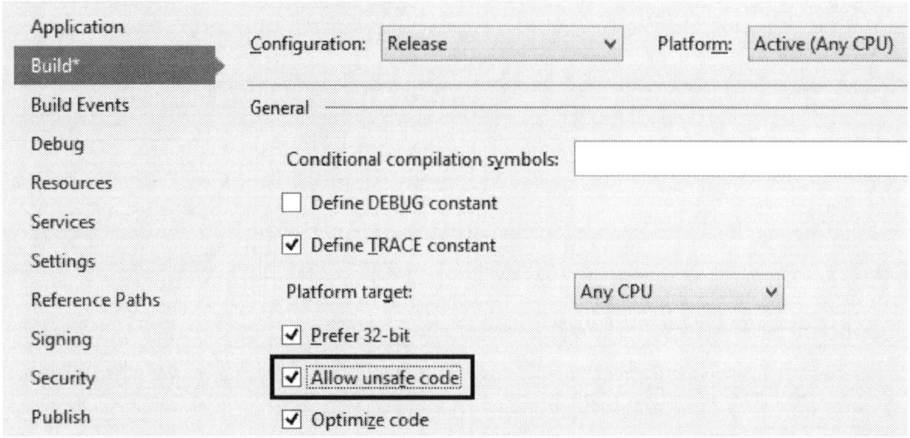

Figure 8-1. *Enabling unsafe code in C# project settings (Visual Studio 2012)*

To use unsafe code, you must first enable compiling unsafe code in C# project settings (see Figure 8-1), which results in passing the /unsafe command-line parameter to the C# compiler. Next, you should mark the region where unsafe code or unsafe variables are permitted, which can be a whole class or struct, a whole method or just a region within a method.

Pinning and GC Handles

Because managed objects located on the GC heap can be relocated during garbage collections occurring at unpredictable times, you must pin them in order to obtain their address and prevent them from being moved around in memory.

Pinning can be done either by using the fixed scope (see example in Listing 8-1) in C# or by allocating a pinning GC handle (see Listing 8-2). P/Invoke stubs, which we will cover later, also pin objects in a way equivalent to the fixed statement. Use fixed if the pinning requirement can be confined to the scope of a function, as it is more efficient than the GC handle approach. Otherwise, use GCHandle.Alloc to allocate a pinning handle to pin an object indefinitely (until you explicitly free the GC handle by calling GCHandle.Free). Stack objects (value types) do not require pinning, because they're not subject to garbage collection. A pointer can be obtained directly for stack-located objects by using the ampersand (&) reference operator.

Listing 8-1. Using fixed scope and pointer casting to reinterpret data in a buffer

```
using (var fs = new FileStream(@"C:\Dev\samples.dat", FileMode.Open)) {
  var buffer = new byte[4096];
  int bytesRead = fs.Read(buffer, 0, buffer.Length);
  unsafe {
    double sum = 0.0;
    fixed (byte* pBuff = buffer) {
      double* pDblBuff = (double*)pBuff;
      for (int i = 0; i < bytesRead / sizeof(double); i++)
        sum += pDblBuff[i];
    }
  }
}
```

■ **Caution**   The pointer obtained from the `fixed` statement must not be used outside the `fixed` scope because the pinned object becomes unpinned when the scope ends. You can use the `fixed` keyword on arrays of value types, on strings and on a specific value type field of a managed class. Be sure to specify structure memory layout.

GC handles are a way to refer to a managed object residing on the GC heap via an immutable pointer-sized handle value (even if the object's address changes), which can even be stored by native code. GC handles come in four varieties, specified by the GCHandleType enumeration: Weak, WeakTrackRessurection, Normal and Pinned. The Normal and Pinned types prevent an object from being garbage collected even if there is no other reference to it. The Pinned type additionally pins the object and enables its memory address to be obtained. Weak and WeakTrackResurrection do not prevent the object from being collected, but enable obtaining a normal (strong) reference if the object hasn't been garbage collected yet. It is used by the WeakReference type.

Listing 8-2. Using a pinning GCHandle for pinning and pointer casting to reinterpret data in a buffer

```
using (var fs=new FileStream(@"C:\Dev\samples.dat", FileMode.Open)) {
  var buffer=new byte[4096];
  int bytesRead=fs.Read(buffer, 0, buffer.Length);
  GCHandle gch=GCHandle.Alloc(buffer, GCHandleType.Pinned);
  unsafe {
    double sum=0.0;
    double* pDblBuff=(double *)(void *)gch.AddrOfPinnedObject();
    for (int i=0; i<bytesRead / sizeof(double); i++)
      sum+= pDblBuff[i];
    gch.Free();
  }
}
```

■ **Caution**   Pinning may cause managed heap fragmentation if a garbage collection is triggered (even by another concurrently running thread). Fragmentation wastes memory and reduces the efficiency of the garbage collector's algorithm. To minimize fragmentation, do not pin objects longer than necessary.

Lifetime Management

In many cases, native code continues to hold unmanaged resources across function calls, and will require an explicit call to free the resources. If that's the case, implement the IDisposable interface in the wrapping managed class, in addition to a finalizer. This will enable clients to deterministically dispose unmanaged resources, while the finalizer should be a last-resort safety net in case you forgot to dispose explicitly.

Allocating Unmanaged Memory

Managed objects taking more than 85,000 bytes (commonly, byte buffers and strings) are placed on the Large Object Heap (LOH), which is garbage collected together with Gen2 of the GC heap, which is quite expensive. The LOH also often becomes fragmented because it is never compacted; rather free spaces are re-used if possible. Both these issues increase memory usage and CPU usage by the garbage collector. Therefore, it is more efficient to use managed memory pooling or to allocate these buffers from unmanaged memory (e.g. by calling

`Marshal.AllocHGlobal`). If you later need to access unmanaged buffers from managed code, use a "streaming" approach, where you copy small chunks of the unmanaged buffer to managed memory and work with one chunk at a time. You can use `System.UnmanagedMemoryStream` and `System.UnmanagedMemoryAccessor` to make the job easier.

Memory Pooling

If you are heavily using buffers to communicate with native code, you can either allocate them from GC heap or from an unmanaged heap. The former approach becomes inefficient for high allocation rates and if the buffers aren't very small. Managed buffers will need to be pinned, which promotes fragmentation. The latter approach is also problematic, because most managed code expects buffers to be managed byte arrays (`byte[]`) rather than pointers. You cannot convert a pointer to a managed array without copying, but this is bad for performance.

■ **Tip** You can look up the `% Time in GC` performance counter under the `.NET CLR Memory` performance counter category to get an estimate of the CPU time "wasted" by the GC, but this doesn't tell you what code is responsible. Use a profiler (see Chapter 2) before investing optimization effort, and see Chapter 4 for more tips on garbage collection performance.

We propose a solution (see Figure 8-2) which provides a copy-free access from both managed and unmanaged code and does not stress the GC. The idea is to allocate large managed memory buffers (segments) which reside on the Large Object Heap. There is no penalty associated with pinning these segments because they're already non-relocatable.

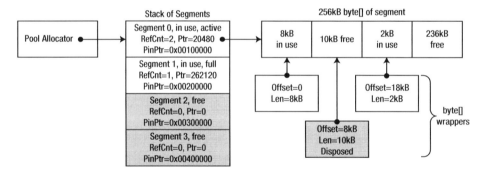

Figure 8-2. *Proposed memory pooling scheme*

A simple allocator, where the allocation pointer (an index actually) of a segment moves only forward with each allocation will then allocate buffers of varying sizes (up to the segment size) and will return a wrapper object around those buffers. Once the pointer approaches the end and an allocation fails, a new segment is obtained from the segment pool and allocation is attempted again.

Segments have a reference count that is incremented for every allocation and decremented when the wrapper object is disposed of. Once its reference count reaches zero, it can be reset, by setting the pointer to zero and optionally zero filling memory, and then returned to the segment pool.

The wrapper object stores the segment's `byte[]`, the offset where data begins, its length, and an unmanaged pointer. In effect, the wrapper is a window into the segment's large buffer. It will also reference the segment in order to decrement the segment in-use count once the wrapper is disposed. The wrapper could provide convenience methods such a safe indexer access which accounts for the offset and verifies that access is within bounds.

Since .NET developers have a habit of assuming that buffer data always begins at index 0 and lasts the entire length of the array, you will need to modify code not to assume that, but to rely on additional offset and length parameters that will be passed along with the buffer. Most .NET BCL methods that work with buffers have overloads which take offset and length explicitly.

The major downside to this approach is the loss of automatic memory management. In order for segments to be recycled, you will have to explicitly dispose of the wrapper object. Implementing a finalizer isn't a good solution, because this will more than negate the performance benefits.

P/Invoke

Platform Invoke, better known as P/Invoke, enables calling C-style functions that are exported by DLLs from managed code. To use P/Invoke, the managed caller declares a `static extern` method, with a signature (parameter types and return value type) equivalent to those of the C function. The method is then marked with the `DllImport` attribute, while specifying at a minimum, the DLL which exports the function.

```
// Native declaration from WinBase.h:
HMODULE WINAPI LoadLibraryW(LPCWSTR lpLibFileName);

// C# declaration:
class MyInteropFunctions {
  [DllImport("kernel32.dll", SetLastError=true)]
  public static extern IntPtr LoadLibrary(string fileName);
}
```

In the preceding code, we define `LoadLibrary` as a function taking a `string` and returning an `IntPtr`, which is a pointer type that cannot be dereferenced directly, thus using it does not render the code unsafe. The `DllImport` attribute specifies that the function is exported by kernel32.dll (which is the main Win32 API DLL) and that the Win32 last error code should be saved so Thread Local Storage so that it will not be overwritten by calls to Win32 functions not done explicitly (e.g. internally by the CLR) . The `DllImport` attribute can also be used to specify the C function's calling convention, string encoding, exported name resolution options, etc.

If the native function's signature contains complex types such as C structs, then equivalent structures or classes must be defined by the managed code, using equivalent types for each field. Relative structure field order, field types and alignment must match to what the C code expects. In some cases, you will need to apply the `MarshalAs` attribute on fields, on function parameters or the return value to modify default marshaling behavior. For example, the managed `System.Boolean` (bool) type can have multiple representations in native code: the Win32 BOOL type is four bytes long and a true value is any non-zero value, while in C++ the bool value is one byte long and the true value equals 1.

In the following code listing, the `StructLayout` attribute that is applied to the `WIN32_FIND_DATA` struct, specifies that a sequential in-memory field layout is desired; without it, the CLR is free to re-arrange fields for better efficiency. The `MarshalAs` attributes applied to the `cFileName` and `cAlternateFileName` fields specify that the strings should be marshaled as fixed-size strings embedded within the structure, as opposed to being just pointers to a string external to the structure.

```
// Native declaration from WinBase.h:
typedef struct _WIN32_FIND_DATAW {
  DWORD dwFileAttributes;
  FILETIME ftCreationTime;
  FILETIME ftLastAccessTime;
  FILETIME ftLastWriteTime;
  DWORD nFileSizeHigh;
  DWORD nFileSizeLow;
  DWORD dwReserved0;
  DWORD dwReserved1;
```

```
  WCHAR   cFileName[MAX_PATH];
  WCHAR   cAlternateFileName[14];
} WIN32_FIND_DATAW;

HANDLE WINAPI FindFirstFileW(__in  LPCWSTR lpFileName,
  __out LPWIN32_FIND_DATAW lpFindFileData);

// C# declaration:
[StructLayout(LayoutKind.Sequential, CharSet=CharSet.Auto)]
struct WIN32_FIND_DATA {
  public uint dwFileAttributes;
  public FILETIME ftCreationTime;
  public FILETIME ftLastAccessTime;
  public FILETIME ftLastWriteTime;
  public uint nFileSizeHigh;
  public uint nFileSizeLow;
  public uint dwReserved0;
  public uint dwReserved1;
  [MarshalAs(UnmanagedType.ByValTStr, SizeConst=260)]
  public string cFileName;
  [MarshalAs(UnmanagedType.ByValTStr, SizeConst=14)]
  public string cAlternateFileName;
}

[DllImport("kernel32.dll", CharSet=CharSet.Auto)]
static extern IntPtr FindFirstFile(string lpFileName, out WIN32_FIND_DATA lpFindFileData);
```

When you call the FindFirstFile method in the preceding code listing, the CLR loads the DLL that is exporting the function (kernel32.dll), locates the desired function (FindFirstFile), and translates parameter types from their managed to native representations (and vice versa). In this example, the input lpFileName string parameter is translated to a native string, whereas writes to the WIN32_FIND_DATAW native structure pointed to by the lpFindFileData parameter are translated to writes to the managed WIN32_FIND_DATA structure. In the following sections, we will describe in detail each of these stages.

PInvoke.net and P/Invoke Interop Assistant

Creating P/Invoke signatures can be hard and tedious. There are many rules to obey and many nuances to know. Producing an incorrect signature can result in hard to diagnose bugs. Fortunately, there are two resources which make this easier: the PInvoke.net website and the P/Invoke Interop Assistant tool.

PInvoke.net is a very helpful Wiki-style website, where you can find and contribute P/Invoke signatures for various Microsoft APIs. PInvoke.net was created by Adam Nathan, a senior software development engineer at Microsoft who previously worked on the .NET CLR Quality Assurance team and has written an extensive book about COM interoperability. You can also download a free Visual Studio add-on to access P/Invoke signatures without leaving Visual Studio.

P/Invoke Interop Assistant is a free tool from Microsoft downloadable from CodePlex, along with source code. It contains a database (an XML file) describing Win32 functions, structures, and constants which are used to generate a P/Invoke signature. It can also generate a P/Invoke signature given a C function declaration, and can generate native callback function declaration and native COM interface signature given a managed assembly.

Figure 8-3 shows Microsoft's P/Invoke Interop Assistant tool showing the search results for "CreateFile" on the left side and the P/Invoke signature along with associated structures is shown on the right. The P/Invoke Interop Assistant tool (along with other useful CLR interop-related tools) can be obtained from http://clrinterop.codeplex.com/.

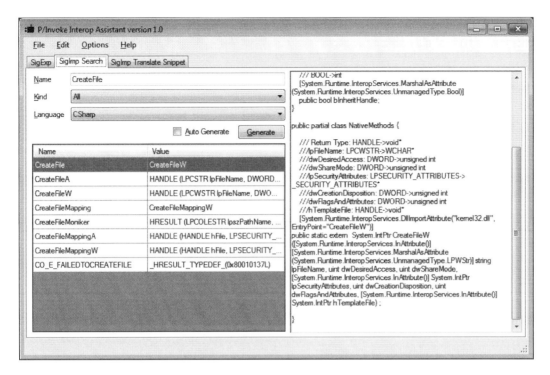

Figure 8-3. *Screenshot of P/Invoke Interop Asssitant showing the P/Invoke signature for* `CreateFile`

Binding

When you first call a P/Invoke'd function, the native DLL and its dependencies are loaded into the process via the Win32 `LoadLibrary` function (if they've not already been loaded). Next, the desired exported function is searched for, possibly searching for mangled variants first. Search behavior depends on the values of the `CharSet` and `ExactSpelling` fields of `DllImport`.

- If `ExactSpelling` is `true`, P/Invoke searches only for a function with the exact name, taking into account only the calling convention mangling. If this fails, P/Invoke will not continue searching for other name variations and will throw an `EntryPointNotFoundException`.

- If `ExactSpelling` is `false`, then behavior is determined by the `CharSet` property:

  - If set to `CharSet.Ansi` (default), P/Invoke searches the exact (unmangled) name first, and then the mangled name (with "A" appended).

  - If set to `CharSet.Unicode`, P/Invoke searches the mangled name first (with "W" appended), and then the unmangled name.

The default value for `ExactSpelling` is `false` for C# and `True` for VB.NET. The `CharSet.Auto` value behaves like `CharSet.Unicode` on any modern operating system (later than Windows ME).

> ■ **Tip** Use the Unicode versions of Win32 functions. Windows NT and beyond are natively Unicode (UTF16).
> If you call the ANSI versions of Win32 functions, strings are converted to Unicode which results in a performance
> penalty, and the Unicode version of the function is called. The .NET string representation is also natively UTF16, so
> marshaling string parameters is faster if they are already UTF16. Design your code and especially the interface to be
> Unicode-compatible, which has globalization benefits as well. Set `ExactSpelling` to `true`, which will speed up initial
> load time by eliminating an unnecessary function search.

Marshaler Stubs

When you first call a P/Invoke'd function, right after loading the native DLL, a P/Invoke marshaler stub will be
generated on demand, and will be re-used for subsequent calls. The marshaler performs the following steps
once called:

1. Checks for callers' unmanaged code execution permissions.
2. Converts managed arguments to their appropriate native in-memory representation, possibly allocating
   memory.
3. Sets thread's GC mode to pre-emptive, so GC can occur without waiting the thread to reach a safe point.
4. Calls the native function.
5. Restores thread GC mode to co-operative.
6. Optionally saves Win32 error code in Thread Local Storage for later retrieval by `Marshal.`
   `GetLastWin32Error`.
7. Optionally converts `HRESULT` to an exception and throws it.
8. Converts native exception if thrown to a managed exception.
9. Converts the return value and output parameters back to their managed in-memory representations.
10. Cleans up any temporarily allocated memory.

P/Invoke can also be used to call managed code from native code. A reverse marshaler stub can be
generated for a delegate (via `Marshal.GetFunctionPointerForDelegate`) if it is passed as a parameter in a
P/Invoke call to a native function. The native function will receive a function pointer in place of the delegate,
which it can call to invoke the managed method. The function pointer points to a dynamically generated stub
which in addition to parameter marshaling, also knows the target object's address (`this` pointer).

In .NET Framework 1.x, marshaler stubs consisted of either generated assembly code (for simple signatures)
or of generated ML (Marshaling Language) code (for complex signatures). ML is an internal byte code and is
executed by an internal interpreter. With the introduction of AMD64 and Itanium support in .NET Framework
2.0, Microsoft realized that implementing a parallel ML infrastructure for every CPU architecture would be a great
burden. Instead, stubs for 64-bit versions of .NET Framework 2.0 were implemented exclusively in generated IL
code. While the IL stubs were significantly faster than the interpreted ML stubs, they were still slower than the x86
generated assembly stubs, so Microsoft opted to retain the x86 implementation. In .NET Framework 4.0, the IL
stub generation infrastructure was significantly optimized, which made IL stubs faster compared even to the x86
assembly stubs. This allowed Microsoft to remove the x86-specific stub implementation entirely and to unify stub
generation across all architectures.

■ **Tip** A function call that crosses the managed-to-native boundary is at least an order of magnitude slower than a direct call within the same environment. If you're in control of both the native and managed code, construct the interface in a way that minimizes native-to-managed round trips (chatty interfaces). Try to combine several "work items" into one call (chunked interfaces). Similarly, combine invocations of several trivial functions (e.g.trivial Get/Set functions) into a façade which does equivalent work in one call.

Microsoft provides a freely downloadable tool called *IL Stub Diagnostics* from CodePlex along with source code. It subscribes to the CLR ETW IL stub generation/cache hit events and displays the generated IL stub code in the UI.

Below we show an annotated example IL marshaling stub, consisting of five sections of code: initialization, marshaling of input parameters, invocation, marshaling back of return value and/or output parameters and cleanup. The marshaler stub is for the following signature:

```
// Managed signature:
[DllImport("Server.dll")]static extern int Marshal_String_In(string s);
// Native Signature:
unmanaged int __stdcall Marshal_String_In(char *s)
```

In the initialization section, the stub declares local (stack) variables, obtains a stub context and demands unmanaged code execution permissions.

```
// IL Stub:
// Code size    153 (0x0099)
.maxstack 3
// Local variables are:
// IsSuccessful, pNativeStrPtr, SizeInBytes, pStackAllocPtr, result, result, result
.locals (int32,native int,int32,native int,int32,int32,int32)

call          native int [mscorlib] System.StubHelpers.StubHelpers::GetStubContext()
// Demand unmanaged code execution permission
call          void [mscorlib] System.StubHelpers.StubHelpers::DemandPermission(native int)
```

In the marshaling section, the stub marshals input parameters native function. In this example, we marshal a single string input parameter. The marshaler may call helper types under the System.StubHelpersnamespace or the System.Runtime.InteropServices.Marshal class to assist in converting of specific types and of type categories from managed to native representation and back. In this example, we call CSTRMarshaler::ConvertToNative to marshal the string.

There's a slight optimization here: if the managed string is short enough, it is marshaled to memory allocated on the stack (which is faster). Otherwise, memory has to be allocated from the heap.

```
    ldc.i4        0x0           // IsSuccessful=0  [push 0 to stack]
    stloc.0                     //       [store to IsSuccessful]
IL_0010:
    nop           // argument {
    ldc.i4        0x0           // pNativeStrPtr=null   [push 0 to stack]
    conv.i                      //       [convert to an int32 to "native int" (pointer)]
    stloc.3                     //       [store result to pNativeStrPtr]
    ldarg.0                     // if (managedString == null)
    brfalse       IL_0042       //     goto IL_0042
    ldarg.0                     // [push managedString instance to stack]
                                // call the get Length property (returns num of chars)
```

```
call              instance int32 [mscorlib] System.String::get_Length()
ldc.i4       0x2          // Add 2 to length, one for null char in managedString and
                          // one for an extra null we put in [push constant 2 to stack]
add                       //        [actual add, result pushed to stack]
                          // load static field, value depends on lang. for non-Unicode
                          // apps system setting
ldsfld       System.Runtime.InteropServices.Marshal::SystemMaxDBCSCharSize
mul                       // Multiply length by SystemMaxDBCSCharSize to get amount of
                          // bytes
stloc.2                   // Store to SizeInBytes
ldc.i4       0x105        // Compare SizeInBytes to 0x105, to avoid allocating too much
                          // stack memory  [push constant 0x105]
                          // CSTRMarshaler::ConvertToNative will handle the case of
                          // pStackAllocPtr == null and will do a CoTaskMemAlloc of the
                          // greater size
ldloc.2                   //        [Push SizeInBytes]
clt                       //        [If SizeInBytes>0x105, push 1 else push 0]
brtrue       IL_0042      //        [If 1 goto IL_0042]
ldloc.2                   // Push SizeInBytes (argument of localloc)
localloc                  // Do stack allocation, result pointer is on top of stack
stloc.3                   // Save to pStackAllocPtr
IL_0042:
ldc.i4       0x1          // Push constant 1 (flags parameter)
ldarg.0                   // Push managedString argument
ldloc.3                   // Push pStackAllocPtr (this can be null)
                          // Call helper to convert to Unicode to ANSI
call native int [mscorlib]System.StubHelpers.CSTRMarshaler::ConvertToNative(int32,string, native int)
stloc.1                   // Store result in pNativeStrPtr,
                          // can be equal to pStackAllocPtr
ldc.i4       0x1          // IsSuccessful=1 [push 1 to stack]
stloc.0                   //        [store to IsSuccessful]
nop
nop
nop
```

In the next section, the stub obtains the native function pointer from the stub context and invokes it. The call instruction actually does more work than we can see here, such as changing the GC mode and catching the native function's return in order to suspend execution of managed code while the GC is in progress and is in a phase that requires suspension of managed code execution.

```
ldloc.1                   // Push pStackAllocPtr to stack,
                          // for the user function, not for GetStubContext
call         native int [mscorlib] System.StubHelpers.StubHelpers::GetStubContext()
ldc.i4       0x14         // Add 0x14 to context ptr
add                       //        [actual add, result is on stack]
ldind.i                   //        [deref ptr, result is on stack]
ldind.i                   //        [deref function ptr, result is on stack]
calli        unmanaged stdcall int32(native int)  // Call user function
```

The following section is actually structured as two sections that handle the "unmarshaling" (conversion of native types to managed types) of the return value and output parameters, respectively. In this example, the native function returns an int which does not require marshaling and is just copied as-is to a local variable. Since there are no output parameters, the latter section is empty.

```
// UnmarshalReturn {
    nop                 // return {
    stloc.s      0x5              // Store user function result (int) into x, y and z
    ldloc.s      0x5
    stloc.s      0x4
    ldloc.s      0x4
    nop                 // } return
    stloc.s      0x6
// } UnmarshalReturn
// Unmarshal {
    nop                 // argument {
    nop                 // } argument
    leave        IL_007e     // Exit try protected block
IL_007e:
    ldloc.s      0x6         // Push z
    ret                      // Return z
// } Unmarshal
```

Finally, the cleanup section releases memory that was allocated temporarily for the sake of marshaling. It performs cleanup in a `finally` block so that cleanup happens even if an exception is thrown by the native function. It may also perform some cleanup only in case of an exception. In COM interop, it may translate an HRESULT return value indicating an error into an exception.

```
// ExceptionCleanup {
IL_0081:
// } ExceptionCleanup
// Cleanup {
    ldloc.0                      // If (IsSuccessful && !pStackAllocPtr)
    ldc.i4       0x0         //        Call ClearNative(pNativeStrPtr)
    ble          IL_0098
    ldloc.3
    brtrue       IL_0098
    ldloc.1
    call         void [mscorlib] System.StubHelpers.CSTRMarshaler::ClearNative(native int)
IL_0098:
    endfinally
IL_0099:
// } Cleanup
.try IL_0010 to IL_007e finally handler IL_0081 to IL_0099
```

In conclusion, the IL marshaler stub is non-trivial even for this trivial function signature. Complex signatures result in even lengthier and slower IL marshaler stubs.

Blittable Types

Most native types share a common in-memory representation with managed code. These types, called *blittable types*, do not require conversion, and are passed as-is across managed-to-native boundaries, which is significantly faster than marshaling non-blittable types. In fact, the marshaler stub can optimize this case even further by pinning a managed object and passing a direct pointer to the managed object to native code, avoiding one or two memory copy operations (one for each required marshaling direction).

A blittable type is one of the following types:

- System.Byte (byte)

- System.SByte (sbyte)

- System.Int16 (short)

- System.UInt16 (ushort)

- System.Int32 (int)

- System.UInt32 (uint)

- Syste.Int64 (long)

- System.UInt64 (ulong)

- System.IntPtr

- System.UIntPtr

- System.Single (float)

- System.Double (double)

In addition, a single-dimensional array of blittable types (where all elements are of the same type) is also blittable, so is a structure or class consisting solely of blittable fields.

A System.Boolean (bool) is not blittable because it can have 1, 2 or 4 byte representation in native code, a System.Char (char) is not blittable because it can represent either an ANSI or Unicode character and a System.String (string) is not blittable because its native representation can be either ANSI or Unicode, and it can be either a C-style string or a COM BSTR and the managed string needs to be immutable (which is risky if the native code modifies the string, breaking immutability). A type containing an object reference field is not blittable, even if it's a reference to a blittable type or an array thereof. Marshaling non-blittable types involves allocation of memory to hold a transformed version of the parameter, populating it appropriately and finally releasing of previously allocated memory.

You can get better performance by marshaling string input parameters manually (see the following code for an example). The native callee must take a C-style UTF-16 string and it should never write to the memory occupied by the string, so this optimization is not always possible. Manual marshaling involves pinning the input string and modifying the P/Invoke signature to take an IntPtr instead of a string and passing a pointer to the pinned string object.

```
class Win32Interop {
  [DllImport("NativeDLL.DLL", CallingConvention=CallingConvention.Cdecl)]
  public static extern void NativeFunc(IntPtr pStr); // takes IntPtr instead of string
}

//Managed caller calls the P/Invoke function inside a fixed scope which does string pinning:
unsafe
{
    string str="MyString";
    fixed (char *pStr=str)     {
      //You can reuse pStr for multiple calls.
      Win32Interop.NativeFunc((IntPtr)pStr);
    }
}
```

Converting a native C-style UTF-16 string to a managed string can also be optimized by using System.String's constructor taking a char* as parameter. The System.String constructor will make a copy of the buffer, so the native pointer can be freed after the managed string has been created. Note that no validation is done to ensure that the string only contains valid Unicode characters.

Marshaling Direction, Value and Reference Types

As mentioned earlier, function parameters can be marshaled by the marshaler stub in either or both directions. Which direction a parameter gets marshaled is determined by a number of factors:

- Whether the parameter is a value or reference type.
- Whether the parameter is being passed by value or by reference.
- Whether the type is blittable or not.
- Whether marshaling direction-modifying attributes (System.RuntimeInteropService.InAttribute and System.RuntimeInteropService. OutAttribute) are applied to the parameter.

For the purposes of this discussion, we define the "in" direction to be the managed to native marshaling direction; conversely the "out" direction is the native to managed direction. Below is a list of default marshaling direction rules:

- Parameters passed by value, regardless whether they're value or reference types, are marshaled in the "in" direction only.
    - You do not need to apply the In attribute manually.
    - StringBuilder is an exception to this rule and is always marshaled "in/out".
- Parameters passed by reference (via the ref C# keyword or the ByRef VB .NET keyword), regardless whether they're value or reference types, are marshaled "in/out".

Specifying the OutAttribute alone will inhibit the "in" marshaling, so the native callee may not see initializations done by the caller. The C# out keyword behaves like ref keyword but adds an OutAttribute.

■ **Tip**   If parameters are not blittable in a P/Invoke call, and you require marshaling in only the "out" direction, you can avoid unnecessary marshaling by using the out C# keyword instead of the ref keyword.

Due to the blittable parameter pinning optimization mentioned above, blittable reference types will get an effective "in/out" marshaling, even if the above rules tell otherwise. You should not rely on this behavior if you need "out" or "in/out" marshaling behavior, but instead you should specify direction attributes explicitly, as this optimization will stop working if you later add a non-blittable field or if this is a COM call that crosses an apartment boundary.

The difference between marshaling value types versus reference types manifests in how they are passed on the stack.

- Value types passed by value are pushed as copies on the stack, so they are effectively always marshaled "in", regardless of modifying attributes.
- Value types passed by reference and reference types passed by value are passed by pointer.
- Reference types passed by reference are passed as pointer to a pointer.

> ■ **Note**   Passing large value type parameters (more than a dozen or so bytes long) by value is more expensive than passing them by reference. The same goes for large return values, where out parameters are a possible alternative.

Code Access Security

The .NET Code Access Security mechanism enables running partially trusted code in a sandbox, with restricted access to runtime capabilities (e.g. P/Invoke) and BCL functionality (e.g. file and registry access). When calling native code, CAS requires that all assemblies whose methods appear in the call stack to have the UnmanagedCode permission. The marshaler stub will demand this permission for each call, which involves walking the call stack to ensure that all code has this permission.

> ■ **Tip**   If you run only fully trusted code or you have other means to ensure security, you can gain a substantial performance increase by placing the SuppressUnmanagedCodeSecurityAttribute on the P/Invoke method declaration, a class (in which case it applies to contained methods), an interface or a delegate.

COM Interoperability

COM was designed for the very purpose of writing components in any COM-capable language/platform and consumption thereof in any (other) COM-capable language/platform. .NET is no exception, and it allows you to easily consume COM objects and expose .NET types as COM objects.

With COM interop, the basic idea is the same as in P/Invoke: you declare a managed representation of the COM object and the CLR created a wrapper object that handles the marshaling. There are two kinds of wrappers: Runtime Callable Wrapper (RCW) which enables managed code to use COM objects (see Figure 8-4), and COM Callable Wrapper (CCW) that enables COM code to call managed types (see Figure 8-5). Third party COM components are often shipped with a Primary Interop Assembly, which contains vendor-approved interop definitions and is strongly named (signed) and installed in the GAC . Other times, you can use the tlbimp. exe tool, which is part of the Windows SDK to auto-generate an interop assembly based on the information contained in the type library.

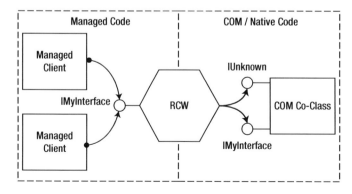

Figure 8-4. *Managed client calling unmanaged COM object*

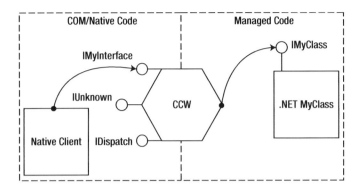

Figure 8-5. *Unmanaged client calling a managed COM object*

COM interop re-uses the P/Invoke parameter marshaling infrastructure, with some changes in defaults (e.g. a string is marshaled to BSTR by default), so the advice provided in the P/Invoke section of this chapter applies here as well.

COM has its own performance issues resulting from COM-specific particularities such as the apartment threading model and a mismatch between the the reference counted nature of COM and the .NET garbage collected approach.

Lifetime Management

When you hold a reference to a COM object in .NET, you are actually holding a reference to an RCW. The RCW always holds a single reference to the underlying COM object and there is only one RCW instance per COM object. The RCW maintains its own reference count, separate from the COM reference count. This reference count's value is usually one but can be greater if a number of interface pointers have been marshaled or if the same interface has been marshaled by multiple threads.

Normally, when the last managed reference to the RCW is gone and there is a subsequent garbage collection at the generation where the RCW resides; the RCW's finalizer runs and it decrements the COM objects's reference count (which was one) by calling the Release method on the IUnknown interface pointer for the COM underlying object. The COM object subsequently destroys itself and releases its memory.

Since the .NET GC runs at non-deterministic times and is not aware of the unmanaged memory burden caused by it holding the RCWs and subsequently COM objects alive, it will not hasten garbage collections and memory usage may become be very high.

If necessary, you can call the Marshal.ReleaseComObject method to explicitly release the object. Each call will decrement RCW's reference count and when it reaches zero, the underlying COM object's reference count will be decremented (just like in the case of the RCW's finalizer running), thus releasing it. You must ensure that you do not continue to use the RCW after calling Marshal.ReleaseComObject. If the RCW reference count is greater than zero, you will need to call Marshal.ReleaseComObject in a loop until the return value equals zero. It is a best practice to call Marshal.ReleaseComObject inside a finally block, to ensure that the release occurs even in the case of an exception being thrown somewhere between the instantiation and the release of the COM object.

Apartment Marshaling

COM implements its own thread synchronization mechanisms for managing cross-thread calls, even for objects not designed for multi-threading. These mechanisms can degrade performance if one is not aware of them. While this issue is not specific for interoperability with .NET, it is nonetheless worth discussing as it is a common pitfall, likely because developers that are accustomed to typical .NET thread synchronizations conventions might be unaware of what COM is doing behind the scenes.

COM assigns objects and threads *apartments* which are boundaries across which COM will marshal calls. COM has several apartment types:

- Single–threaded apartment (STA), each hosts a single thread, but can host any number of objects. There can be any number of STA apartments in a process.

- Multi–threaded apartment (MTA), hosts any number of threads and any number of objects,but there is only one MTA apartment in a process. This is the default for .NET threads.

- Neutral-threaded apartment (NTA), hosts objects but not threads. There is only one NTA apartment in a process.

A thread is assigned to an apartment when a call is made to `CoInitialize` or `CoInitializeEx` to initialize COM for that thread. Calling `CoInitialize` will assign the thread to a new STA apartment, while `CoInitializeEx` allows you to specify either an STA or an MTA assignment. In .NET, you do not call those functions directly, but instead mark a thread's entry point (or `Main`) with the `STAThread` or `MTAThread` attribute. Alternatively, you can call `Thread.SetApartmentState` method or the `Thread.ApartmentState` property before a thread is started. If not otherwise specified, .NET initializes threads (including the main thread) as MTA.

COM objects are assigned to apartments based on the *ThreadingModel* registry value, which can be:

- Single – object resides in the default STA.

- Apartment (STA) – object must reside in any STA, and only that STA's thread is allowed to call the object directly. Different instances can reside in different STA.

- Free (MTA) - object resides in the MTA. Any number of MTA threads can call it directly and concurrently. Object must ensure thread-safety.

- Both – object resides in the creator's apartment (STA or MTA). In essense, it becomes either STA-like or MTA-like object once created.

- Neutral – object resides in the neutral apartment and never requires marshaling. This is the most efficient mode.

Refer to Figure 8-6 for a visual representation of apartments, threads and objects.

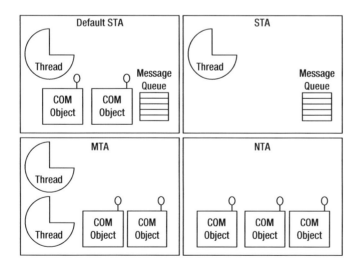

Figure 8-6. *Process division into COM apartments*

If you create an object with a threading model incompatible with that of the creator thread's apartment, you will receive an interface pointer which actually points to a proxy. If the COM object's interface needs to be passed to a different thread belonging to a different apartment, the interface pointer should not be passed directly, but instead needs to be marshaled. COM will return a proxy object as appropriate.

Marshaling involves translating the function's call (including parameters) to a message which will be posted to the recipient STA apartment's message queue. For STA objects, this is implemented as a hidden window whose window procedure receives the messages and dispatches calls to the COM object via a stub. In this way, STA COM objects are always invoked by the same thread, which is obviously thread-safe.

When the caller's apartment is incompatible with the COM object's apartment, a thread switch and cross-thread parameter marshaling occurs.

▓ **Tip** Avoid the cross-thread performance penalty by matching the COM object's apartment with the creating thread's apartment. Create and use apartment threaded (STA) COM objects on STA threads, and free-threaded COM objects on MTA threads. COM objects marked as supporting both modes can be used from either thread without penalty.

CALLING STA OBJECTS FROM ASP.NET

ASP.NET executes pages on MTA threads by default. If you call STA objects, they undergo marshaling. If you predominantly call STA objects, this will degrade performance. You can remedy this by marking pages with the ASPCOMPAT attribute, as follows:

```
<%@Page Language = "vb" AspCompat = "true" %>
```

Note that page constructors still executes in an MTA thread, so defer creating STA objects to Page_Load and Page_Init events.

TLB Import and Code Access Security

Code Access Security does the same security checking as in P/Invoke. You can use the /unsafe switch with the tlbimp.exe utility which will emit the SuppressUnmanagedCodeSecurity attribute on generated types. Use this only in full-trust environments as this may introduce security issues.

NoPIA

Prior to .NET Framework 4.0, you had to distribute interop assemblies or Primary Interop Assemblies (PIA) alongside with your application or add-in. These assemblies tend to be large (even more so compared to the code that uses them), and they are not typically installed by the vendor of the COM component; instead they are installed as redistributable packages, because they are not required for the operation of the COM component itself. Another reason for not installing the PIAs is that they have to be installed in the GAC, which imposes a .NET Framework dependency on the installer of an otherwise completely native application.

Starting with .NET Framework 4.0, the C# and VB.NET compilers can examine which COM interfaces and which methods within them are required, and can copy and embed only the required interface definitions into the caller assembly, eliminating the need to distribute PIA DLLs and reducing code size. Microsoft calls this feature NoPIA. It works both for Primary Interop Assemblies and for interop assemblies in general.

PIA assemblies had an important feature called type equivalence. Since they have a strong name and are put into the GAC, different managed components can exchange the RCWs, and from .NET's perspective, they would have equivalent type. In contrast, interop assemblies generated by tlbimp.exe would not have this feature, since each component would have its own distinct interop assembly. With NoPIA, since there is a strongly named assembly is not used, Microsoft came up with a solution which treats RCWs from different assemblies as the same type, as long as the interfaces have the same GUID.

To enable NoPIA, select Properties on the interop assembly under References, and set "Embed Interop Types" to True (see Figure 8-7).

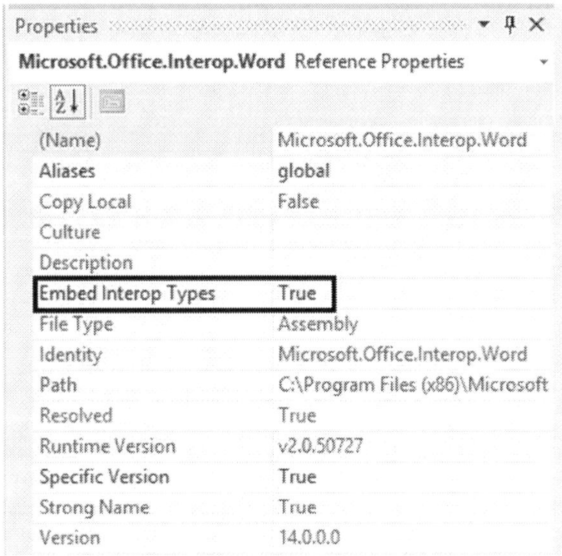

Figure 8-7. *Enabling NoPIA in interop assembly reference properties*

Exceptions

Most COM interface methods report success or failure via an HRESULT return value. Negative HRESULT values (with most significant bit set) indicate failure, while zero (S_OK) or positive values report success. Additionally, a COM object may provide richer error information by calling the SetErrorInfo function, passing an IErrorInfo object which is created by calling CreateErrorInfo. When calling a COM method via COM interop, the marshaler stub converts the HRESULT into a managed exception according to the HRESULT value and the data contained inside the IErrorInfo object. Since throwing exceptions is relatively expensive, COM functions that fail frequently will negatively impact performance. You can suppress automatic exception translation by marking methods with the PreserveSigAttribute. You will have to change the managed signature to return an int, and the retval parameter will become an "out" parameter.

C++/CLI Language Extensions

C++/CLI is a set of C++ language extensions, which enables creating hybrid managed and native DLLs. In C++/CLI, you can have both managed and unmanaged classes or functions even within the same .cpp file. You can use both managed types as well as native C and C++ types, just as you would in ordinary C++, i.e. by including a header and linking against the library. These powerfulcapabilities can be used to construct managed wrapper types callable from any .NET language as well as native wrapper classes and functions (exposed as .dll, .lib and .h files) which are callable by native C/C++ code.

Marshaling in C++/CLI is done manually, and the developer is in bettercontrol and more aware of marshaling performance penalties. C++/CLI can be successfully used in scenarios with which P/Invoke cannot cope, such as marshaling of variable-length structures. Another advantage to C++/CLI is that you can simulate a chunky interface approach even if you do not control the callee's code, by calling native methods repeatedly without crossing the managed-to-native boundary each time.

In the code listing below, we implement a native `NativeEmployee` class and a managed `Employee` class, wrapping the former. Only the latter is accessible from managed code.

If you look at the listing, you'll see that `Employee`'s constructor showcases two techniques of managed to native string conversion: one that allocates `GlobalAlloc` memory that needs to be released explicitly and one that temporarily pins the managed string in memory and returns a direct pointer. The latter method is faster, but it only works if the native code expects a UTF-16 null-terminated string, and you can guarantee that no writes occur to the memory pointed to by the pointer. Furthermore, pinning managed objects for a long time can lead to memory fragmentation (see Chapter 4), so if said requirements are not satisfied, you will have to resort to copying.

`Employee`'s `GetName` method showcases three techniques of native to managed string conversion: one that uses the `System.Runtime.InteropServices.Marshal` class, one that uses the `marshal_as` template function (that we will discuss later) which is defined in the msclr/marshal.h header file and finally one that uses `System.String`'s constructor, which is the fastest.

`Employee`'s `DoWork` method takes a managed array or managed strings, and converts that into an array of `wchar_t` pointers, each pointing to a string; in essence it's an array of C-style strings. Managed to native string conversions are done via the `marshal_context`'s `marshal_as` method. In contrast to `marshal_as` global function, `marshal_context` is used for conversions which require cleanup. Usually these are managed to unmanaged conversions that allocate unmanaged memory during the call to `marshal_as` that needs to be released once it's not longer required. The `marshal_context` object contains a linked list of cleanup operations that are executed when it is destroyed.

```
#include <msclr/marshal.h>
#include <string>
#include <wchar.h>
#include <time.h>

using namespace System;
using namespace System::Runtime::InteropServices;

class NativeEmployee {
public:
  NativeEmployee(const wchar_t *employeeName, int age)
    : _employeeName(employeeName), _employeeAge(age) { }

  void DoWork(const wchar_t **tasks, int numTasks) {
    for (int i = 0; i < numTasks; i++) {
      wprintf(L"Employee %s is working on task %s\n",
              _employeeName.c_str(), tasks[i]);
    }
  }
}
```

```cpp
  int GetAge() const {
    return _employeeAge;
  }

  const wchar_t *GetName() const {
    return _employeeName.c_str();
  }

private:
  std::wstring _employeeName;
  int _employeeAge;
};

#pragma managed

namespace EmployeeLib {
  public ref class Employee {
  public:
    Employee(String ^employeeName, int age) {
      //OPTION 1:
      //IntPtr pEmployeeName = Marshal::StringToHGlobalUni(employeeName);
      //m_pEmployee = new NativeEmployee(
      //  reinterpret_cast<wchar_t *>(pEmployeeName.ToPointer()), age);
      //Marshal::FreeHGlobal(pEmployeeName);

      //OPTION 2 (direct pointer to pinned managed string, faster):
      pin_ptr<const wchar_t> ppEmployeeName = PtrToStringChars(employeeName);
      _employee = new NativeEmployee(ppEmployeeName, age);
    }

    ~Employee() {
      delete _employee;
      _employee = nullptr;
    }

    int GetAge() {
      return _employee->GetAge();
    }

    String ^GetName() {
      //OPTION 1:
      //return Marshal::PtrToStringUni(
      //  (IntPtr)(void *) _employee->GetName());

      //OPTION 2:
      return msclr::interop::marshal_as<String ^>(_employee->GetName());

      //OPTION 3 (faster):
      return gcnew String(_employee->GetName());
    }
```

```
  void DoWork(array<String^>^ tasks) {
    //marshal_context is a managed class allocated (on the GC heap)
    //using stack-like semantics. Its IDisposable::Dispose()/d'tor will
    //run when exiting scope of this function.
    msclr::interop::marshal_context ctx;
    const wchar_t **pTasks = new const wchar_t*[tasks->Length];
    for (int i = 0; i < tasks->Length; i++) {
      String ^t = tasks[i];
      pTasks[i] = ctx.marshal_as<const wchar_t *>(t);
    }
    m_pEmployee->DoWork(pTasks, tasks->Length);
    //context d'tor will release native memory allocated by marshal_as
    delete[] pTasks;
  }

private:
  NativeEmployee *_employee;
};
}
```

In summary, C++/CLI offers fine control over marshaling and does not require duplicating function declarations, which is error prone, especially when you often change the native function signatures.

The marshal_as Helper Library

In this section, we will elaborate on the marshal_as helper library provided as part of Visual C++ 2008 and later.

marshal_as is a template library for simplified and convenient marshaling of managed to native types and vice versa. It can marshal many native string types, such as char *, wchar_t *, std::string, std::wstring, CStringT<char>, CStringT<wchar_t>, BSTR, bstr_t and CComBSTR to managed types and vice versa. It handles Unicode/ANSI conversions and handles memory allocations/release automatically.

The library is declared and implemented inline in marshal.h (for base types), in marshal_windows.h (for Windows types), in marshal_cppstd.h (for STL data types) and in marshal_atl.h (for ATL data types).

marshal_as can be extended to handle conversion of user-defined types. This helps avoid code duplication when marshaling the same type in many places and allows having a uniform syntax for marshaling of different types.

The following code is an example of extending marshal_as to handle conversion of a managed array of strings to an equivalent native array of strings.

```
namespace msclr  {
 namespace interop  {
   template<>
   ref class context_node<const wchar_t**, array<String^>^> : public context_node_base {
   private:
     const wchar_t** _tasks;
     marshal_context _context;
   public:
     context_node(const wchar_t**& toObject, array<String^>^ fromObject) {
       //Conversion logic starts here
       _tasks = NULL;
       const wchar_t **pTasks = new const wchar_t*[fromObject->Length];
       for (int i = 0; i < fromObject->Length; i++) {
         String ^t = fromObject[i];
         pTasks[i] = _context.marshal_as<const wchar_t *>(t);
       }
```

```
      toObject = _tasks = pTasks;
    }

    ~context_node() {
      this->!context_node();
    }

  protected:
    !context_node() {
      //When the context is deleted, it will free the memory
      //allocated for the strings (belongs to marshal_context),
      //so the array is the only memory that needs to be freed.
      if (_tasks != nullptr) {
        delete[] _tasks;
        _tasks = nullptr;
      }
    }
  };
 }
}
//You can now rewrite Employee::DoWork like this:
void DoWork(array<String^>^ tasks) {
  //All unmanaged memory is freed automatically once marshal_context
  //gets out of scope.
  msclr::interop::marshal_context ctx;
  _employee->DoWork(ctx.marshal_as<const wchar_t **>(tasks), tasks->Length);
}
```

IL Code vs. Native Code

An unmanaged class will by default be compiled to IL code in C++/CLI rather than to machine code. This can degrade performance relative to optimized native code, because Visual C++ compiler can optimize code better than the JIT can.

You can use #pragma unmanaged and #pragma managed before a section of code to override complication behavior. Additionally, in a VC++ project you can also enable C++/CLI support for individual compilation units (.cpp files).

Windows 8 WinRT Interop

Windows Runtime (WinRT) is the new platform designed for Windows 8 Metro-style applications. WinRT is implemented in native code (i.e. .NET Framework is not used by WinRT), but you can target WinRT from C++/CX, .NET languages or JavaScript. WinRT replaces a large portion of Win32 and .NET BCL, which become inaccessible. WinRT places an emphasis on asynchrony, making it mandatory for any operation potentially taking more than 50ms to complete. This is done to ensure smooth UI performance which is especially important for touch-based user interfaces like Metro.

WinRT is built on top of an advanced version of COM. Below are some differences between WinRT and COM:

- Objects are created using RoCreateInstance.

- All objects implement the IInspectable interface which in turn derives from the familiar IUnknown interface.

- Supports .NET-style properties, delegates and events (instead of sinks).

- Supports parameterized interfaces ("generics").

- Uses the .NET metadata format (.winmd files) instead of TLB and IDL.

- All types derive from Platform::Object.

Despite borrowing many ideas from .NET, WinRT is implemented entirely in native code, so the CLR is not required when calling WinRT from a non-.NET language.

Microsoft implemented *language projections* that map WinRT concepts to language-specific concepts, whether the language in C++/CX, C# or JavaScript. For example, C++/CX is a new language extension of C++ which manages reference counting automatically, translates WinRT object activation (RoActivateInstance) to a C++ constructor, converts HRESULTs to exceptions, converts "retval" arguments to return values, etc.

When the caller and callee are both managed, the CLR is smart enough to make the call directly and there is not inerop involved. For calls that cross a native to managed boundary, regular COM interop is involved. When both the caller and callee are implemented in C++, and the callee's header files are available to the caller, no COM interop is involved and the call is very fast, otherwise, a COM QueryInterface needs to be done.

Best Practices for Interop

The following is a summary list of best practices for high-performance interop:

- Design interfaces to avoid native-managed transitions, by chunking (combining) work.

- Reduce round trips with a façade.

- Implement IDisposable if unmanaged resources are held across calls.

- Consider using memory pooling or unmanaged memory.

- Consider using unsafe code for re-interpreting data (e.g. in network protocols).

- Explicitly name the function you call and use ExactSpelling=true.

- Use blittable parameter types whenever possible.

- Avoid Unicode to ANSI conversions where possible.

- Manually marshall strings to/from IntPtr.

- Use C++/CLI for better control and performance for C/C++ and COM interop.

- Specify [In] and [Out] attributes to avoid unnecessary marshaling.

- Avoid long lifetime for pinned objects.

- Consider calling ReleaseComObject.

- Consider using SuppressUnmanagedCodeSecurityAttribute for performance-critical full- trust scenarios.

- Consider using TLBIMP /unsafe for performance-critical full-trust scenarios.

- Reduce or avoid COM cross-apartment calls.

- If appropriate, use ASPCOMPAT attribute in ASP.NET to reduce or avoid COM cross-apartment calls.

Summary

In this chapter, you have learned about unsafe code, about how the various interop mechanisms are implemented, how each implementation detail can have a profound impact on performance, and how to mitigate it. You've been introduced to best practices and techniques for improving interop performance and making coding easier and less error prone (e.g. help with P/Invoke signature generation and the marshal_as library).

CHAPTER 9

Algorithm Optimization

At the heart of some applications lie specialized algorithms designed for a specific domain and based on assumptions that do not hold universally. Other applications rely on well-tested algorithms that fit many domains and have been relevant for decades in the entire field of computer software. We believe that every software developer can benefit and obtain insight from some of the crown jewels of algorithms research, as well as the algorithm categories on which software frameworks are based. Although some parts of this chapter might be somewhat difficult if you do not have a strong mathematical background, they are well worth the effort.

This chapter gently brushes against some of the pillars of computer science and reviews several examples of immortal algorithms and their complexity analysis. Supplied with these examples, you should feel more comfortable using existing algorithms, adapting them to your needs, and inventing your own.

■ **Note**   This is not a textbook on algorithms research, nor an introductory text into the most important algorithms in modern computer science. This chapter is deliberately short to make it explicitly clear that you cannot learn from it all you need to know. We have not delved into formal definitions in any detail. For example, our treatment of Turing machines and languages is not at all rigorous. For a textbook introduction to algorithms, consider Cormen, Leiserson, Rivest, and Stein's "Introduction to Algorithms" (MIT Press, 2001) and Dasgupta, Papadimitriou, and Vazirani's "Algorithms" (soon to appear, currently available online as a draft).

Taxonomy of Complexity

Chapter 5 had the chance to briefly mention the complexity of some operations on the .NET Framework's collections and some collections of our own implementation. This section defines more accurately what Big-Oh complexity means and reviews the main complexity classes known in computability and complexity theory.

Big-Oh Notation

When we discussed the complexity of a lookup operation on a List<T> in Chapter 5, we said it had runtime complexity $O(n)$. What we meant to say informally is that, when you have a list of 1,000 items and are trying to find in it another item, then the *worst-case* running time of that operation is 1,000 iterations through the list—namely, if the item is not already in the list. Thus, we try to estimate the order of magnitude of the running time's growth as the inputs become larger. When specified formally, however, the Big-Oh notation might appear slightly confusing:

Suppose that the function T(A;n) returns the number of computation steps required to execute the algorithm A on an input size of n elements, and let f(n) be a monotonic function from positive integers to positive integers. Then, T(A;n) is O(f(n)), if there exists a constant c such that for all n, T(A;n)≤cf(n).

In a nutshell, we can say that an algorithm's runtime complexity is $O(f(n))$, if $f(n)$ is an upper bound on the actual number of steps it takes to execute the algorithm on an input of size n. The bound does not have to be tight; for example, we can also say that List<T> lookup has runtime complexity $O(n^4)$. However, using such a loose upper bound is not helpful, because it fails to capture the fact that it *is* realistic to search a List<T> for an element even if it has 1,000,000 elements in it. If List<T> lookup had tight runtime complexity $O(n^4)$, it would be highly inefficient to perform lookups even on lists with several thousand elements.

Additionally, the bound might be tight for some inputs but not tight for others; for example, if we search the list for an item that happens to be its first element, the number of steps is clearly constant (one!) for all list sizes—this is why we mentioned *worst-case* running time in the preceding paragraphs.

Some examples of how this notation makes it easier to reason about running time and compare different algorithms include:

- If one algorithm has runtime complexity $2n^3+4$ and another algorithm has runtime complexity $\frac{1}{2}n^3-n^2$, we can say that both algorithms have runtime complexity $O(n^3)$, so they are equivalent as far as Big-Oh complexity is concerned (try to find the constant c that works for each of these running times). It is easy to prove that we can omit all but the largest term when talking about Big-Oh complexity.

- If one algorithm that has runtime complexity n^2 and another algorithm has runtime complexity $100n+5000$, we can still assert that the first algorithm is slower on large inputs, because it has Big-Oh complexity $O(n^2)$, as opposed to $O(n)$. Indeed, for $n=1,000$, it is already the case that the first algorithm runs significantly slower than the second.

Similar to the definition of an upper bound on runtime complexity, there are also lower bounds (denoted by $\Omega(f(n))$) and tight bounds (denoted by $\Theta(f(n))$). They are less frequently used to discuss algorithm complexity, however, so we omit them here.

THE MASTER THEOREM

The *master theorem* is a simple result that provides a ready-made solution for analyzing the complexity of many recursive algorithms that decompose the original problem into smaller chunks. For example, consider the following code, which implements the *merge sort* algorithm:

```
public static List<T> MergeSort(List<T> list) where T : IComparable<T> {
    if (list.Count <= 1) return list;
    int middle = list.Count / 2;
    List<T> left = list.Take(middle).ToList();
    List<T> right = list.Skip(middle).ToList();
    left = MergeSort(left);
    right = MergeSort(right);
    return Merge(left, right);
}
```

```
private List<T> Merge(List<T> left, List<T> right) where T : IComparable<T>{
  List<T> result = new List<T>();
  int i = 0, j = 0;
  while (i<left.Count || j<right.Count) {
    if (i<left.Count && j<right.Count) {
      if (left[i].CompareTo(right[j])<= 0)
        result.Add(left[i++]);
      else
        result.Add(right[j++]);
    } else if (i<left.Count) {
      result.Add(left[i++];
    } else {
      result.Add(right++);
    }
  }
  return result;
}
```

Analyzing this algorithm's runtime complexity requires solving the *recurrence equation* for its running time, $T(n)$, which is given recursively as $T(n) = 2T(n/2) + O(n)$. The explanation is that, for every invocation of `MergeSort`, we recurse into `MergeSort` for each half of the original list and perform linear-time work merging the lists (clearly, the `Merge` helper method performs exactly n operations for an original list of size n).

One approach to solving recurrence equations is guessing the outcome, then trying to prove (usually by mathematical induction) the correctness of the result. In this case, we can expand some terms and see if a pattern emerges:

$$T(n) = 2T(n/2) + O(n) = 2(2T(n/4) + O(n/2)) + O(n) = 2(2(2T(n/8) + O(n/4)) + O(n/2)) + O(n) = \ldots$$

The master theorem provides a closed-form solution for this recurrence equation and many others. According to the master theorem, $T(n) = O(n \log n)$, which is a well-known result about the complexity of merge sort (in fact, it holds for θ, as well as O). For more details about the master theorem, consult the Wikipedia article at `http://en.wikipedia.org/wiki/Master_theorem`.

Turing Machines and Complexity Classes

It is common to refer to algorithms and problems as being "in *P*" or "in *NP*" or "*NP*-complete". These refer to different complexity classes. The classification of problems into complexity classes helps computer scientists easily identify problems that have reasonable (*tractable*) solutions and reject or find simplifications for problems that do not.

A *Turing machine* (*TM*) is a theoretical computation device that models a machine operating on an infinite *tape* of *symbols*. The machine's head can read or write one symbol at a time from the tape, and internally the machine can be in one of a finite number of *states*. The device's operation is fully determined by a finite set of *rules* (an algorithm), such as "when in state Q and the symbol on the tape is 'A', write 'a' " or "when in state P and the symbol on the tape is 'a', move the head to the right and switch to state S". There are also two special states: the *start state* from which the machine begins operation and the *end state*. When the machine reaches the end state, it is common to say it loops forever or simply halts execution. Figure 9-1 shows an example of a Turing machine's definition—the circles are states, and the arrows indicate state transitions in the syntax `read;write;head_move_direction`.

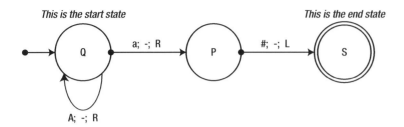

This is the start state

This is the end state

Figure 9-1. *A state diagram of a simple Turing machine. The leftmost arrow points into the initial state, Q. The looped arrow shows that when the machine is in state Q and reads the symbol A, it moves to the right and remains in state Q*

When discussing the complexity of algorithms on a Turing machine, there is no need to reason in vague "iterations"—a computation step of a TM is a single state transition (including a transition from a state to itself). For example, when the TM in Figure 9-1 starts with the input "AAAa#" on its tape, it performs exactly four computation steps. We can generalize this to say that, for an input of n 'A's followed by "a#", the machine performs $O(n)$ steps. (Indeed, for such an input of size n, the machine performs exactly $n+2$ steps, so the definition of $O(n)$ holds, for example, with the constant $c = 3$.)

Modeling real-world computation using a Turing machine is quite difficult—it makes for a good exercise in an undergraduate course on automata theory, but has no practical use. The amazing result is that every C# program (and, in fact, every algorithm that can be executed on a modern computer) can be translated—laboriously—to a Turing machine. Roughly speaking, if an algorithm written in C# has runtime complexity $O(f(n))$, then the same algorithm translated to a Turing machine has runtime complexity of $O(f^2(n))$. This has very useful implications on analyzing algorithm complexity: if a problem has an efficient algorithm for a Turing machine, then it has an efficient algorithm for a modern computer; if a problem does not have an efficient algorithm for a Turing machine, then it, typically, does not have an efficient algorithm for a modern computer.

Although we could call $O(n^2)$ algorithms efficient and any "slower" algorithms inefficient, complexity theory takes a slightly different stance. P is the set of all problems a Turing machine can solve in polynomial time—in other words, if A is a problem in P (with input of size n), then there exists a Turing machine that produces the desired result on its tape within *polynomial time* (i.e. within $O(n^k)$ steps for some natural number k). In many subfields of complexity theory, problems in P are considered easy—and algorithms that run in polynomial time are considered efficient, even though k and, therefore, the running time can be very large for some algorithms.

All of the algorithms considered so far in this book are efficient if we embrace this definition. Still, some are "very" efficient and others less so, indicating that this separation is not sufficiently subtle. You might even ask whether there are any problems that are not in P, problems that do not have efficient solutions. The answer is a resounding yes—and, in fact, from a theoretical perspective, there are *more* problems that do not have efficient solutions than problems that do.

First, we consider a problem that a Turing machine cannot solve, regardless of efficiency. Then, we see there are problems a Turing machine can solve, but not in polynomial time. Finally, we turn to problems for which *we do not know* whether there is a Turing machine that can solve them in polynomial time, but strongly suspect that there is not.

The Halting Problem

From a mathematical perspective, there are more problems than Turing machines (we say that Turing machines are "countable" and problems are not), which means there must be infinitely many problems that cannot be solved by Turing machines. This class of problems is often called *undecidable* problems.

WHAT DO YOU MEAN BY "COUNTABLE"?

In mathematics, there are many kinds of "infinite". It is easy to see that there are an infinite number of Turing machines—after all, you could add a dummy state that does nothing to any Turing machine and obtain a new, larger Turing machine. Similarly, it is easy to see that there are an infinite number problems—this requires a formal definition of a problem (as a "language") but leads to the same result. However, it is not obvious why there are "more" problems than Turing machines, especially since the number of both is infinite.

The set of Turing machines is said to be *countable*, because there is a one-to-one correspondence from natural numbers (1, 2, 3, …) to Turing machines. It might not be immediately obvious how to construct this correspondence, but it is possible, because Turing machines can be described as finite strings and the set of *all* finite strings is countable.

However, the set of problems (languages) is *not* countable, because a one-to-one correspondence from natural numbers to languages does not exist. A possible proof is along the following lines: consider the set of problems corresponding to all real numbers, where, for any real number r, the problem is to print the number or to recognize whether the number has been supplied as input. A well-known result (Cantor's Theorem) is that the real numbers are uncountable, and, hence, this set of problems is uncountable as well.

To summarize, this seems like an unfortunate conclusion. Not only are there problems that cannot be solved (decided) by a Turing machine, but there are many *more* such problems than problems that can be solved by a Turing machine. Luckily, a great many problems *can* be solved by Turing machines, as the incredible evolution of computers in the 20th century shows, theoretical results notwithstanding.

The *halting problem*, which we now introduce, is undecidable. The problem is as follows: receive as input a program T (or a description of a Turing machine) and an input w to the program; return TRUE if T halts when executed on w and FALSE if it does not halt (enters an infinite loop).

You could even translate this problem to a C# method that accepts a program's code as a string:

```
public static bool DoesHaltOnInput(string programCode, string input) { ... }
```

…or even a C# method that takes a delegate and an input to feed it:

```
public static bool DoesHaltOnInput(Action<string> program, string input) { ... }
```

Although it may appear there is a way to analyze a program and determine whether it halts or not (e.g. by inspecting its loops, its calls to other methods, and so on), it turns out that there is neither a Turing machine nor a C# program that can solve this problem. How does one reach this conclusion? Obviously, to say a Turing machine can solve a problem, we only need to demonstrate the Turing machine—but, to say that there exists no Turing machine to solve a particular problem, it appears that we have to go over all possible Turing machines, which are infinite in number.

As often is the case in mathematics, we use a proof by contradiction. Suppose someone came up with the method DoesHaltOnInput, which tests whether Then we could write the following C# method:

```
public static void Helper(string programCode, string input) {
  bool doesHalt = DoesHaltOnInput(programCode, input);
  if (doesHalt) {
    while (true) {} //Enter an infinite loop
  }
}
```

Now all it takes is to call DoesHaltOnInput on the source of the Helper method (the second parameter is meaningless). If DoesHaltOnInput returns true, the Helper method enters an infinite loop; if DoesHaltOnInput returns false, the Helper method does not enter an infinite loop. This contradiction illustrates that the DoesHaltOnInput method does not exist.

■ **Note** The halting problem is a humbling result; it demonstrates, in simple terms, that there are limits to the computational ability of our computing devices. The next time you blame the compiler for not finding an apparently trivial optimization or your favorite static analysis tool for giving you false warnings you can see will never occur, remember that statically analyzing a program and acting on the results is often undecidable. This is the case with optimization, halting analysis, determining whether a variable is used, and many other problems that might be easy for a developer given a specific program but cannot be generally solved by a machine.

There are many more undecidable problems. Another simple example stems again from the counting argument. There are a countable number of C# programs, because every C# program is a finite combination of symbols. However, there are uncountably many real numbers in the interval [0,1]. Therefore, there must exist a real number that cannot be printed out by a C# program.

NP-Complete Problems

Even within the realm of decidable problems—those that can be solved by a Turing machine—there are problems that do not have efficient solutions. Computing a perfect strategy for a game of chess on an $n \times n$ chessboard requires time *exponential* in n, which places the problem of solving the generalized chess game outside of P. (If you like checkers and dislike computer programs playing checkers better than humans, you should take some solace in the fact that generalized checkers is not in P either.)

There are problems, however, that are thought to be less complex, but for which we do not yet have a polynomial algorithm. Some of these problems would prove quite useful in real-life scenarios:

- The *traveling salesman* problem: Find a path of minimal cost for a salesman who has to visit n different cities.

- The *maximum clique* problem: Find the largest subset of nodes in a graph such that every two nodes in the subset are connected by an edge.

- The *minimum cut* problem: Find a way to divide a graph into two subsets of nodes such that there are a minimal number of edges crossing from one subset to the other.

- The *Boolean satisfiability* problem: Determine whether a Boolean formula of a certain form (such as "A and B or C and not A") can be satisfied by an assignment of truth values to its variables.

- The *cache placement* problem: Decide which data to place in cache and which data to evict from cache, given a complete history of memory accesses performed by an application.

These problems belong in another set of problems called *NP*. The problems in *NP* are characterized as follows: if A is a problem in *NP*, then there exists a Turing machine that can *verify* the solution of A for an input of size n in polynomial time. For example, verifying that a truth assignment to variables is legal and solves the Boolean satisfiability problem is clearly very easy, as well as linear in the number of variables. Similarly, verifying that a subset of nodes is a clique is very easy. In other words, these problems have easily verifiable solutions, but it is not known whether there is a way to efficiently come up with these solutions.

Another interesting facet of the above problems (and many others) is that if *any* has an efficient solution, then they *all* have an efficient solution. The reason is that they can be *reduced* from one to another. Moreover, if *any* of these problems has an efficient solution, which means that problem is in *P*, then the entire *NP* complexity class collapses into *P* such that *P* = *NP*. Arguably the biggest mystery in theoretical computer science today is whether *P* = *NP* (most computer scientists believe these complexity classes are not equal).

Problems that have this collapsing effect on *P* and *NP* are called *NP-complete* problems. For most computer scientists, showing that a problem is *NP*-complete is sufficient to reject any attempts to devise an efficient algorithm for it. Subsequent sections consider some examples of *NP*-complete problems that have acceptable approximate or probabilistic solutions.

Memoization and Dynamic Programming

Memoization is a technique that preserves the results of intermediate computations if they will be needed shortly afterwards, instead of recomputing them. It can be considered a form of caching. The classic example comes from calculating Fibonacci numbers, which is often one of the first examples used to teach recursion:

```
public static ulong FibonacciNumber(uint which) {
  if (which == 1 || which == 2) return 1;
  return FibonacciNumber(which-2)+FibonacciNumber(which-1);
}
```

This method has an appealing look, but its performance is quite appalling. For inputs as small as 45, this method takes a few seconds to complete; finding the 100th Fibonacci number using this approach is simply impractical, as its complexity grows exponentially.

One of the reasons for this inefficiency is that intermediate results are calculated more than once. For example, FibonacciNumber(10) is calculated recursively to find FibonacciNumber(11) and FibonacciNumber(12), and again for FibonacciNumber(12) and FibonacciNumber(13), and so on. Storing the intermediate results in an array can improve this method's performance considerably:

```
public static ulong FibonacciNumberMemoization(uint which) {
  if (which == 1 || which == 2) return 1;
  ulong[] array = new ulong[which];
  array[0] = 1; array[1] = 1;
  return FibonacciNumberMemoization(which, array);
}
private static ulong FibonacciNumberMemoization(uint which, ulong[] array) {
  if (array[which-3] == 0) {
    array[which-3] = FibonacciNumberMemoization(which-2, array);
  }
  if (array[which-2] == 0) {
    array[which-2] = FibonacciNumberMemoization(which-1, array);
  }
  array[which-1] = array[which-3]+array[which-2];
  return array[which-1];
}
```

This version finds the 10,000th Fibonacci number in a small fraction of a second and scales linearly. Incidentally, this calculation can be expressed in even simpler terms by storing only the last two numbers calculated:

```
public static ulong FibonacciNumberIteration(ulong which) {
  if (which == 1 || which == 2) return 1;
  ulong a = 1, b = 1;
  for (ulong i = 2; i<which; ++i) {
    ulong c = a+b;
    a = b;
    b = c;
  }
  return b;
}
```

▓ **Note**   It is worth noting that Fibonacci numbers have a closed formula based on the golden ratio
(see http://en.wikipedia.org/wiki/Fibonacci_number#Closed-form_expression for details).
However, using this closed formula to find an accurate value might involve non-trivial arithmetic.

The simple idea of storing results required for subsequent calculations is useful in many algorithms that break down a big problem into a set of smaller problems. This technique is often called *dynamic programming*. We now consider two examples.

Edit Distance

The *edit distance* between two strings is the number of character substitutions (deletions, insertions, and replacements) required to transform one string into the other. For example, the edit distance between "cat" and "hat" is 1 (replace 'c' with 'h'), and the edit distance between "cat" and "groat" is 3 (insert 'g', insert 'r', replace 'c' with 'o'). Efficiently finding the edit distance between two strings is important in many scenarios, such as error correction and spell checking with replacement suggestions.

The key to an efficient algorithm is breaking down the larger problem into smaller problems. For example, if we know that the edit distance between "cat" and "hat" is 1, then we also know that the edit distance between "cats" and "hat" is 2—we use the sub-problem already solved to devise the solution to the bigger problem. In practice, we wield this technique more carefully. Given two strings in array form, $s[1\ldots m]$ and $t[1\ldots n]$, the following hold:

- The edit distance between the empty string and t is n, and the edit distance between s and the empty string is m (by adding or removing all characters).

- If $s[i] = t[j]$ and the edit distance between $s[1\ldots i-1]$ and $t[1\ldots j-1]$ is k, then we can keep the i-th character and the edit distance between $s[1\ldots i]$ and $t[1\ldots j]$ is k.

- If $s[i] \neq t[j]$, then the edit distance between $s[1\ldots i]$ and $t[1\ldots j]$ is the minimum of:

    - The edit distance between $s[1\ldots i]$ and $t[1\ldots j-1]$, +1 to insert $t[j]$;

    - The edit distance between $s[1\ldots i-1]$ and $t[1\ldots j]$, +1 to delete $s[i]$;

    - The edit distance between $s[1\ldots i-1]$ and $t[1\ldots j-1]$, +1 to replace $s[i]$ by $t[j]$.

The following C# method finds the edit distance between two strings by constructing a table of edit distances for each of the substrings and then returning the edit distance in the ultimate cell in the table:

```
public static int EditDistance(string s, string t) {
  int m = s.Length, n = t.Length;
  int[,] ed = new int[m,n];
```

```
for (int i = 0; i<m; ++i) {
  ed[i,0] = i+1;
}
for (int j = 0; j<n; ++j) {
  ed[0,j] = j+1;
}
for (int j = 1; j<n; ++j) {
  for (int i = 1; i<m; ++i) {
    if (s[i] == t[j]) {
      ed[i,j] = ed[i-1,j-1]; //No operation required
    } else {                 //Minimum between deletion, insertion, and substitution
      ed[i,j] = Math.Min(ed[i-1,j]+1, Math.Min(ed[i,j-1]+1, ed[i-1,j-1]+1));
    }
  }
}
return ed[m-1,n-1];
}
```

The algorithm fills the edit distances table column-by-column, such that it never attempts to use data not yet calculated. Figure 9-2 illustrates the edit distances table constructed by the algorithm when run on the inputs "stutter" and "glutton".

	g	l	u	t	t	o	n
s	1	2	3	4	5	6	7
t	2	2	3	3	4	5	6
u	3	3	2	3	4	5	6
t	4	4	3	2	3	4	5
t	5	5	4	3	2	3	4
e	6	6	5	4	3	3	4
r	7	7	6	5	4	4	4

Figure 9-2. The edit distances table, completely filled out

This algorithm uses $O(mn)$ space and has running time complexity of $O(mn)$. A comparable recursive solution that did not use memoization would have exponential running time complexity and fail to perform adequately even for medium-size strings.

All-Pairs-Shortest-Paths

The *all-pairs-shortest-paths* problem is to find the shortest distances between every two pairs of vertices in a graph. This can be useful for planning factory floors, estimating trip distances between cities, evaluating the required cost of fuel, and many other real-life scenarios. The authors encountered this problem in one of their consulting engagements. This was the problem description provided by the customer (see Sasha Goldshtein's blog post at http://blog.sashag.net/archive/2010/12/16/all-pairs-shortest-paths-algorithm-in-real-life.aspx for the original story):

- We are implementing a service that manages a set of physical backup devices. There is a set of conveyor belts with intersections and robot arms that manipulate backup tapes across the room. The service gets requests, such as "transfer a fresh tape *X* from storage cabinet 13 to backup cabinet 89, and make sure to pass through formatting station *C* or *D*".

- When the system starts, we calculate all shortest routes from every cabinet to every other cabinet, including special requests, such as going through a particular computer. This information is stored in a large hashtable indexed by route descriptions and with routes as values.

- System startup with 1,000 nodes and 250 intersections takes more than 30 minutes, and memory consumption reaches a peak of approximately 5GB. This is not acceptable.

First, we observe that the constraint "make sure to pass through formatting computer *C* or *D*" does not pose significant additional challenge. The shortest path from *A* to *B* going through *C* is the shortest path from *A* to *C* followed by the shortest path from *C* to *B* (the proof is almost a tautology).

The Floyd-Warshall algorithm finds the shortest paths between every pair of vertices in the graph and uses decomposition into smaller problems quite similar to what we have seen before. The recursive formula, this time, uses the same observation made above: the shortest path from *A* to *B* goes through some vertex *V*. Then to find the shortest path from *A* to *B*, we need to find first the shortest path from *A* to *V* and then the shortest path from *V* to *B*, and concatenate them together. Because we do not know what *V* is, we need to consider all possible intermediate vertices—one way to do so is by numbering them from 1 to *n*.

Now, the length of the shortest path (*SP*) from vertex *i* to vertex *j* using only the vertices 1,…,*k* is given by the following recursive formula, assuming there is no edge from *i* to *j*:

$$SP(i, j, k) = min\{ SP(i, j, k\text{-}1), SP(i, k, k\text{-}1) + SP(k, j, k\text{-}1) \}$$

To see why, consider the vertex *k*. Either the shortest path from *i* to *j* uses this vertex or it does not. If the shortest path does not use the vertex *k*, then we do not have to use this vertex and can rely on the shortest path using only the vertices 1,…,*k*-1. If the shortest path uses the vertex *k*, then we have our decomposition—the shortest path can be sewn together from the shortest path from *i* to *k* (that uses only the vertices 1,…,*k*-1) and the shortest path from *k* to *j* (that uses only the vertices 1,…,*k*-1). See Figure 9–3 for an example.

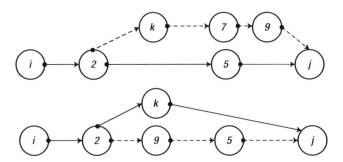

***Figure* 9-3.** *In the upper part of the diagram, the shortest path from i to j (through vertices 2 and 5) does not use the vertex k. Hence, we can restrict ourselves to the shortest path using vertices 1,…,k-1. In the lower part, the shortest path from i to j uses vertex k. Hence the shortest path from i to j is the shortest path from i to k, sewn together with the shortest path from k to j*

To get rid of the recursive calls, we use memoization—this time we have a three-dimensional table to fill, and, after finding the values of *SP* for all pairs of vertices and all values of *k*, we have the solution to the all-pairs-shortest-paths problem.

We can further reduce the amount of storage space by noting that, for every pair of vertices *i, j*, we do not actually need all the values of *k* from 1 to *n*—we need only the minimum value obtained so far. This makes the table two-dimensional and the storage only $O(n^2)$. The running time complexity remains $O(n^3)$, which is quite incredible considering that we find the shortest path between every two vertices in the graph.

Finally, when filling the table, we need to record for each pair of vertices *i, j* the next vertex *x* to which we should proceed if we want to find the actual shortest path between the vertices. The translation of these ideas to C# code is quite easy, as is reconstructing the path based on this last observation:

```
static short[,] costs;
static short[,] next;

public static void AllPairsShortestPaths(short[] vertices, bool[,] hasEdge) {
  int N = vertices.Length;
  costs = new short[N, N];
  next = new short[N, N];
  for (short i = 0; i<N; ++i) {
    for (short j = 0; j<N; ++j) {
      costs[i, j] = hasEdge[i, j] ? (short)1 : short.MaxValue;
      if (costs[i, j] == 1)
        next[i, j] = -1; //Marker for direct edge
    }
  }
  for (short k = 0; k<N; ++k) {
    for (short i = 0; i<N; ++i) {
      for (short j = 0; j<N; ++j) {
        if (costs[i, k]+costs[k, j]<costs[i, j]) {
          costs[i, j] = (short)(costs[i, k]+costs[k, j]);
          next[i, j] = k;
        }
      }
    }
  }
}
public string GetPath(short src, short dst) {
    if (costs[src, dst] == short.MaxValue) return "<no path>";
    short intermediate = next[src, dst];
    if (intermediate == -1)
        return "->"; //Direct path
    return GetPath(src, intermediate)+intermediate+GetPath(intermediate, dst);
}
```

This simple algorithm improved the application performance dramatically. In a simulation with 300 nodes and an average fan-out of 3 edges from each node, constructing the full set of paths took 3 seconds and answering 100,000 queries about shortest paths took 120ms, with only 600KB of memory used.

Approximation

This section considers two algorithms that do not offer an accurate solution to the posed problem, but the solution they give can be an adequate *approximation*. If we look for the maximum value of some function $f(x)$, an algorithm that returns a result that is always within a factor of c of the actual value (which may be hard to find) is called a *c-approximation* algorithm.

Approximation is especially useful with *NP*-complete problems, which do not have known polynomial algorithms. In other cases, approximation is used to find solutions more efficiently than by completely solving the problem, sacrificing some accuracy in the process. For example, a $O(\log n)$ 2-approximation algorithm may be more useful for large inputs than an $O(n^3)$ precise algorithm.

Traveling Salesman

To perform a formal analysis, we need to formalize somewhat the *traveling salesman* problem referred to earlier. We are given a graph with a weight function w that assigns the graph's edges positive values—you can think of this weight function as the distance between cities. The weight function satisfies the triangle inequality, which definitely holds if we keep to the analogy of traveling between cities on a Euclidean surface:

For all vertices x, y, z $$w(x, y) + w(y, z) \geq w(x, z)$$

The task, then, is to visit every vertex in the graph (every city on the salesman's map) exactly once and return to the starting vertex (the company headquarters), making sure the sum of edge weights along this path is minimal. Let $wOPT$ be this minimal weight. (The equivalent decision problem is *NP*-complete, as we have seen.)

The approximation algorithm proceeds as follows. First, construct a *minimal spanning tree* (MST) for the graph. Let $wMST$ be the tree's total weight. (A minimal spanning tree is a subgraph that touches every vertex, does not have cycles, and has the minimum total edge weight of all such trees.)

We can assert that $wMST \leq wOPT$, because $wOPT$ is the total weight of a *cyclic* path that visits every vertex; removing any edge from it produces a spanning tree, and $wMST$ is the total weight of the *minimum* spanning tree. Armed with this observation, we produce a 2-approximation to $wOPT$ using the minimum spanning tree as follows:

1. Construct an MST. There is a known $O(n \log n)$ greedy algorithm for this.

2. Traverse the MST from its root by visiting every node and returning to the root. The total weight of this path is $2wMST \leq 2wOPT$.

3. Fix the resulting path such that no vertex is visited more than once. If the situation in Figure 9-4 arises—the vertex y was visited more than once—then fix the path by removing the edges (x, y) and (y, z) and replacing them with the edge (x, z). This can only *decrease* the total weight of the path because of the triangle inequality.

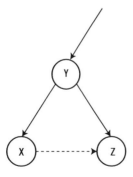

Figure 9-4. *Instead of traversing Y twice, we can replace the path (X, Y, Z) with the path (X, Z)*

The result is a 2-approximation algorithm, because the total weight of the path produced is still, at most, double the weight of the optimal path.

Maximum Cut

We are given a graph and need to find a *cut*—a grouping of its vertices into two disjoint sets—such that the number of edges crossing between the sets (crossing the cut) is *maximal*. This is known as the *maximum cut* problem, and solving it is quite useful for planning in many engineering fields.

We produce a very simple and intuitive algorithm that yields a 2-approximation:

1. Divide the vertices into two arbitrary disjoint sets, A and B.

2. Find a vertex v in A that has more neighbors in A than in B. If not found, halt.

3. Move v from A to B and go back to step 2.

First, let A be a subset of the vertices and v a vertex in A. We denote by $\deg_A(v)$ the number of vertices in A that v has an edge with (i.e. the number of its neighbors in A). Next, given two subsets A, B of the vertices, we denote by $e(A, B)$ the number of edges between vertices in two different sets and by $e(A)$ the number of edges between vertices in the set A.

When the algorithm terminates, for each v in A, it holds that $\deg_B(v) \geq \deg_A(v)$—otherwise the algorithm would repeat step 2. Summing over all the vertices, we obtain that $e(A, B) \geq \deg_B(v_1) + \ldots + \deg_B(v_k) \geq \deg_A(v_1) + \ldots + \deg_A(v_k) \geq 2e(A)$, because every edge on the right hand side was counted twice. Similarly, $e(A, B) \geq 2e(B)$ and, therefore, $2e(A, B) \geq 2e(A) + 2e(B)$. From this we obtain $2e(A, B) \geq e(A, B) + e(A) + e(B)$, but the right hand side is the total number of edges in the graph. Therefore, the number of edges crossing the cut is at least one-half the total number of edges in the graph. The number of edges crossing the cut cannot be larger than the total number of edges in the graph, so we have a 2-approximation.

Finally, it is worth noting that the algorithm runs for a number of steps that is linear in the number of edges in the graph. Whenever step 2 repeats, the number of edges crossing the cut increases by at least 1, and it is bounded from above by the total number of edges in the graph, so the number of steps is also bounded from above by that number.

Probabilistic Algorithms

When considered approximation algorithms, we were still bound by the requirement of producing a deterministic solution. There are some cases, however, in which introducing a source of randomness into an algorithm can provide probabilistically sound results, although it becomes no longer possible to *guarantee* absolutely the algorithm's correctness or bounded running time.

Probabilistic Maximum Cut

It turns out that a 2-approximation of the maximum cut problem can be obtained by randomly selecting the two disjoint sets (specifically, flipping a coin for each vertex to decide whether it goes into A or B). By probabilistic analysis, the expected number of edges crossing the cut is ½ the total number of edges.

To show that the expected number of edges crossing the cut is ½ the total number of edges, consider the probability that a specific edge (u, v) is crossing the cut. There are four alternatives with equal probability ¼: the edge is in A; the edge is in B; v is in A, and u is in B; and v is in B, and u is in A. Therefore, the probability the edge is crossing the cut is ½.

For an edge e, the expected value of the indicator variable Xe (that is equal to 1 when the edge is crossing the cut) is ½. By linearity of expectation, the expected number of edges in the cut is ½ the number of edges in the graph.

Note that we can no longer trust the results of a single round, but there are derandomization techniques (such as the method of conditional probabilities) that can make success very likely after a small constant number of rounds. We have to prove a bound on the probability that the number of edges crossing the cut is smaller than ½ the number of edges in the graph—there are several probabilistic tools, including Markov's inequality, that can be used to this end. We do not, however, perform this exercise here.

Fermat Primality Test

Finding the prime numbers in a range is an operation we parallelized in Chapter 6, but we never got as far as looking for a considerably better algorithm for testing a single number for primality. This operation is important in applied cryptography. For example, the RSA asymmetric encryption algorithm used ubiquitously on the Internet relies on finding large primes to generate encryption keys.

A simple result from number theory known as *Fermat's little theorem* states that, if p is prime, then for all numbers $1 \leq a \leq p$, the number a^{p-1} has remainder 1 when divided by p (denoted $a^{p-1} \boxtimes 1 \pmod{p}$). We can use this idea to devise the following probabilistic primality test for a candidate n:

1. Pick a random number a in the interval $[1, n]$, and see if the equality from Fermat's little theorem holds (i.e. if a^{p-1} has remainder 1 when divided by p).

2. Reject the number as composite, if the equality does not hold.

3. Accept the number as prime or repeat step 1 until the desired confidence level is reached, if the equality holds.

For most composite numbers, a small number of iterations through this algorithm detects that it is composite and rejects it. All prime numbers pass the test for any number of repetitions, of course.

Unfortunately, there are infinitely many numbers (called Carmichael numbers) that are not prime but will pass the test for every value of a and any number of iterations. Although Carmichael numbers are quite rare, they are a sufficient cause of concern for improving the Fermat primality test with additional tests that can detect Carmichael numbers. The Miller-Rabin primality test is one example.

For composite numbers that are not Carmichael, the probability of selecting a number a for which the equality does not hold is more than ½. Thus, the probability of wrongly identifying a composite number as prime shrinks exponentially as the number of iterations increases: using a sufficient number of iterations can decrease arbitrarily the probability of accepting a composite number.

Indexing and Compression

When storing large amounts of data, such as indexed web pages for search engines, compressing the data and accessing it efficiently on disk is often more important than sheer runtime complexity. This section considers two simple examples that minimize the amount of storage required for certain types of data, while maintaining efficient access times.

Variable Length Encoding

Suppose you have a collection of 50,000,000 positive integers to store on disk and you can guarantee that every integer will fit into a 32-bit int variable. A naïve solution would be to store 50,000,000 32-bit integers on disk, for a total of 200,000,000 bytes. We seek a better alternative that would use significantly less disk space. (One reason for compressing data on disk might be to load it more quickly into memory.)

Variable length encoding is a compression technique suitable for number sequences that contain many small values. Before we consider how it works, we need to guarantee that there *will* be many small values in the sequence—which currently does not seem to be the case. If the 50,000,000 integers are uniformly distributed in the range $[0, 2^{32}]$, then more than 99% will not fit in 3 bytes and require a full 4 bytes of storage. However, we can sort the numbers prior to storing them on disk, and, instead of storing the numbers, store the gaps. This trick is called *gap compression* and likely makes the numbers much smaller, while still allowing us to reconstruct the original data.

For example, the series (38, 14, 77, 5, 90) is first sorted to (5, 14, 38, 77, 90) and then encoded using gap compression to (5, 9, 24, 39, 13). Note that the numbers are much smaller when using gap compression, and the average number of bits required to store them has gone down significantly. In our case, if the 50,000,000 integers were uniformly distributed in the range $[0, 2^{32}]$, then many gaps would very likely fit in a single byte, which can contain values in the range [0, 256].

Next, we turn to the heart of *variable byte length encoding*, which is just one of a large number of methods in information theory that can compress data. The idea is to use the most significant bit of every byte to indicate whether it is the last byte that encodes a single integer or not. If the bit is off, go on to the next byte to reconstruct the number; if the bit is on, stop and use the bytes read so far to decode the value.

For example, the number 13 is encoded as 10001101—the high bit is on, so this byte contains an entire integer and the rest of it is simply the number 13 in binary. Next, the number 132 is encoded as 00000001˙10000100. The first byte has its high bit off, so remember the seven bits 0000001, and the second byte has its high bit on, so append the seven bits 0000000 and obtain 10000100, which is the number 132 in binary. In this example, one of the numbers was stored using just 1 byte, and the other using 2 bytes. Storing the gaps obtained in the previous step using this technique is likely to compress the original data almost four-fold. (You can experiment with randomly generated integers to establish this result.)

Index Compression

To store an index of words that appear on web pages in an efficient way—which is the foundation of a crude search engine—we need to store, for each word, the page numbers (or URLs) in which it appears, compressing the data, while maintaining efficient access to it. In typical settings, the page numbers in which a word appears do not fit in main memory, but the dictionary of words just might.

Storing on disk the page numbers in which dictionary words appear is a task best left to variable length encoding—which we just considered. However, storing the dictionary itself is somewhat more complex. Ideally, the dictionary is a simple array of entries that contain the word itself and a disk offset to the page numbers in which the words appears. To enable efficient access to this data, it should be sorted—this guarantees $O(\log n)$ access times.

Suppose each entry is the in-memory representation of the following C# value type, and the entire dictionary is an array of them:

```
struct DictionaryEntry {
  public string Word;
  public ulong  DiskOffset;
}
DictionaryEntry[] dictionary = ...;
```

As Chapter 3 illustrates, an array of value types consists solely of the value type instances. However, each value type contains a reference to a string; for n entries, these references, along with the disk offsets, occupy $16n$ bytes on a 64-bit system. Additionally, the dictionary words themselves take up valuable space, and each dictionary word—stored as a separate string— has an extra 24 bytes of overhead (16 bytes of object overhead + 4 bytes to store the string length + 4 bytes to store the number of characters in the character buffer used internally by the string).

We can considerably decrease the amount of space required to store the dictionary entries by concatenating all dictionary words to a single long string and storing offsets into the string in the DictionaryEntry structure (see Figure 9-5). These concatenated dictionary strings are rarely longer than 2^{24} bytes = 16MB, meaning the index field can be a 3-byte integer instead of an 8-byte memory address:

```
[StructLayout(LayoutKind.Sequential, Pack = 1, Size = 3)]
struct ThreeByteInteger {
  private byte a, b, c;
  public ThreeByteInteger() {}
  public ThreeByteInteger(uint integer) ...
  public static implicit operator int(ThreeByteInteger tbi) ...
}
struct DictionaryEntry {
  public ThreeByteInteger LongStringOffset;
  public ulong            DiskOffset;
}
class Dictionary {
  public DictionaryEntry[] Entries = ...;
  public string            LongString;
}
```

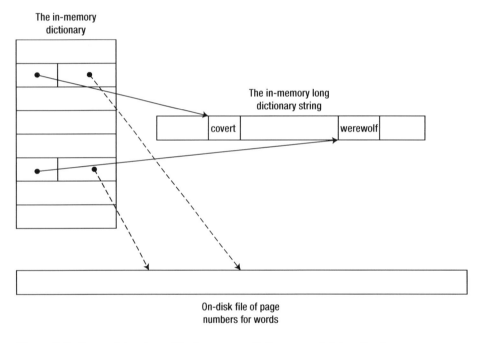

Figure 9-5. *General structure of the in-memory dictionary and string directory*

The result is that we maintain binary search semantics over the array—because the entries have uniform size—but the amount of data stored is significantly smaller. We saved almost $24n$ bytes for the string objects in memory (there is now just one long string) and another $5n$ bytes for the string references replaced by offset pointers.

Summary

This chapter examines some of the pillars of theoretical computer science, including runtime complexity analysis, computability, algorithm design, and algorithm optimization. As you have seen, algorithm optimization is not restricted to the ivory tower of academia; there are real-life situations where choosing the proper algorithm or using a compression technique can make a considerable performance difference. Specifically, the sections on dynamic programming, index storage, and approximation algorithms contain recipes that you can adapt for your own applications.

The examples in this chapter are not even the tip of the iceberg of complexity theory and algorithms research. Our primary hope is that, by reading this chapter, you learned to appreciate some of the ideas behind theoretical computer science and practical algorithms used by real applications. We know that many .NET developers rarely encounter the need to invent a completely new algorithm, but we still think it is important to understand the taxonomy of the field and have some examples of algorithms on your tool belt.

CHAPTER 10

Performance Patterns

This chapter contains a variety of topics we haven't had the opportunity to discuss elsewhere. Although small, they are extremely important for high-performance applications. There is no unifying thread to guide you through this chapter but the desire to obtain top-notch performance in simple tight loops and complex applications alike.

We begin the chapter with JIT compiler optimizations, which are vital for good performance of CPU-bound applications. Next, we discuss startup performance, which can be critical for client applications that exercise the user's patience. Finally, we discuss processor-specific optimizations, including data- and instruction-level parallelism, and several smaller topics.

JIT Compiler Optimizations

Earlier in this book we have seen the importance of some optimizations performed by the JIT compiler. Specifically, in Chapter 3 we have discussed inlining in some detail when investigating the method dispatch sequences for virtual and non-virtual methods. In this section we summarize the primary optimizations performed by the JIT compiler, and how to make sure your code does not thwart the JIT compiler's ability to carry out these optimizations. JIT optimizations mostly affect the performance of CPU-bound applications, but are relevant, to some extent, to other types of programs as well.

To inspect these optimizations you must attach the debugger to a running process—the JIT compiler will not perform optimizations when it detects the presence of a debugger. Specifically, when you attach to the process you must make sure that the methods you want to inspect have already been called and compiled.

If for some reason you would like to disable JIT optimizations—for example, to make debugging easier in face of inlining and tail calls (discussed later)—you don't have to modify the code or use a Debug build. Instead, you can create an .ini file that has the same name as your application executable (for example, MyApp.ini) and put the following three lines in it. When placed next to your executable on the next launch, it will inhibit the JIT compiler from performing any optimizations.

```
[.NET Framework Debugging Control]
GenerateTrackingInfo=1
AllowOptimize=0
```

Standard Optimizations

There are some standard optimizations performed by every optimizing compiler, even simple ones. For example, the JIT is able to reduce the following C# code to only a couple of x86 machine code instructions:

```
//Original C# code:
static int Add(int i, int j) {
```

```
  return i+j;
}
static void Main() {
  int i=4;
  int j=3*i+11;
  Console.WriteLine(Add(i, j));
}

; Optimized x86 assembly code
call 682789a0                      ; System.Console.get_Out()
mov ecx,eax
mov edx,1Bh                        ; Add(i,j) was folded into its result, 27 (0x1B)
mov eax,dword ptr [ecx]            ; the rest is standard invocation sequence for the
mov eax,dword ptr [eax+38h]        ; TextWriter.WriteLine virtual method
call dword ptr [eax+14h]
```

■ **Note**   It is not the C# compiler that performs this optimization. If you inspect the generated IL code, the local variables are there, as is the call to the Add method. The JIT compiler is responsible for all optimizations.

This optimization is called *constant folding*, and there are many similar simple optimizations, such as *common subexpression reduction* (in a statement like a + (b * a) – (a * b * c), the value a * b need only be calculated once). The JIT compiler performs these standard optimizations, but often fares considerably worse compared to optimizing compilers such as the Microsoft Visual C++ compiler. The reason is that the JIT compiler has a very constrained execution environment, and must be able to compile methods quickly to prevent significant delays when they are first called.

Method Inlining

This optimization often reduces code size and almost always decreases execution time by replacing method call sites with the callee's body. As we have seen in Chapter 3, virtual methods are not inlined by the JIT compiler (even if a sealed method is called on a derived type); interface methods undergo partial inlining with speculative execution; only static and non-virtual methods can always be inlined. For performance critical code, such as simple properties and methods on very commonly accessed infrastructure classes, make sure to avoid virtual methods and interface implementations.

The exact criteria used by the JIT compiler to determine which methods to inline are not publicly available. Some heuristics can be discovered by experimentation:

- Methods with complex call graphs (e.g. loops) are not inlined.

- Methods with exception handling are not inlined.

- Recursive methods are not inlined.

- Methods that have non-primitive value type parameters, local variables, or return values are not inlined.

- Methods with bodies larger than 32 bytes of IL are not inlined. (The MethodImplOptions.AggressiveInlining value of the [MethodImpl] attribute overrules this limitation.)

In recent versions of the CLR, some artificial limitations on inlining were removed. For example, as of .NET 3.5 SP1, the 32-bit JIT compiler is able to inline methods that accept *some* non-primitive value type parameters, like Chapter 3's Point2D. The changes made in that release replace operations on value types by equivalent operations on primitive types under certain conditions (Point2D is transformed to two ints), and allow better optimization of struct-related code in general, such as copy propagation, redundant assignment elimination, and others. For example, consider the following trivial code:

```
private static void MethodThatTakesAPoint(Point2D pt) {
  pt.Y = pt.X ^ pt.Y;
  Console.WriteLine(pt.Y);
}

Point2D pt;
pt.X = 3;
pt.Y = 5;
MethodThatTakesAPoint(pt);
```

Using the CLR 4.5 JIT compiler, this entire section of code is compiled to the moral equivalent of Console.WriteLine(6), which is the result of 3 ^ 5. The JIT compiler is able to use inlining and constant propagation on the custom value type. When using the CLR 2.0 JIT compiler, an actual call to the method is emitted at the call site, and inside the method there is no visible optimization:

```
; calling code
mov eax,3
lea edx,[eax+2]
push edx
push eax
call dword ptr ds:[1F3350h] (Program.MethodThatTakesAPoint(Point2D), mdToken: 06000003)

; method code
push ebp
mov ebp,esp
mov eax,dword ptr [ebp+8]
xor dword ptr [ebp+0Ch],eax
call mscorlib_ni+0x22d400 (715ed400) (System.Console.get_Out(), mdToken: 06000773)
mov ecx,eax
mov edx,dword ptr [ebp+0Ch]
mov eax,dword ptr [ecx]
call dword ptr [eax+0BCh]
pop ebp
ret 8
```

Although there is no way to *force* inlining if the JIT compiler is not willing to perform it, there is a way to turn off inlining. The MethodImplOptions.NoInlining value of the [MethodImpl] attribute disables inlining of the specific method on which it is placed—incidentally, this is quite useful for micro-benchmarking, discussed in Chapter 2.

Range-Check Elimination

When accessing array elements, the CLR must make sure that the index used to access the array is within the bounds of the array. If this check was not made, memory safety would be compromised; you could initialize a byte[] object and index it with negative and positive indices to read/write any location in memory. Although absolutely necessary, this range check has a performance cost of a few instructions. Below is the code emitted by the JIT compiler for a standard array access:

```
//Original C# code:
uint[] array = new uint[100];
array[4] = 0xBADC0FFE;
```

```
; Emitted x86 assembly instructions
mov ecx,offset 67fa33aa          ; type of array element
mov edx,64h                      ; array size
call 0036215c                    ; creates a new array (CORINFO_HELP_NEWARR_1_VC)
cmp dword ptr [eax+4],4          ; eax+4 contains the array length, 4 is the index
jbe NOT_IN_RANGE                 ; if the length is less than or equal the index, jump away
mov dword ptr [eax+18h],0BADC0FFEh ; the offset was calculated at JIT time (0x18=8+4*4)
; Rest of the program's code, jumping over the NOT_IN_RANGE label
NOT_IN_RANGE:
call clr!JIT_RngChkFail          ; throws an exception
```

There is a specific case in which the JIT compiler can eliminate the range-check for accessing array elements—an indexed for loop that visits every array element. Without this optimization, accessing arrays would always be slower than in unmanaged code, which is an unacceptable performance hit for scientific applications and memory-bound work. For the following loop, the JIT compiler will eliminate the range check:

```
//Original C# code:
for (int k=0; k<array.Length; ++k) {
    array[k]=(uint)k;
}
```

```
; Emitted x86 assembly instructions (optimized)
xor edx,edx                      ; edx=k=0
mov eax,dword ptr [esi+4]        ; esi=array, eax=array.Length
test eax,eax                     ; if the array is empty,
jle END_LOOP                     ; skip the loop
NEXT_ITERATION:
mov dword ptr [esi+edx*4+8],edx  ; array[k]=k
inc edx                          ; ++k
cmp eax,edx                      ; as long as array.Length>k,
jg NEXT_ITERATION                ; jump to the next iteration
END_LOOP:
```

There is only a single check during the loop, and it's the check that makes sure the loop terminates. However, the array access inside the loop is *not* checked—the highlighted line writes to the k-th element in the array without making sure (again) that k is within the array bounds.

Unfortunately, it is also fairly easy to impede this optimization. Some changes to the loop, which appear quite innocent, may have the adverse effect of forcing a range check when accessing the array:

```
//The range-check elimination occurs
for (int k=0; k<array.Length - 1; ++k) {
    array[k]=(uint)k;
}
```

```
//The range-check elimination occurs
for (int k=7; k<array.Length; ++k) {
    array[k]=(uint)k;
}
```

```
//The range-check elimination occurs
//The JIT removes the -1 from the bounds check and starts from the second element
for (int k=0; k<array.Length - 1; ++k) {
    array[k+1]=(uint)k;
}
```

```
//The range-check elimination does not occur
for (int k=0; k<array.Length / 2; ++k) {
    array[k * 2]=(uint)k;
}
```

```
//The range-check elimination does not occur
staticArray=array; //"staticArray" is a static field of the enclosing class
for (int k=0; k<staticArray.Length; ++k) {
    staticArray[k]=(uint)k;
}
```

To summarize, range-check elimination is a fragile optimization, and you would do well to make sure that performance-critical sections of your code enjoy this optimization, even if it means that you have to inspect the assembly code generated for your program. For more details on range-check elimination and additional corner cases, see the article "Array Bounds Check Elimination in the CLR" by Dave Detlefs on http://blogs.msdn.com/b/clrcodegeneration/archive/2009/08/13/array-bounds-check-elimination-in-the-clr.aspx.

Tail Call

Tail calling is an optimization that reuses the stack frame of an existing method to call another method. This optimization is very useful for many types of recursive algorithms. In fact, some recursive methods can be as efficient as iteration-based ones if tail call optimization is employed pervasively. Consider the following recursive method, which calculates the greatest common divisor of two integers:

```
public static int GCD(int a, int b) {
  if (b == 0) return a;
  return GCD(b, a % b);
}
```

Clearly, the recursive invocation of GCD(b, a % b) is not subject to inlining—it is a recursive invocation, after all. However, because the caller and callee's stack frames are fully compatible, and because the caller does not do anything after the recursive invocation, a possible optimization would be to rewrite this method as follows:

```
public static int GCD(int a, int b) {
START:
  if (b == 0) return a;
  int temp=a % b;
  a=b;
  b=temp;
  goto START;
}
```

This rewrite does away with all method invocations—effectively, the recursive algorithm has been turned into an iterative one. Although you could perform this rewrite by hand every time you encountered the possibility, the JIT compiler will do it automatically under some circumstances. Below are two versions of the GCD method—the first compiled with the CLR 4.5 32-bit JIT compiler and the second with the CLR 4.5 64-bit JIT compiler:

```
; 32-bit version, parameters are in ECX and EDX
push ebp
mov ebp,esp
push esi
mov eax,ecx     ; EAX=a
mov ecx,edx     ; ECX=b
test ecx,ecx    ; if b == 0, returning a
jne PROCEED
```

```
pop esi
pop ebp
ret
PROCEED:
cdq
idiv eax,ecx      ; EAX=a / b, EDX=a % b
mov esi,edx
test esi,esi      ; if a % b == 0, returning b (inlined base of recursion)
jne PROCEED2
mov eax,ecx
jmp EXIT
PROCEED2:
mov eax,ecx
cdq
idiv eax,esi
mov ecx,esi       ; recursive call on the next line
call dword ptr ds:[3237A0h] (Program.GCD(Int32, Int32), mdToken: 06000004)
EXIT:
pop esi
pop ebp
ret               ; reuses return value (in EAX) from recursive return

; 64-bit version, parameters in ECX and EDX
sub rsp,28h       ; construct stack frame - happens only once!
START:
mov r8d,edx
test r8d,r8d      ; if b == 0, return a
jne PROCEED
mov eax,ecx
jmp EXIT
PROCEED:
cmp ecx,80000000h
jne PROCEED2:
cmp r8d,0FFFFFFFFh
je OVERFLOW       ; miscellaneous overflow checks for arithmetic
xchg ax,ax        ; two-byte NOP (0x66 0x90) for alignment purposes
PROCEED2:
mov eax,ecx
cdq
idiv eax,r8d      ; EAX=a / b, EDX=a % b
mov ecx,r8d       ; reinitialize parameters
mov r8d,edx       ; . . .
jmp START         ; and jump back to the beginning (no function call)
xchg ax,ax        ; two-byte NOP (0x66 0x90) for alignment purposes
EXIT:
add rsp,28h
ret
OVERFLOW:
call    clr!JIT_Overflow
nop
```

It becomes evident that the 64-bit JIT compiler uses the tail call optimization to get rid of the recursive method invocation, whereas the 32-bit JIT compiler does not. A detailed treatment of the conditions that the two

JIT compilers use for determining whether tail call can be employed is beyond the scope of this book—below are some of the heuristics:

- The 64-bit JIT compiler is quite relaxed in terms of tail calling, and will often perform a tail call even if the language compiler (e.g. the C# compiler) did not suggest it by using the `tail.` IL prefix.

    - Calls followed by additional code (other than returning from the method) are not subject to tail calling. (Slightly relaxed in CLR 4.0.)

    - Calls to a method that returns a different type than the caller.

    - Calls to a method that has too many parameters, unaligned parameters, or parameter/return types that are large value types. (Relaxed considerably in CLR 4.0.)

- The 32-bit JIT compiler is less inclined to perform this optimization, and will emit tail calls only if instructed to do so by the `tail.` IL prefix.

■ **Note**   A curious aspect of tail calling implications is the case of an infinite recursion. If you have a bug with the recursion's base case that would cause an infinite recursion, but the JIT compiler was able to turn the recursive method call into a tail call, the usual `StackOverflowException` outcome that is the result of infinite recursion turns into an infinite loop!

More details on the `tail.` IL prefix used to suggest tail calling to reluctant JIT compilers and on the criteria used by the JIT compiler to perform tail calling are available online:

- The `tail.` IL prefix, which the C# compiler does not emit, but is used frequently by functional language compilers (including F#) is described on the MSDN, as part of the `System.Reflection.Emit` class page: `http://msdn.microsoft.com/en-us/library/system.reflection.emit.opcodes.tailcall.aspx`.

- The list of conditions for performing a tail call in the JIT compiler (prior to CLR 4.0) is detailed in David Broman's article, "Tail call JIT conditions", at `http://blogs.msdn.com/b/davbr/archive/2007/06/20/tail-call-jit-conditions.aspx`.

- The tail calling optimization changes in the CLR 4.0 JIT compiler are described in depth in the article "Tail Call Improvements in .NET Framework 4", at `http://blogs.msdn.com/b/clrcodegeneration/archive/2009/05/11/tail-call-improvements-in-net-framework-4.aspx`.

Startup Performance

For client applications, quick startup is a great first impression to make on the user or a potential client evaluating the product or taking a demo. However, the more complex the application, the harder it is to maintain acceptable startup times. It's important to differentiate between *cold startup*, when the application is launched for the first time after the system has just finished booting, and *warm startup*, when the application is launched (not for the first time) after the system has been used for some time. Always-on system services or background agents need fast cold startup times, so as to prevent the system startup sequence and user logon from taking too long. Typical client applications such as email clients and Web browsers might get away with slightly longer cold startup times, but users will expect them to launch rapidly when the system has been used for a while. Most users will want short startup times in both cases.

There are several factors that go into long startup times. Some of them are relevant only for cold startup; others are relevant for both types of startup.

- I/O operations—to launch the application, Windows and the CLR must load from the disk the application's assemblies as well as .NET Framework assemblies, CLR DLLs, and Windows DLLs. This factor is relevant mostly for cold startup.

- JIT compilation—every method called for the first time during application startup must be compiled by the JIT compiler. Because code compiled by the JIT is not preserved when the application terminates, this factor is relevant for both cold and warm startup.

- GUI initialization—depending on your GUI framework (Metro, WPF, Windows Forms, etc.), there are GUI-specific initialization steps that must take place for the user interface to be displayed. This factor is relevant for both types of startup.

- Loading application-specific data—your application might require some information from files, databases, or Web services to display its initial screen. This factor is relevant for both types of startup, unless your application employs some caching scheme for this data.

We have several measurement tools at our disposal to diagnose long startup times and their likely causes (see Chapter 2). Sysinternals Process Monitor can point to I/O operations performed by the application's process, regardless of whether Windows, the CLR, or the application code initiated them. PerfMonitor and the `.NET CLR JIT` performance counter category can help diagnose excessive JIT compilation during application startup. Finally, "standard" profilers (in sampling or instrumentation modes) can determine how your application is spending its time during startup.

Additionally, there is a simple experiment you can perform that will tell you whether I/O is the primary cause of slow startup times: time your application's cold startup and warm startup scenarios (you should use a clean hardware environment for these tests, and make sure there are no unnecessary services or other initialization taking place in the cold startup test). If the warm startup is significantly faster than the cold startup, I/O is the chief culprit.

Improving your application-specific data loading is up to you; every guideline we can issue would be too general to use in practice (other than providing a splash screen to stretch your users' patience...). However, we can offer several remedies for poor startup performance that originates from I/O operations and JIT compilation. Optimizing your application's startup time can cut it down in half or more, in some cases.

Pre-JIT Compilation with NGen (Native Image Generator)

Although the JIT compiler is very convenient and compiles methods only when they are called, there is still a performance cost that your application pays whenever the JIT runs. The .NET Framework offers an optimization tool, called *Native Image Generator* (NGen.exe), which can compile your assemblies to machine code (*native images*) before runtime. If every assembly your application requires is pre-compiled in this manner, there will be no need to load the JIT compiler and to use it during application startup. Although the generated native image is likely to be larger than the original assembly, in most cases the amount of disk I/O on cold startup actually decreases, because the JIT compiler itself (clrjit.dll) and metadata for referenced assemblies aren't read from disk.

Pre-compilation has another advantageous effect—native images can be shared between processes, unlike code that the JIT compiler emits at runtime. If several processes on the same machine use a native image for some assembly, physical memory consumption is lower than in the JIT-compiled case. This is especially important in shared-system scenarios, when multiple users connect through Terminal Services sessions to a single server, and run the same application.

To pre-compile your application, all you need to do is point the NGen.exe tool, which resides in the .NET Framework's directory, to your application's main assembly (typically an .exe file). NGen will proceed to locate all the static dependencies your main assembly has and pre-compile them all to native images. The resulting native

images are stored in a cache that you do not have to manage—it is stored next to the GAC, in the
C:\Windows\Assembly\NativeImages_* folders by default.

▓ **Tip**   Because the CLR and NGen manage the native image cache automatically, you should *never* copy the native
images from one machine to another. The only supported way to pre-compile managed assemblies on a specific
system is to run the NGen tool on *that* system. The ideal time to do this would be during the application's installation
(NGen even supports a "defer" command, which will queue pre-compilation to a background service). This is what
the. NET Framework installer does for frequently used .NET assemblies.

Below is a complete example of using NGen to pre-compile a simple application that consists of two
assemblies—the main .exe file, and an auxiliary .dll referenced by it. NGen successfully detects the dependency
and pre-compiles both assemblies to native images:

```
> c:\windows\microsoft.net\framework\v4.0.30319\ngen install Ch10.exe

Microsoft (R) CLR Native Image Generator - Version 4.0.30319.17379
Copyright (c) Microsoft Corporation.  All rights reserved.

Installing assembly D:\Code\Ch10.exe
1>    Compiling assembly D:\Code\Ch10.exe (CLR v4.0.30319) ...
2>    Compiling assembly HelperLibrary, ... (CLR v4.0.30319) ...
```

At runtime, the CLR uses the native images and does not require clrjit.dll to be loaded at all (in the lm
command's output below, clrjit.dll is not listed). Type method tables (see Chapter 3), also stored in the native
images, point to the pre-compiled versions inside the native image boundaries.

```
0:007 > lm
start      end         module name
01350000 01358000   Ch10        (deferred)
2f460000 2f466000   Ch10_ni     (deferred)
30b10000 30b16000   HelperLibrary_ni    (deferred)
67fa0000 68eef000   mscorlib_ni    (deferred)
6b240000 6b8bf000   clr         (deferred)
6f250000 6f322000   MSVCR110_CLR0400    (deferred)
72190000 7220a000   mscoreei    (deferred)
72210000 7225a000   MSCOREE     (deferred)
74cb0000 74cbc000   CRYPTBASE   (deferred)
74cc0000 74d20000   SspiCli     (deferred)
74d20000 74d39000   sechost     (deferred)
74d40000 74d86000   KERNELBASE    (deferred)
74e50000 74f50000   USER32      (deferred)
74fb0000 7507c000   MSCTF       (deferred)
75080000 7512c000   msvcrt      (deferred)
75150000 751ed000   USP10       (deferred)
753e0000 75480000   ADVAPI32    (deferred)
75480000 75570000   RPCRT4      (deferred)
75570000 756cc000   ole32       (deferred)
75730000 75787000   SHLWAPI     (deferred)
```

```
75790000 757f0000   IMM32      (deferred)
76800000 7680a000   LPK        (deferred)
76810000 76920000   KERNEL32   (deferred)
76920000 769b0000   GDI32      (deferred)
775e0000 77760000   ntdll      (pdb symbols)


0:007> !dumpmt -md 2f4642dc
EEClass:          2f4614c8
Module:           2f461000
Name:             Ch10.Program
mdToken:          02000002
File:             D:\Code\Ch10.exe
BaseSize:         0xc
ComponentSize:    0x0
Slots in VTable:  6
Number of IFaces in IFaceMap: 0
--------------------------------------
MethodDesc Table
   Entry MethodDe   JIT Name
68275450 68013524 PreJIT System.Object.ToString()
682606b0 6801352c PreJIT System.Object.Equals(System.Object)
68260270 6801354c PreJIT System.Object.GetHashCode()
68260230 68013560 PreJIT System.Object.Finalize()
2f464268 2f46151c PreJIT Ch10.Program..ctor()
2f462048 2f461508 PreJIT Ch10.Program.Main(System.String[])


0:007> !dumpmt -md 30b141c0
EEClass:          30b114c4
Module:           30b11000
Name:             HelperLibrary.UtilityClass
mdToken:          02000002
File:             D:\Code\HelperLibrary.dll
BaseSize:         0xc
ComponentSize:    0x0
Slots in VTable:  6
Number of IFaces in IFaceMap: 0
--------------------------------------
MethodDesc Table
   Entry MethodDe   JIT Name
68275450 68013524 PreJIT System.Object.ToString()
682606b0 6801352c PreJIT System.Object.Equals(System.Object)
68260270 6801354c PreJIT System.Object.GetHashCode()
68260230 68013560 PreJIT System.Object.Finalize()
30b14158 30b11518 PreJIT HelperLibrary.UtilityClass..ctor()
30b12048 30b11504 PreJIT HelperLibrary.UtilityClass.SayHello()
```

Another useful option is the "update" command, which forces NGen to recalculate the dependencies for all native images in the cache and pre-compile again any modified assemblies. You would use this after installing an update on the target system, or during development.

■ **Note**   Theoretically, NGen could use a completely different—and larger—set of optimizations than what the JIT compiler uses at runtime. After all, NGen is not as time-bound as the JIT compiler. However, at the time of writing, NGen has no optimizations up its sleeve other than those the JIT compiler employs.

When using CLR 4.5 on Windows 8, NGen does not passively wait for your instructions to pre-compile application assemblies. Instead, the CLR generates assembly usage logs that are processed by NGen's background maintenance task. This task decides, periodically, which assemblies would benefit from pre-compilation, and runs NGen to create native images for them. You can still use NGen's "display" command to review the native image cache (or inspect its files from a command line prompt), but much of the burden of deciding which assemblies would benefit from pre-compilation is now at the CLR's discretion.

Multi-Core Background JIT Compilation

Starting in CLR 4.5, you can instruct the JIT compiler to generate a profile of methods executed during application startup, and use that profile on subsequent application launches (including cold startup scenarios) to compile these methods in the background. In other words, while your application's main thread is initializing, the JIT compiler executes on background threads such that methods are likely to be already compiled by the time they are needed. The profile information is updated on each run, so it will remain fresh and up to date even if the application is launched for hundreds of times with different configurations.

■ **Note**   This feature is enabled by default in ASP.NET and Silverlight 5 applications.

To opt into using multi-core background JIT compilation, you call two methods on the `System.Runtime.ProfileOptimization` class. The first method tells the profiler where the profiling information can be stored, and the second method tells the profiler which startup scenario is being executed. The purpose of the second method is to distinguish between considerably different scenarios, such that the optimization is tailored for the specific scenario. For example, an archiving utility may be invoked with a "display files in archive" parameter, which requires one set of methods, and a "create compressed archive from directory" parameter, which requires a completely different set of methods:

```
public static void Main(string[] args) {
  System.Runtime.ProfileOptimization.SetProfileRoot(
    Path.GetDirectoryName(Assembly.GetExecutingAssembly().Location));
  if (args[0] == "display") {
    System.Runtime.ProfileOptimization.StartProfile("DisplayArchive.prof");
  } else if (args[0] == "compress") {
    System.Runtime.ProfileOptimization.StartProfile("CompressDirectory.prof");
  }
  //...More startup scenarios
  //The rest of the application's code goes here, after determining the startup scenario
}
```

Image Packers

A common approach to minimizing I/O transfer costs is by compressing the original data. After all, it would make little sense to download a 15GB uncompressed Windows installation if it can fit—in compressed form—on a single DVD. The same idea can be used with managed applications stored on disk. Compressing the application and decompressing it only after loading it into memory can significantly decrease cold startup costs by reducing the number of I/O operations performed on startup. Compression is a double-edged sword, because of CPU time required to decompress the application's code and data in memory, but it can be worthwhile to pay the price in CPU time when reducing cold startup costs is critical, such as with a kiosk application that has to launch as quickly as possible after the system is turned on.

There are several commercial and open source compression utilities for applications (usually called *packers*). If you use a packer, make sure it can compress .NET applications—some packers will only work well with unmanaged binaries. One example of a tool that compresses .NET applications is MPress, which is freely available online at http://www.matcode.com/mpress.htm. Another example is the Rugland Packer for .NET Executables (RPX), an open source utility published at http://rpx.codeplex.com/. Below is some sample output from RPX when run on a very small application:

```
> Rpx.exe Shlook.TestServer.exe Shlook.Common.dll Shlook.Server.dll

Rugland Packer for (.Net) eXecutables 1.3.4399.43191
█                                                                █ 100.0%
Unpacked size      :.............27.00 KB
Packed size        :.............13.89 KB
Compression        :.............48.55%
_____

Application target is the console
_____

Uncompressed size :.............27.00 KB
Startup overhead   :.............5.11 KB
Final size         :.............19.00 KB
_____

Total compression :.............29.63%
```

Managed Profile-Guided Optimization (MPGO)

Managed profile guided optimization (MPGO) is a tool introduced in Visual Studio 11 and CLR 4.5 that optimizes the on-disk layout of native images produced by NGen. MPGO generates profile information from a specified period of the application's execution and embeds it in the assembly. Subsequently, NGen uses this information to optimize the layout of the generated native image.

MPGO optimizes native image's layout in two primary ways. First, MPGO makes sure that code and data which are used frequently (hot data) are placed together on disk. As a result, there will be fewer page faults and disk reads for hot data, because more hot data fits on a single page. Second, MPGO places potentially writable data together on disk. When a data page that is shared with other processes is modified, Windows creates a private copy of the page for the modifying process to use (this is known as *copy-on-write*). As a result of MPGO's optimization, fewer shared pages are modified, resulting in less copies and lower memory utilization.

To run MPGO on your application, you need to provide the list of assemblies to instrument, an output directory in which to place the optimized binaries, and a timeout after which profiling should stop. MPGO instruments the application, runs it, analyzes the results, and creates optimized native images for the assemblies you specified:

```
> mpgo.exe -scenario Ch10.exe -assemblylist Ch10.exe HelperLibrary.dll -OutDir . –NoClean

Successfully instrumented assembly D:\Code\Ch10.exe
Successfully instrumented assembly D:\Code\HelperLibrary.dll

<output from the application removed>

Successfully removed instrumented assembly D:\Code\Ch10.exe
Successfully removed instrumented assembly D:\Code\HelperLibrary.dll
Reading IBC data file: D:\Code\Ch10.ibc
The module D:\Code\Ch10-1.exe, did not contain an IBC resource
Writing profile data in module D:\Code\Ch10-1.exe
Data from one or more input files has been upgraded to a newer version.
Successfully merged profile data into new file D:\Code\Ch10-1.exe
Reading IBC data file: D:\Code\HelperLibrary.ibc
The module D:\Code\HelperLibrary-1.dll, did not contain an IBC resource
Writing profile data in module D:\Code\HelperLibrary-1.dll
Data from one or more input files has been upgraded to a newer version.
Successfully merged profile data into new file D:\Code\HelperLibrary-1.dll
```

▧ **Note** When the optimization completes, you need to run NGen again on the optimized assemblies to create final native images that benefit from MPGO. Running NGen on assemblies is covered earlier in this chapter.

At the time of writing, there were no plans to introduce MPGO into the Visual Studio 2012 user interface. The command line tool is the only way to add these performance gains to your application. Because it relies on NGen, this is another optimization that is best performed after installation time on the target machine.

Miscellaneous Tips for Startup Performance

There are several additional tips we didn't mention earlier that might be able to shave a few more seconds off your application's startup time.

Strong Named Assemblies Belong in the GAC

If your assemblies have strong names, make sure to place them in the global assembly cache (GAC). Otherwise, loading the assembly requires touching almost every page to verify its digital signature. Verification of strong names when the assembly is not placed in the GAC will also diminish any performance gains from NGen.

Make Sure Your Native Images Do Not Require Rebasing

When using NGen, make sure that your native images do not have base address collisions, which require rebasing. Rebasing is an expensive operation that involves modifying code addresses at runtime, and creates copies of otherwise shared code pages. To view the native image's base address, use the dumpbin.exe utility with the /headers flag, as follows:

```
> dumpbin.exe /headers Ch10.ni.exe

Microsoft (R) COFF/PE Dumper Version 11.00.50214.1
Copyright (C) Microsoft Corporation.  All rights reserved.


Dump of file Ch10.ni.exe

PE signature found

File Type: DLL

FILE HEADER VALUES
             14C machine (x86)
               4 number of sections
        4F842B2C time date stamp Tue Apr 10 15:44:28 2012
               0 file pointer to symbol table
               0 number of symbols
              E0 size of optional header
            2102 characteristics
                   Executable
                   32 bit word machine
                   DLL

OPTIONAL HEADER VALUES
             10B magic # (PE32)
           11.00 linker version
               0 size of code
               0 size of initialized data
               0 size of uninitialized data
               0 entry point
               0 base of code
               0 base of data
        30000000 image base (30000000 to 30005FFF)
            1000 section alignment
             200 file alignment
            5.00 operating system version
            0.00 image version
            5.00 subsystem version
               0 Win32 version
            6000 size of image
<more output omitted for brevity>
```

To change the native image's base address, change the base address in the project properties in Visual Studio. The base address can be located on the Build tab, after opening the Advanced dialog (see Figure 10-1).

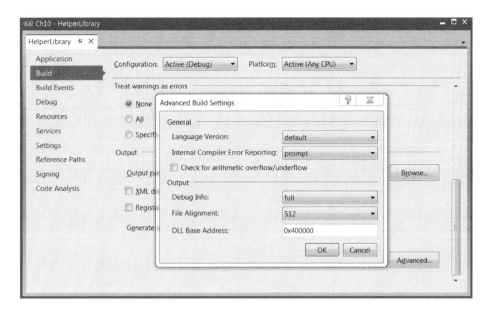

Figure 10-1. *Visual Studio Advanced Build Settings dialog, which allows modifying the base address for the native image that NGen generates*

As of .NET 3.5 SP1, NGen opts-in to use Address Space Layout Randomization (ASLR) when the application is running on Windows Vista or a newer platform. When using ASLR, base load addresses for images are randomized across runs for security reasons. Under this configuration, rebasing assemblies to avoid base address collisions is not important on Windows Vista and newer platforms.

Reduce the Total Number of Assemblies

Reduce the number of assemblies loaded by your application. Each assembly load incurs a constant cost, regardless of its size, and inter-assembly references and method calls may be more costly at runtime. Large applications that load hundreds of assemblies are not uncommon, and their startup times can be reduced by several seconds if assemblies are merged to only a few binaries.

Processor-Specific Optimization

Theoretically, .NET developers should never be concerned with optimizations tailored to a specific processor or instruction set. After all, the purpose of IL and JIT compilation is to allow managed applications to run on any hardware that has the .NET Framework installed, and to remain indifferent to operating system bitness, processor features, and instruction sets. However, squeezing the last bits of performance from managed applications may require reasoning at the assembly language level, as we have seen throughout this book. At other times, understanding processor-specific features is a first step for even more significant performance gains.

In this short section we will review some examples of optimization tailored to specific processor features, optimization that might work well on one machine and break on another. We focus mostly on Intel processors, especially the Nehalem, Sandy Bridge and Ivy Bridge families, but most of the guidance will also be relevant to AMD processors. Because these optimizations are perilous and sometimes unrepeatable, you should not use these examples as definitive guidance, but only as motivation for reaping more performance from your applications.

Single Instruction Multiple Data (SIMD)

Data-level parallelism, also known as *Single Instruction Multiple Data* (SIMD), is a feature of modern processors that enables the execution of a single instruction on a large set of data (larger than the machine word). The de-facto standard for SIMD instruction sets is SSE (Streaming SIMD Extensions), used by Intel processors since Pentium III. This instruction set adds new 128-bit registers (with the XMM prefix) as well as instructions that can operate on them. Recent Intel processors introduced *Advanced Vector Extensions* (AVX), which is an extension of SSE that offers 256-bit registers and even more SIMD instructions. Some examples of SSE instructions include:

- Integer and floating-point arithmetic

- Comparisons, shuffling, data type conversion (integer to floating-point)

- Bitwise operations

- Minimum, maximum, conditional copies, CRC32, population count (introduced in SSE4 and later)

You might be wondering whether instructions operating on these "new" registers are slower than their standard counterparts. If that were the case, any performance gains would be deceiving. Fortunately, that is not the case. On Intel i7 processors, a floating-point addition (FADD) instruction on 32-bit registers has throughput of one instruction per cycle and latency of 3 cycles. The equivalent ADDPS instruction on 128-bit registers also has throughput of one instruction per cycle and latency of 3 cycles.

LATENCY AND THROUGHPUT

Latency and throughput are common terms in general performance measurements, but especially so when discussing the "speed" of processor instructions:

- An instruction's latency is the time (usually measured in clock cycles) it takes to execute one instance of the instruction from start to finish.

- An instruction's throughput is the number of instructions of the same type that can be executed in a unit of time (usually measured in clock cycles).

If we say that FADD has latency of 3 cycles, it means that a single FADD operation will take 3 cycles to complete. If we say that FADD has throughput of one instruction per cycle, it means that by issuing multiple instances of FADD concurrently the processor is able to sustain an execution rate of one instruction per cycle, which will like require three of these instructions to execute concurrently.

Very often, an instruction's throughput is significantly better than its latency because processors can issue and execute multiple instructions in parallel (we will return to this subject later).

Using these instructions in high-performance loops can provide up to 8× performance gains compared to naïve sequential programs that operate on a single floating-point or integer value at a time. For example, consider the following (admittedly trivial) code:

```
//Assume that A, B, C are equal-size float arrays
for (int i=0; i<A.length; ++i) {
  C[i]=A[i]+B[i];
}
```

The standard code emitted by the JIT in this scenario is the following:

```
; ESI has A, EDI has B, ECX has C, EDX is the iteration variable
xor edx,edx
cmp dword ptr [esi+4],0
jle END_LOOP
NEXT_ITERATION:
fld dword ptr [esi+edx*4+8]        ; load A[i], no range check
cmp edx,dword ptr [edi+4]          ; range check before accessing B[i]
jae OUT_OF_RANGE
fadd dword ptr [edi+edx*4+8]       ; add B[i]
cmp edx,dword ptr [ecx+4]          ; range check before accessing C[i]
jae OUT_OF_RANGE
fstp dword ptr [ecx+edx*4+8]       ; store into C[i]
inc edx
cmp dword ptr [esi+4],edx          ; are we done yet?
jg NEXT_ITERATION
END_LOOP:
```

Each loop iteration performs a single FADD instruction that adds two 32-bit floating-point numbers. However, by using 128-bit SSE instructions, four iterations of the loop can be issued at a time, as follows (the code below performs no range checks and assumes that the number of iterations is equally divisible by 4):

```
xor edx, edx
NEXT_ITERATION:
movups xmm1, xmmword ptr [edi+edx*4+8]    ; copy 16 bytes from B to xmm1
movups xmm0, xmmword ptr [esi+edx*4+8]    ; copy 16 bytes from A to xmm0
addps xmm1, xmm0                          ; add xmm0 to xmm1 and store the result in xmm1
movups xmmword ptr [ecx+edx*4+8], xmm1    ; copy 16 bytes from xmm1 to C
add edx, 4                                ; increase loop index by 4
cmp edx, dword ptr [esi+4]
jg NEXT_ITERATION
```

On an AVX processor, we could move even more data around in each iteration (with the 256-bit YMM* registers), for an even bigger performance improvement:

```
xor edx, edx
NEXT_ITERATION:
vmovups ymm1, ymmword ptr [edi+edx*4+8]    ; copy 32 bytes from B to ymm1
vmovups ymm0, ymmword ptr [esi+edx*4+8]    ; copy 32 bytes from A to ymm0
vaddps ymm1, ymm1, ymm0                    ; add ymm0 to ymm1 and store the result in ymm1
vmovups ymmword ptr [ecx+edx*4+8], ymm1    ; copy 32 bytes from ymm1 to C
add edx, 8                                 ; increase loop index by 8
cmp edx, dword ptr [esi+4]
jg NEXT_ITERATION
```

▤ **Note**   The SIMD instructions used in these examples are only the tip of the iceberg. Modern applications and games use SIMD instructions to perform complex operations, including scalar product, shuffling data around in registers and memory, checksum calculation, and many others. Intel's AVX portal is a good way to learn thoroughly what AVX can offer: http://software.intel.com/en-us/avx/

The JIT compiler uses only a small number of SSE instructions, even though they are available on practically every processor manufactured in the last 10 years. Specifically, the JIT compiler uses the SSE MOVQ instruction to copy medium-sized structures through the XMM* registers (for large structures, REP MOVS is used instead), and uses SSE2 instructions for floating point to integer conversion and other corner cases. The JIT compiler *does not* auto-vectorize loops by unifying iterations, as we did manually in the preceding code listings, whereas modern C++ compilers (including Visual Studio 2012) do.

Unfortunately, C# doesn't offer any keywords for embedding inline assembly code into your managed programs. Although you could factor out performance-sensitive parts to a C++ module and use .NET interoperability to access it, this is often clumsy. There are two other approaches for embedding SIMD code without resorting to a separate module.

A brute-force way to run arbitrary machine code from a managed application (albeit with a light interoperability layer) is to dynamically emit the machine code and then call it. The Marshal.GetDelegateForFunctionPointer method is key, as it returns a managed delegate pointing to an unmanaged memory location, which may contain arbitrary code. The following code allocates virtual memory with the EXECUTE_READWRITE page protection, which enables us to copy code bytes into memory and then execute them. The result, on an Intel i7-860 CPU, is a more than 2× improvement in execution time!

```
[UnmanagedFunctionPointer(CallingConvention.StdCall)]
delegate void VectorAddDelegate(float[] C, float[] B, float[] A, int length);

[DllImport("kernel32.dll", SetLastError=true)]
static extern IntPtr VirtualAlloc(
  IntPtr lpAddress, UIntPtr dwSize, IntPtr flAllocationType, IntPtr flProtect);

//This array of bytes has been produced from the SSE assembly version – it is a complete
//function that accepts four parameters (three vectors and length) and adds the vectors
byte[] sseAssemblyBytes={ 0x8b, 0x5c, 0x24, 0x10, 0x8b, 0x74, 0x24, 0x0c, 0x8b, 0x7c, 0x24,
                          0x08, 0x8b, 0x4c, 0x24, 0x04, 0x31, 0xd2, 0x0f, 0x10, 0x0c, 0x97,
                          0x0f, 0x10, 0x04, 0x96, 0x0f, 0x58, 0xc8, 0x0f, 0x11, 0x0c, 0x91,
                          0x83, 0xc2, 0x04, 0x39, 0xda, 0x7f, 0xea, 0xc2, 0x10, 0x00 };
IntPtr codeBuffer=VirtualAlloc(
    IntPtr.Zero,
    new UIntPtr((uint)sseAssemblyBytes.Length),
    0x1000 | 0x2000, //MEM_COMMIT | MEM_RESERVE
    0x40            //EXECUTE_READWRITE
);
Marshal.Copy(sseAssemblyBytes, 0, codeBuffer, sseAssemblyBytes.Length);
VectorAddDelegate addVectors=(VectorAddDelegate)
  Marshal.GetDelegateForFunctionPointer(codeBuffer, typeof(VectorAddDelegate));
//We can now use 'addVectors' to add vectors!
```

A completely different approach, which unfortunately isn't available on the Microsoft CLR, is extending the JIT compiler to emit SIMD instructions. This is the approach taken by *Mono.Simd*. Managed code developers who use the Mono .NET runtime can reference the Mono.Simd assembly and use JIT compiler support that converts operations on types such as Vector16b or Vector4f to the appropriate SSE instructions. For more information about Mono.Simd, see the official documentation at http://docs.go-mono.com/index.aspx?link=N:Mono.Simd.

Instruction-Level Parallelism

Unlike data-level parallelism, which relies on specific instructions to operate on larger chunks of data at a time, *instruction-level parallelism* (ILP) is a mechanism that executes several instructions simultaneously on the same processor. Modern processors have a deep pipeline with several types of execution units, such as a unit for accessing memory, a unit for performing arithmetic operations, and a unit for decoding CPU instructions. Pipelines enable the execution of multiple instructions to overlap as long as they are not competing for the same parts of the pipeline and as long as there are no *data dependencies* between them. Data dependencies arise when an instruction requires the result of another instruction that executes before it; for example, when an instruction reads from a memory location to which the previous instruction has written.

■ **Note**   Instruction-level parallelism is *not* related to parallel programming, which we discussed in Chapter 6. When using parallel programming APIs the application runs multiple threads on multiple processors. Instruction-level parallelism enables a single thread, on a single processor, to execute multiple instructions at once. Unlike parallel programming, ILP is more difficult to control and depends heavily on program optimization.

In addition to pipelining, processors employ so-called *superscalar execution*, which uses multiple redundant units on the same processor to perform multiple operations of the same type at once. Furthermore, to minimize the impact of data dependencies on parallel instruction execution, processors will execute instructions out of their original order as long as it does not violate any data dependencies. By adding *speculative execution* (primarily by attempting to guess which side of a branch is going to be taken, but by other means as well), the processor is very likely to be able to execute additional instructions even if the next instruction in the original program order cannot be executed because of a data dependency.

Optimizing compilers are renowned for organizing the instruction sequence to maximize instruction level parallelism. The JIT compiler does not do a particularly good job, but the out-of-order execution capabilities of modern processors may offset it. However, poorly-specified programs can affect performance considerably by introducing unnecessary data dependencies—especially into loops—thus limiting instruction-level parallelism.

Consider the following three loops:

```
for (int k = 1; k < 100; ++k) {
    first[k] = a * second[k] + third[k];
}
for (int k = 1; k < 100; ++k) {
    first[k] = a * second[k] + first[k - 1];
}
for (int k = 1; k < 100; ++k) {
    first[k] = a * first[k - 1] + third[k];
}
```

We executed these loops on one of our test machines with arrays of 100 integers, for a million iterations every time. The first loop ran for ~ 190ms, the second for ~ 210ms, and the third for ~ 270ms. This is a substantial performance difference that stems from instruction-level parallelism. The first loop's iterations don't have any data dependencies—multiple iterations can be issued on the processor in any order and execute concurrently in the processor's pipeline. The second loop's iterations introduce a data dependency—to assign first[k], the code depends on first[k-1]. However, at least the multiplication (which must complete before the addition takes place) can be issued without data dependencies. In the third loop, the situation is as bad as it gets: even the multiplication can't be issued without waiting for the data dependency from the previous iteration.

Another example is finding the maximum value in an array of integers. In a trivial implementation, each iteration depends on the currently established maximum from the previous iteration. Curiously, we can apply here the same idea encountered in Chapter 6—aggregation and then summation over local results. Specifically, finding the maximum of the entire array is equivalent to finding the maxima over the even and odd elements, and then performing one additional operation to find the global maximum. Both approaches are shown below:

```
//Naïve algorithm that carries a dependency from each loop iteration to the next
int max = arr[0];
for (int k = 1; k < 100; ++k) {
  max = Math.Max(max, arr[k]);
}
```

```
//ILP-optimized algorithm, which breaks down some of the dependencies such that within the
//loop iteration, the two lines can proceed concurrently inside the processor
int max0 = arr[0];
int max1 = arr[1];
for (int k = 3; k < 100; k += 2) {
  max0 = Math.Max(max0, arr[k-1]);
  max1 = Math.Max(max1, arr[k]);
}
int max = Math.Max(max0, max1);
```

Unfortunately, the CLR JIT compiler undermines this particular optimization by emitting less-than-optimal machine code for the second loop. In the first loop, the important values fit in registers—max and k are stored in registers. In the second loop, the JIT compiler isn't able to fit all the values in registers; if max1 or max0 are placed in memory instead, the loop's performance degrades considerably. The corresponding C++ implementation provides the expected performance gains—the first unrolling operation improves execution time by a factor of two, and unrolling again (using four local maxima) shaves off another 25%.

Instruction-level parallelism can be combined with data-level parallelism. Both examples considered here (the multiply-and-add loop and the maximum calculation) can benefit from using SIMD instructions for additional speedups. In the case of maxima, the PMAXSD SSE4 instruction operates on two sets of four packed 32-bit integers and finds the respective maxima of each pair of integers in the two sets. The following code (using the Visual C++ intrinsics from <smmintrin.h>) runs 3× faster than the previously best version and 7× faster than the naïve original:

```
__m128i max0 = *(__m128i*)arr;
for (int k = 4; k < 100; k += 4) {
  max0 = _mm_max_epi32(max0, *(__m128i*)(arr+k)); //Emits PMAXSD
}
int part0 = _mm_extract_epi32(max0, 0);
int part1 = _mm_extract_epi32(max0, 1);
int part2 = _mm_extract_epi32(max0, 2);
int part3 = _mm_extract_epi32(max0, 3);
int finalmax = max(part0, max(part1, max(part2, part3)));
```

When you minimize data dependencies to gain from instruction-level parallelism, the data-level parallelization (sometimes called *vectorization*) often turns up instantaneously for even bigger performance wins.

MANAGED VS. UNMANAGED CODE

A common concern voiced by .NET opponents is that the managed aspects of the CLR introduce a performance cost and render unviable the development of high-performance algorithms using C#, the .NET Framework, and the CLR. Throughout this book, and even in this chapter, we've seen several performance pitfalls that you must be aware of if you want to squeeze every bit of performance from your managed applications. Unfortunately, there will *always* be cases where unmanaged code (written in C++, C, or even hand-crafted assembly) will have better performance than its managed counterpart.

We do not intend to analyze and categorize every example off the Web where a C++ algorithm was demonstrated to be somewhat more efficient than its C# version. Still, there are some common themes that arise more often than others:

- Strictly CPU-bound numeric algorithms tend to run faster in C++, even after applying specific optimizations in C#. The reasons tend to fluctuate between array bounds checks (which the JIT compiler optimizes away only in some cases, and only for single-dimensional arrays), SIMD instructions employed by C++ compilers, and other optimizations at which C++ compilers excel such as sophisticated inlining and smart register allocation.

- Certain memory management patterns are detrimental to the GC's performance (as we have seen in Chapter 4). At times, C++ code can get memory management "right" by using pooling or reusing unmanaged memory obtained from other sources, where .NET code would struggle.

- C++ code enjoys more direct access to Win32 APIs, and does not require interoperability support, such as parameter marshaling and thread state transitions (discussed in Chapter 8). High-performance applications that exhibit a chatty interface with the operating system may run slower in .NET due to this interoperability layer.

David Piepgrass's excellent CodeProject article, "Head-to-head benchmark: C++ vs. NET" (available at `http://www.codeproject.com/Articles/212856/Head-to-head-benchmark-Csharp-vs-NET`), busts some of the misconceptions around managed code performance. For example, Piepgrass demonstrates that .NET collections are much faster in some cases than their C++ STL equivalents; the same applies to reading file data line-by-line using `ifstream` vs. `StreamReader`. On the other hand, some of his benchmarks emphasize the deficiencies that still exist in the 64-bit JIT compiler, and the lack of SIMD intrinsics on the CLR (which we discussed earlier) is another contributing factor to C++'s advantage.

Exceptions

Exceptions are not an expensive mechanism if used correctly and sparingly. There are simple guidelines that you can follow to steer clear of the risks involved with throwing too many exceptions and incurring a significant performance cost:

- Use exceptions for exceptional conditions: if you expect an exception to happen frequently, consider programming defensively instead of throwing an exception. There are exceptions to this rule (pun intended), but in high-performance scenarios, a condition that occurs 10% of the time should not be handled by throwing an exception.

- Check for exceptional conditions before invoking a method that can throw an exception. Examples of this approach are the `Stream.CanRead` property and the `TryParse` family of static methods on value types (e.g. `int.TryParse`).

- Do not throw exceptions as a control flow mechanism: don't throw an exception to exit a loop, to stop reading from a file, or to return information from a method.

The biggest performance costs associated with throwing and handling exceptions can be categorized into several buckets:

- Constructing an exception requires a stack walk (to fill in the stack trace), which gets more expensive the deeper the stack is.

- Throwing and handling an exception requires interacting with unmanaged code—the Windows Structured Exception Handling (SEH) infrastructure—and running through a chain of SEH handlers on the stack.

- Exceptions divert control flow and data flow from hot regions, causing page faults and cache misses as cold data and code are accessed.

To understand whether exceptions are causing a performance problem, you can use the .NET CLR Exceptions performance counter category (for more on performance counters, see Chapter 2). Specifically, the # of Exceps Thrown / sec counter can help pinpoint potential performance problems if thousands of exceptions are thrown per second.

Reflection

Reflection has a bad reputation for being a performance hog in many complex applications. Some of this reputation is justified: there are extremely expensive operations that you can perform using Reflection, such as invoking a function by its name using Type.InvokeMember or creating an object instance using a late-bound parameter list using Activator.CreateInstance. The main costs when invoking methods or setting field values through Reflection stem from the work that has to happen in the background—instead of strongly-typed code that can be compiled by the JIT to machine instructions, code that uses Reflection is effectively interpreted at runtime through a series of costly method calls.

For example, invoking a method using Type.InvokeMember requires determining which method to invoke using metadata and overload resolution, making sure the specified arguments match the method's parameters, performing type coercions if necessary, verifying any security concerns, and finally executing the method call. Because Reflection is heavily based on object parameters and return values, boxing and unboxing may add an additional extra cost.

■ **Note** For more performance tips surrounding .NET Reflection APIs from an internal perspective, consider Joel Pobar's MSDN Magazine article, "Dodge Common Performance Pitfalls to Craft Speedy Applications", available online at http://msdn.microsoft.com/en-us/magazine/cc163759.aspx.

Often enough, Reflection can be eliminated from performance-critical scenarios by using some form of *code generation*—instead of reflecting over unknown types and invoking methods/properties dynamically, you can generate code (for each type) that will do so in a strongly-typed fashion.

Code Generation

Code generation is often used by serialization frameworks, Object/Relational Mappers (ORMs), dynamic proxies, and other performance-sensitive code that needs to work with dynamic, unknown types. There are several ways to dynamically generate code in the .NET Framework, and there are many third-party code generation frameworks, such as LLBLGen and T4 templates.

- Lightweight Code Generation (LCG), a.k.a. DynamicMethod. This API can be used to generate a method without creating a type and assembly to contain it. For small chunks of code, this is the most efficient code generation mechanism. Emitting code in an LCG method requires the ILGenerator class, which works directly with IL instructions.

- The System.Reflection.Emit namespace contains APIs that can be used to generate assemblies, types, and methods—on the IL level.

- Expression trees (in the `System.Linq.Expression` namespace) can be used to create lightweight expressions from a serialized representation.

- The `CSharpCodeProvider` class can be used to directly compile C# source code (provided as a string or read from a file) to an assembly.

Generating Code from Source

Suppose that you are implementing a serialization framework that writes out an XML representation of arbitrary objects. Using Reflection to obtain non-null public field values and write them out recursively is fairly expensive, but makes for a simple implementation:

```
//Rudimentary XML serializer - does not support collections, cyclic references, etc.
public static string XmlSerialize(object obj) {
  StringBuilder builder=new StringBuilder();
  Type type=obj.GetType();
  builder.AppendFormat("<{0} Type='{1}'">", type.Name, type.AssemblyQualifiedName);
  if (type.IsPrimitive || type == typeof(string)) {
    builder.Append(obj.ToString());
  } else {
    foreach (FieldInfo field in type.GetFields()) {
      object value=field.GetValue(obj);
      if (value !=null) {
        builder.AppendFormat("<{0}>{1}</{0}>", field.Name, XmlSerialize(value));
      }
    }
  }
  builder.AppendFormat("</{0}>", type.Name);
  return builder.ToString();
}
```

Instead, we could generate strongly-typed code to serialize a specific type and invoke that code. Using `CSharpCodeProvider`, the gist of the implementation looks as follows:

```
public static string XmlSerialize<T>(T obj){
  Func<T,string> serializer = XmlSerializationCache<T>.Serializer;
  if (serializer == null){
    serializer = XmlSerializationCache<T>.GenerateSerializer();
  }
  return serializer(obj);
}

private static class XmlSerializationCache<T>{
  public static Func<T,string> Serializer;
  public static Func<T,string> GenerateSerializer() {
    StringBuilder code=new StringBuilder();
    code.AppendLine("using System;");
    code.AppendLine("using System.Text;");
    code.AppendLine("public static class SerializationHelper {");
    code.AppendFormat("public static string XmlSerialize({0} obj) {{", typeof(T).FullName);
    code.AppendLine("StringBuilder result=new StringBuilder();");
    code.AppendFormat("result.Append(\"<{0} Type='{1}'">\");",
                      typeof(T).Name, typeof(T).AssemblyQualifiedName);
```

```
    if (typeof(T).IsPrimitive || typeof(T) == typeof(string)) {
      code.AppendLine("result.AppendLine(obj.ToString());");
    } else {
      foreach (FieldInfo field in typeof(T).GetFields()) {
        code.AppendFormat("result.Append(\"<{0}>\");", field.Name);
        code.AppendFormat("result.Append(XmlSerialize(obj.{0}));", field.Name);
        code.AppendFormat("result.Append(\"</{0}>\");", field.Name);
      }
    }
    code.AppendFormat("result.Append(\"</{0}>\");", typeof(T).Name);
    code.AppendLine("return result.ToString();");
    code.AppendLine("}");
    code.AppendLine("}");

    CSharpCodeProvider compiler=new CSharpCodeProvider();
    CompilerParameters parameters=new CompilerParameters();
    parameters.ReferencedAssemblies.Add(typeof(T).Assembly.Location);
    parameters.CompilerOptions="/optimize+";
    CompilerResults results=compiler.CompileAssemblyFromSource(parameters, code.ToString());
    Type serializationHelper=results.CompiledAssembly.GetType("SerializationHelper");
    MethodInfo method=serializationHelper.GetMethod("XmlSerialize");
    Serializer=(Func<T,string>)Delegate.CreateDelegate(typeof(Func<T,string>), method);
    return Serializer;
  }
}
```

The Reflection-based part has moved such that it is only used once to generate strongly-typed code—the result is cached in a static field and reused every time a certain type must be serialized. Note that the serializer code above has not been extensively tested; it is merely a proof of concept that demonstrates the idea of code generation. Simple measurements indicate that the code-generation-based approach is more than twice as fast as the original, Reflection-only code.

Generating Code Using Dynamic Lightweight Code Generation

Another example stems from the network protocol parsing domain. Suppose that you have a large stream of binary data, such as network packets, and you have to parse it to retrieve from it packet headers and select parts of the payload. For example, consider the following packet header structure (this is a completely fictional example—TCP packet headers are not arranged that way):

```
public struct TcpHeader {
  public uint SourceIP;
  public uint DestIP;
  public ushort SourcePort;
  public ushort DestPort;
  public uint Flags;
  public uint Checksum;
}
```

Retrieving such a structure from a stream of bytes is a trivial task in C/C++, and doesn't even require copying any memory if accessed by pointer. In fact, retrieving *any* structure from a stream of bytes would be trivial:

```
template<typename T>
const T* get_pointer(const unsigned char* data, int offset) {
  return (T*)(data+offset);
}
```

```
template<typename T>
const T get_value(const unsigned char* data, int offset) {
  return *get_pointer(data, offset);
}
```

In C# things are more complicated, unfortunately. There are numerous ways of reading arbitrary data from a stream. One possibility would be to use Reflection to go over the type's fields and read them from the stream of bytes individually:

```
//Supports only some primitive fields, does not recurse
public static void ReadReflectionBitConverter<T>(byte[] data, int offset, out T value) {
  object box = default(T);
  int current = offset;
  foreach (FieldInfo field in typeof(T).GetFields()) {
    if (field.FieldType == typeof(int)) {
      field.SetValue(box, BitConverter.ToInt32(data, current));
      current += 4;
    } else if (field.FieldType == typeof(uint)) {
      field.SetValue(box, BitConverter.ToUInt32(data, current));
      current += 4;
    } else if (field.FieldType == typeof(short)) {
      field.SetValue(box, BitConverter.ToInt16(data, current));
      current += 2;
    } else if (field.FieldType == typeof(ushort)) {
      field.SetValue(box, BitConverter.ToUInt16(data, current));
      current += 2;
    }
    //...many more types omitted for brevity
    value = (T)box;
  }
}
```

When executed 1,000,000 times over a 20-byte TcpHeader structure on one of our test machines, this method took an average of 170ms to execute. Although the running time might seem not too bad, the amount of memory allocated by all the boxing operations is considerable. Additionally, if you consider a realistic network rate of 1Gb/s, it's reasonable to expect tens of millions of packets per second, which means we would have to spend most of our CPU time reading structures from the incoming data.

A considerably better approach involves the Marshal.PtrToStructure method, which is designed to convert an unmanaged chunk of memory to a managed structure. Using it requires pinning the original data to retrieve a pointer to its memory:

```
public static void ReadMarshalPtrToStructure<T>(byte[] data, int offset, out T value) {
  GCHandle gch = GCHandle.Alloc(data, GCHandleType.Pinned);
  try {
    IntPtr ptr = gch.AddrOfPinnedObject();
    ptr += offset;
    value = (T)Marshal.PtrToStructure(ptr, typeof(T));
  } finally {
    gch.Free();
  }
}
```

This version fares considerably better, at an average of 39ms for 1,000,000 packets. This is a significant performance improvement, but Marshal.PtrToStructure still forces a heap memory allocation because it returns an object reference, and this is still not fast enough for tens of millions of packets per second.

In Chapter 8 we discussed C# pointers and unsafe code, and it seems to be a great opportunity to use them. After all, the C++ version is so easy precisely because it uses pointers. Indeed, the following code is much faster at 0.45ms for 1,000,000 packets—an incredible improvement!

```
public static unsafe void ReadPointer(byte[] data, int offset, out TcpHeader header) {
  fixed (byte* pData=&data[offset]) {
    header=*(TcpHeader*)pData;
  }
}
```

Why is this method so fast? Because the entity responsible for copying data around is no longer an API call like Marshal.PtrToStructure—it's the JIT compiler itself. The assembly code generated for this method can be inlined (indeed, the 64-bit JIT compiler chooses to do so) and can use 3-4 instructions to copy memory around (e.g., using the MOVQ instruction on 32-bit systems to copy 64 bits at a time). The only problem is that the ReadPointer method we devised is not generic, unlike its C++ counterpart. The knee-jerk reaction is to implement a generic version of it—

```
public static unsafe void ReadPointerGeneric<T>(byte[] data, int offset, out T value) {
  fixed (byte* pData=&data[offset]) {
    value=*(T*)pData;
  }
}
```

—which does not compile! Specifically, T* is not something you can write in C#, anywhere, because there is no generic constraint to guarantee that a pointer to T can be taken (and only blittable types, discussed in Chapter 8, can be pinned and pointed to). Because no generic constraint is available to express our intent, it would seem that we have to write a separate version of ReadPointer for each type, which is where code generation comes back into play.

TYPEDREFERENCE AND TWO UNDOCUMENTED C# KEYWORDS

Desperate times call for desperate measures, and in this case the desperate measures are pulling out two undocumented C# keywords, __makeref and __refvalue (supported by equally undocumented IL opcodes). Together with the TypedReference struct these keywords are used in some low-level interoperability scenarios with C-style variable length method argument lists (which require another undocumented keyword, __arglist).

TypedReference is a small struct that has two IntPtr fields—Type and Value. The Value field is a pointer to a value, which can be a value type or a reference type, and the Type field is its method table pointer. By creating a TypedReference that points to a value type's location, we can reinterpret memory in a strongly-typed fashion, as our scenario requires, and use the JIT compiler to copy memory, as in the ReadPointer case.

```
//We are taking the parameter by ref and not by out because we need to take its address,
//and __makeref requires an initialized value.
public static unsafe void ReadPointerTypedRef<T>(byte[] data, int offset, ref T value) {
  //We aren't actually modifying 'value' -- just need an lvalue to start with
  TypedReference tr=__makeref(value);
  fixed (byte* ptr=&data[offset]) {
    //The first pointer-sized field of TypedReference is the object address, so we
```

```
    //overwrite it with a pointer into the right location in the data array:
    *(IntPtr*)&tr=(IntPtr)ptr;
    //__refvalue copies the pointee from the TypedReference to 'value'
    value=__refvalue(tr, T);
  }
}
```

This nasty compiler magic still has a cost, unfortunately. Specifically, the __makeref operator is compiled by the JIT compiler to call clr!JIT_GetRefAny, which is an extra cost compared to the fully-inlinable ReadPointer version. The result is an almost 2× slowdown—this method takes 0.83ms to execute 1,000,000 iterations. Incidentally, this is still the fastest *generic* approach we will see in this section.

To avoid writing a separate copy of the ReadPointer method for each type, we'll use Lightweight Code Generation (the DynamicMethod class) to generate code. First, we inspect the IL generated for the ReadPointer method:

```
.method public hidebysig static void ReadPointer(
uint8[] data, int32 offset, [out] valuetype TcpHeader& header) cil managed
{
  .maxstack 2
  .locals init ([0] uint8& pinned pData)
  ldarg.0
  ldarg.1
  ldelema uint8
  stloc.0
  ldarg.2
  ldloc.0
  conv.i
  ldobj TcpHeader
  stobj TcpHeader
  ldc.i4.0
  conv.u
  stloc.0
  ret
}
```

Now all we have to do is emit IL where TcpHeader is replaced by the generic type argument. In fact, thanks to the excellent *ReflectionEmitLanguage* plugin for .NET Reflector (available at http://reflectoraddins.codeplex. com/wikipage?title=ReflectionEmitLanguage), which converts methods to the Reflection.Emit API calls required to generate them, we don't even have to write the code by hand—although it admittedly required a few minor fixes:

```
static class DelegateHolder<T>
{
  public static ReadDelegate<T>Value;
  public static ReadDelegate<T>CreateDelegate() {
    DynamicMethod dm=new DynamicMethod("Read", null,
      new Type[] { typeof(byte[]), typeof(int), typeof(T).MakeByRefType() },
      Assembly.GetExecutingAssembly().ManifestModule);
    dm.DefineParameter(1, ParameterAttributes.None, "data");
    dm.DefineParameter(2, ParameterAttributes.None, "offset");
    dm.DefineParameter(3, ParameterAttributes.Out, "value");
    ILGenerator generator=dm.GetILGenerator();
```

```
        generator.DeclareLocal(typeof(byte).MakePointerType(), pinned: true);
        generator.Emit(OpCodes.Ldarg_0);
        generator.Emit(OpCodes.Ldarg_1);
        generator.Emit(OpCodes.Ldelema, typeof(byte));
        generator.Emit(OpCodes.Stloc_0);
        generator.Emit(OpCodes.Ldarg_2);
        generator.Emit(OpCodes.Ldloc_0);
        generator.Emit(OpCodes.Conv_I);
        generator.Emit(OpCodes.Ldobj, typeof(T));
        generator.Emit(OpCodes.Stobj, typeof(T));
        generator.Emit(OpCodes.Ldc_I4_0);
        generator.Emit(OpCodes.Conv_U);
        generator.Emit(OpCodes.Stloc_0);
        generator.Emit(OpCodes.Ret);
        Value=(ReadDelegate<T>)dm.CreateDelegate(typeof(ReadDelegate<T>));
        return Value;
    }
}
public static void ReadPointerLCG<T>(byte[] data, int offset, out T value)
{
    ReadDelegate<T> del=DelegateHolder<T>.Value;
    if (del == null) {
        del=DelegateHolder<T>.CreateDelegate();
    }
    del(data, offset, out value);
}
```

This version takes 1.05ms for 1,000,000 packets, which is more than twice as long as ReadPointer, but still more than two orders of magnitude faster than the original Reflection-based approach—another win for code generation. (The performance loss compared to ReadPointer is due the need to fetch the delegate from a static field, check for null, and invoke the method through a delegate.)

Summary

However different, the optimization tips and techniques discussed in this chapter are critical for implementing high-performance CPU-bound algorithms and designing the architecture of complex systems. By making sure your code takes advantage of the built-in JIT optimizations as well as any specific instructions the processor has to offer, by reducing as much as possible the startup times of your client applications, and by steering clear of expensive CLR mechanisms such as Reflection and exceptions, you will assuredly squeeze every bit of performance from your managed software.

In the next and final chapter we will discuss the performance characteristics of Web applications, primarily in the ASP.NET domain, and introduce specific optimizations that are relevant only to Web servers.

■ ■ ■

CHAPTER 11

Web Application Performance

Web applications are designed to handle hundreds and even thousands of requests per second. To build such applications successfully, it is important to identify potential performance bottlenecks and to do everything you can to prevent them from occurring. But handling and preventing bottlenecks in ASP.NET applications is not confined to your code alone. From the time a web request reaches the server to the time it reaches your application's code, it passes through an HTTP pipeline and then through the IIS pipeline, only to reach another pipeline, the ASP.NET's pipeline, and only then does it reach your code. And when you finish handling the request, the response is sent down those pipelines until it is eventually received by the client's machine. Every one of these pipelines is a potential bottleneck, so improving the performance of ASP.NET applications actually means improving both *your* code and the performance of the pipeline.

When discussing ways to improve the performance of ASP.NET applications, one has to look further than just the application itself, and examine the way various parts that make a web application affect its overall performance. The overall performance of a web application is comprised of the following:

- The application's code

- The ASP.NET environment

- The hosting environment (in most cases, IIS)

- The network

- The client-side (not discussed in this book)

In this chapter we will briefly discuss tools for performance testing of web applications and explore various ways, from each of the above mentioned subjects, which can help us improve the overall performance of our web application. Toward the end of the chapter, we will discuss the need and implications of scaling web applications and how to avoid known pitfalls when scaling.

Testing the Performance of Web Applications

Before you start making changes to your web application, you need to know if your application is performing well or not—is it up to the requirements specified in the SLA (service level agreement)? Does it behave differently under load? Are there any general issues which can be improved? To know all this and more we need to use testing and monitoring tools that can help us identify pitfalls and bottlenecks in our web application.

In Chapter 2 we discussed some general-purpose analysis tools to detect performance issues in code, such as the Visual Studio and ANTS profilers, but there are additional tools that can assist you in testing, measuring, and investigating the "web" part of your application.

This is just a brief introduction to the world of web application performance testing. For a more thorough description and guidance on how to plan, execute, and analyze web application performance testing, you can refer to the "Performance Testing Guidance for Web Applications" MSDN article (`http://msdn.microsoft.com/library/bb924375`).

Visual Studio Web Performance Test and Load Test

Among the testing features that are available in Visual Studio Ultimate is the Web Performance test, which enables you to evaluate the response time and throughput of a web application. With the Web Performance test, you can record the HTTP requests and responses which are generated when browsing a web application, as shown in Figure 11-1. (This is supported directly in Internet Explorer only.)

Figure 11-1. *Recording a web application with Web Test Recorder*

Once a recording has taken place, you can use that recording to test the performance of the web application, as well as test its correctness, by matching the new responses with the previously recorded responses.

Web Performance tests allow you to customize the flow of the test. You can change the order of requests and add new requests of your own, insert loops and conditions to the flow, change the headers and content of requests, add validation rules for responses, and even customize the entire test flow by converting it to code and editing the generated code.

Using the Web Performance test on its own has its benefits, but in order to test the performance of your web application under stress, use the Web Performance test in conjunction with Visual Studio's Load Test feature. This Visual Studio feature enables you to simulate loads on the system where multiple users are calling it concurrently, performing different operations on it, and to test how the system behaves during that time, by collecting various performance information such as performance counters and event logs.

▦ **Caution**   It is advisable that you do not load test a public web site, only your own web sites and web applications. Load testing a public web site may be interpreted as a denial-of-service (DOS) attack, causing your machine or even your local network to be banned from accessing the web site.

Combining Load Test with the recordings of the Web Performance test, we can simulate dozens and even hundreds of users, concurrently accessing our web application, simulating calls to various pages with different parameters in each request.

To properly simulate hundreds of users, it is advisable that you use *test agents*. Test agents are machines that receive testing instructions from a controller machine, perform the required tests, and send the results back to the controller. The use of test agents helps in reducing the stress on the testing machine (not the machine being tested), because a single machine simulating hundreds of users may suffer from performance degradation, causing the test to produce faulty results.

During load test we can monitor various performance counters that can point out how our application behaves under stress, for example by checking if requests are queued in ASP.NET, if the duration of a request is increasing over time, and if requests are getting timed out because of faulty configuration.

By running load tests with various scenarios, such as different number of concurrent users or different types of networks (slow/fast), we can learn a lot on how our web application works under stress, and from the recorded data derive conclusions on ways we can improve its overall performance.

HTTP Monitoring Tools

Network monitoring tools that can sniff HTTP communication, such as Wireshark, NetMon, HTTP Analyzer, and Fiddler, can assist us in identifying issues with the HTTP requests and responses send to and from our web application. With the help of monitoring tools, we can verify various issues which can affect the performance of our web application. For example:

- **Properly using the browser's cache**. By looking at the HTTP traffic, we can identify which responses are returned without caching headers, and whether requests are sent with the proper "match" headers when the requested content has already been cached.

- **Number and size of messages**. Monitoring tools show each request and response, the time it took for each message to be received, and the size of each message, allowing you to track down requests that are sent too often, large requests and responses, and requests that are taking too long to process.

- **Applying compression**. By viewing the requests and responses, you can verify that requests are being sent with the *Accept-Encoding* header to enable GZip compression, and that your web server returns a compressed response accordingly.

- **Synchronized communication**. Some HTTP monitoring tools can show a timeline of the requests and which process generated which request, so we can verify whether our client application is able to send multiple requests at once, or are requests being synchronized due to lack of outgoing connections. For example, you can use this feature to detect how many concurrent connections a browser can open to a specific server, or check if your .NET client application is using the default two connections restriction enforced by `System.Net.ServicePointManager`.

Some tools, such as Fiddler, can also export the recorded traffic as a Visual Studio Web Performance test, so you can use Web Test and Load Test to test web applications that are called from client applications and browsers other than Internet Explorer. For example, you can monitor HTTP-based WCF calls from a .NET client application, export them as a Web Test, and use the Load Test to stress test your WCF service.

Web Analyzing Tools

Another set of tools that can be used to identify issues with web applications are web analysis tools, such as Yahoo!'s YSlow and Google's Page Speed. Web analyzing tools do more than just analyze the traffic itself, looking for missing caching headers and non-compressed responses. They analyze the HTML page itself to detect problems that can affect the performance of loading and rendering pages, such as:

- Large HTML structures that can affect the rendering time.

- HTML, CSS, and JavaScript content that can be shrunk in size by using minifications techniques.

- Large images that can be scaled down to reduce their size and match their dimensions in the HTML page.

- JavaScript code that can be executed after the page is loaded instead of during, to allow pages to load faster.

Improving Web Performance on the Server

There are many ways to improve the performance of code in ASP.NET applications. Some improvements can be made using techniques that are valid for both ASP.NET applications and desktop applications, such as using threads or Tasks for non-dependent asynchronous operations, but there are also some improvements that relate to the way you write your ASP.NET code, whether it is a WebForm's code-behind, or an ASP.NET MVC Controller. These changes, however small, can help utilize your server better, allowing the application to run faster, and handle more concurrent requests.

Cache Commonly Used Objects

The processing of a request in a web application often requires the use of fetched data, usually from a remote location such as a database, or a web service. These data lookups are expensive operations, often causing latency in response time. Instead of fetching the data for each operation, that data can be pre-fetched once, and stored in-memory, in some sort of a caching mechanism. New requests that will come in after the data was fetched can use the cached data instead of fetching it again from its original source. The caching paradigm is often described as:

1. If the data is already cached, use it.

2. Else:

    a. Fetch the data.

    b. Store it in the cache.

    c. Use it.

■ **Caution**   Since several requests can access the same cached object at any given time, causing the same object be referenced from multiple threads, it is expected that an update to a cached object will be done responsibly, whether by treating it as immutable (changes to a cached object will require cloning it, making the changes on the new copy, and then updating the cache with the cloned object), or by using locking mechanisms to make sure it is not being updated by other threads.

Many developers use ASP.NET's Application state collection as a sort of caching mechanism, because it provides an in-memory caching store, accessible for all users and sessions. Using the Application collection is quite simple:

```
Application["listOfCountries"]=countries; // Store a value in the collection
countries=(IEnumerable<string>)Application["listOfCountries"]; // Get the value back
```

When using the Application collection, the resources which are stored in memory and accumulated over time can eventually fill the server memory, causing the ASP.NET application to start using paged memory from disk, or even fail due to lack of memory. Therefore, ASP.NET provides a special caching mechanism, which provides some sort of management over cached items, freeing unused items when memory is lacking.

ASP.NET caching, accessible through the Cache class, provides an extensive caching mechanism, which in addition to storing resources also allows you to:

- Define an expiration for a cached object, either by specified a TimeSpan or a fixed DateTime. Once the allotted life time of the cached object expires, the object will automatically be removed from the cache.

- Define priority for cached objects. When there is a memory lack and objects need to be freed, the priority can assist the cache mechanism to decide which objects are less "important."

- Define validity for a cached object by adding dependencies, such as an SQL dependency. For example, if the cached object is a result of an SQL query, an SQL dependency can be set, so changes in the database that affects the results returned from the query will invalidate the cached object.

- Attach callbacks to cached objects, so when an object is being removed from the cache, the callback is invoked. Using callbacks can assist in retrieving updated resource information when expiration or invalidation occurs in the cache.

Adding items to the cache is as simple as adding items to a dictionary:

```
Cache["listOfCountries"]=listOfCountries;
```

When adding an item to the cache using the above code, the cached item will have the default priority of Normal and will not use any expiration or dependency checks. For example, to add an item to the cache with a sliding expiration, use the Insert method:

```
Cache.Insert("products", productsList,
  Cache.NoAbsoluteExpiration, TimeSpan.FromMinutes(60), dependencies: null);
```

▨ **Note**   The Cache class also provides the Add method. Unlike the Insert method, the Add method will throw an exception if the cache already contains an item with the same key parameter.

The cache access paradigm, using ASP.NET's Cache class is usually implemented as follows:

```
object retrievedObject=null;

retrievedObject=Cache["theKey"];
if (retrievedObject == null) {
  //Lookup the data somewhere (database, web service, etc.)
  object originalData=null;
  ...
```

```
  //Store the newly retrieved data in the cache
  Cache["theKey"]=originalData;
  retrievedObject=originalData;
}
//Use the retrieved object (either from the cache or the one that was just cached)
...
```

You'll notice that the first line of code attempts to retrieve the object from the cache, without first checking whether it exists in the cache. This is because objects can be removed from the cache at any time by other requests or by the cache mechanism itself, so an item can be removed from the cache between checking and retrieval.

Using Asynchronous Pages, Modules, and Controllers

When IIS passes a request to ASP.NET, the request is queued to the thread pool, and a worker thread is assigned to handle the request whether it is a request for a simple HTTP handler, a page within an ASP.NET WebForm application, or a controller within an ASP.NET MVC application.

Since the number of worker threads in the thread pool is limited (defined by the value set for processModel►maxWorkerThreads section in the web.config), then that implies ASP.NET is also limited by the number of threads, or requests, it can execute simultaneously.

The thread limit is usually high enough to support small-to-medium web applications that need to handle only several dozens of concurrent requests. However, if your web application is required to handle hundreds of requests concurrently, you should keep reading this section.

The limit on the number of concurrently executing requests encourages developers to try to minimize the execution time of requests, but what happens when the execution of a request depends on some other I/O operation, such as calling a web service, or waiting for a database operation to complete? In this case the execution time of the requests is highly dependent on the time it takes to get the information back from the remote process, and during that time the worker thread attached to the request is occupied and cannot be freed for another request.

Eventually, when the number of currently executing requests exceeds the limit of the thread pool, new requests will be placed in a special waiting queue. When the number of queued requests exceeds the limit of the queue, incoming requests will fail, returning an HTTP 503 response ("service unavailable").

▨ **Note** The limitation of the thread pool and requests queue is defined for ASP.NET applications in the processModel section of the web.config file, and is controlled partially by the processModel►autoConfig attribute.

In modern web applications, where I/O operations are an inevitable part of our system's design (calling web services, querying databases, reading from network file storages, etc.), this behavior often leads to having many running threads waiting on I/O and only several threads actually performing CPU consuming tasks. This often leads to a low utilization of the server's CPU, which cannot be used by other requests since there are no more free threads for the incoming requests.

In web applications where many requests start by fetching data from web services or databases, it is common to see low CPU utilization even with high user load. You can use performance counters to check the CPU utilization of your web application, by checking the Processor\% CPU Utilization counter in conjunction with the ASP.NET Applications\Requests/Sec and ASP.NET\Requests Queued counters.

If some of your requests are executing lengthy I/O operations, then there is no need to hold the worker thread until completion. With ASP.NET you can write asynchronous pages, controllers, handlers, and modules, which enable you to return worker threads back to the thread pool while your code is waiting for an I/O operation to complete, and once completed, to grab a worker thread from the pool to complete the execution of the request. From the end-user's point of view, the page will still seem to take some time to load, since the server is holding the request until the processing is complete and the response is ready to be sent back.

By changing I/O-bound requests to use asynchronous processing instead of synchronous processing, you can increase the number of worker threads available for CPU-intensive requests, enabling your server to better utilize its CPU(s) and prevent requests from being queued.

Creating an Asynchronous Page

If you have an ASP.NET Web Forms application, and you wish to create an async page, first you will need to mark the page as async:

```
<%@ Page Async="true" ...
```

Once marked as async, create a new PageAsyncTask object and pass it the delegates for the begin, end, and timeout methods. After creating the PageAsyncTask object, call the Page.RegisterAsyncTask method to start the asynchronous operation.

The following code shows how to start a lengthy SQL query using the PageAsyncTask:

```
public partial class MyAsyncPage : System.Web.UI.Page {
  private SqlConnection _sqlConnection;
  private SqlCommand _sqlCommand;
  private SqlDataReader _sqlReader;

  IAsyncResult BeginAsyncOp(object sender, EventArgs e, AsyncCallback cb, object state) {
    //This part of the code will execute in the original worker thread,
    //so do not perform any lengthy operations in this method
    _sqlCommand=CreateSqlCommand(_sqlConnection);
    return _sqlCommand.BeginExecuteReader(cb, state);
  }
  void EndAsyncOp(IAsyncResult asyncResult) {
    _sqlReader=_sqlCommand.EndExecuteReader(asyncResult);
    //Read the data and build the page's content
    ...
  }
  void TimeoutAsyncOp(IAsyncResult asyncResult) {
    _sqlReader=_sqlCommand.EndExecuteReader(asyncResult);
    //Read the data and build the page's content
    ...
  }

  public override void Dispose() {
    if (_sqlConnection !=null) {
      _sqlConnection.Close();
    }
    base.Dispose();
  }

  protected void btnClick_Click(object sender, EventArgs e) {
    PageAsyncTask task=new PageAsyncTask(
      new BeginEventHandler(BeginAsyncOp),
      new EndEventHandler(EndAsyncOp),
      new EndEventHandler(TimeoutAsyncOp),
      state:null);
    RegisterAsyncTask(task);
  }
}
```

Another way of creating async pages is by using completion events, such as the ones created when using web services or WCF services-generated proxies:

```
public partial class MyAsyncPage2 : System.Web.UI.Page {
  protected void btnGetData_Click(object sender, EventArgs e) {
    Services.MyService serviceProxy = new Services.MyService();
    //Attach to the service's xxCompleted event
    serviceProxy.GetDataCompleted += new
      Services.GetDataCompletedEventHandler(GetData_Completed);
    //Use the Async service call which executes on an I/O thread
    serviceProxy.GetDataAsync();
  }
  void GetData_Completed (object sender, Services. GetDataCompletedEventArgs e) {
    //Extract the result from the event args and build the page's content
  }
}
```

In the above example the page is also marked as Async, as the first example, but there is no need to create the PageAsyncTask object, since the page automatically receives notification when the xxAsync method is called, and after the xxCompleted event is fired.

■ **Note**   When setting the page to async, ASP.NET changes the page to implement the IHttpAsyncHandler instead of the synchronous IHttpHandler. If you wish to create your own asynchronous generic HTTP handler, create a generic HTTP handler class which implements the IHttpAsyncHandler interface.

Creating an Asynchronous Controller

Controller classes in ASP.NET MVC can also be created as asynchronous controllers, if they perform lengthy I/O operations. To create an asynchronous controller you will need to perform these steps:

1. Create a controller class that inherits from the AsyncController type.

2. Implement a set of action methods for each async operation according to the following convention, where *xx* is the name of the action: xxAsync and xxCompleted.

3. In the xxAsync method, call the AsyncManager.OutstandingOperations.Increment method with the number of asynchronous operations you are about to perform.

4. In the code which executes during the return of the async operation, call the AsyncManager.OutstandingOperations.Decrement method to notify the operation has completed.

For example, the following code shows a controller with an asynchronous action named *Index*, which calls a service that returns the data for the view:

```
public class MyController : AsyncController {
  public void IndexAsync() {
    //Notify the AsyncManager there is going to be only one Async operation
    AsyncManager.OutstandingOperations.Increment();
    MyService serviceProxy = new MyService();

    //Register to the completed event
```

```
  serviceProxy.GetDataCompleted+= (sender, e) =>{
    AsyncManager.Parameters["result"]=e.Value;
    AsyncManager.OutstandingOperations.Decrement();
  };
  serviceProxy.GetHeadlinesAsync();
}
public ActionResult IndexCompleted(MyData result) {
  return View("Index", new MyViewModel { TheData=result });
}
}
```

Tweaking the ASP.NET Environment

In addition to our code, every incoming request and outgoing response has to go through ASP.NET's
components. Some of ASP.NET's mechanisms were created to serve the developer's needs, such as the ViewState
mechanism, but can affect the overall performance of our application. When fine-tuning ASP.NET applications
for performance, it is advisable to change the default behavior of some of these mechanisms, although changing
them may sometimes require changing the way your application code is constructed.

Turn Off ASP.NET Tracing and Debugging

ASP.NET Tracing enables developers to view diagnostic information for requested pages, such as execution time
and path, session state, and HTTP headers list.

Although tracing is a great feature and provides added value when developing and debugging ASP.NET
applications, it has some effects on the overall performance of the application, due to the tracing mechanism
and the collection of data which is performed on each request. Therefore, if you have enabled tracing during
development, turn it off before deploying your web application to the production environment, by changing the
trace settings in the web.config:

```
<configuration>
  <system.web>
    <trace enabled="false"/>
  </system.web>
</configuration>
```

▓ **Note**   The default value of trace, if not specified otherwise in the web.config, is disabled (enabled="false"),
so removing the trace settings from the web.config file will also disable it.

When creating new ASP.NET web applications, one of the things automatically added to the application's
web.config file is the system.web➤compilation configuration section with the debug attribute set to true:

```
<configuration>
  <system.web>
    <compilation debug="true" targetFramework="4.5" />
  </system.web>
</configuration>
```

■ **Note**   This is the default behavior when creating ASP.NET web applications in Visual Studio 2012 or 2010. In prior versions of Visual Studio the default behavior was to set the debug setting to `false`, and when the developer first tried to debug the application, a dialog appeared asking permission to change the setting to `true`.

The issue with this setting is that developers often neglect to change the setting from `true` to `false` when they deploy the application to production, or even do it intentionally to get more detailed exception information. In fact, keeping this setting can lead to several performance problems:

- Scripts that are downloaded using the WebResources.axd handler, for example when using validation controls in pages, will not be cached by the browser. When setting the debug flag to `false`, responses from this handler will be returned with caching headers, allowing browsers to cache the response for future visits.

- Requests will not timeout when debug is set to `true`. Although this is very convenient when debugging the code, this behavior is less desired in production environments when such requests can lead to the server not being able to handle other incoming requests, or even cause extensive CPU usage, increased memory consumption and other resource allocation issues.

- Setting the debug flag to false will enable ASP.NET to define timeouts for requests according to the `httpRuntime`➤`executionTimeout` configuration settings (the default value is 110 seconds).

- JIT optimizations will not be applied to the code when running with debug = true. JIT optimizations are one of the most important advantages of .NET and can efficiently improve the performance of your ASP.NET application without requiring you changing your code. Setting `debug` to `false` will allow the JIT compiler to perform its deeds, making your application perform faster and more efficient.

- The compilation process does not use batch compilations when using debug = true. Without batch compilation an assembly will be created for each page and user control, causing the web application to load dozens and even hundreds of assemblies during runtime; loading that many assemblies may cause future memory exceptions due to fragmented address space. When the debug mode is set to false, batch compilation is used, generating a single assembly for the user controls, and several assemblies for the pages (pages are grouped to assemblies according to their use of user controls).

Changing this setting is very easy: either remove the debug attribute entirely from the configuration, or set it to false:

```
<configuration>
  <system.web>
    <compilation debug="false" targetFramework="4.5" />
  </system.web>
</configuration>
```

In case you fear forgetting to change this setting when deploying applications to production servers, you can force *all* ASP.NET applications in a server to ignore the debug setting by adding the following configuration in the server's machine.config file:

```
<configuration>
  <system.web>
    <deployment retail="true"/>
  </system.web>
</configuration>
```

Disable View State

View state is the technique used in ASP.NET Web Forms applications to persist a page's state into the rendered HTML output (ASP.NET MVC applications do not use this mechanism). View state is used to allow ASP.NET to keep the state of a page between postbacks performed by the user. The view state data is stored in the HTML output by serializing the state, encrypting it (not set by default), encoding it to a Base64 string, and storing it in a hidden field. When the user posts back the page, the content is decoded, and then deserialized back to the view state dictionary. Many server controls use the view state to persist their own state, for example storing their property values in the view state.

Although very useful and powerful, this mechanism generates a payload that, when placed in the page as a Base64 string, can increase the size of the response by a magnitude. For example, a page containing a single GridView with paging, bounded to a list of 800 customers, will generate an output HTML 17 KB in size, out of which 6 KB is the view state field—this is because `GridView` controls store their data source in the view state. In addition, using view state requires serializing and deserializing the view state on each request, which adds additional overhead to the processing of the page.

■ **Tip** The payload created by using view state is usually not noticeable by clients that access a web server in their own local area network. This is because LANs are usually very fast and able to transfer very large pages in a matter of milliseconds (an optimal 1Gb LAN can reach a throughput of ~40–100 MB/s, depending on hardware). However, the payload of the view state is most notable when using slow wide area networks, such as the Internet.

If you do not require the use of the view state, it is advisable to disable it. View state can be disabled for the entire application by disabling it in the web.config file:

```
<system.web>
  <pages enableViewState="false"/>
</system.web>
```

If you don't wish to disable view state for the entire application, it can also be disabled for a single page and all of its controls:

```
<%@ Page EnableViewState="false" ... %>
```

You can also disable view state per control:

```
<asp:GridView ID="gdvCustomers" runat="server" DataSourceID="mySqlDataSource"
              AllowPaging="True" EnableViewState="false"/>
```

Prior to ASP.NET 4, disabling the view state in the page made it impossible to re-enable it for specific controls in the page. As of ASP.NET 4, a new approach was added to allow disabling view state on a page, but re-enabling it for specific controls. This is achieved in ASP.NET 4 by using the ViewStateMode property. For example, the following code disables the view state for the entire page, excluding the GridView control:

```
<%@ Page EnableViewState = "true" ViewStateMode = "Disabled" ... %>

<asp:GridView ID = "gdvCustomers" runat = "server" DataSourceID = "mySqlDataSource"
            AllowPaging = "True" ViewStateMode = "Enabled"/>
```

■ **Caution**   Disabling the view state by setting the EnableViewState to false will override any setting done to the ViewStateMode. Therefore, if you wish to use the ViewStateMode, make sure EnableViewState is set to true or omitted (the default value is true).

Server-Side Output Cache

Although ASP.NET pages are considered dynamic in content, you often end up in scenarios where the dynamic content of a page does not necessarily change over time. For example, a page can receive the ID of a product and return an HTML content describing that product. The page itself is dynamic, because it can return different HTML content for different products, but the product page for a specific product does not change that often, at least not until the product details themselves change in the database.

Continuing our product example, to prevent our page from requerying the database every time a product is requested, we may want to cache that product information in a local cache so we can access it faster, but still we will need to render the HTML page every time. Instead of caching the data we need, ASP.NET offers a different caching mechanism, the ASP.NET Output Cache, which caches the outputted HTML itself.

By using output cache, ASP.NET can cache the rendered HTML so subsequent requests will automatically receive the rendered HTML without needing to execute our page's code. Output cache is supported in ASP.NET Web Forms for caching pages, as well as in ASP.NET MVC for caching controller actions.

For example, the following code uses output cache to cache the view returned by an ASP.NET MVC controller's action for 30 seconds:

```
public class ProductController : Controller {
  [OutputCache(Duration = 30)]
  public ActionResult Index() {
    return View();
  }
}
```

If the index action in the above example received an ID parameter and returned a view displaying specific product information, we would need to cache several versions of the output, according to the different IDs the action receives. Output cache, therefore, supports not just a single caching of the output, but also supports caching different outputs of the same action according to the parameters passed to that action. The following code shows how to alter the action to cache outputs according to an ID parameter passed to the method:

```
public class ProductController : Controller {
  [OutputCache(Duration = 30, VaryByParam = "id")]
  public ActionResult Index(int id) {
    //Retrieve the matching product and set the model accordingly
    ...
    return View();
  }
}
```

▨ **Note** In addition to varying by query string parameters, output cache can also vary the cached output by the request's HTTP headers, such as the Accept-Encoding and Accept-Language header. For example, if your action returns content in different languages according to the Accept-Language HTTP header, you can set the output cache to vary by that header, creating a different cached version of the output for each requested language.

If you have the same caching settings for different pages or actions, you can create a caching profile, and use that profile instead of repeating the caching settings over and over again. Caching profiles are created in the web. config, under the system.web➤caching section. For example, the following configuration declares a caching profile which we want to use in several pages:

```
<system.web>
  <caching>
    <outputCacheSettings>
      <outputCacheProfiles>
        <add name="CacheFor30Seconds" duration="30" varyByParam="id"/>
      </outputCacheProfiles>
    </outputCacheSettings>
  </caching>
</system.web>
```

Now the profile can be used for our Index action, instead of repeating the duration and parameter:

```
public class ProductController : Controller {
  [OutputCache(CacheProfile="CacheFor30Seconds")]
  public ActionResult Index(int id) {
    //Retrieve the matching product and set the model
    ...
    return View();
  }
}
```

We can also use the same caching profile in an ASP.NET web form, by using the OutputCache directive:

```
<%@ OutputCache CacheProfile="CacheEntityFor30Seconds" %>
```

▨ **Note** By default, the ASP.NET output cache mechanism keeps the cached content in the server's memory. As of ASP.NET 4, you can create your own output cache provider to be used instead of the default one. For example, you can write your own custom provider which stores the output cache to disk.

Pre-Compiling ASP.NET Applications

When compiling an ASP.NET Web application project, a single assembly is created to hold all application's code. However, web pages (.aspx) and user controls (.ascx) are not compiled, and deployed as-is to the server. The first time the web application starts (upon first request), ASP.NET dynamically compiles the web pages and user controls, and places the compiled files in the ASP.NET Temporary Files folder. This dynamic compilation increases the response time of first requests, causing users to experience a slow-loading web site.

To resolve this issue, web applications can be pre-compiled, including all code, pages, and user controls, by using the ASP.NET compilation tool (Aspnet_compiler.exe). Running the ASP.NET compilation tool in production servers can reduce the delay users experience on first requests. To run the tool, follow these steps:

1. Open a command prompt in your production server.

2. Navigate to the *%windir%\Microsoft.NET* folder

3. Navigate to either the *Framework* or *Framework64* folder, according to the whether the web application's application pool is configured to support 32-bit applications or not (for 32-bit operating systems, the *Framework* folder is the only option).

4. Navigate to the framework version's folder, according to the .NET framework version used by the application pool (*v2.0.50727* or *v4.0.30319*).

5. Enter the following command to start the compilation (replace *WebApplicationName* with the virtual path of your application):

    ```
    Aspnet_compiler.exe -v /WebApplicationName
    ```

Fine-Tuning the ASP.NET Process Model

When a call is made to an ASP.NET application, ASP.NET uses a worker thread to handle the request. Sometimes, the code in our application can itself create a new thread, for example when calling out to a service, thus reducing the number of free threads in the thread pool.

To prevent exhaustion of the thread pool, ASP.NET automatically performs several adjustments to the thread pool, and applies several limitations on the number of requests that can execute at any given by. These settings are controlled from three main configuration sections—the system.web➤processModel section, the system.web➤httpRuntime section, and the system.net➤connectionManagement section.

■ **Note** The httpRuntime and connectionManagement sections can be set from within the application's web. config file. The processModel section, however, can only be changed in the *machine.config* file.

The processModel section controls thread pool limitations such as minimum and maximum number of worker threads, while the httpRuntime section defines limitations related to available threads, such as the minimum number of available threads that must exist in order to keep processing incoming requests. The connectionManagement section controls the maximum number of outgoing HTTP connections per address.

All of the settings have default values, however, since some of these values are set a bit low, ASP.NET includes another setting, the autoConfig setting, which tweaks some of the settings to achieve optimal performance. This setting, which is part of the processModel configuration section exists since ASP.NET 2.0, and is automatically set to true.

The autoConfig setting controls the following settings (the default values below were obtained from the Microsoft Knowledge Base article KB821268 at http://support.microsoft.com/?id=821268):

*   processModel➤maxWorkerThreads. Changes the maximum amount of worker threads in the thread pool from 20× the number of cores to 100× the number of cores.

*   processModel➤maxIoThreads. Changes the maximum amount of I/O threads in the thread pool from 20× the number of cores to 100× the number of cores.

*   httpRuntime➤minFreeThreads. Changes the minimum number of available threads that are required to allow the execution of new requests from 8 to 88× the number of cores.

- `httpRuntime➤minLocalFreeThreads`. Changes the minimum number of available threads that are required to allow the execution of new local requests (from the local host) from 4 to 76× the number of cores.

- `connectionManagement➤maxConnections`. Changes the maximum number of concurrent connections from 10 to 12× the number of cores.

Although the above defaults were set in order to achieve optimized performance, there may be cases when you will need to change them, in order to achieve better performance, depending on the scenario you encounter with your web application. For example, if your application calls out to services, you may need to increase the number of maximum concurrent connections to allow more requests to connect to backend services at the same time. The following configuration shows how to increase the number of maximum connection:

```
<configuration>
  <system.net>
    <connectionManagement>
      <add address = "*" maxconnection = "200" />
    </connectionManagement>
  </system.net>
</configuration>
```

In other scenarios, for example when web applications tend to get many requests upon starting, or have a sudden burst of requests, you may need to change the minimum number of worker threads in the thread pool (the value you specify is multiplied at runtime by the number of cores on the machine). To perform this change, apply the following configuration in the machine.config file:

```
<configuration>
  <system.web>
    <processModel autoConfig = "true" minWorkerThreads = "10"/>
  </system.web>
</configuration>
```

Before you rush to increase the size of minimum and maximum threads, consider the side effects this change may have on your application: if you allow too many requests to run concurrently, this may lead to excessive CPU usage and high memory consumption, which can eventually crash your web application. Therefore, after changing these settings, you must perform load test to verify the machine can sustain that many requests.

Configuring IIS

As our web application's hosting environment, IIS has some influence on its overall performance, for example, the smaller the IIS pipeline is, less code will be executed on each request. There are mechanisms in IIS which can be used to increase our application's performance regarding latency and throughput, as well as some mechanisms which, when tuned properly, can improve the overall performance of our application.

Output Caching

We already saw that ASP.NET provides its own mechanism for output caching, so why does IIS need yet another mechanism for output caching? The answer is quite simple: there are other content types we want to cache, not only ASP.NET pages. For example, we may want to cache a set of static image files that are frequently requested, or the output of a custom HTTP handler. For that purpose, we can use the output cache provided by IIS.

IIS has two types of output cache mechanisms: user-mode cache and kernel-mode cache.

User-Mode Cache

Just like ASP.NET, IIS is capable of caching responses in-memory, so subsequent requests are answered automatically from memory without accessing static files from disk, or invoking server-side code.

To configure the output cache for your web application, open the IIS Manager application, select your web application, open the *Output Caching* feature. Once opened, click the *Add...* link from the *Actions* pane to add a new cache rule, or select an existing rule to edit it.

To create a new user-mode cache rule, add a new rule, type the file name extension you wish to cache, and check the *User-mode caching* checkbox in the *Add Cache Rule* dialog, as shown in Figure 11-2.

Figure 11-2. *The Add Cache Rule dialog*

Once you checked the checkbox, you can select when the cached item will be removed from memory, such as after the file has been updated or after some time has passed since the content was first cached. File changes is more suitable for static files, whereas time interval is more suitable for dynamic content. By pressing the *Advanced* button you can also control how the cache will store different versions of the output (options are according to query string or HTTP headers).

Once you add a caching rule, its configuration will be stored in your application's web.config file, under the `system.webServer`➤caching section. For example, setting the rule to cache .aspx pages, causes them to expire after 30 minutes, and varies the output by the Accept-Language HTTP header will generate the following configuration:

```
<system.webServer>
  <caching>
    <profiles>
      <add extension=".aspx" policy="CacheForTimePeriod" kernelCachePolicy="DontCache"
          duration="00:00:30" varyByHeaders="Accept-Language" />
    </profiles>
  </caching>
</system.webServer>
```

Kernel-Mode Cache

Unlike user-mode cache, which stores the cached content in the IIS's worker process memory, kernel-mode caching stored cached content in the HTTP.sys kernel-mode driver. Using kernel-mode caching provides faster response time, however it is not always supported. For example, kernel-mode caching cannot be used when the request contains a query string, or when the request is not an anonymous request.

Setting up a cache rule for kernel-mode is done in a similar manner to user-mode caching. In the rules dialog, check the *Kernel-mode caching* checkbox, and then select the caching monitoring setting you wish to use.

You can use both kernel-mode and user-mode caching in the same rule. When both modes are used, kernel-mode caching is attempted first. If not successful, for example, when the request contains a query string, the user-mode caching is applied.

▓ **Tip** When using a time interval for monitoring with both kernel-mode and user-mode set, make sure the time interval is identical in both settings, otherwise the interval for kernel-mode will be used for both.

Application Pool Configuration

Application pools control how IIS creates and maintains the worker processes which eventually host our code. When you install IIS and ASP.NET several application pools are created, according to the .NET framework versions installed on the web server, to which you can add new pools as you install more web applications on the server. When an application pool is created, it has some default settings which control its behavior. For example, every application pool, when created, has a default setting for the idle timeout after which the application pool shuts down.

Understanding the meaning of some of these settings can help you configure the way the application pool works, so it will serve your application's needs more precisely.

Recycling

By changing the recycling settings you can control when the application pool restarts the worker process. For example, you can set that the worker process be recycled every couple of hours, or when it exceeds a certain amount of memory. If your web application consumes a lot of memory over time (for example due to stored objects), increasing the number of recycles can help maintain its overall performance. On the other hand, if your web application performs normally, reducing the number of recycles will prevent loss of state information.

■ **Tip**   You can use the `ASP.NET\Worker Process Restarts` performance counter to check the number of times your application pool recycled itself and the recycling frequency. If you see many recycles with no apparent reason, try to correlate the results with the application's memory consumption and CPU usage to verify it hasn't crossed any thresholds defined in the application pool configuration.

Idle Timeouts

The default setting of an application pool shuts down the pool after 20 minutes of inactivity. If you expect such idle timeframes, for example when all the users go out for lunch, you may want to increase the timeout period, or even cancel it.

Processor Affinity

By default, an application pool is configured to use all the cores available in the server. If you have any special background process running on the server which needs as much CPU time as it can get, you can tweak the affinity of the pool to use only specific cores, freeing the other cores for the background process. Of course this will also require you to set the background process's affinity so it won't compete with the worker process over the same cores.

Web Garden

The default behavior of an application pool is to start one worker process which handles all the requests for the application. If your worker process handles several requests at once, and those requests compete for the same resource by locking on it, you may end up with contention, causing latency in returning responses. For example, if your application is using a proprietary caching mechanism that has locks that prevent concurrent requests from inserting items to the cache, requests will start to synchronize one after the other, causing latencies that will be hard to detect and fix. Although we can sometimes fix the code to use less locking, it is not always possible. Another way of resolving this contention issue is to spin up multiple worker processes, all running the same application, and each handling its own set of requests, thus lowering the contention rate in the application.

Another scenario where running several processes of the same web application is useful, is when you have a 64-bit IIS server running a 32-bit web application. 64-bit servers usually have lots of memory, but 32-bit applications can only use up to 2 GB memory, which often leads up to frequent GC cycles and probably frequent application pool recycles. By spinning two or three worker processes for a 32-bit web application, the application can better utilize the server's available memory and reduce the number of GC cycles and application pool recycles it requires.

In the IIS application pool configuration, you can set the maximum number of worker processes that are permitted to service requests. Increasing the value to more than 1 (which is the default), will spin more worker processes as requests come in, up to the defined maximum. An application pool that has more than one worker process is referred to as a "Web Garden." Each time a connection is made from a client, it is assigned to a worker process which services the requests from that client from now on, allowing the requests from multiple users to be balanced between the processes, hopefully lowering to contention rate.

Note that using web gardens has its disadvantages. Multiple worker processes take up more memory, they prevent the use of the default in-proc session state, and when multiple worker processes are running on the same machine you may find yourself dealing with local resource contention, for example if both worker processes try to use the same log file.

Optimizing the Network

Even if you write code that runs fast and you have a hosting environment that has a high throughput, still one of the more problematic bottlenecks of web applications is the bandwidth of your clients and the amount of data and number of requests that the client passes through the network. There are several techniques that can help reduce the number of requests and the size of the responses, some of them are easy as configuring IIS, while others require some more attention to in the application's code.

Apply HTTP Caching Headers

One of the ways to conserve bandwidth is to make sure that all the content that is not going to change for some time will be cached in the browser. Static content, such as images, scripts, and CSS files are good candidates for browser cache, but also dynamic content such as .aspx and .ashx files can often be cached if the content is not getting updated often.

Setting Cache Headers for Static Content

Static files are usually sent back to the client with two caching headers:

- **ETag**. This HTTP header is set by IIS to contain a calculated hash, based on the last modification date of the requested content. For static content, such as image files and CSS files, IIS sets the ETag according to the last modification date of the file. When subsequent requests are sent with the previously cached ETag value, IIS calculates the ETag for the requested file, and if it does not match the client's ETag, the requested file is sent back. If the ETags match, an HTTP 304 (Not Modified) response is sent back. For subsequent requests, the value of the cached *ETag* is placed in the *If-None-Match* HTTP header.

- **Last-Modified**. IIS sets this HTTP header to the last modification date of the requested file. This is an additional caching header which provides a backup in case IIS's ETag support is disabled. When a subsequent request containing the last modified date is sent to the server, IIS verifies the last modification time of the file and decides whether to respond with the content of the file, if the modification time has changed, or with an HTTP 304 response. For subsequent requests, the value of the cached *Last-Modified* is placed in the *If-Modified-Since* HTTP header.

These caching headers will ensure that content is not sent back to the client if the client already has the recent version, but it still requires that a request will be sent from the client to the server to verify that the content hasn't changed. If you have static files in your application that you know probably won't change in the next couple of weeks, or even months, such as your company's logo or script files that are not going to be changed until the next version of the application, you may want to set caching headers that will allow the client to cache that content and reuse it without verifying with the server if the content has changed every time that content is requested. This behavior can be achieved by using either the Cache-Control HTTP header with max-age or the Expires HTTP header. The different between max-age and Expires is that max-age sets a sliding expiration value while Expires allows you to set a fixed point in time (date + time) when the content will expire. For example, setting the max-age to 3600 will allow the browser to use the cached content for one hour (3600 seconds = 60 minutes = 1 hour) automatically, without sending requests to the server to validate it. Once the content expires, either due to the sliding window expiration or due to the arrival of the fixed expiration time, it is marked as stale. When a new request is made to a stale content, the browser will send a request to the server asking for newer content.

> ■ **Tip**   You can verify no requests are being sent for cached content by using HTTP monitoring tools, such as Fiddler, and inspecting which requests are sent to the server. If you notice a request being sent although it was supposed to be cached, check the response of that request to verify the existence of the max-age / Expires headers.

Using max-age / Expires together with the ETag / Last-Modified ensures that a request that is sent after the content has expired can return with an HTTP 304 response if the content on the server hasn't actually changed. The response in this case will contain a new max-age / Expires HTTP header.

In most browsers, clicking the Refresh button (or pressing F5) will force the browser to refresh the cache by ignoring the max-age / Expires header, and sending requests for cached content even if the content has yet to expire. The requests will still have the If-Modified-Since / If-None-Match headers, if applicable, so that the server can return a 304 response if the content is still up-to-date.

To set max-age, add the following configuration to your web.config file:

```
<system.webServer>
  <staticContent>
    <clientCache cacheControlMode="UseMaxAge" cacheControlMaxAge="0:10:00" />
  </staticContent>
</system.webServer>
```

The above configuration will cause all responses sent for static content to have the Cache-Control HTTP header with the max-age attribute set to 600 seconds.

To use the Expires header, change the `clientCache` element configuration as shown in the following sample:

```
<system.webServer>
  <staticContent>
    <clientCache cacheControlMode="UseExpires" httpExpires="Wed, 11 Jul 2013 6:00:00 GMT"/>
  </staticContent>
</system.webServer>
```

The above configuration will make all static content expire on July 11, 2013, at 6 AM.

If you wish to have different max-age or expiration settings for different content, such as have a fixed expiration for JavaScript files and a 100 day sliding window for images, you can use the location section to apply different configuration to different parts of the application, as shown in the following example:

```
<location path="Scripts">
  <system.webServer>
    <staticContent>
      <clientCache cacheControlMode="UseExpires" httpExpires="Wed, 11 Jul 2013 6:00:00 GMT" />
    </staticContent>
  </system.webServer>
</location>
<location path="Images">
  <system.webServer>
    <staticContent>
      <clientCache cacheControlMode="UseMaxAge" cacheControlMaxAge="100.0:00:0" />
    </staticContent>
  </system.webServer>
</location>
```

■ **Note**   You must use a fully formatted date and time to set the Expires header. Also, according to the HTTP specifications, the Expires header's date must not exceed a year from the current date.

Setting Cache Headers for Dynamic Content

Static files have modification dates that can be used to verify if a cached content has changed or not. Dynamic content, however, does not have a modification date, because every time a dynamic content is requested it is recreated and its modification date is actually the current date, therefore headers such as ETag and Last-Modified are not relevant when dealing with dynamic content.

Having said that, if you look at the content of a dynamic page, you may find a way to express the modification date of that content, or maybe calculate an ETag for it. For example, if a request is sent to retrieve product information from the database, the product table might hold a last update date column that can be used to set the Last-Modified header. If the database table doesn't have a last update column, you can try calculating an MD5 hash from the entity's fields and set the ETag to the result. When a subsequent request is sent to the server, the server can recalculate the MD5 hash for the entity, and if none of the fields has changed, the ETags will be identical and the server can return an HTTP 304 response.

For example, the following code sets the Last-Modified cache header in a dynamic page to the last update date of a product:

```
Response.Cache.SetLastModified(product.LastUpdateDate);
```

If you don't have the last update date, you can set the ETag to an MD5 hash calculated by the entity's properties, as demonstrated in the following code:

```
Response.Cache.SetCacheability(HttpCacheability.ServerAndPrivate);

//Calculate MD5 hash
System.Security.Cryptography.MD5 md5 = System.Security.Cryptography.MD5.Create();
string contentForEtag = entity.PropertyA + entity.NumericProperty.ToString();
byte[] checksum = md5.ComputeHash(System.Text.Encoding.UTF8.GetBytes(contentForEtag));

//Create an ETag string from the hash.
//ETag strings must be surrounded with double quotes, according to the standard
string etag = "\"" + Convert.ToBase64String(checksum, 0, checksum.Length) + "\"";
Response.Cache.SetETag(etag);
```

■ **Note**   The default cacheability mode of requests in ASP.NET prevents the use of ETags. To support ETags, we need to change the cacheability mode to `ServerAndPrivate`, allowing content to be cached on the server-side and on the client-side, but not on shared machines, such as proxies.

When receiving a request containing an ETag, you can compare the calculated ETag with the ETag supplied by the browser, and if they match, respond with a 304 response, as shown in the following code:

```
if (Request.Headers["If-None-Match"] == calculatedETag) {
  Response.Clear();
  Response.StatusCode = (int)System.Net.HttpStatusCode.NotModified;
  Response.End();
}
```

If you have any assumptions on the life span of the dynamic content, you can also apply values to the max-age or Expires headers. For example, if you assume that a discontinued product will not be changed, you can set the page returned for the product to expire in one year, as follow:

```
if (productIsDiscontinued)
  Response.Cache.SetExpires(DateTime.Now.AddYears(1));
```

You can also do the same using the Cache-Control max-age header:

```
if (productIsDiscontinued)
  Response.Cache.SetMaxAge(TimeSpan.FromDays(365));
```

Instead of setting the response's expiration in code, you can specify it in the .aspx file as an output cache directive. For example, if the product information shown in the product page can be cached for 10 minutes (600 seconds) in the client, you can set the product page's output cache directive to the following:

```
<%@ Page ... %>
<%@ OutputCache Duration="600" Location="Client"%>
```

When using the OutputCache directive, the specified duration is output to the response's HTTP headers as both max-age and expires (expires is calculated from the current date).

Turn on IIS Compression

With the exception of multimedia files (sound, images, and videos) and binary files, such as Silverlight and Flash components, most of the content returned from our web server is text-based, such as HTML, CSS, JavaScript, XML, and JSON. By using IIS compression, those textual responses can be shrunk in size, allowing a quicker response with smaller payloads. With the use of IIS compression, responses can be reduced in size up to 50–60 percent of their original size, and sometimes even more than that. IIS supports two types of compression, static and dynamic. To use IIS compression, make sure you first install the static and dynamic compression IIS components.

Static Compression

When using static compression in IIS, compressed content is stored on disk, so for subsequent requests for the resource, the already compressed content will be returned without the need to perform the compression again. By only compressing the content once, you pay with disk space, but reduce CPU usage and latency that is usually the result of using compression.

Static compression is useful for files that don't usually change (therefore "static"), such as CSS files, JavaScript files, but even if the original file changes, IIS will notice the change, and will recompress the updated file.

Note that compression works best for text files (*.htm, *.txt, *.css) and even for binary files, such as Microsoft Office documents (*.doc, *.xsl), but doesn't work that well for files which are already compressed, such as image files (*.jpg, *.png) and compressed Microsoft Office documents (.docx, .xslx).

Dynamic Compression

When using dynamic compression, IIS performs the compression each time a resource is requested, without storing the post-compression content. This means every time the resource is requested it will be compressed before being sent to the client, incurring both CPU usage and some latency due to the compression process. Dynamic compression, therefore, is more suitable for content that changes often, such as ASP.NET pages.

Since dynamic compression increases the CPU usage, it is advisable that you check your CPU utilization after turning on the compression, to verify it does not put too much strain on the CPU.

Configuring Compression

The first thing that needs to be done to use compression is to enable either static compression, dynamic compression, or both. To enable compression in IIS, open the IIS Manager application, select your machine, click the *Compression* option, and select which compression features your wish to use, as shown in Figure 11-3:

 Compression

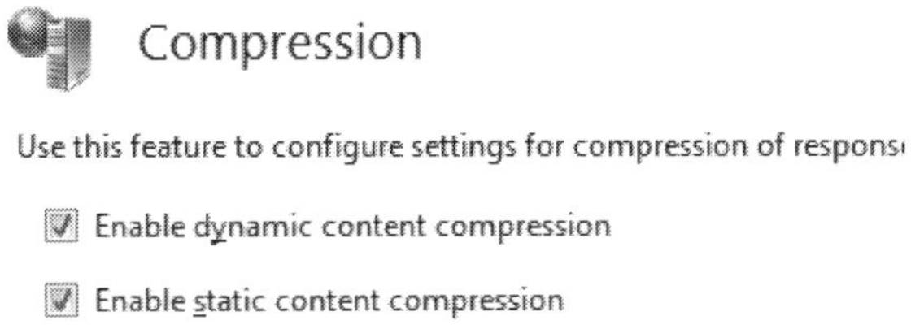

Use this feature to configure settings for compression of response

☑ Enable dynamic content compression

☑ Enable static content compression

Figure 11-3. Enabling dynamic and static compression in the IIS Manager application

You can also use the *Compression* dialog to set static compression settings, such as the folder where the cached content will be stored, and the minimum file size eligible for compression.

After selecting which compression types are active, you can go ahead and select which MIME types will be statically compressed and which will be dynamically compressed. Unfortunately, IIS doesn't support changing these settings from the IIS Manager application, so you will need to change it manually in the IIS configuration file, applicationHost.config, which is located in the *%windir%\System32\inetsrv\config* folder. Open the file and search for the < httpCompression > section, you should already see several MIME types defined for static compression and several other types for dynamic compression. In addition to the already specified MIME types, you can add additional types which you use in your web applications. For example, if you have AJAX calls that return JSON responses, you may want to add dynamic compression support for those responses. The following configuration shows how to dynamic compression support for JSON (existing content was removed for brevity):

```
<httpCompression>
  <dynamicTypes>
    <add mimeType="application/json; charset=utf-8" enabled="true" />
  </dynamicTypes>
</httpCompression>
```

■ **Note**   After adding new MIME types to the list, it is advised that you verify the compression is indeed working by checking the responses with HTTP sniffing tools, such as Fiddler. Compressed responses should have the Content-Encoding HTTP header, and it should be set to either gzip or deflate.

IIS Compression and Client Applications

In order for IIS to compress outgoing responses, it needs to know that the client application can handle compressed responses. Therefore, when a client application sends a request to the server, it needs to add the Accept-Encoding HTTP header and set it to either gzip or deflate.

Most known browsers add this header automatically, so when using a browser with a web application or a Silverlight application, IIS will respond with compressed content. However, in .NET applications, when sending HTTP requests with the HttpWebRequest type, the Accept-Encoding header is not automatically added, and you will need to add it manually. Furthermore, `HttpWebRequest` will not try to decompress responses unless it is set to expect compressed responses. For example, if you are using an `HttpWebRequest` object, you will need to add the following code to be able to receive and decompress compressed responses:

```
var request = (HttpWebRequest)HttpWebRequest.Create(uri);
request.Headers.Add(HttpRequestHeader.AcceptEncoding, "gzip,deflate");
request.AutomaticDecompression = DecompressionMethods.GZip | DecompressionMethods.Deflate;
```

Other HTTP communication objects, such as an ASMX web service proxy or a `WebClient` object, also support IIS compression, but need to be manually configured to send the header and decompress the response. As for HTTP-based WCF services, prior to WCF 4, .NET clients using either a service reference or a channel factory did not support IIS compression. As of WCF 4, IIS compression is supported automatically, both for sending the header and decompressing the response.

Minification and Bundling

When working with web applications, you often work with pages that use several JavaScript and CSS files. When a page has several links to external resources, loading the page in a browser becomes a lengthy operation, since the user will often need to wait until the page and all of its related styles and scripts are downloaded and parsed. When working with external resources we face two problems:

1. The number of requests the browser needs to send and wait for the response. The more requests there are, the more time it will take the browser to send all requests, since browsers are limited by the number of concurrent connections they can have to a single server (for example, in IE 9 the number of concurrent requests per server is 6).

2. The size of the response, which affects the overall time it takes the browser to download all the responses. The larger the responses, the more time it will take for the browser to download the response. This may also affect the browser's ability to begin sending new requests if hitting the maximum number of concurrent requests.

To resolve this issue we need a technique that will both enable us to lower the size of responses and reduce the number of requests (and therefore responses). With ASP.NET MVC 4 and in ASP.NET 4.5, this technique is now built in to the framework and is called "bundling and minification."

Bundling refers to the ability to bundle a set of files into one URL which when requested, returns all the files concatenated as one response, and minification refers to the reduction of size of a style or script file by removing whitespaces, and in the case of script files, renaming variables and functions so they use less characters, therefore taking less space.

The use of minification together with compression can significantly reduce the size of responses. For example, the size of the jQuery 1.6.2 script file before minification is 240 kb. After compression the file size is approximately 68 kb. The minified version of the original file is 93 kb, a bit bigger than the compressed version, but after applying compression to the minified file, the size comes down to only 33 kb, about 14 percent of the original file size.

To create a minified bundle, first install the Microsoft.AspNet.Web.Optimization NuGet package, and add a reference to the `System.Web.Optimization` assembly. Once added, you can use the `BundleTable` static class to create new bundles for scripts and styles. The bundling should be set prior to loading pages, therefore you should place the bundling code in the *global.asax*, in the `Application_Start` method. For example, the following code creates a bundle named *MyScripts* (accessible from the virtual *bundles* folder) with three script files which will automatically be minified:

```
protected void Application_Start() {
  Bundle myScriptsBundle = new ScriptBundle("~/bundles/MyScripts").Include(
    "~/Scripts/myCustomJsFunctions.js",
```

```
    "~/Scripts/thirdPartyFunctions.js",
    "~/Scripts/myNewJsTypes.js");

  BundleTable.Bundles.Add(myScriptsBundle);
  BundleTable.EnableOptimizations = true;
}
```

▓ **Note**   By default, bundling and minification only work when the web application's compilation mode is set to release. To enable bundling even when in debug mode, we set `EnableOptimizations` to `true`.

To use the bundle which was created, add the following script line to the page:

```
<%= Scripts.Render("~/bundles/MyScripts") %>
```

When the page is rendered, the above line will be replaced with a < script > tag that points to the bundle, for example the above line may translate to the following HTML:

```
<script src = "/bundles/MyScript?v = XGaE5OlO_bpMLuETD5_XmgfU5dchi8GOSSBExK294I41"
        type = "text/javascript" ></script>
```

By default, the bundle and minification framework sets the response to expire after one year, so the bundle will remain in the browser's cache and served from the cache. To prevent bundles from becoming stale, each bundle has a token which is placed in the URL's query string. If any of the files are removed from the bundle, if new files are added, or if the bundled files are changed, the token will change, and the next request to the page will generate a different URL with a different token, making the browser request for the new bundle.

In a similar manner, we can create a bundle for CSS files:

```
Bundle myStylesBundle = new StyleBundle("~/bundles/MyStyles")
      .Include("~/Styles/defaultStyle.css",
               "~/Styles/extensions.css",
               "~/Styles/someMoreStyles.js");

BundleTable.Bundles.Add(myStylesBundle);
```

And use the bundle in a page:

```
<%= Styles.Render("~/bundles/MyStyles") %>
```

Which will render a < link > element:

```
<link href = "/bundles/MyStyles?v = ji3nO1pdg6VLv3CVUWntxgZNf1zRciWDbm4YfW-yORI1"
      rel = "stylesheet" type = "text/css" />
```

The bundling and minification framework also supports custom transformations, allowing the creation of specialized transform classes, for example to create your own custom minification for JavaScript files.

Use Content Delivery Networks (CDNs)

One of the performance issues related to web applications is the latency involved with accessing resources over the network. End-users who use the same local network as the web server usually have good response time, but once your web application goes global and users from all over the world access it over the Internet, distant users, such as users from other continents, will probably suffer from longer latencies and slower bandwidth due to network problems.

One solution to the location problem is to spread multiple instances of the web server in different locations, geographically dispersed, so end-users will always be geographically close to one of the servers. Of course this creates a whole management issue since you will need to replicate and synchronize servers all the time, and possibly instruct each end-user to use a different URL according to where they are in the world.

That is where Content Delivery Networks (CDNs) come in. A CDN is a collection of web servers, placed in different locations around the globe, allowing end-users to always be close to your web application's content. When using CDNs, you actually use the same address of the CDN all over the world, but the local DNS in your area translates that address to the actual CDN server which is closest to your location. Various Internet companies, such as Microsoft, Amazon, and Akamai have their own CDNs which you can use for a certain fee.

The following scenario describes the common use of a CDN:

1. You set up your CDN and point it to where the original content is.

2. The first time an end-user accesses the content through the CDN, the local CDN server connects to your web server, pulls the content from it, caches it in the CDN server, and returns the content to the end-user.

3. For subsequent requests, the CDN server returns the cached content without contacting your web server, allowing for quicker response times, and possibly faster bandwidth.

▓ **Note**   In addition to serving your end-users faster, the use of a CDN also reduces the number of requests for static content your web server needs to handle, allowing it to dedicate most of its resources for handling dynamic content.

To achieve the first step, you will need to choose the CDN provider you wish to use, and configure your CDN as instructed by its provider. Once you have the address of the CDN, simply change the links for your static content (images, styles, scripts) to point to the CDN address. For example, if you upload your static content to Windows Azure blob storage and register your content with Windows Azure CDN, you can change the URLs in your pages to point to the CDN like so:

```
<link href="http://az18253.vo.msecnd.net/static/Content/Site.css"
      rel="stylesheet" type="text/css" />
```

For debugging purposes you can replace the static URL with a variable that will allow you to control whether to use a local address or the CDN's address. For example, the following Razor code constructs the URL by prefixing it with the CDN address provided by the CdnUrl application setting from the *web.config* file:

```
@using System.Web.Configuration
<script src="@WebConfigurationManager.AppSettings["CdnUrl"]/Scripts/jquery-1.6.2.js"
        type="text/javascript"></script>
```

When debugging your web application, change the CdnUrl to an empty string to get the content from your local web server.

Scaling ASP.NET Applications

So you've improved the performance of your web application by incorporating everything you learned here, maybe even applied some other techniques to boost things up, and now your application is working great, and is as optimized as it can be. You put your application to production, everything works great for the first couple of weeks, but then additional users start using the web site, and more new users are joining every day, increasing the number of requests your server has to handle, and suddenly, your server starts to choke. It may begin with requests taking longer than usual, your worker process starts to use more memory and more CPU, and eventually requests give in to timeouts, and HTTP 500 ("Internal Server Error") messages are filling your log files.

What has gone wrong? Should you try to improve the performance of your application again? More users will join and again you'll be in the same situation. Should you increase the machine's memory, or add more CPUs? There's a limit to the amount of scale-up you can do on a single machine. It's time to face the facts—you need to scale out to more servers.

Scaling out web applications is a natural process that has to occur at some point in the life cycle of web applications. One server can hold dozens and even thousands of concurrent users, but it cannot handle that kind of stress for that long. Session state filling up the server's memory, threads getting starved because there are no more threads available, and context-switching that occurs too often will eventually increase the latency and lower the throughput of your single server.

Scaling Out

From an architectural point of view, scaling is not hard: just buy another machine or two (or ten), place the servers behind a load-balancer, and from there on, all should be OK. The problem is that usually it's not that easy.

One of the major issues developers face when having to scale is how to handle *server affinity*. For example, when you use a single web server, the session state of your users is kept in-memory. If you add another server, how will you make those session objects available to it? How will you synchronize the sessions between the servers? Some web developers tend to solve this issue by keeping the state in the server and having an affinity between the client and the server. Once a client connects to one of the servers through the load balancer, the load balancer will, from that point on, keep sending all of that client's requests to the same web server, this is also referred to as a "sticky" session. Using sticky sessions is a workaround, not a solution, since it does not allow you to truly balance the work between the servers. It is easy getting to a situation where one of the servers is handling too many users, whereas other servers are not handling requests at all, because all of their clients already disconnected.

So the real solution for good scalability is not to rely on your machine's memory, whether its regarding the state you keep for your users, or the cache you store in-memory to boost performance. Why does storing cache on a machine become problematic when scaling? Just think what will happen when a user sends a request that causes the cache to be updated: the server that got the request will update its in-memory cache, but other servers won't know of this change, and if they also have a copy of that cached object, it will become stale and cause application-wide inconsistencies. One of the ways you might choose to solve this issue is by synchronizing cached objects between servers. Although possible, this solution adds another layer of complexity to the architecture of your web application, not to mention the amount of chatter your servers are going to have between them.

ASP.NET Scaling Mechanisms

Scaling out to multiple servers requires an out-of-process state management. ASP.NET has two built-in out-of-process mechanisms for state management:

- **State Service**. The state service is a Windows service that provides state management for multiple machines. This service is installed automatically when installing the .NET framework, but is turned off by default. You can simply choose which machine will run the state service, and configure all other machines to use it. Although state service enables several machines to use the same session store, it does not provide persistency, so if something happens to the machine hosting the service, the entire session state of your web farm will be lost.

- **SQL Server**. ASP.NET supports storing the session state in SQL Server. Storing state in SQL Server gives the same sharing abilities as that of the state service, but it also enables the persistency of the state, so even if your web servers fail, and if the SQL Server fails, the state information can be restored.

For caching, the solution in most cases is to use a distributed cache mechanism, such as Microsoft's AppFabric Cache, NCache, or Memcached which is an open-source distributed cache. With distributed cache, you can take several servers and combine their memory into one distributed memory, which is used as a cache store for your cached data. Distributed caches offer abstraction of location so you don't need to know where each piece of data is located, notification services so you can know when something has changed, and high-availability to make sure that even if one of the cache servers fails, the data is not lost.

Some distributed caches, such as AppFabric Cache and Memcached also have custom Session State and Cache providers for ASP.NET.

Scaling Out Pitfalls

Although not relevant to performance, it is a good place to mention some other issues you should be aware of when scaling out your web application. Certain parts in web applications require the use of a special security keys to generate unique identifiers that prevent tampering and spoofing the web application. For example, a unique key is used when creating Forms Authentication cookies, and when encrypting view state data. By default, the security keys for a web application are generated each time the application pool starts. For a single server this might not be a problem, but when you scale out your server into multiple servers this will pose a problem, since each server will have its own unique key. Consider the following scenario: a client sends a request to server A and gets back a cookie signed with server A's unique key, then the client sends a new request to server B with the cookie it received before. Since server B has a different unique key, the validation of the cookie's content will fail and an error will be returned.

You can control how these keys are generated in ASP.NET by configuring the machineKey section in your web.config. When scaling out web applications to multiple servers, you need to configure the machine key to use the same pre-generated key in all the servers by hard-coding it into the application's configuration.

Another issue relating to scaling out and the use of unique keys is the ability to encrypt sections in web.config files. Sensitive information located in the web.config file is often encrypted when the application is deployed to production servers. For example, the connectionString section can be encrypted to prevent the username and password to the database from being discovered. Instead of encrypting the web.config file separately in each server after deployment, making the deployment process tedious, you can generate one encrypted web.config file and deploy it to all the servers. To be able to do that, all you need to do is to create an RSA key container and import it once in all the web servers.

■ **Note**   To learn more about generating machine keys and applying them to the application's configuration, consult the Microsoft Knowledge Base document KB312906 (http://support.microsoft.com/?id=312906). For more information on generating the RSA key container, read the "Importing and Exporting Protected Configuration RSA Key Containers" MSDN article (http://msdn.microsoft.com/library/yxw286t2).

Summary

In the beginning of this chapter, we argued that the overall performance of a web application is controlled not only by your code, but also by various parts of the pipeline. We started this chapter by examining some testing and analyzing tools that can assist you in locating the bottlenecks in your web applications. By proper testing, and using monitoring and analysis tools, you can easily track down problems, and significantly improve the performance of your web application. From there, we went over the pipeline, identifying different parts of it that can be modified to make your application either work faster, work smarter, or provide smaller payloads so they can be sent more quickly. After going over this chapter, you are now aware to how small changes, such as working properly with client-side caching, can help reduce the number of requests your server has to deal with, resolving some bottleneck issues many applications are facing.

Later on in the chapter, we realized that a single server will not be able to handle all of your client's requests, so planning ahead for scaling and applying scalable solutions beforehand, such as distributed cache and out-of-process state management, will enable you to scale easier once you've reached the point where one server is just not enough. Finally, in this chapter we only explored different techniques of improving the server-side of your web application, leaving another side for you to explore—the client side.

This is the last chapter of this book. Throughout its eleven chapters, you have seen how to measure and improve application performance, how to parallelize .NET code and run your algorithms on the GPU, how to navigate the complexities of the .NET type system and garbage collector, how to choose collections wisely and when to implement your own, and even how to use the latest-and-greatest processor features to squeeze additional performance for your CPU-bound software. Thank you for following us on this journey, and best of luck improving the performance of your applications!

Index

▨ H

▨ I

23550512R00200

Made in the USA
Lexington, KY
18 June 2013